Business Law I

Mercer County Community College

Jeffrey F. Beatty | Susan S. Samuelson

CENGAGE
Learning™

Australia • Brazil • Japan • Korea • Mexico • Singapore • Spain • United Kingdom • United States

CENGAGE
Learning™

Business Law I: Mercer County Community College

Jeffrey F. Beatty I Susan S. Samuelson

Executive Editor:
Maureen Staudt
Michael Stranz

Senior Project Development Manager:
Linda de Stefano

Marketing Specialist:
Sara Mercurio
Lindsay Shapiro

Production/Manufacturing Manager:
Donna M. Brown

PreMedia Supervisor:
Joel Brennecke

Rights & Permissions Specialist:
Kalina Hintz
Todd Osborne

Cover Image:
Getty Images*

For product information and technology assistance, contact us at
Cengage Learning Customer & Sales Support, 1-800-354-9706

For permission to use material from this text or product,
submit all requests online at **cengage.com/permissions**
Further permissions questions can be emailed to
permissionrequest@cengage.com

ISBN-13: 978-1-111-05511-0

ISBN-10: 1-111-05511-4

Cengage Learning
5191 Natorp Boulevard
Mason, Ohio 45040
USA

Cengage Learning is a leading provider of customized learning solutions with office locations around the globe, including Singapore, the United Kingdom, Australia, Mexico, Brazil, and Japan. Locate your local office at:
international.cengage.com/region

Cengage Learning products are represented in Canada by
Nelson Education, Ltd.

For your lifelong learning solutions, visit **www.cengage.com/custom**

Visit our corporate website at **www.cengage.com**

Printed in the United States of America

Acknowledgements

The content of this text has been adapted from the following product(s):

Introduction to Business Law
Beatty/Samuelson ISBN-10: (0-324-31142-7)
ISBN-13: (978-0-324-31142-6)

Table Of Contents

1

Introduction to Law

Law is powerful. Law is essential. And law is fascinating. We hope this book will persuade you of all three ideas.

Three Important Ideas About Law

POWER

The law displays its muscle every day, to people from all walks of life. A driver is seriously injured in an automobile accident, and the jury concludes the car had a design defect. The jurors award her $29 million. A senior vice-president congratulates himself on a cagey stock purchase but is horrified to receive, not profits, but a prison sentence. A homeless person, ordered by local police to stop panhandling, ambles into court and walks out with an order permitting him to beg on the city's streets. The strong reach of the law touches us all. To understand something that powerful is itself power.

Suppose, some years after graduation, you are a midlevel manager at Sublime Corp., which manufactures and distributes video games and related hardware and software. You are delighted with this important position in an excellent company—and especially glad you bring legal knowledge to the job. Sarah, an expert at computer-generated imagery, complains that Rob, her boss, is constantly touching her and making lewd comments. That is sexual harassment, and your knowledge of *employment law* helps you respond promptly and carefully. You have dinner with Jake, who has his own software company. Jake wants to manufacture an exciting new video game in cooperation with Sublime, but you are careful not to create a binding deal. (*Contract law.*) Jake mentions that a similar game is already on the market. Do you have the right to market one like it? That answer you already know. (*Intellectual property law.*)

The next day a letter from the Environmental Protection Agency asks how your company disposes of toxic chemicals used to manufacture computer drives. You can discuss it efficiently with in-house counsel, because you have a working knowledge of administrative law. LuYu, your personnel manager, reports that a silicon chip worker often seems drowsy; she suspects drug use. Does she have the right to test him? (*Constitutional law* and *employment law.*) On the other hand, if she fails to test him, could Sublime Corp. be liable for any harm the worker does? (*Tort law* and *agency law.*)

In a mere week, you might use your legal training a dozen times, helping Sublime to steer clear of countless dangers. During the coming year you encounter many other legal issues, and you and your corporation benefit from your skills.

It is not only as a corporate manager that you will confront the law. As a voter, investor, juror, entrepreneur, and community member, you will influence and be affected by the law. Whenever you take a stance about a legal issue, whether in the corporate office, the voting booth, or as part of local community groups, you help to create the social fabric of our nation. Your views are vital. This book will offer you knowledge and ideas from which to form and continually reassess your legal opinions and values.

IMPORTANCE

We depend upon laws for safe communities, functioning economies, and personal liberties. An easy way to gauge the importance of law is to glance through any newspaper, and read about nations that lack a strong system of justice. Notice that these countries cannot insure physical safety and personal liberties. They also fail to offer economic opportunity for most citizens. We may not always like the way our legal system works, but we depend on it for a functioning society.

FASCINATION

Law is intriguing. When the jury awarded $29 million against an auto manufacturer for a defective car design, it certainly demonstrated the law's power. But was the jury's decision right? Should a company have to pay that much for one car accident? Maybe the jury was reacting emotionally. Or perhaps the anger caused by terrible trauma should be part of a court case. These are not abstract speculations for philosophers. Verdicts such as this may cause each of us to pay more for our next automobile. Then again, we may be driving safer cars.

Sources of Contemporary Law

It would be nice if we could look up "the law" in one book, memorize it, and then apply it. But the law is not that simple. Principles and rules of law actually come from many different sources. Why is this so?

We inherited a complex structure of laws from England. Additionally, ours is a nation born in revolution and created, in large part, to protect the rights of its people from the government. The Founding Fathers created a national government but insisted the individual states maintain control in many areas. As a result, each state has its own government with exclusive power over many important areas of our lives. What the Founding Fathers created was **federalism: a double-layered system of government, with the national government and state governments each exercising important but limited powers.** To top it off, the Founders guaranteed many rights to the people alone, ordering national and state governments to keep clear. They achieved all of this in one remarkable document, the United States Constitution.

CONSTITUTIONS

United States Constitution

The United States Constitution, adopted in 1789 by the original 13 colonies, is the supreme law of the land.[1] Any law that conflicts with it is void. This Federal Constitution, as it is also known, does three basic things. First, it establishes the national government of the United States, with its three branches. The Constitution creates the Congress, with a Senate and a House of Representatives, and prescribes what laws Congress may pass. The same document establishes the office of the president and the duties that go with it. And it creates the third branch of government, the federal courts, describing what cases they may hear.

Second, the Constitution ensures the states retain all power not given to the national government. This simple idea has meant that state governments play an important role in all of our lives. Major issues of family law, criminal law, property law, and many other areas are regulated predominantly by the various states.

Third, the Constitution guarantees many basic rights to the American people. Most of these rights are found in the amendments to the Constitution. The First

---

[1] The complete text of the Constitution appears in Appendix A.

Amendment guarantees the rights of free speech, free press, and the free exercise of religion. The Fourth, Fifth, and Sixth Amendments protect the rights of any person accused of a crime. Other amendments ensure that the government treats all people equally and that it pays for any property it takes from a citizen. Merely by creating a limited government of three branches and guaranteeing basic liberties to all citizens, the Constitution became one of the most important documents ever written.

State Constitutions

In addition to the Federal Constitution, each state has a constitution that establishes its own government. All states have an executive (the governor), a legislature, and a court system. Thus there are two entire systems of government affecting each of us: a federal government, with power over the entire country, and a state government, exercising those powers that the United States Constitution did not grant to the federal government. This is federalism at work.

STATUTES

The second important source of law is statutory law. The Constitution gave to the United States Congress the power to pass laws on many subjects. **Laws passed by Congress are called statutes.** For example, the Constitution allows Congress to pass statutes about the military: to appropriate money, reorganize divisions, and close bases. You can find any federal statute, on any subject, at the Web site of the United States House of Representatives, which is **http://www.house.gov/.**

    State legislatures also pass statutes. Each state constitution allows the legislature to pass laws on a wide variety of subjects. All state legislatures, for example, may pass statutes about family law issues such as divorce and child custody.

COMMON LAW AND EQUITY

The common law originated in England, as lawyers began to record decisions and urge judges to follow earlier cases. As judges started to do that, the earlier cases, called precedent, took on steadily greater importance. Eventually, judges were obligated to follow precedent. **The principle that precedent is binding on later cases is *stare decisis,* which means "let the decision stand."** *Stare decisis* makes the law predictable, and this in turn enables businesses and private citizens to plan intelligently. We will see this principle at work later in this chapter.

    Sometimes a judge refused to hear a case, ruling that no such claims were legal. The injured party might then take his case to the Chancellor, in London, whose status in the king's council gave him unique, flexible powers. This Court of Chancery had no jury. The court's duty was to accomplish what "good conscience" required, that is, an equitable result. This more creative use of a court's power became known as equity.

    Principles of equity traveled to the colonies along with the common-law rules. All states permit courts to use equitable powers. An example of a contemporary equitable power is an **injunction,** a court order that someone stop doing something. Suppose a music company is about to issue a new compact disk by a well-known singer, but a composer claims that the recording artist has stolen his song. The composer, claiming copyright violation, could seek an injunction to prevent the company from issuing the compact disk. Every state has a trial court that can issue injunctions and carry out other equitable relief. There is no jury in an equity case.

Sources of Law

50 State Governments

State Constitution
• establishes the state government
• guarantees the rights of state residents

One Federal Government

United States Constitution
• establishes limited federal government
• protects states' power
• guarantees liberty of citizens

Legislative Branch

State Legislature

• passes statutes on state law
• creates state agencies

Executive Branch

Governor

• proposes statutes
• signs or vetoes statutes
• oversees state agencies
• issues executive orders

Judicial Branch

State Courts

• create state common law
• interpret statutes
• review constitutionality of statutes and other acts

Administrative Agencies
• oversee day-to-day application of law in dozens of commercial and other areas

Legislative Branch

Congress

• passes statutes
• ratifies treaties
• creates administrative agencies

Executive Branch

President

• proposes statutes
• signs or vetoes statutes
• oversees administrative agencies
• issues executive orders

Judicial Branch

Federal Courts

• interpret statutes
• create (limited) federal common law
• review the constitutionality of statutes and other legal acts

Administrative Agencies
• oversee day-to-day application of law in dozens of commercial and other areas

Federal Form of Government. Principles and rules of law come from many sources. The government in Washington creates and enforces law throughout the nation. But 50 state governments exercise great power in local affairs. And citizens enjoy constitutional protection from both state and federal government. The Founding Fathers wanted this balance of power and rights, but the overlapping authority creates legal complexity.

ADMINISTRATIVE LAW

In a society as large and diverse as ours, the executive and legislative branches of government cannot oversee all aspects of commerce. Congress passes statutes about air safety, but U.S. senators do not stand around air traffic towers, serving coffee to keep everyone awake. The executive branch establishes rules concerning how foreign nationals enter the United States, but presidents are reluctant to sit on the dock of the bay, watching the ships come in. **Administrative agencies** do this day-to-day work.

Most administrative agencies are created by Congress or by a state legislature. Familiar examples at the federal level are the Federal Communications Commission (FCC), which regulates most telecommunications; the Federal Trade Commission (FTC), which oversees interstate trade; and the Immigration and Naturalization Service (INS), which controls our nation's borders. At the state level, regulators set insurance rates for all companies in the state, control property development and land use, and regulate many other issues.

Criminal and Civil Law

It is a crime to embezzle money from a bank, to steal a car, to sell cocaine. **Criminal law concerns behavior so threatening that society outlaws it altogether.** Most criminal laws are statutes, passed by Congress or a state legislature. The government itself prosecutes the wrongdoer, regardless of what the bank president or car owner wants. A district attorney, paid by the government, brings the case to court. The injured party, for example the owner of the stolen car, is not in charge of the case, although she may appear as a witness. The government will seek to punish the defendant with a prison sentence, a fine, or both. If there is a fine, the money goes to the state, not to the injured party.

Civil law is different, and most of this book is about civil law. **The civil law regulates the rights and duties between parties.** Tracy agrees in writing to lease you a 30,000-square-foot store in her shopping mall. She now has a legal duty to make the space available. But then another tenant offers her more money, and she refuses to let you move in. Tracy has violated her duty, but she has not committed a crime. The government will not prosecute the case. It is up to you to file a civil lawsuit. Your case will be based on the common law of contract. You will also seek equitable relief, namely an injunction ordering Tracy not to lease to anyone else. You should win the suit, and you will get your injunction and some money damages. But Tracy will not go to jail.

Some conduct involves both civil and criminal law. Suppose Tracy is so upset over losing the court case that she becomes drunk and causes a serious car accident. She has committed the crime of driving while intoxicated, and the state will prosecute. Tracy may be fined or imprisoned. She has also committed negligence, and the injured party will file a lawsuit against her, seeking money.

LAW AND MORALITY

Law is different from morality, yet the two are obviously linked. There are many instances when the law duplicates what all of us would regard as a moral position. It is negligence to drive too fast in a school district, and few would dispute the moral value of that law. And similarly with contract law: If the owner of land agrees in writing to sell property to a buyer at a stated price, the seller must go through with the deal, and the legal outcome matches our moral expectations.

On the other hand, we have had laws that we now clearly regard as immoral. Seventy-five years ago, a factory owner could legally fire a worker for any reason at all—including, for example, her religion. Today, we would say it is immoral to fire a worker because of her faith—and the law prohibits it.

Finally, there are legal issues where the morality is not so clear. Suppose you serve alcohol to a guest who becomes intoxicated and then causes an automobile accident, seriously injuring a pedestrian. Should you, the social host, be liable? This is an issue of tort liability, which we examine in Chapter 5. As with many topics in this book, the problem has no easy answer. As you learn the law, you will have an opportunity to reexamine your own moral beliefs. One of the goals of Chapter 2, on ethics, is to offer you some new tools for that task.

Working with the Book's Features

In this section we introduce a few of the book's features, and discuss how you can use them effectively. We will start with cases.

ANALYZING A CASE

A law case is the decision a court has made in a civil lawsuit or criminal prosecution. Cases are the heart of the law and an important part of this book. Reading them effectively takes practice. The following decision in a civil suit is a good place to start.

This case begins with violence outside a nightclub. Lindie Osborne, an innocent young woman out for a night on the town, is viciously struck by a drunken karate expert. Obviously the thug who attacked her is responsible for the harm done. But is the nightclub also liable? That is no theoretical question, because the hooligan is likely to have little or no money.

CASE SUMMARY

OSBORNE v. STAGES MUSIC HALL, INC.

312 Ill. App. 3d 141; 726 N.E.2d 728; 2000 Ill. App. LEXIS157; 244 Ill. Dec. 753
Illinois Court of Appeals, 2000

FACTS: Stages Music Hall owned the Metro Club in Chicago. Karl Trujillo and his friend Daniel Hosneola became intoxicated while at the Metro and got into a violent fight with eight of the club's bouncers. Trujillo, trained in the martial arts, knocked down two of the employees, but the bouncers finally ejected the young men, who remained outside the door, clamoring for readmission.

Meanwhile, Lindie Osborne and her friend Michelle Becht were leaving the Metro. As Becht exited, one of the young men slapped her in the face. Osborne hurried outside, but as she approached her friend, Trujillo spun on his heel and kicked her in the face. Osborne fell to the ground. The two men left the scene but were later arrested.

Osborne suffered two facial fractures that required permanent plates and pins to be inserted in her jaw, which was wired shut for six weeks. She sued Stages, but the trial court gave a directed verdict for Stages, meaning that it dismissed the case. The court declared that Stages had no duty to protect Osborne because the incident took place on a public sidewalk, and because Trujillo's assault was not foreseeable. Osborne appealed.

ISSUE: Did Stages have a duty to protect Osborne from Trujillo's attack?

DECISION: Yes, Stages did have a duty to protect Osborne. Reversed and remanded to the trial court.

REASONING: An injured plaintiff can only recover if the defendant had a duty to her. In deciding whether to impose this burden, courts examine the foreseeability of the injury and the consequences to the defendant.

Metro's bouncers knew that Trujillo and Hosneola were intoxicated, combative, and angry. After they ejected the two men, they made no effort to supervise the area outside the club, even though earlier in the evening they had erected barriers to control foot traffic. In other words, they exported the club's problem to the sidewalk, and then allowed two female patrons to walk directly into the danger. The club was obligated to guard against such a foreseeable assault. Stages did have a duty to Osborne.

The burden on Stages is not excessive. It might have been enough for the club simply to warn the two women of the peril. A jury should decide exactly what steps a bar must take in these circumstances. The case is remanded for a new trial. ◢

Analysis

Let's take it from the top. The case is called *Osborne v. Stages Music Hall, Inc.* Lindie Osborne is the plaintiff, the person who is suing. Stages Music Hall, Inc., which owns the Metro Club, is being sued, and is called the defendant. In this example, the plaintiff's name happens to appear first, but that is not always true. When a defendant loses a trial and files an appeal, *some* courts reverse the names of the parties.

The next line gives the legal citation, which indicates where to find the case in a law library. We explain in the footnote how to locate a book if you plan to do research.[2]

The *Facts* section provides a background to the lawsuit, written by the authors of this text. The court's own explanation of the facts is often many pages long, and may involve complex matters irrelevant to the subject covered in this book, so we relate only what is necessary.

The *Issue* section is very important. It tells you what the court had to decide—and why you are reading the case.

The *Decision.* This is the court's answer to the issue posed. A court's decision is often referred to as its *holding.* The court rules that Stages did have a duty to Osborne. The court *reverses* the trial court's decision, meaning it declares the lower court's ruling wrong and void. The judges also *remand* the case to the trial court, that is, send it back down to the lower court, for a new trial. If this court had agreed with the trial court's decision, the judges would have *affirmed* the lower court's ruling, meaning to uphold it.

---

[2] If you want to do legal research, you need to know where to find particular legal decisions. A case citation guides you to the correct volume(s). The full citation of our case is: *Osborne v. Stages Music Hall, Inc.*, 312 Ill. App. 3d 141, 726 N.E.2d 728, 2000 Ill. App. Lexis 157. The string of numbers identifies three different books in which you can find the full text of this decision. The first citation is to "Ill.App.3d," which means the official court reporter of the state of Illinois, third set. Illinois, like most states, reports its law cases in a series of numbered volumes. After the volumes reach the number 999, most reporters start over with a second set of volumes and then a third. This case appears in volume 312 of the third set of Illinois reporters. If you go to a law library and find that book, you can then turn to page 141 and—*voilà!*—you have the case. The decision is also reported in another set of volumes, called the regional reporters. This series of law reports is grouped by geographic region. Illinois is included in the northeast region, so our case appears in volume 726 of the second set of the northeast reporter, at page 728. Finally, most cases are now available online. The third citation is to the electronic law library operated by LEXIS. Once you are connected to the LEXIS service, typing "2000 Ill. App. Lexis 157" in the appropriate box will bring the Metro Club and its rowdy patrons right into your computer.

The *Reasoning.* This section explains why the court reached its decision. The actual written decision may be three paragraphs or 75 pages. Some judges offer us lucid prose, while others seem intent on torturing the reader. Judges frequently digress and often discuss matters that are irrelevant to the issue on which this text is focusing. For those reasons, we have taken the court's explanation and cast it in our own words. If you are curious about the full opinion, you can always look it up.

Let us examine the reasoning. The court begins with a general point of law, applicable to many cases. The judges point out that a defendant is liable only if he has a duty to the plaintiff. Whether there is such a duty depends on the foreseeability of the injury and the potential burden placed on the defendant. The judges are emphasizing that courts do not reach decisions arbitrarily. They attempt to make thoughtful choices, consistent with earlier rulings, that make good sense for the general public.

The court then describes the key facts that it will use to decide whether Stages had a duty to Osborne. The judges note that the club's bouncers knew the two disorderly men were drunk and dangerous. Yet after evicting the men from the club, the bouncers neither supervised the sidewalk, nor warned departing patrons of the obvious danger. The bouncers rid themselves of an unpleasant problem and left it for everyone else to cope with the resulting risk. The court concludes that an injury was easy to foresee, and that as a result Stages did have a duty to Osborne. Finally, the judges explain that imposing a duty on the club is not a particularly heavy burden, because the club might have fulfilled this duty simply by warning its patrons of the danger.

Why does the court not specify what Metro should have done? The judges are leaving that decision to the jury, which will have several questions to answer: What would a reasonable club have done to prevent the harm? Did the Metro club do enough? (Almost certainly not, since they did nothing.) How severe were Osborne's injuries? How much money does the Metro owe her? The jury will consider all of these questions, if the parties go through with the second trial. In all likelihood, though, now that an appeals court has ruled that Metro *did* have a duty, the defendant will be eager to settle out of court. The most important issue of the case is decided: Metro does not escape liability merely because the attack occurred outside.

UPDATE

In this feature, we ask students to find a current article on an issue discussed in the text. The goal is for you to apply the principles of this course to current events—this material is very real! You may use periodicals from the library or articles from any electronic database. The article should be dated within the past two months.

Find an article on nightclub liability. What did the club allegedly do or fail to do? Is this a civil or criminal case? What outcome do you anticipate? How could the owner have avoided the problem?

"YOU BE THE JUDGE"

Many cases involve difficult decisions for juries and judges. Often both parties have legitimate, opposing arguments. Most chapters in this book will have a feature called "You Be the Judge," in which we present the facts of a case but not the court's holding. We offer you two opposing arguments based on the kinds of claims the lawyers made in court. We leave it up to you to debate and decide which position is stronger or to add your own arguments to those given. The following case is another negligence lawsuit, with issues similar to those in the Osborne case. A suicide caused a distraught family to sue a rock singer and music producer. Once again the defendants asked the judge to dismiss the case. They pointed out, correctly, that a negligence case requires a plaintiff to prove that the defendant could have foreseen the type of harm that occurred. Could Ozzy Osbourne have foreseen this sad outcome to one of his songs? You be the judge.

YOU BE THE JUDGE

McCOLLUM v. CBS, INC.

202 Cal. App. 3d 989, 249 Cal. Rptr. 187, 1988 Cal. App. LEXIS 909
California Court of Appeal, 1988

FACTS: John McCollum, 19 years old, was an alcoholic with serious emotional problems. He listened over and over to music recorded by Ozzy Osbourne on CBS records, particularly two albums called *Blizzard of Oz* and *Diary of a Madman*. He usually listened to the music on the family stereo in the living room because the sound was most intense there. One Friday evening, though, he went to his bedroom and lay on his bed, listening to more Osbourne music. He placed a loaded .22 caliber handgun to his right temple and pulled the trigger.

McCollum's parents sued Osbourne and CBS records, claiming that they negligently aided and encouraged John to commit suicide. The parents' argument was that Osbourne's songs were designed to appeal to unstable youths, and that the message of some of his music explicitly urged death. One of the songs John had listened to before his death was "Suicide Solution," which included these lyrics:

> *Wine is fine but whiskey's quicker*
> *Suicide is slow with liquor*
> *Take a bottle drown your sorrows*
> *Then it floods away tomorrows*
> *Now you live inside a bottle*
> *The reaper's travelling at full throttle*
> *It's catching you but you don't see*
> *The reaper is you and the reaper is me*
> *Breaking law, knocking doors*
> *But there's no one at home*
> *Made your bed, rest your head*
> *But you lie there and moan*
> *Where to hide, Suicide is the only way out*
> *Don't you know what it's really about.*[3]

The trial court dismissed the lawsuit, ruling that the plaintiff had not made out a valid negligence claim. The court ruled the First Amendment's free speech provision protected the rights of Osbourne and CBS to publish any music they wanted. In addition, the court found that the defendants could not have foreseen that anyone would respond to the lyrics by taking his own life. With no foreseeability, the court ruled, the plaintiffs' case must fail. The parents appealed.

YOU BE THE JUDGE: Was McCollum's suicide foreseeable?

ARGUMENT FOR THE PARENTS: Your honors, for years Ozzy Osbourne has been well known as the "madman" of rock and roll. The words and music of his songs revolve around bizarre, antisocial beliefs, emphasizing death and satanic worship. Many of his songs suggest that life is hopeless and suicide is not only acceptable but desirable. Now one of his devoted fans has acted on Osbourne's advice and killed himself. The defendants share responsibility for this tragic death.

Osbourne and CBS knew that many of Osbourne's fans struggled with self-identity, alienation, and substance abuse. Both defendants aggressively targeted this market and reaped enormous profits. They realized that the confused youths who adored Osbourne were precisely those most vulnerable to vicious advice. Yet in spite of their knowledge, both defendants churned out songs such as "Suicide Solution," urging troubled, chemically addicted young people to kill themselves. Not

---

[3] Words and music by John Osbourne, Robert Daisley, and Randy Rhoads. TRO © Copyright 1981 Essex Music International, Inc., New York, New York and Kord Music Publishers, London, England. Used by permission.

only was it foreseeable that one of Osbourne's fans would sooner or later take his life, it was inevitable. The only way to ensure this doesn't occur again is to permit a jury to hear the parents' case and, if it is persuaded by the evidence, to award the grieving parents damages.

ARGUMENT FOR OSBOURNE AND CBS: Your honors, we all agree that this death was tragic and unnecessary. But the plaintiffs delude themselves if they think Mr. Osbourne and CBS bear any responsibility. The fact is that John McCollum was deeply troubled and alcoholic. He was responsible for his life—and for his own death. Next to the young man himself, of course, those who bear the greatest responsibility for his sad life and gruesome end are his parents, the plaintiffs in this case. Mr. Osbourne

and CBS sympathize with the parents' bereavement, but not with their attempt to foist responsibility onto others.

If the plaintiffs' farfetched foreseeability argument were the law—which it is not—every singer, writer, and film and television producer would be at risk of several thousand lawsuits every year. Under their theory, a producer who made a bank robbery movie would be liable for every robbery that took place afterward, as would every author or singer who ever mentioned the subject. The First Amendment was written to ensure that we do have access to arts and entertainment, and to prohibit efforts at silencing artists with outlandish lawsuits. This death was never foreseeable, and no jury should ever hear the case. ▌

Chapter Conclusion

We depend upon the law to give us a stable nation and economy, a fair society, a safe place to live and work. But while law is a vital tool for crafting the society we want, there are no easy answers about how to create it. In a democracy, we all participate in the crafting. Legal rules control us, yet we create them. A working knowledge of the law can help build a successful career—and a solid democracy.

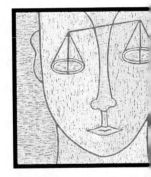

Chapter Review

1. Our federal system of government means that law comes from a national government in Washington, D.C. and from 50 state governments.

2. The primary sources of contemporary law are:

    *   United States Constitution and state constitutions.

    *   Statutes, which are drafted by legislatures.

    *   Common law, which is the body of cases decided by judges, as they follow earlier cases, known as precedent; and

    *   Administrative law, the rules and decisions made by federal and state administrative agencies.

3. Criminal law concerns behavior so threatening to society that it is outlawed altogether. Civil law deals with duties and disputes between parties, not outlawed behavior.

PRACTICE TEST

Matching Questions

Match the following terms with their definitions:

___ **A.** Statute   **1.** Law created by judges.

___ **B.** Administrative Agencies   **2.** Let the decision stand.

___ **C.** Common law   **3.** A law passed by Congress or a state legislature.

___ **D.** *Stare decisis*   **4.** The supreme law of the land.

___ **E.** United States Constitution   **5.** The Internal Revenue Service; the Federal Communications Commission; the Federal Trade Commission.

True/False Questions

Circle true or false:

1. T F The idea that current cases must be decided based on earlier cases is called legal positivism.

2. T F Civil lawsuits are brought to court by the injured party, but criminal cases must be prosecuted by the government.

3. T F Congress established the federal government by passing a series of statutes.

4. T F The federal government has three branches: executive, legislative, and administrative.

5. T F Law is different from morality, but the two are closely linked.

Multiple-Choice Questions

6. More American law comes from one country than from any other. Which country?

(a) France.   (d) Spain

(b) England.   (e) Canada

(c) Germany

7. Under the United States Constitution, power that is not expressly given to the federal government is retained by

(a) The courts   (d) The states and the people

(b) The Congress   (e) International treaty

(c) The Founding Fathers

8. The 25 nations of the European Union sometimes struggle to create a unified policy that works for all of the countries, while still permitting each member nation to maintain adequate power over its own affairs. With what legal principle are they struggling?

(a) Jurisprudence   (d) Federalism

(b) Precedent   (e) Morality

(c) Strict construction.

9. Judges use precedent to create what kind of law?

(a) Common law   (d) Local law

(b) Statutes   (e) Empirical law

(c) National law

10. Rebecca leaves a store at night and enters the store's parking lot. Before she can reach her car, she is robbed at gunpoint. Rebecca sues the store. When a court decides whether the store had a *duty* to prevent this harm, what issue will the judges focus on?

   (a) Federalism

   (b) Equity

   (c) Legal realism

   (d) Morality

   (e) Foreseeability

Short-Answer Questions

11. Union organizers at a hospital wanted to distribute leaflets to potential union members, but hospital rules prohibited leafletting in areas of patient care, hallways, cafeterias, and any areas open to the public. The National Labor Relations Board (NLRB) ruled that these restrictions violated the law and ordered the hospital to permit the activities in the cafeteria and coffee shop. The NLRB cannot create common law or statutory law. What kind of law was it creating?

12. Bill and Diane are hiking in the woods. Diane walks down a hill to fetch fresh water. Bill meets a stranger, who introduces herself as Katrina. Bill sells a kilo of cocaine to Katrina, who then flashes a badge and mentions how much she enjoys her job at the Drug Enforcement Administration. Diane, heading back to camp with the water, meets Freddy, a motorist whose car has overheated. Freddy is late for a meeting where he expects to make a $30 million profit; he's desperate for water for his car. He promises to pay Diane $500 tomorrow if she will give him the pail of water, which she does. The next day, Bill is in jail and Freddy refuses to pay for Diane's water. Explain the criminal law/civil law distinction and what it means to Bill and Diane. Who will do what to whom, with what results?

13. The stock market crash of 1929 and the Great Depression that followed were caused in part because so many investors blindly put their money into stocks they knew nothing about. During the 1920s it was often impossible for an investor to find out what a corporation was planning to do with its money, who was running the corporation, and many other vital things. Congress responded by passing the Securities Act of 1933, which required a corporation to divulge more information about itself before it could seek money for a new stock issue. What kind of law did Congress create? Explain the relationship between voters, Congress, and the law.

14. Ethics: The greatest of all Chinese lawgivers, Confucius, did not esteem written laws. He believed that good rulers were the best guarantee of justice. Does our legal system rely primarily on the rule of law or the rule of people? Which do you instinctively trust more? Confucius himself was an extraordinarily wise man. How does that fact influence your analysis?

15. Role Reversal: Each Practice Test contains one Role Reversal feature, in which we challenge you to create your own exam question. The goal is to think creatively and accurately. Crafting questions is a good way to reinforce what you understand and recognize the areas you need to review. Your professor may ask you to submit the questions in writing or electronically or to prepare an overhead slide.

   The question should be challenging enough that the average student will need to stop and think, but clear enough that there is only one answer. Useful questions can be formatted as essay, short answer, or multiple choice. Notice that some exam questions are very direct, while others require deeper analysis. Here are two examples. The first focuses on a definition.

   Question: An injunction is:

   (a) A decision by an appeals court affirming the trial court.

   (b) A decision by an appeals court reversing a trial court.

   (c) A decision by an appeals court sending a decision back down to a lower court.

   (d) A theory of law requiring that current cases be decided based on earlier decisions.

   (e) A judge's order that someone stop doing something.

   As you know, the correct answer is "e."

   The next question demands that the student spot the issue of law involved (foreseeability) and correctly apply it to the facts provided.

   Question: Marvin asks Sheila, a qualified auto mechanic, to fix his engine, which constantly stalls (stops) while driving. When Marvin returns, Sheila informs him that the engine is now "Perfect—runs like a top." Marvin drives home along Lonesome

Highway. Suddenly the car stalls. Sheila has not fixed it. Marvin pulls over and begins the long walk to the nearest telephone. A blimp flies overhead, advertising "Top" brand tires. Tragically, the blimp suddenly plummets to earth and explodes 20 feet from Marvin, seriously injuring him. Marvin sues Sheila. Sheila's best defense is that:

(a) The falling blimp is so bizarre that Sheila could never have foreseen it.

(b) Sheila made reasonable efforts to fix the engine.

(c) Marvin should have checked the engine himself.

(d) Marvin should have carried a cell phone with him in case of emergencies.

(e) Sheila is a qualified mechanic and her work is presumptively sufficient.

The correct answer is "a." Notice that the same facts could be used as an essay question, simply by deleting the multiple-choice answers. Now it is your turn for Role Reversal: draft a multiple-choice question focusing on federalism.

Internet Research Problem

Take a look at **http://www.courttv.com**. Find two current cases that interest you: one civil, one criminal. Explain the different roles played by each type of law, and summarize the issues in the respective cases.

You can find further practice problems in the Online Quiz at **http://beatty.westbuslaw.com** or in the Study Guide that accompanies this text.

2

Business Ethics and Social Responsibility

Arthur Haupt is a 79-year-old retired waiter who lives with his black cat, Max, in a tidy, 650-square-foot apartment in Chicago's Rienzi Plaza apartment building. He works 20 hours a week, shelving books at Loyola University's law library, earning $6.95 an hour. He also gets Social Security and two modest pensions. His total income last year was $18,713. His monthly rent in this federally subsidized apartment is $352. Market rent for an equivalent apartment would be as high as $1,644.

Last fall, Haupt's landlord notified him that he might be evicted. Nationally, landlords have taken about 125,000 units out of the federal subsidy program. At the same time, demand for subsidized housing is rising, in part because big cities such as Chicago are tearing down their old public housing projects and telling residents to find subsidized apartments instead. Where will Arthur Haupt go?

The landlord, Sheldon Baskin, is not a bad guy. Twenty years ago, he and his partners signed a contract with the federal government, promising to build and maintain an apartment building for low-income Chicagoans. In exchange, the government guaranteed a steady stream of rent. But now the contract on Rienzi Plaza is set to expire. Baskin could make a

larger profit on the building, either by selling it, converting it to condominiums, or renting to unsubsidized tenants who could pay more. What does Baskin owe to his investors?

The Rienzi tenants and community groups have begun looking for a white knight—someone who could buy the building and preserve its low-income housing. Two for-profit organizations that specialize in investing in "affordable" housing expressed interest in buying Rienzi, but neither has made an offer.

Meanwhile, Mr. Baskin asked government officials how much more rent they would pay if he extended his contract for five years. Officials said they would have to hire an outside consultant to do a market study, a task that would take months—long past the deadline by which federal regulations require Mr. Baskin to announce his decision.[1] ▪

Business is an enormously powerful tool that corporate managers can use to accomplish many goals. They may wish to earn a good living, even to become wealthy, but they can also use their business skills to cure the ill, feed the hungry, entertain the bored, and in many other ways affect their community, their country, and their world.

This book is primarily about the impact of law on business. But law is only one set of rules that governs business; ethics is another. **Ethics is the study of how people ought to act.** Law and ethics are often in harmony. Most reasonable people agree that murder should be prohibited. But law and ethics are not always compatible. In some cases, it might be *ethical* to commit an *illegal* act; in others, it might be *unethical* to be *legal*. A 75-year-old man confined to a wheelchair robbed a bank in San Diego of $70 so that he could buy heart medicine. That was illegal—was it unethical?

Or what about Martin Luther King, Jr., who was arrested in Birmingham, Alabama in 1963 for leading illegal sit-ins and marches to protest laws that discriminated against African Americans. When eight local clergymen criticized his activities, King offered this defense:

> [W]hen you suddenly find your tongue twisted as you seek to explain to your
> six-year-old daughter why she can't go to the public amusement park that has just
> been advertised on television, and see tears welling up when she is told that Fun-
> town is closed to colored children . . . [W]hen you take a cross-country drive and
> find it necessary to sleep night after night in the uncomfortable corners of your
> automobile because no motel will accept you . . . How can [we] advocate breaking
> some laws and obeying others? . . . I agree with St. Augustine that "an unjust law
> is not law at all."[2]

The other chapters of this book focus on legal issues, but this chapter concentrates on ethics. In all of the examples in this chapter, the activities are *legal*, but are they *ethical?*

---

[1] Based on the article: Jonathan Eig, "Landlord's Dilemma: Help Poor Tenants or Seek More Profits." *The Wall Street Journal,* July 17, 2001, p. 1.

[2] Martin Luther King, Jr., "Letter from Birmingham Jail." *The Christian Century,* June 12, 1963.

Why Bother with Ethics?

Business schools teach students how to maximize the profitability of an enterprise, large or small. Some people argue that, in the *long run*, ethical behavior does indeed maximize profitability. But they must mean the *very* long run, because to date there is little evidence that ethical behavior necessarily pays financially, either in the short or the long run.

For instance, when a fire destroyed the Malden Mills factory in Lawrence, Massachusetts, its 70-year-old owner, Aaron Feuerstein, could have shut down the business, collected the insurance money, and sailed off into retirement. But a layoff of the factory's 3,000 employees would have been a major economic blow to the region. So instead Feuerstein kept the workers on the payroll making the company's patented Polartec fabric, while he rebuilt the factory. However, five years after the fire, Malden Mills filed bankruptcy papers. The company was not able to pay off the loans it had incurred to keep the business going.

In contrast, unethical behavior is no bar to financial success. The first antitrust laws in America were designed, at least in part, to restrain John D. Rockefeller's unethical activities. Yet, four generations later, his name is still synonymous with wealth and his numerous heirs can live comfortably on their inheritance from him.

If ethical behavior does not necessarily pay and unethical behavior sometimes does, why bother with ethics?

SOCIETY AS A WHOLE BENEFITS FROM ETHICAL BEHAVIOR

John Akers, the former chairman of IBM, argues that, without ethical behavior, a society cannot be economically competitive. He puts it this way:

> *Ethics and competitiveness are inseparable. No society anywhere will compete very long or successfully with people stabbing each other in the back; with people trying to steal from each other; with everything requiring notarized confirmation because you can't trust the other fellow; with every little squabble ending in litigation; and with government writing reams of regulatory legislation, tying business hand and foot to keep it honest. There is no escaping this fact: the greater the measure of mutual trust and confidence in the ethics of a society, the greater its economic strength.*[3]

PEOPLE FEEL BETTER WHEN THEY BEHAVE ETHICALLY

Every businessperson has many opportunities to be dishonest. Consider how one person felt when he *resisted* temptation:

> *Occasionally a customer forgot to send a bill for materials shipped to us for processing . . . It would have been so easy to rationalize remaining silent. After all, didn't they deserve to lose because of their inefficiency? However, upon instructing our staff to inform the parties of their errors, I found them eager to do so. Our honesty was beneficial in subtle ways. The "inefficient" customer remained loyal*

---

[3] David Grier, "Confronting Ethical Dilemmas," unpublished manuscript of remarks at the Royal Bank of Canada, Sept. 19, 1989.

for years . . . [O]ur highly moral policy had a marvelously beneficial effect on our employees. Through the years, many an employee visited my office to let me know that they liked working for a "straight" company.[4]

Profitability is generally not what motivates managers to care about ethics. Managers want to feel good about themselves and the decisions they have made; they want to sleep at night. Their decisions—to lay off employees, install safety devices in cars, burn a cleaner fuel—affect peoples' lives.

The Web site **http://www.yourtruehero.org** offers examples of ordinary people who have inspired others with their ethical behavior.

UNETHICAL BEHAVIOR CAN BE VERY COSTLY

Unethical behavior is a risky business strategy—it may lead to disaster. An engaged couple made a reservation, and put down a $1,500 deposit, to hold their wedding reception at a New Hampshire restaurant. Tragically, the bride died of asthma four months before the wedding. Invoking the terms of the contract, the restaurant owner refused to return the couple's deposit. In a letter to the groom, he admitted, "Morally, I would of course agree that the deposit should be returned." When newspapers reported this story, customers deserted the restaurant and it was forced into bankruptcy—over a $1,500 disagreement.[5] Unethical behavior does not always damage a business, but it certainly has the potential of destroying a company overnight. So why take the risk?

Even if unethical behavior does not devastate a business, it can cause other, subtler damage. In one survey, a majority of those questioned said that they had witnessed unethical behavior in their workplace and that this behavior had reduced productivity, job stability, and profits. Unethical behavior in an organization creates a cynical, resentful, and unproductive workforce.

So why bother with ethics? Because society benefits when managers behave ethically. Because ethical managers have happier, more satisfying lives. And because unethical behavior can destroy a business faster than a snake can bite.

What Is Ethical Behavior?

It is one thing to decide, in theory, that being ethical is good; in practice, it can be much more difficult to make the right decisions. Supreme Court Justice Potter Stewart once said that he could not define pornography, but he knew it when he saw it. Many people feel the same way about ethics—that somehow, instinctively, they know what is right and wrong. In real life, however, ethical dilemmas are often not black and white, but many shades of gray. The purpose of this section is to analyze the following ethics checklist as an aid to managers in making tough decisions:

* What are the facts?

* What are the critical issues?

---

[4] Hugh Aaron, "Doing the Right Thing in Business." *The Wall Street Journal,* June 21, 1993, p. A10.

[5] John Milne, "N.H. Restaurant Goes Bankrupt in Wake of Wedding Refund Flap." *The Boston Globe,* Sept. 9, 1994, p. 25.

- Who are the stakeholders?

- What are the alternatives?

- What are the ethical implications of each alternative?

    - Is it legal?

    - How would it look in the light of day?

    - What are the consequences?

    - Does it violate important values?

    - Does it violate the Golden Rule?

    - Is it just?

    - Has the process been fair?

ANALYZING THE ETHICS CHECKLIST

What Are the Facts?

Although this question seems obvious, people often forget in the heat of battle to listen to (and, more importantly, to hear) all the different viewpoints. It is crucial to discover the facts, firsthand, from the people involved.

What Are the Critical Issues?

In analyzing ethical dilemmas, expand your thinking to include all the important issues. Avoid a narrow focus that encompasses only one or two aspects. In the case of the New Hampshire restaurant that refused to refund a deposit, the owner focused on the narrow legal issue. His interpretation of the contract was correct. But if the owner had expanded his thinking to include consideration for his customers, he might have reached a different decision.

Who Are the Stakeholders?

Stakeholders are all the people potentially affected by the decision. That list might include subordinates, bosses, shareholders, suppliers, customers, members of the community in which the business operates, society as a whole, or even more remote stakeholders, such as future generations.

What Are the Alternatives?

The next step is to list the reasonable alternatives. A creative manager may find a clever solution that is a winner for everyone. What alternatives might be available to Sheldon Baskin, the landlord who faced a dilemma in the opening scenario?

What Are the Ethical Implications of Each Alternative?

Is the Alternative Legal?   Illegal may not always be synonymous with unethical, but, as a general rule, you need to think long and hard about the ethics of any illegal activities.

How Would the Alternative Look in the Light of Day?   If your activities were reported on the evening news, how would you feel? Proud? Embarrassed? Horrified? Undoubtedly, sexual harassment would be virtually eliminated if people thought that their parents, spouse, or partner would shortly see a video replay of the offending behavior.

What Are the Consequences of This Alternative?   Ask yourself: Am I hurting anyone by this decision? Which alternative will cause the greatest good (or the least harm) to the most people? For example, you would like to fire an incompetent employee. That decision will clearly have adverse consequences for him. But the other employees in your division will benefit, and so will the shareholders of your company. You should look with a particularly critical eye if an alternative benefits you while harming others.

This approach to decision making was first developed by two 19th-century English philosophers, Jeremy Bentham and John Stuart Mill. Bentham and Mill argued that all decisions should be evaluated according to how much happiness they create. This philosophy is called **utilitarianism.**

Does the Alternative Violate Important Values?   In addition to consequences, consider fundamental values. It is possible to commit an act that does not harm anyone else, but is still the wrong thing to do. Suppose, for instance, that you are away from home and have the opportunity to engage in a temporary sexual liaison. You are absolutely certain that your spouse will never find out and your partner for the night will have no regrets or guilt. There would be no negative consequences, but you believe that infidelity is wrong, regardless of the consequences, so you resist temptation.

Some people question whether, as a diverse, heterogeneous society (not to mention world), we have common values. But throughout history, and across many different cultures, common values do appear, such as: consideration, courage, integrity, and self-control. Although reasonable people may disagree about a precise list of important values, most would agree that values matter. Try compiling your own list of values and then check it periodically to see if you are living up to it in your business and personal life.

Does the Alternative Violate the Golden Rule?   We all know the Golden Rule: Do unto others as you would have them do unto you. If one of the alternatives you are considering would be particularly unpleasant when done to you, reconsider.

Immanuel Kant, an 18th-century German philosopher, took the Golden Rule one step further with a concept he called the **categorical imperative.** According to Kant, you should not do something unless you would be willing for everyone else to do it, too (and not just to you). Imagine that you could cheat on an exam without getting caught. You might gain some short-term benefit—a higher grade. But what would happen if everyone cheated? The professor would have to make the exams harder or curve everyone's grade down. If your school developed a reputation for cheating, you might not be able to find a job after graduation. Cheating works only if most people are honest. To take advantage of everyone else's honesty is contemptible.

Is the Alternative Just?   Are you respecting individual rights such as liberty (privacy, free speech, and religious freedom), welfare (employment, housing, food, education), and equality? Would it be just to fire an employee because her political views differ from your own?

Has the Process Been Fair?   Unequal outcomes are acceptable, provided they are the result of a fair process. At the end of a poker game, some players have won and others lost, but no one can complain that the result was unfair, unless players cheated. In a business context, a fair process means applying the same set of rules to everyone. If three of your subordinates are vying for the same promotion, it would be unfair to let one state her case to you but not the others.

Applying the Ethics Checklist: Making Decisions

An organization has responsibilities to customers, employees, shareholders, and society generally, both here and overseas. The purpose of this section is to apply the ethics checklist to actual business dilemmas. The checklist does not lead to one particular solution; rather it is a method to use in thinking through ethics problems. The goal is for you to reach a decision that satisfies you.

ORGANIZATION'S RESPONSIBILITY TO SOCIETY

Facts.   In the United States, teenagers routinely list alcohol commercials among their favorite advertisements. Adolescents who frequently see ads for alcohol are more likely to believe that drinkers are attractive, athletic, and successful. They are also more likely to drink, drink excessively, and drink in hazardous situations, such as when driving a car.

Then Secretary of Health and Human Services, Louis W. Sullivan publicly denounced the test marketing of Uptown, a high-tar cigarette targeted at African Americans. He called it "contemptible that the tobacco industry has sought to increase their market" among minorities because this population was "already bearing more than its fair share of smoking-related illness and mortality." Comedian Jay Leno joked that R. J. Reynolds named the cigarette Uptown "because the word 'genocide' was already taken."[6]

A promotion for Request Jeans shows a man pinning a naked woman against a shower wall. In Canada, an advertisement features childlike model Kate Moss lying naked on a couch. Above the couch is a picture of the product being promoted—Calvin Klein's Obsession for Men.

Critical Issues.   Is it ethical to entice teenagers into drinking or African Americans into smoking? What about glorifying rape to sell jeans?

Stakeholders.   Ad designers are primarily responsible to their firms and the firms' clients. After all, designers are paid to sell product, not to make the world a better place. But do the designers have any responsibility to the people who see the advertisements? Or to society as a whole?

Alternatives.   Firms have at least four alternatives in dealing with issues of ethics in advertising. They can:

- Ignore ethics and simply strive to create promotions that sell the most product

- Try, in a general way, to minimize racism, sexism, and other exploitation

---

[6] Richard W. Pollay, Jung S. Lee, and David Carter-Whitney, "Separate, But Not Equal: Racial Segmentation in Cigarette Advertising," *Journal of Advertising*, Mar. 1992, vol. 21, no. 1, p. 45.

- Include, as part of the development process, a systematic, focused review of the underlying messages contained in their advertisements; or

- Refuse to create any ads that are potentially demeaning, insensitive, or dangerous, recognizing that such a stand may lead to a loss of clients.

Ethical Implications.   All of these alternatives are perfectly legal. And, far from the ad executives being embarrassed if the ads see the light of day, the whole purpose of ads is to be seen. As for the consequences, the ads may help clients sell their products. But a manager might question whether these ads violate fundamental values. Are they showing consideration for others? Do they encourage self-control? As for the Golden Rule, how would an advertising executive feel about an ad in which he was being sexually assaulted? Are these ads just? Do they violate principles of equality? Is the process by which they have been created fair? Have those who may be adversely affected by them had an opportunity to be heard?

ORGANIZATION'S RESPONSIBILITY TO ITS CUSTOMERS

In this chapter's opening scenario, landlord Sheldon Baskin faced a dilemma: His contract with the federal government was set to expire, so he would soon have the right to evict the poor and elderly tenants in Rienzi Plaza. What would you do if you were Baskin? What obligation does he have to the tenants? To his investors? Is it fair to them if he decides to subsidize the rents of low-income tenants? What about the community? Does it benefit from having elderly members? How will Baskin feel about himself if he puts these elderly tenants out on the street? Or if *The Wall Street Journal* runs a front-page article about his eviction plans? On the other hand, could he argue that it is the government's responsibility to house the poor and elderly? Is there any compromise solution?

ORGANIZATION'S RESPONSIBILITY TO ITS EMPLOYEES

Which deal would you rather have?

- *Plan A:* Your company has a 401(k) pension plan. Federal law permits you to contribute a certain amount tax free each year. You can then invest that money in a choice of mutual funds. In addition, for every dollar you put in, your employer will contribute a dollar of company stock. However, you cannot sell this company stock until you are 50 years old. The good news is that, if the stock market—and your company—prosper, your retirement years will indeed be golden. The downside is that if the stock market or your company declines, you could be like one of the tenants in Rienzi Plaza, unable to pay your rent.

- *Plan B:* The amount of your pension is guaranteed by the company, regardless of how the market performs. This guarantee is backed up by a federal agency. In addition, as part of your annual bonus, you are given company stock that you can sell at any time. Moreover, when you invest in your special 401(k) plan, the company guarantees a minimum annual return of 12%.

Enron Corp. offered Plan A to its rank-and-file employees; Plan B was reserved for top executives. At one point, 60% of the assets in the Plan A 401(k) was invested in Enron stock. As this stock plummeted in value from $80 a share to under $1, many employees were unable to sell out because they had not yet turned 50. Even worse, as the stock price sank, the company imposed a month-long "blackout" prohibiting all employees from selling any stock in the 401(k) while a new plan administrator took over. Less than a month after the blackout ended, the company filed for bankruptcy. As a result, the 401(k) plans lost $1.3 billion of their $2.1 billion worth.

Is it ethical for top executives to set up two such different pension/savings plans for company employees? Supporters of 401(k) plans argue that offering top executives a better pension is no more unfair than paying them higher wages. Moreover, the 401(k) plans are better than nothing, which is what companies would offer if these plans were not available. One could even argue that these plans are good for employees: The matching employer contributions entice many workers into saving money that they might otherwise just spend. And the plans are good for employers: A company can meet its obligations with transfers of company stock, which are much cheaper to make than the cash payments required by traditional plans. Moreover, companies like having their stock in the friendly hands of employees. The younger employees whom companies want to attract rarely object to a 401(k) pension plan because they do not appreciate the significant disadvantages—and companies have not been eager to educate them.

Should companies do more than meet the minimum requirements of the pension laws? How much more? Would a generous pension plan for all employees benefit the company by attracting valuable workers or harm the company by decreasing its profits?

ORGANIZATION'S RESPONSIBILITY TO ITS SHAREHOLDERS

Ford Motor Company was founded by William C. Ford, Jr.'s great-grandfather, Henry. The younger Ford is an avid environmentalist and also head of the company that bears his name. He shares the concern of many environmentalists that automobile exhaust contributes to global warming. Ford Motor recently announced that it would increase the fuel economy of its sport utility vehicles (SUVs) by 25% (about 5 miles per gallon). This decision comes shortly after Congress, partly in response to lobbying by automobile manufacturers, refused to increase national fuel economy standards.

About a fifth of the vehicles Ford sells each year are SUVs. Because these heavy cars are gas inefficient, Ford has barely been able to meet existing federal standards. To achieve the higher fuel economy it has announced, the company will make more auto parts out of lighter aluminum and will redesign the SUV engines. The cost of implementing these changes could be substantial, but the company has decided not to pass the costs on to consumers. The plan is controversial within the company itself, because some insiders believe that consumers would prefer more powerful cars to more gas-efficient ones.

Milton Friedman, a Nobel laureate in economics, famously observed, "The one and only social responsibility of business is to increase its profits."[7] He argued that an executive should act for the benefit of the owners of the company. His primary responsibility is to them. If an individual wishes to support other responsibilities, such as a charity, a church, a city, or a country, let him do so with his own time and money, not that of the shareholders.

---

[7] Milton Friedman, "The Social Responsibility of Business Is to Increase Its Profits," *The New York Times Magazine,* Sept. 13, 1970, p. 32.

If you were a shareholder of Ford Motor Company, would you support the fuel efficiency initiative? Perhaps you would prefer to earn higher returns on your stock so that you could give money to other projects you consider more compelling (finding an AIDS vaccine, for example). Should William Ford, who inherited his company stock, have the right to spend company funds to support his pet projects? If the air needs to be cleaner or the schools richer, why shouldn't private donors or public institutions be responsible, not one company's shareholders?

Do executives have an obligation to be socially responsible? Ford officials argue that their fuel economy initiative may be profitable—it might increase sales enough to make up for the lower profit per car. Moreover, an environmentally friendly image may help sales of all its cars, not just SUVs. By voluntarily increasing its own fuel standards, Ford may head off tighter federal regulation.

UPDATE

Find a current news article about fuel economy standards. Have other automobile manufacturers (here and abroad) followed Ford's lead? Did Ford sales increase enough to offset the cost of making these design changes? Did Ford's stock price rise or fall after the company announced its intention to increase fuel economy?

ORGANIZATION'S RESPONSIBILITY OVERSEAS

An American company's ethical obligations do not end at the border. What ethical duties does an American manager owe to stakeholders in countries where the culture and economic circumstances are very different?

Here is a typical story from Guatemala:

"My father left home a long time ago. My mother supported me and my five brothers and sisters by selling tortillas and corn. Our house was a tin shack on the side of the road. We were crowded with all of us in one room, especially when it rained and the roof and sides leaked. One day the police came and cleared us all out. The owners of the land said we couldn't come back unless we paid rent. How could we afford that? I was 12 and my mother said it was time for me to work. But most people won't hire children. "Lots of other kids shine shoes or beg, but I heard that the maquila [clothing factory] was willing to hire children if we would work as hard as older people.

"I can keep up with the grown-ups. We work from 6:00 in the morning to 6:30 at night, with half an hour break at noon. We have no other breaks the whole rest of the day. If I don't work fast enough, they hit me, not too hard, and threaten to fire me. Sometimes, if there is too much work to do, they'll lock the doors and not let us out until everything is finished.

"I earn $30 a week and without that money, we would not have enough to eat. My mother hopes all of my brothers and sisters can get jobs in the factory, too. Of course, I'd rather be in school where I could wear a uniform and have friends. Then I could get a job as a clerk at the medical clinic. I would find people's files and tell them how long before the doctor could see them."

This description paints a distasteful picture indeed: Children being beaten as they work 12-hour days. Should American companies (and consumers) buy goods that are produced in sweatshop factories? Jeffrey Sachs, a leading economist and adviser to developing nations, says, "My concern is not that there are too many sweatshops but that there are too few."[8] Why would he support sweatshops and child labor?

Historically, poor children have worked. Indeed, for many people and for many centuries, the point of having children was to create a supply of free labor to help support the family. In England in 1860, almost 40% of 14-year-old boys worked, and that was not just a few hours at Burger Box, but more likely 60 hours a week. That percentage is higher than in Africa or India today. For a child in a desperately poor family, the choice is not work or school, it is work, starvation, or prostitution. (For a history of sweatshops in America, work your way over to **http://americanhistory.si.edu/sweatshops/**.)

Industrialization has always been the first stepping-stone out of dire poverty—it was in England, it is now in the Third World. Eventually, higher productivity leads to higher wages. During the past 50 years, Taiwan and South Korea welcomed sweatshops. During the same period, India resisted what it perceived to be foreign exploitation. Although all three countries started at the same economic level, Taiwan and South Korea today have much lower levels of infant mortality and much higher levels of education than India.[9]

When governments or customers try to force Third World factories to pay higher wages, the factory owners typically either relocate to lower-wage countries or mechanize, thereby reducing the need for workers. In either case, the local economy suffers.

The difference, however, between the 21st and the 19th centuries is that now there are wealthy countries able to help their poorer neighbors. In the 19th century, England was among the richest countries, so it was on its own to solve its economic problems. Is America ethically obligated to assist people around the world who live in abject poverty? Already, owing to pressure from activists, many companies have introduced better conditions in their factories. Workers are less likely to be beaten. They can go to the bathroom without asking permission. They might even receive rudimentary medical care. Manufacturing processes use fewer dangerous chemicals. Factories are cleaner, with better lighting and more ventilation. But hours are still long and wages low.

Many of these sweatshops produce clothing. As a consumer, how much would you be willing to pay in higher clothing prices to eliminate sweatshops and child labor? As a taxpayer, how much are you willing to pay in taxes to subsidize Third World incomes so that sweatshops and child labor are no longer necessary?

---

[8] Allen R. Meyerson, "In Principle, A Case for More 'Sweatshops,'" *The New York Times*, June 22, 1997, p. E5.

[9] The data in this and the preceding paragraph are from Nicholas D. Kristof and Sheryl WuDunn, "Two Cheers for Sweatshops," *The New York Times Magazine*, Sept. 24, 2000, p. 70.

Chapter Conclusion

Even employees who are ethical in their personal lives may find it difficult to uphold their standards at work if those around them behave differently. Managers wonder what they can do to create an ethical environment in their companies. The surest way to infuse ethics throughout an organization is for top executives to behave ethically themselves. Few employees will bother to "do the right thing" unless they observe that their bosses value and support such behavior. To ensure a more ethical world, managers must be an example for others, both within and outside their organizations.

For further discussion and updates on ethical issues, check in at **http://ethics.acusd.edu/index.html**.

Chapter Review

1. There are at least three reasons to be concerned about ethics in a business environment:

   * Society as a whole benefits from ethical behavior.

   * People feel better when they behave ethically.

   * Unethical behavior can be very costly.

2. The ethics checklist:

   * What are the facts?

   * What are the critical issues?

   * Who are the stakeholders?

   * What are the alternatives?

* What are the ethical implications of each alternative?

   * Is it legal?

   * How would it look in the light of day?

   * What are the consequences?

   * Does it violate important values?

   * Does it violate the Golden Rule?

   * Is it just?

   * Has the process been fair?

PRACTICE TEST

Matching Questions

Match the following people with their views:

___ **A.** Martin Luther King, Jr.

___ **B.** John Akers

___ **C.** Immanuel Kant

___ **D.** Milton Friedman

___ **E.** Jeremy Bentham and John Stuart Mill

1. Argued that "Ethics and competitiveness are inseparable."

2. Argued that all decisions should be evaluated according to how much utility they create.

3. Argued that "The one and only social responsibility of business is to increase its profits."

4. Argued that "An unjust law is not law at all."

5. Argued that you should not do something unless you would be willing for everyone else to do it, too.

Short-Answer Questions

1. Executives were considering the possibility of moving their company to a different state. They wanted to determine if employees would be willing to relocate, but they did not want the employees to know the company was contemplating a move because the final decision had not yet been made. Instead of asking the employees directly, the company hired a firm to carry out a telephone survey. When calling the employees, these "pollsters" pretended to be conducting a public opinion poll and identified themselves as working for the new state's chamber of commerce. Has this company behaved in an ethical manner? Would there have been a better way to obtain this information?

2. Rap artist Ice-T and his band, Body Count, recorded a song called *Cop Killer,* in which the singer gleefully anticipates slitting a policeman's throat. (The lyrics to this song are available at **http://www.cleat.org/ remember/TimeWarner/lyrics.html**.) Time Warner, Inc. produced this song and other gangsta rap recordings with violent and sexually degrading lyrics. Recorded music is an important source of profits for the company. If Time Warner renounces rap albums, its reputation in the music business—and future profits— might suffer. This damage could spill over into the multimedia market, which is crucial to Time Warner's future. What decision would you make if you were CEO of Time Warner?

3. H. B. Fuller Company of St. Paul is a leading manufacturer of industrial glues. Its mission statement says the company "will conduct business legally and ethically." It has endowed a university chair in business ethics and donates 5% of its profits to charity. But now it is under attack for selling its shoemakers' glue, Resistol, in Central America. Many homeless children in these countries have become addicted to Resistol's fumes. So widespread is the problem that glue sniffers in Central America are called "resistoleros." Glue manufacturers in Europe have added a foul-smelling oil to their glue that discourages abusers. Fuller fears that the smell may also discourage legitimate users. What should Fuller do?

4. According to the Electronic Industries Association, questionable returns have become the toughest problem plaguing the consumer electronics industry. Some consumers purchase electronic equipment to use once or twice for a special occasion and then return it—a radar detector for a weekend getaway or a camcorder to videotape a wedding. Or a customer might return a cordless telephone because he cannot figure out how it works. The retailer's staff lacks the expertise to help, so they refund the customer's money and ship the phone back to the manufacturer labeled as defective. Excessive and unwarranted returns force manufacturers to repackage and reship perfectly good products, imposing extra costs that squeeze their profits and raise prices to consumers. One retailer returned a cordless telephone that was two years old and had been chewed up by a dog. What ethical obligations do consumers and retailers have in these circumstances?

5. Genentech, Inc. manufactures Protropin, a genetically engineered version of the human growth hormone. This drug's purpose is to enhance the growth of short children. Protropin is an important product for Genentech, accounting for more than one third of the company's total revenue of $217 million. Although the drug is approved for the treatment of children whose bodies make inadequate quantities of growth hormone, many doctors prescribe it for children with normal amounts of growth hormone who simply happen to be short. There is no firm evidence that the drug actually increases growth for short children with normal growth hormone. Moreover, many people question whether it is appropriate to prescribe such a powerful drug for cosmetic reasons, especially when the drug may not work. Nor is there proof that it is safe over the long term. Is Genentech behaving ethically? Should it discourage doctors from prescribing the drug to normal, short children?

6. ROLE REVERSAL: Write one or two paragraphs that could be used as an essay question describing an ethical dilemma that you have faced in your own life.

Internet Research Problem

Go to **http://www.mapnp.org/library/ethics/ethxgde.htm** and click on Ethics Tools: Resolving Ethical Dilemmas (with Real-to-Life Examples). Outline the steps you would take to resolve one of these dilemmas. Use the ethics checklist in this chapter to guide you.

You can find further practice problems in the Online Quiz at **http://beatty.westbuslaw.com** or in the Study Guide that accompanies this text.

3

Courts, Litigation, and Alternative Dispute Resolution

Tony Caruso had not returned for dinner, and his wife, Karen, was nervous. She put on some sandals and hurried across the dunes, a half mile to the ocean shore. She soon came upon Tony's dog, Blue, tied to an old picket fence. Tony's shoes and clothing were piled neatly nearby. Karen and friends searched frantically throughout the evening. A little past midnight, Tony's body washed ashore, his lungs filled with water. A local doctor concluded he had accidentally drowned.

Karen and her friends were not the only ones distraught. Tony had been partners with Beth Smiles in an environmental consulting business, Enviro-Vision. They were good friends, and Beth was emotionally devastated. When she was able to focus on business issues, Beth filed an insurance claim with the Coastal Insurance Group. Beth hated to think about Tony's death in financial terms, but she was relieved that the struggling business would receive $2 million on the life insurance policy.

Several months after filing the claim, Beth received this reply from Coastal: "Under the policy issued to Enviro-Vision, we are liable in the amount of $1 million in the event of Mr. Caruso's death. If his death is accidental, we are liable to pay double indemnity of $2 million. But pursuant to section H(5) death by suicide is not covered. After a thorough investigation, we have concluded that Anthony Caruso's death was an act of suicide. Your claim is denied in its entirety." Beth was furious. She was convinced Tony was incapable of suicide. And her company could not afford the $2 million loss. She decided to consult her lawyer, Chris Pruitt.

Three Fundamental Areas of Law

This case is a fictionalized version of several real cases based on double indemnity insurance policies. In this chapter we follow Beth's dispute with Coastal from initial interview through appeal, using it to examine three fundamental areas of law: the structure of our court systems, litigation, and alternative dispute resolution.

When Beth Smiles meets with her lawyer, Chris Pruitt brings a second attorney from his firm, Janet Booker, who is an experienced **litigator**, that is, a lawyer who handles court cases. If they file a lawsuit, Janet will be in charge, so Chris wants her there for the first meeting. Janet probes about Tony's home life, the status of the business, his personal finances, everything. Beth becomes upset that Janet doesn't seem sympathetic, but Chris explains that Janet is doing her job: She needs all the information, good and bad.

LITIGATION VERSUS ALTERNATIVE DISPUTE RESOLUTION

Janet starts thinking about the two methods of dispute resolution: litigation and alternative dispute resolution. **Litigation** refers to lawsuits, the process of filing claims in court, trying the case, and living with the court's ruling. **Alternative dispute resolution** is any other formal or informal process used to settle disputes without resorting to a trial. It is increasingly popular with corporations and individuals alike because it is generally cheaper and faster than litigation.

Alternative Dispute Resolution

Janet Booker knows that even after expert legal help, vast expense, and years of work, litigation may leave clients unsatisfied. If she can use alternative dispute resolution (ADR) to create a mutually satisfactory solution in a few months, for a fraction of the cost, she is glad to do it. In most cases the parties **negotiate,** whether personally or through lawyers. Fortunately, the great majority of disputes are resolved this way. Negotiation often begins as soon as a dispute arises and may last a few days or several years.

MEDIATION

Mediation is the fastest-growing method of dispute resolution in the United States. Here, a neutral person, called a mediator, attempts to coax the two disputing parties toward a voluntary settlement.

A mediator does not render a decision in the dispute, but uses a variety of skills to prod the parties toward agreement. Mediators must earn the trust of both parties, listen closely, diffuse anger and fear, explore common ground, cajole the parties into different perspectives, and build the will to settle. Good mediators do not need a law degree, but they must have a sense of humor and low blood pressure.

ARBITRATION

In this form of ADR, the parties agree to bring in a neutral third party, but with a major difference: The arbitrator has the power to impose an award. The arbitrator allows each side equal time to present its case and, after deliberation, issues a binding decision, generally without giving reasons. Unlike mediation, arbitration ensures that there will be a final result, although the parties lose control of the outcome. Arbitration is generally faster and cheaper than litigation.

Parties in arbitration give up many rights that litigants retain, including discovery. *Discovery,* as we see below, allows the two sides in a lawsuit to obtain, before trial, documentary and other evidence from the opponent. Arbitration permits both sides to keep secret many files that would have to be divulged in a court case, potentially depriving the opposing side of valuable evidence. A party may have a stronger case than it realizes, and the absence of discovery may permanently deny it that knowledge.

Janet Booker proposes to Coastal Insurance that they use ADR to expedite a decision in their dispute. Coastal rejects the offer. Coastal's lawyer, Rich Stewart, insists that suicide is apparent.

It is a long way to go before trial, but Janet has to prepare her case. The first thing she thinks about is where to file the lawsuit.

Court Systems

The United States has more than 50 systems of courts. One nationwide system of *federal* courts serves the entire country. In addition, each *state* has its court system. The state and federal courts are in different buildings, have different judges, and hear different kinds of cases. Each has special powers and certain limitations.

STATE COURTS

The typical state court system forms a pyramid, as Exhibit 3.1 shows. You may use the Internet to learn the exact names and powers of the courts in your state. Go to **http://www.state.[name of state].gov**, and click on "agencies," "courts," or a similar link.

Trial Courts

Almost all cases start in trial courts, the ones endlessly portrayed on television and in film. There is one judge and there will often (but not always) be a jury. This is the only court to hear testimony from witnesses and receive evidence. **Trial courts determine the facts of a particular dispute and apply to those facts the law given by earlier appellate court decisions.**

In the Enviro-Vision dispute, the trial court will decide all important facts that are in dispute. Did Tony Caruso die? Did he drown? Assuming he drowned, was his death accidental or suicide? Once the jury has decided the facts, it will apply the law to those facts. If Tony Caruso died accidentally, contract law provides that Beth Smiles is entitled to double indemnity benefits. If the jury decides he killed himself, Beth gets nothing.

Jurisdiction refers to a court's power to hear a case. A plaintiff may start a lawsuit only in a court that has jurisdiction over that kind of case. Some state trial courts have very limited jurisdiction, while others have the power to hear almost any case. In Exhibit 3.1, notice that some courts have power only to hear cases of small claims, domestic relations, and so forth.

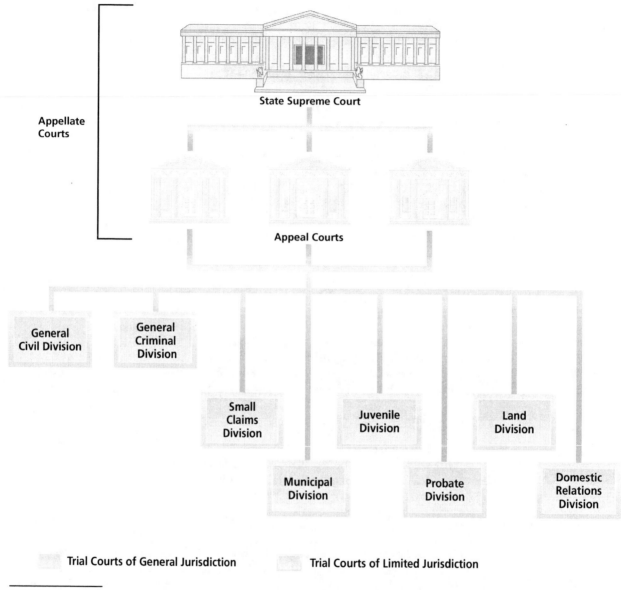

State Supreme Court

Appellate
Courts

Appeal Courts

General Civil Division	General Criminal Division

Small Claims Division

Juvenile Division

Land Division

Municipal Division

Probate Division

Domestic Relations Division

Trial Courts of General Jurisdiction   Trial Courts of Limited Jurisdiction

Exhibit 3.1

Appellate Courts

Appellate courts are entirely different from trial courts. Three or more judges hear the case. There are no juries, ever. These courts do not hear witnesses or take new evidence. They hear appeals of cases already tried below. **Appeal courts generally accept the facts given to them by trial courts and review the trial record to see if the court made errors of law.**

An appeal court reviews the trial record to make sure that the lower court correctly applied the law to the facts. If the trial court made an **error of law,** the appeal court may require a new trial. Suppose the jury concludes that Tony Caruso committed suicide, but votes to award Enviro-Vision $1 million because it feels sorry for Beth Smiles. That is an error of law: If Tony committed suicide, Beth is entitled to nothing. An appellate court will reverse the decision, declaring Coastal the victor.

The party that loses at the trial court generally is entitled to be heard at the intermediate court of appeals. The party filing the appeal is the **appellant.** The party opposing the appeal (because it won at trial) is the **appellee.** A party that loses at the court of appeals may *ask* the state supreme court to hear an appeal, but the state's highest court may choose not to accept the case.

FEDERAL COURTS

As discussed in Chapter 1, federal courts are established by the United States Constitution, which limits what kinds of cases can be brought in any federal court. For our purposes, two kinds of civil lawsuits are permitted in federal court: federal question cases and diversity cases.

Federal Question Cases

A claim based on the United States Constitution, a federal statute, or a federal treaty is called a federal question case.[1] Federal courts have jurisdiction over these cases. If the Environmental Protection Agency orders Logging Company not to cut in a particular forest, and Logging Company claims that the agency has wrongly deprived it of its property, that suit is based on a federal statute (a law passed by Congress) and is thus a federal question. Enviro-Vision's potential suit merely concerns an insurance contract. The federal district court has no federal question jurisdiction over the case.

Diversity Cases

Even if no federal law is at issue, federal courts have jurisdiction when (1) the plaintiff and defendant are citizens of different states and (2) the amount in dispute exceeds $75,000. The theory behind diversity jurisdiction is that courts of one state might be biased against citizens of another state. To ensure fairness, the parties have the option of federal court.

Enviro-Vision is located in Oregon and Coastal Insurance is incorporated in Georgia.[2] They are citizens of different states and the amount in dispute far exceeds $75,000. Janet could file this case in United States District Court based on diversity jurisdiction.

Trial Courts

United States District Courts are the primary trial courts in the federal system. The nation is divided into about 94 districts, and each has a district court. States with smaller populations have one district, while those with larger populations have several districts. There are also specialized trial courts such as Bankruptcy Court,

---

[1] 28 U.S.C. §1331 governs federal question jurisdiction and 28 U.S.C. §1332 covers diversity jurisdiction.

[2] For diversity purposes, a corporation is a citizen of the state in which it is incorporated and the state in which it has its principal place of business.

Tax Court, and others which are, you will be happy to know, beyond the scope of this book.

Appellate Courts

United States Courts of Appeals.   These are the intermediate courts of appeals. As the map below shows, they are divided into "circuits," most of which are geographical areas. For example, an appeal from the Northern District of Illinois would go to the Court of Appeals for the Seventh Circuit. You will find an interactive map of the District and Circuit Courts at **http://www.uscourts.gov/links.html**.

United States Supreme Court.   This is the highest court in the country. There are nine justices on the Court. One justice is the chief justice and the other eight are associate justices. When they decide a case, each justice casts an equal vote. For a face-to-face meeting with Supreme Court justices, past and present, introduce yourself to **http://oyez.nwu.edu**.

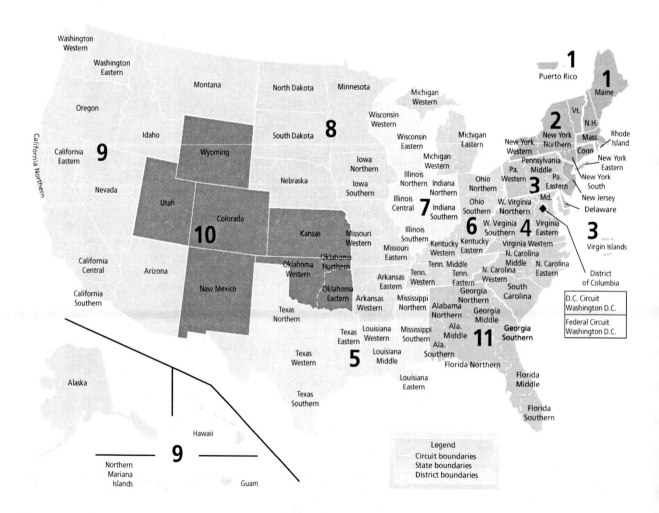

Litigation

Janet Booker decides to file the Enviro-Vision suit in the Oregon trial court. She thinks that a state court judge may take the issue more seriously than a federal district court judge.

PLEADINGS

The documents that begin a lawsuit are called the **pleadings.** The most important are the complaint and the answer.

Complaint

The plaintiff files in court a **complaint,** which is a short, plain statement of the facts she is alleging and the legal claims she is making. The purpose of the complaint is to inform the defendant of the general nature of the claims and the need to come into court and protect his interests.

Janet Booker files the complaint, as shown below. Since Enviro-Vision is a partnership, she files the suit on behalf of Beth, personally.

STATE OF OREGON

CIRCUIT COURT

Multnomah County   Civil Action No._____

Elizabeth Smiles,

Plaintiff

                                                                        JURY TRIAL DEMANDED

v.

Coastal Insurance Company, Inc.,

Defendant

COMPLAINT

Plaintiff Elizabeth Smiles states that:

1. She is a citizen of Multnomah County, Oregon.

2. Defendant Coastal Insurance Company, Inc., is incorporated under the laws of Georgia and has as its usual place of business 148 Thrift Street, Savannah, Georgia.

3. On or about July 5, 2006, plaintiff Smiles ("Smiles"), Defendant Coastal Insurance Co, Inc. ("Coastal") and Anthony Caruso entered into an insurance contract ("the contract"), a copy of which is annexed hereto as Exhibit "A." This contract was signed by all parties or their authorized agents, in Multnomah County, Oregon.

4. The contract obligates Coastal to pay to Smiles the sum of two million dollars ($2 million) if Anthony Caruso should die accidentally.

5. On or about September 18, 2006, Anthony Caruso accidentally drowned and died while swimming.

6. Coastal has refused to pay any sum pursuant to the contract.

7. Coastal has knowingly, willingly and unreasonably refused to honor its obligations under the contract.

WHEREFORE, plaintiff Elizabeth Smiles demands judgment against defendant Coastal for all monies due under the contract; demands triple damages for Coastal's knowing, willing, and unreasonable refusal to honor its obligations; and demands all costs and attorney's fees, with interest.

ELIZABETH SMILES,

By her attorney,

   [Signed]

Janet Booker

Pruitt, Booker & Bother

983 Joy Avenue

Portland, OR

October 18, 2006

Answer

Coastal has 20 days in which to file an answer. Coastal's **answer is a brief reply to each of the allegations in the complaint.** The answer tells the court and the plaintiff exactly what issues are in dispute. Since Coastal admits that the parties entered into the contract that Beth claims they did, there is no need for her to prove that in court. The court can focus its attention on the issue that Coastal disputes: whether Tony Caruso died accidentally.

If the defendant fails to answer in time, the plaintiff will ask for a **default judgment,** meaning a decision that the plaintiff wins without a trial.

Class Actions

Suppose Janet uncovers evidence that Coastal denies 80% of all life insurance claims, calling them suicide. She could ask the court to permit a **class action.** If the court granted her request, she would represent the entire group of plaintiffs, including those who are unaware of the lawsuit or even unaware they were harmed. Class actions can give the plaintiffs much greater leverage, since the defendant's potential liability is vastly increased. Because Janet has no such evidence, she decides not to pursue a class action.

Discovery

Discovery is the critical, pre-trial opportunity for both parties to learn the strengths and weaknesses of the opponent's case.

The theory behind civil litigation is that the best outcome is a negotiated settlement and that parties will move toward agreement if they understand the opponent's case. That is likeliest to occur if both sides have an opportunity to examine the evidence their opponent will bring to trial. Further, if a case does go all the way to trial, efficient and fair litigation cannot take place in a courtroom filled, like a piñata, with surprises. In television dramas, witnesses say astonishing things that amaze the courtroom. In real trials, the lawyers know in advance the answers to practically all questions asked because discovery has allowed them to see the opponent's documents and question its witnesses. The following are the most important forms of discovery.

Interrogatories.   These are written questions that the opposing party must answer, in writing, under oath.

Depositions.   These provide a chance for one party's lawyer to question the other party, or a potential witness, under oath. The person being questioned is the **deponent.** Lawyers for both parties are present.

Production of Documents and Things.   Each side may ask the other side to produce relevant documents for inspection and copying; to produce physical objects, such as part of a car alleged to be defective; and for permission to enter on land to make an inspection, for example, at the scene of an accident.

Physical and Mental Examination.   A party may ask the court to order an examination of the other party, if his physical or mental condition is relevant, for example, in a case of medical malpractice.

Janet Booker begins her discovery with interrogatories. Her goal is to learn Coastal's basic position and factual evidence and then follow up with more detailed questioning during depositions. Her interrogatories ask for every fact Coastal relied on in denying the claim. She asks for the names of all witnesses, the identity of all documents, and the descriptions of all things or objects that they considered. She requests the names of all corporate officers who played any role in the decision and of any expert witnesses Coastal plans to call.

Coastal has 30 days to answer Janet's interrogatories. Before it responds, Coastal mails to Janet a notice of deposition, stating its intention to depose Beth Smiles. Beth and Janet will go to the office of Coastal's lawyer, and Beth will answer questions under oath. But at the same time Coastal sends this notice, it sends 25 other notices of deposition. It will depose Karen Caruso as soon as Beth's deposition is over. Coastal also plans to depose all seven employees of Enviro-Vision; three neighbors who lived near Tony and Karen's beach house; two policemen who participated in the search; the doctor and two nurses involved in the case; Tony's physician; Jerry Johnson, Tony's tennis partner; Craig Bergson, a college roommate; a couple who had dinner with Tony and Karen a week before his death; and several other people.

Rich, the Coastal lawyer, proceeds to take Beth's deposition. It takes two full days. He asks about Enviro-Vision's past and present. He learns that Tony appeared to have won their biggest contract ever from Rapid City, Oregon, but that he then lost it when he had a fight with Rapid City's mayor. He inquires into Tony's mood, learns that he was depressed, and probes in every direction he can to find evidence of suicidal motivation. Janet and Rich argue frequently over questions and whether Beth should have to answer them. At times Janet is persuaded and permits Beth to answer; at other times she instructs Beth not to answer. For example, toward the end of the second day, Rich asks Beth whether she and Tony had been sexually involved. Janet instructs Beth not to answer. This fight necessitates a trip into court. As both lawyers know, **the parties are entitled to discover anything that could reasonably lead to valid evidence.** Rich wants his questions answered, and files a motion to compel discovery. The judge will have to decide whether Rich's questions are reasonable.

A **motion** is a formal request to the court. Before, during, and after trial, both parties will file many motions. A **motion to compel discovery** is a request to the court for an order requiring the other side to answer discovery. The judge rules that Beth must discuss Tony's romantic life only if Coastal has evidence that he was involved with someone outside his marriage. Because the company lacks any such evidence, the judge denies Coastal's motion.

At the same time, the judge hears Beth's **motion for a protective order.** Beth claims that Rich has scheduled too many depositions; the time and expense are a huge burden to a small company. The judge limits Rich to 10 depositions. Rich cancels several depositions, including that of Craig Bergson, Tony's old roommate. As we will see, Craig knows crucial facts about this case, and Rich's decision not to depose him will have major consequences.

Judges rule on many discovery motions, often with dramatic effect, as the following case demonstrates.

CASE SUMMARY

KLUPT v. KRONGARD

126 Md. App. 179; 728 A.2d 727; 1999 Md. App. LEXIS 86
Court of Special Appeals of Maryland, 1999

FACTS: Carle Klupt invented a disposable cardboard videocassette. He formed a corporation, Sharbar, Inc., to develop and market the product. Alvin Krongard and a few associates paid $115,000 to Klupt for a chance to participate in the manufacture and sale of the cassette. Three years later, Krongard and his associates sued Klupt and Sharbar, claiming that the defendants had fraudulently persuaded them to enter into the deal, in other words, had lied in order to get their investment. Klupt, in turn, sued the plaintiffs, asserting that the Krongard group had actually attempted to seize control of the business in violation of their agreement.

The plaintiffs served requests on Klupt for all documents (in writing or any other medium) relating to oral or written communications between the parties. The plaintiffs also scheduled a deposition of Klupt, but the defendant repeatedly objected to dates. Klupt also changed lawyers from time to time, causing further delay. When the trial court ordered him to appear on a specific date, Klupt claimed he had another deposition

scheduled for the same date, but that later turned out to be false.

When he finally appeared for deposition, Klupt produced only four pages of notes from phone conversations with the plaintiffs. He then managed to delay the deposition six more months. When it resumed, Klupt was forced to concede that in fact he had tape-recorded all of his phone calls for many years and had possessed hundreds of recorded calls between the parties. However, in the gap between depositions, he had destroyed the tapes.

Arguing that this was gross abuse of the discovery process, the plaintiffs moved to dismiss Klupt's claims. The trial court granted the motion, and Klupt appealed.

ISSUE: Did the trial court abuse its discretion by dismissing Klupt's claims?

DECISION: Affirmed. The trial court did not abuse its discretion by dismissing Klupt's claims.

REASONING: Appellate courts prefer not to second-guess trial judges on discovery rulings, and will reverse only when the lower court has abused its discretion. However, dismissing a claim is a grave penalty, appropriate only in cases of extraordinary misconduct.

During discovery, Klupt prepared false, back-dated memoranda. He also deliberately concealed many tapes from the court and even from his own lawyer. The tapes were clearly subject to discovery, because they were reasonably calculated to enable the other party to find admissible evidence. Klupt admitted that he had smashed the tapes with a hammer, at a time when the lawsuit was already several months old. The trial judge did not abuse his discretion in dismissing Klupt's claims.

Summary Judgment

When discovery is completed, both sides may consider seeking summary judgment. **Summary judgment is a ruling by the court that no trial is necessary because there are no essential facts in dispute.** The purpose of a trial is to determine the facts of the case, that is, to decide who did what to whom, why, when, and with what consequences. If there are no relevant facts in dispute, then there is no need for a trial.

Suppose Joe sues EZBuck Films, claiming that the company's new movie, *Lover Boy*, violates the copyright of a screenplay that he wrote, called *Love Man*. Discovery establishes that the two stories are suspiciously similar. But EZBuck's lawyer also learns that Joe sold the copyright for *Love Man* to HotShot Pix. EZBuck may or may not have violated a copyright, but there is no need for a trial because Joe cannot win even if there is a copyright violation. He does not own the copyright. When EZBuck moves for summary judgment, the court will grant the motion, terminating the case before trial.

In the following case, the defendant won summary judgment, meaning that the case never went to trial. And yet, this was only the beginning of trouble for that defendant, William Jefferson Clinton.

CASE SUMMARY

JONES v. CLINTON

990 F. Supp. 657, 1998 U.S. Dist. LEXIS 3902
United States District Court for the Eastern District of Arkansas, 1998

FACTS: In 1991, Bill Clinton was governor of Arkansas. Paula Jones worked for a state agency, the Arkansas Industrial Development Commission (AIDC). When Clinton became president, Jones sued him, claiming that he had sexually harassed her. She alleged that, in May 1991, the governor arranged for her to meet him in a hotel room in Little Rock, Arkansas. When they were alone, he put his hand on her leg and slid it toward her pelvis. She escaped from his grasp, exclaimed, "What are you doing?" and said she was "not that kind of girl." She was upset and confused, and sat on a sofa near the door. She claimed that Clinton approached her, "lowered his trousers and underwear, exposed his penis and told her to kiss it." Jones was horrified, jumped up, and said she had to leave. Clinton responded by saying, "Well, I don't want to make you do anything you don't want to do," and pulled his pants up. He added that if she got in trouble for leaving work, Jones should "have Dave call me immediately and I'll take care of it." He also said, "You are smart. Let's keep this between ourselves." Jones remained at AIDC until February 1993, when she moved to California because of her husband's job transfer.

President Clinton denied all of the allegations. He also filed for summary judgment, claiming that Jones had not alleged facts that justified a trial. Jones opposed the motion for summary judgment.

ISSUE: Was Clinton entitled to summary judgment or was Jones entitled to a trial?

DECISION: Jones failed to make out a claim of sexual harassment. Summary judgment is granted for the president.

REASONING: To establish this type of sexual harassment case, a plaintiff must show that her refusal to submit to unwelcome sexual advances resulted in specific harm to her job.

Jones received every merit increase and cost-of-living allowance for which she was eligible. Her only job transfer involved a minor change in working conditions, with no reduction in pay or benefits. Jones claims that she was obligated to sit in a less private area, often with no work to do, and was the only female employee not to receive flowers on Secretary's Day. However, even if these allegations are true, all are trivial and none is sufficient to create a sexual harassment suit. Jones has demonstrated no specific harm to her job. ◢

In other words, the court acknowledged that there were factual disputes, but concluded that even if Jones proved each of her allegations, she would still lose the case, because her allegations fell short of a legitimate case of sexual harassment. Jones appealed the case. Later the same year, as the appeal was pending and the House of Representatives was considering whether to impeach President Clinton, the parties settled the dispute. Clinton, without acknowledging any of the allegations, agreed to pay Jones $850,000 to drop the suit.

Janet and Rich each consider moving for summary judgment, but both correctly decide that they would lose. There is one major fact in dispute: Did Tony Caruso commit suicide? Only a jury may decide that issue. As long as there is some evidence supporting each side of a key factual dispute, the court may not grant summary judgment.

Well over 90% of all lawsuits are settled before trial. But the parties in the Enviro-Vision dispute seem unable to compromise, and are headed for trial.

Trial

ADVERSARY SYSTEM

Our system of justice assumes that the best way to bring out the truth is for the two contesting sides to present the strongest case possible to a neutral factfinder. Each side presents its witnesses and then the opponent has a chance to cross-examine. The **adversary system** presumes that by putting a witness on the stand and letting both lawyers "go at" her, the truth will emerge.

The judge runs the trial. Each lawyer sits at a large table near the front. Beth, looking tense and unhappy, sits with Janet. Rich Stewart sits with a Coastal executive. In the back of the courtroom are benches for the public. Today there are only a few spectators. One is Tony's old roommate, Craig Bergson, who has a special interest in the trial.

RIGHT TO JURY TRIAL

Not all cases are tried to a jury. As a general rule, both plaintiff and defendant have a right to demand a jury trial when the lawsuit is one for money damages. For example, in a typical contract lawsuit, such as Beth's insurance claim, both plaintiff and defendant have a jury trial right whether they are in state or federal court. Even in such a case, though, the parties may waive the jury right, meaning they agree to try the case to a judge.

If the plaintiff is seeking an equitable remedy, such as an injunction (an order not to do something), there is no jury right for either party. Equitable rights come from the old Court of Chancery in England, where there was never a jury. Even today, only a judge may give an equitable remedy.

Although jury selection for some cases takes many days, in the Enviro-Vision case the first day of the hearing ends with the jury selected. In the hallway outside the court, Rich offers Janet $200,000 to settle. Janet reports the offer to Beth and they agree to reject it. Craig Bergson drives home, emotionally confused. Only three weeks before his death, Tony had accidentally met his old roommate and they had had several drinks. Craig believes that what Tony told him answers the riddle of this case.

OPENING STATEMENTS

The next day, each attorney makes an opening statement to the jury, summarizing the proof he or she expects to offer, with the plaintiff going first. Janet focuses on Tony's successful life, his business and strong marriage, and the tragedy of his accidental death.[3]

Rich works hard to establish a friendly rapport with the jury. He expresses regret about the death. Nonetheless, suicide is a clear exclusion from the policy. If insurance companies are forced to pay claims they did not bargain for, everyone's insurance rates will go up.

BURDEN OF PROOF

In civil cases, the plaintiff has the **burden of proof.** That means that the plaintiff must convince the jury that its version of the case is correct; the defendant is not obligated to disprove the allegations.

The plaintiff's burden in a civil lawsuit is to prove its case by a **preponderance of the evidence.** The plaintiff must convince the jury that his or her version of the facts is at least *slightly* more likely than the defendant's version. Some courts describe this as a "51–49" persuasion, that is, that plaintiff's proof must "just tip" credibility in its favor. By contrast, in a criminal case, the prosecution must demonstrate **beyond a reasonable doubt that the defendant is guilty.** The burden of proof in a criminal case is much tougher because the likely consequences are, too. See Exhibit 3.2.

PLAINTIFF'S CASE

Since the plaintiff has the burden of proof, Janet puts in her case first. She wants to prove two things. First, that Tony died. That is easy, since the death certificate clearly demonstrates it and since Coastal does not seriously contest it. Second, in order to win double indemnity damages, she must show that the death was

---

[3] Janet Booker has dropped her claim for triple damages against Coastal. To have any hope of such a verdict, she would have to show that Coastal had no legitimate reason at all for denying the claim. Discovery has convinced her that Coastal will demonstrate some rational reasons for what it did.

accidental. She will do this with the testimony of the witnesses she calls, one after the other. Her first witness is Beth. When a lawyer asks questions of her own witness, it is **direct examination.** Janet brings out all the evidence she wants the jury to hear: that the business was basically sound, though temporarily troubled, that Tony was a hard worker, why the company took out life insurance policies, and so forth.

Then Rich has a chance to **cross-examine** Beth, which means to ask questions of an opposing witness. He will try to create doubt in the jury's mind. He asks Beth only questions for which he is certain of the answers, based on discovery. Rich gets Beth to admit that the firm was not doing well the year of Tony's death; that Tony had lost the best client the firm ever had; that Beth had reduced salaries; and that Tony had been depressed about business.

Janet uses her other witnesses, Tony's friends, family, and coworkers, to fortify the impression that his death was accidental.

DEFENDANT'S CASE

Rich now puts in his case, exactly as Janet did, except that he happens to have fewer witnesses. He calls the examining doctor, who admits that Tony could have committed suicide by swimming out too far. On cross-examination, Janet gets the doctor to acknowledge that he has no idea whether Tony intentionally drowned. Rich also questions several neighbors as to how depressed Tony had seemed and how unusual it was that Blue was tied up. Some of the witnesses Rich deposed, such as the tennis partner Jerry Johnson, have nothing that will help Coastal's case, so he does not call them.

Craig Bergson, sitting in the back of the courtroom, thinks how different the trial would have been had he been called as a witness. When he and Tony had the fateful drink, Tony had been distraught: Business was terrible, he was involved in an extramarital affair that he could not end, and he saw no way out of his problems. He had no one to talk to and had been hugely relieved to speak with Craig. Several times Tony had said, "I just can't go on like this. I don't want to, anymore." Craig thought Tony seemed suicidal and urged him to see a therapist Craig knew. Tony had said that it was good advice, but Craig is unsure whether Tony sought any help.

This evidence would have affected the case. Had Rich Stewart known of the conversation, he would have deposed Craig and the therapist. Coastal's case would have been far stronger, perhaps overwhelming. But Craig's evidence will never be heard. Facts are critical. Rich's decision to depose other witnesses and omit Craig may influence the verdict more than any rule of law.

Closing Argument

Both lawyers sum up their case to the jury, explaining how they hope the jury will interpret what they have heard. Judge Rowland instructs the jury as to its duty. He tells them that they are to evaluate the case based only on the evidence they heard at trial, relying on their own experience and common sense.

He explains the law and the burden of proof, telling the jury that it is Beth's obligation to prove that Tony died. If Beth has proven that Tony died, she is entitled to $1 million; if she has proven that his death was accidental, she is entitled to $2 million. However, if Coastal has proven suicide, Beth receives nothing. Finally, he states that if they are unable to decide between accidental death and suicide, there is a legal presumption that it was accidental. Rich asks Judge Rowland to rephrase the "legal presumption" part, but the judge declines.

Verdict

The jury deliberates informally, with all jurors entitled to voice their opinion. Some deliberations take two hours; some take two weeks. Many states require a unanimous verdict; others require only, for example, a 10–2 vote in civil cases.

This case presents a close call. No one saw Tony die. Yet even though they cannot know with certainty, the jury's decision will probably be the final word on whether he took his own life. After a day and a half of deliberating, the jury notifies the judge that it has reached a verdict. Rich Stewart quickly makes a new offer: $350,000. Beth hesitates but turns it down.

The judge summons the lawyers to court, and Beth goes as well. The judge asks the foreman if the jury has reached a decision. He states that it has: The jury finds that Tony Caruso drowned accidentally, and awards Beth Smiles $2 million.

Appeals

Two days later, Rich files an appeal to the court of appeal. The same day, he phones Janet and increases his settlement offer to $425,000. Beth is tempted but wants Janet's advice. Janet says the risks of an appeal are that the court will order a new trial, and they would start all over. But to accept this offer is to forfeit over $1.5 million. Beth is unsure what to do. The firm desperately needs cash now. Janet suggests they wait until oral argument, another eight months.

Rich files a brief arguing that there were two basic errors at the trial: first, that the jury's verdict is clearly contrary to the evidence; and second, that the judge gave the wrong instructions to the jury. Janet files a reply brief, opposing Rich on both issues. In her brief, Janet cites many cases that she claims are **precedent:** earlier decisions by the state supreme court on similar or identical issues.

Appeal Court Options

The court of appeal can **affirm** the trial court, allowing the decision to stand. The court may **modify** the decision, for example, by affirming that the plaintiff wins but decreasing the size of the award. (That is unlikely here; Beth is entitled to $2 million or nothing.) The court might **reverse and remand,** meaning it nullifies the lower court's decision and returns the case to the trial court for a new trial. Or it could simply **reverse,** turning the loser (Coastal) into the winner, with no new trial.

Janet and Beth talk. Beth is very anxious and wants to settle. She does not want to wait four or five months, only to learn that they must start all over. With Beth's approval, Janet phones Rich and offers to settle for $1.2 million. Rich snorts, "Yeah, right." Then he snaps, "750,000. Take it or leave it. Final offer." After a short conversation with her client, Janet calls back and accepts the offer.

Litigation

1. Pleadings	2. Discovery	3. Pretrial Motions
Complaint	Interrogatories	Class action
Answer	Depositions	Summary judgment
	Production of documents and things	
	Physical and mental examinations	

4. Trial	5. Jury's Role	6. Appeals
Voir dire	Judge's instructions	Affirm
Opening statements	Deliberation	Modify
Plaintiff's case	Verdict	Reverse
Defendant's case		Remand
Closing argument		

Chapter Conclusion

No one will ever know for sure whether Tony took his own life. Craig Bergson's evidence might have tipped the scales in favor of Coastal. But even that is uncertain, since the jury could have found him unpersuasive. After two years, the case ends with a settlement and uncertainty—both typical lawsuit results. The vaguely unsatisfying feeling about it all is only too common and indicates why litigation is best avoided—by reasonable negotiation.

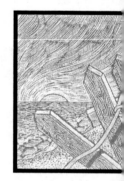

Chapter Review

1. Alternative dispute resolution (ADR) is any formal or informal process to settle disputes without a trial. Mediation and arbitration are the two most common forms.

2. There are many systems of courts, one federal and one in each state. A federal court will hear a case only if it involves a federal question or diversity jurisdiction.

3. Trial courts determine facts and apply the law to the facts; appeal courts generally accept the facts found by the trial court and review the trial record for errors of law.

4. A complaint and an answer are the two most important pleadings, that is, documents that start a lawsuit.

5. Discovery is the critical pretrial opportunity for both parties to learn the strengths and weaknesses of the opponent's case. Important forms of discovery include interrogatories, depositions, production of documents and objects, physical and mental examinations, and requests for admission.

6. A motion is a formal request to the court.

7. Summary judgment is a ruling by the court that no trial is necessary because there are no essential facts in dispute.

8. Generally, both plaintiff and defendant may demand a jury in any lawsuit for money damages.

9. The plaintiff's burden of proof in a civil lawsuit is preponderance of the evidence, meaning that its version of the facts must be at least slightly more persuasive than the defendant's. In a criminal prosecution, the government must offer proof beyond a reasonable doubt in order to win a conviction.

10. The verdict is the jury's decision in a case.

11. An appeal court has many options. The court may affirm, upholding the lower court's decision; modify, changing the verdict but leaving the same party victorious; reverse, transforming the loser into the winner; and/or remand, sending the case back to the lower court.

PRACTICE TEST

Matching Questions

Match the following terms with their definitions:

___ **A.** Arbitration

___ **B.** Diversity jurisdiction

___ **C.** Mediation

___ **D.** Interrogatories

___ **E.** Deposition

1. A pretrial procedure involving written questions to be signed under oath.

2. A form of ADR in which the parties themselves craft the settlement.

3. A pretrial procedure involving oral questions answered under oath.

4. The power of a federal court to hear certain cases between citizens of different states.

5. A form of ADR which leads to a binding decision.

True/False Questions

Circle true or false:

1. T F   One advantage of arbitration is that it provides the parties with greater opportunities for discovery than litigation does.

2. T F   In the United States there are many separate courts, but only one court *system*, organized as a pyramid.

3. T F   If we are listening to witnesses testify, we must be in a trial court.

4. T F   About one half of all lawsuits settle before trial.

5. T F   In a lawsuit for money damages, both the plaintiff and the defendant are generally entitled to a jury.

Multiple-Choice Questions

6. A federal court has the power to hear

   (a) Any case.

   (b) Any case between citizens of different states.

   (c) Any criminal case.

   (d) Appeals of any cases from lower courts.

   (e) Any lawsuit based on a federal statute.

7. Before trial begins, a defendant in a civil lawsuit believes that even if the plaintiff proves everything he has alleged, the law requires the defendant to win. The defendant should

   (a) Request arbitration.

   (b) Request a mandatory verdict.

   (c) Move for recusal.

   (d) Move for summary judgment.

   (e) Demand mediation.

8. In a civil lawsuit
   (a) The defendant is presumed innocent until proven guilty.
   (b) The defendant is presumed guilty until proven innocent.
   (c) The plaintiff must prove her case by a preponderance of the evidence.
   (d) The plaintiff must prove her case beyond a reasonable doubt.
   (e) The defendant must establish his defenses to the satisfaction of the court.

9. Mack sues Jasmine, claiming that she caused an automobile accident. At trial, Jasmine's lawyer is asking her questions about the accident. This is
   (a) An interrogatory
   (b) A deposition
   (c) Direct examination
   (d) Cross-examination
   (e) Opening statement

10. Jurisdiction refers to
    (a) The jury's decision.
    (b) The judge's instructions to the jury.
    (c) Pretrial questions posed by one attorney to the opposing party.
    (d) The power of a court to hear a particular case.
    (e) A decision by an appellate court to send the case back to the trial court.

Short-Answer Questions

11. State which court(s) have jurisdiction as to each of these lawsuits:
    (a) Pat wants to sue his next-door neighbor Dorothy, claiming that Dorothy promised to sell him the house next door.
    (b) Paula, who lives in New York City, wants to sue Dizzy Movie Theatres, whose principal place of business is Dallas. She claims that while she was in Texas on holiday, she was injured by their negligent maintenance of a stairway. She claims damages of $30,000.
    (c) Phil lives in Tennessee. He wants to sue Dick, who lives in Ohio. Phil claims that Dick agreed to sell him 3,000 acres of farmland in Ohio, worth over $2 million.
    (d) Pete, incarcerated in a federal prison in Kansas, wants to sue the United States government. He claims that his treatment by prison authorities violates three federal statutes.

12. Students are now suing schools for sexual harassment. The cases raise important issues about the limits of discovery. In a case in Petaluma, California, a girl claimed that she was harassed for years and that the school knew about it and failed to act. According to press reports, she alleges that a boy stood up in class and asked, "I have a question. I want to know if [Jane Doe] has sex with hot dogs." In discovery, the school district sought the parents' therapy records, the girl's diary, and a psychological evaluation of the girl. Should they get those things?

13. ETHICS: Trial practice is dramatically different in Britain. The lawyers for the two sides, called solicitors, do not go into court. Courtroom work is done by different lawyers, called barristers. The barristers are not permitted to interview any witnesses before trial. They know the substance of what each witness intends to say, but do not rehearse questions and answers, as in the United States. Which approach do you consider more effective? More ethical? What is the purpose of a trial? Of pretrial preparation?

14. You plan to open a store in Chicago, specializing in beautiful rugs imported from Turkey. You will work with a native Turk who will purchase and ship the rugs to your store. You are wise enough to insist on a contract establishing the rights and obligations of both parties and would prefer an ADR clause. But you want to be sensitive to different cultures and do not want a clause that will magnify a problem or alienate the parties. Is there some way you can accomplish all of this?

15. Claus Scherer worked for Rockwell International and was paid over $300,000 per year. Rockwell fired Scherer for alleged sexual harassment of several workers, including his secretary, Terry Pendy. Scherer sued in United States District Court, alleging that Rockwell's real motive in firing him was his high salary.

Rockwell moved for summary judgment, offering deposition transcripts of various employees. Pendy's deposition detailed instances of harassment, including comments about her body, instances of unwelcome touching, and discussions of extramarital affairs. Another deposition, from a Rockwell employee who investigated the allegations, included complaints by other employees as to Scherer's harassment. In his own deposition, which he offered to oppose summary judgment, Scherer testified that he could not recall the incidents alleged by Pendy and others. He denied generally that he had sexually harassed anyone. The district court granted summary judgment for Rockwell. Was its ruling correct?

16. ROLE REVERSAL: Write a multiple-choice question that illustrates the unique significance of summary judgment. First, be sure you understand when and why a party is entitled to summary judgment.

Internet Research Problem

You may be called for jury duty before long. Read the summary of the juror's responsibilities at **http://www.placer.ca.gov/courts/jury.htm**. Some people try hard to get out of jury duty. Why is that a problem in a democratic society?

You can find further practice problems in the Online Quiz at **http://beatty.westbuslaw.com** or in the Study Guide that accompanies this text.

4

Constitutional, Statutory, Administrative, and Common Law

Gregory Johnson was angry. On a public street in Dallas, the young man lit an American flag on fire, protesting the nearby political convention. Law officers arrested and convicted him of violating Texas law, but Johnson appealed his case all the way to the United States Supreme Court, claiming that the First Amendment protected this form of demonstration. Did it? Should it? Which has a higher social value, Johnson's urge to protest, or the government's decision to protect the flag? How do we decide the issue? Where do we find the law that will answer this question? In this chapter, we look at four vital sources of law: the United States Constitution, statutes, administrative agencies, and the common law.

Let us consider a very different—yet related—question. What if a state legislature passes a law prohibiting new construction along a lakefront? This measure will protect the environment, and keep beaches open for all of us. In the process, though, it will render some very expensive waterfront property worthless, because the owners will not be able to build. Whose interest is more important, that of the public or that of the property owners?

Does your state have the power to prohibit flag burning? If so, does that mean it could outlaw a campaign poster on your front lawn? Prohibit political protest entirely? Ban waterfront development? How much power have we granted to the government? What rights do the people retain? Those important questions lead to our first law source.

CONSTITUTIONAL LAW

Government Power

The Constitution of the United States is the greatest legal document ever written. No other written constitution has lasted so long, governed so many, or withstood such challenge.

In 1783, 13 American colonies gained surprising independence from Great Britain. Four years later, the colonies sent delegates to craft a new constitution, but the men (no women among them) faced conflicts on a basic issue. How much power should the federal government be given? The Framers, as they have come to be called because they made or "framed" the original document, had to compromise. **The Constitution is a series of compromises about power.**

SEPARATION OF POWERS

One method of limiting power was to create a national government divided into three branches, each independent and equal. Each branch would act as a check on the power of the other two, avoiding the despotic rule that had come from London. Article I of the Constitution created a Congress, which was to have legislative power. Article II created the office of president, defining the scope of executive power. Article III established judicial power by creating the Supreme Court and permitting additional federal courts.

Consider how the three separate powers balance one another: Congress was given the power to pass statutes, a major grant of power. But the president was permitted to veto legislation, a nearly equal grant. Congress, in turn, had the right to override the veto, ensuring that the president would not become a dictator. The president was allowed to appoint federal judges and members of his cabinet, but only with a consenting vote from the Senate.

FEDERALISM

The national government was indeed to have considerable power, but it would still be *limited* power. Article I, section 8, enumerates those issues on which Congress may pass statutes. If an issue is not on the list, Congress has no power to legislate. Thus Congress may create and regulate a post office because postal service is on the list. But Congress may not pass statutes regulating child custody in a divorce: That issue is not on the list. Only the states may legislate child custody issues.

Power Granted

CONGRESSIONAL POWER

Article I of the Constitution creates the Congress with its two houses. Representation in the House of Representatives is proportionate with a state's population, but each state elects two senators. Congress may perform any of the functions enumerated in Article I, section 8, such as imposing taxes, spending money, creating copyrights, supporting the military, declaring war, and so forth. None of these rights is more important than the authority to raise and spend money (the "power of the purse"), because every branch of government is dependent upon Congress for its money.

One of the most important items on this list of congressional powers concerns trade.

Interstate Commerce

"The Congress shall have power to regulate commerce with foreign nations, and among the several states." This is the **Commerce Clause: Congress is authorized to regulate trade between states.** For example, if Congress passed a law imposing a new tax on all trucks engaged in interstate transportation, the law is valid. Congress can regulate television broadcasts because many of them cross state lines.

States have less power in this area. **A state statute that discriminates against interstate commerce is unconstitutional and void.** Suppose that Ohio, in order to protect its dairy industry, imposes a special tax on milk produced outside the state. That law discriminates against interstate trade, and violates the Commerce Clause.

EXECUTIVE POWER

Article II of the Constitution defines the executive power. Once again the Constitution gives powers in general terms. **The basic job of the president is to enforce the nation's laws.** Three of his key powers concern appointment, legislation, and foreign policy.

Appointment

As we see later in this chapter, administrative agencies play a powerful role in business regulation. The president nominates the heads of most of them. These choices dramatically influence what issues the agencies choose to pursue and how aggressively they do it. For example, a president who believes that it is vital to protect our natural resources may appoint a forceful environmentalist to run the Environmental Protection Agency, whereas a president who dislikes federal regulations will choose a more passive agency head.

Legislation

The president and his advisers propose bills to Congress and lobby hard for their passage. The executive also has the veto power.

Foreign Policy

The president conducts the nation's foreign affairs, coordinating international efforts, negotiating treaties, and so forth. The president is also the commander in chief of the armed forces, meaning that he heads the military.

JUDICIAL POWER

Article III of the Constitution creates the Supreme Court and permits Congress to establish lower courts within the federal court system. Federal courts have two key functions: adjudication and judicial review.

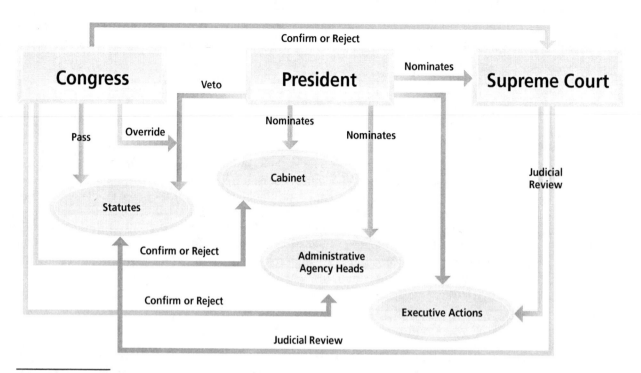

Exhibit 4.1
The Constitution established a federal government of checks and balances. Congress may pass statutes; the president may veto them; and Congress may override the veto. The president nominates cabinet officers, administrative heads, and Supreme Court justices, but the Senate must confirm his nominees. Finally, the Supreme Court (and lower federal courts) exercise judicial review over statutes and executive actions. Unlike the other checks and balances, judicial review is not provided for in the Constitution, but is a creation of the Court itself in *Marbury v. Madison.*

Adjudicating Cases

The federal court system hears criminal and civil cases. All prosecutions of federal crimes begin in United States District Court. That same court has limited jurisdiction to hear civil lawsuits, a subject discussed in Chapter 3, on dispute resolution.

Judicial Review

Judicial review refers to the power of federal courts to declare a statute or governmental action unconstitutional and void. The courts can examine acts from any branch of federal or state government. If Ohio did pass a tax on milk produced in other states, a federal court would declare the law void, as a violation of the Commerce Clause. Exhibit 4.1 illustrates the balance among Congress, the president, and the Court.

Is judicial review good for the nation? Those who oppose it argue that federal court judges are all appointed, not elected, and that we should not permit judges to nullify a statute passed by elected officials because that diminishes the people's role in their government. Those who favor judicial review insist that there must be one cohesive interpretation of the Constitution and the judicial branch is the logical one to provide it. This dispute about power simmers continuously beneath the surface and occasionally comes to the boil.

CASE SUMMARY

YOUNGSTOWN SHEET & TUBE Co. v. SAWYER

343 U.S. 579, 72 S. Ct. 863, 1952 U.S. LEXIS 2625
United States Supreme Court, 1952

FACTS: During the Korean War, steel companies and the unions were unable to reach a contract. The union notified the companies that they would strike, beginning April 9, 1952. President Truman declared steel essential to the war effort and ordered his Secretary of Commerce, Sawyer, to take control of the steel mills and keep them running. Sawyer immediately ordered the presidents of the various companies to serve as operating managers for the United States.

On April 30, the federal district court issued an injunction to stop Sawyer from running the mills. That same day the United States Court of Appeals "stayed" the injunction, i.e., it permitted Sawyer to keep operating the mills. The Supreme Court quickly granted certiorari, heard arguments May 12, and issued its decision June 2—at least five years faster than most cases reach final decision.

ISSUE: Did President Truman have the constitutional power to seize the steel mills?

DECISION: The President lacked the constitutional power to seize the mills. The District Court's injunction is affirmed.

REASONING: If the president had authority to issue the seizure order, it had to come from the Constitution. There is no express authorization of such power in the document. The president, though, argues that his power is implied from the clauses stating that the executive power shall be vested in a president, that he shall take care that the laws be faithfully executed, and that he shall be commander in chief.

Under our constitutional system, the commander in chief has no power to take possession of private property. That is a job for the nation's lawmakers, not for its military authorities.

The executive power clauses also fail to support the president's seizure order. The president is given power to *execute* the laws, not to *make* them. The Constitution permits the president to recommend bills he considers wise and veto those he finds defective; however, it is the Congress alone that passes the laws. The Framers gave the lawmaking power to Congress in good times and bad. The seizure order is void. ◢

UPDATE

Find an article that describes a recent Supreme Court decision declaring a statute unconstitutional. What was the purpose of the statute? Why did the justices nullify the law? Do you agree with the Court's decision? For a look at the current justices, the full text of famous cases, and a calendar of pending cases, see **http://supct.law.cornell.edu/supct/**. You can tour the Court itself and even hear some of the justices read their opinions at **http://oyez.nwu.edu**.

Protected Rights

The original Constitution was silent about the rights of citizens. This alarmed many, who feared that the new federal government would have unlimited power over their lives. So in 1791 the first 10 amendments, known as the Bill of Rights, were added to the Constitution, guaranteeing many liberties directly to individual citizens.

The amendments to the Constitution protect the people of this nation from the power of state and federal government. The **First Amendment** guarantees rights of free speech, free press, and religion; the **Fourth Amendment** protects against illegal searches; the **Fifth Amendment** ensures due process; the **Sixth Amendment** demands fair treatment for defendants in criminal prosecutions; and the **Fourteenth Amendment** guarantees equal protection of the law. We consider the First, Fifth, and Fourteenth Amendments in this chapter and the Fourth, Fifth, and Sixth Amendments in Chapter 7, on crime.

The "people" who are protected include citizens and, for most purposes, corporations. Corporations are considered persons and receive most of the same protections. The great majority of these rights also extend to citizens of other countries who are in the United States.

Constitutional rights generally protect only against governmental acts. The Constitution generally does not protect us from the conduct of private parties, such as corporations or other citizens. Constitutional protections apply to federal, state, and local governments.

FIRST AMENDMENT: FREE SPEECH

The First Amendment states that "Congress shall make no law . . . abridging the freedom of speech . . ." In general, we expect our government to let people speak and hear whatever they choose. The Framers believed democracy would only work if the members of the electorate were free to talk, argue, listen, and exchange viewpoints in any way they wanted. If a city government prohibited an antiabortion group from demonstrating, its action would violate the First Amendment. Government officers may not impose their political beliefs on the citizens. The government may regulate the *time, place,* and *manner* of speech, for example by prohibiting a midnight rally, or insisting that demonstrators remain within a specified area. But outright prohibitions are unconstitutional.

"Speech" includes symbolic conduct. Does that mean flag burning is permissible? You be the judge.

CASE SUMMARY

TEXAS v. JOHNSON

491 U.S. 397, 109 S. Ct. 2533, 1989 U.S. LEXIS 3115
United States Supreme Court, 1989

FACTS: Outside the Republican National Convention in Dallas, Gregory Johnson participated in a protest against policies of the Reagan administration. Participants gave speeches and handed out leaflets. Johnson burned an American flag. He was arrested and convicted under a Texas statute that prohibited desecrating the flag, but the Texas Court of Criminal Appeals reversed on the grounds that the conviction violated the First Amendment. Texas appealed to the United States Supreme Court. The Court concluded that flag burning *was* in fact symbolic speech, and that it *could* therefore receive First Amendment protection. The question was, *should* it be protected?

YOU BE THE JUDGE

Does the First Amendment protect flag burning?

ARGUMENT FOR TEXAS: For more than 200 years, the American flag has occupied a unique position as the symbol of our nation, a special place that justifies a governmental prohibition against flag burning. In the Revolutionary War, the flag served to unite the struggling colonies. More recently, in the First and Second World Wars, thousands of our countrymen and women died defending the flag. Nearly 6,000 Americans died just on the small island of Iwo Jima, in order to raise a flag there.

No other American symbol has been so universally admired and honored. Surely it is the height of hypocrisy to burn this glorious emblem of freedom and then demand in a courtroom that the liberty which the flag symbolizes guarantees the right to destroy the banner itself.

ARGUMENT FOR JOHNSON: The government may not prohibit the expression of an idea simply because society finds it offensive. Could the government prohibit the burning of state flags? Copies of the Constitution? How are we to decide which symbols deserve special treatment? Judges are not entitled to force their own political perspectives on the populace.

The way to preserve the flag's special role is not to punish those who feel differently about these matters. It is to persuade them that they are wrong. We do not consecrate the flag by punishing its desecration, for in doing so we dilute the freedom that this cherished emblem represents.

Fifth Amendment: Due Process and The Takings Clause

Ralph is a first-semester senior at State University, where he majors in finance. With a 3.6 grade point average and outstanding recommendations, he has an excellent chance of admission to an elite business school—until his life suddenly turns upside down. Professor Watson, who teaches Ralph in marketing, notifies the school's dean that the young man plagiarized material that he included in his recent paper. Dean Holmes reads Watson's report and sends Ralph a brief letter: "I find that you have committed plagiarism in violation of school rules. Your grade in Dr. Watson's marketing course is an 'F.' You are hereby suspended from the University for one full academic year."

Ralph is shocked. He is convinced he did nothing wrong, and wants to tell his side of the story, but Dean Holmes refuses to speak with him. What can he do? The first step is to read the Fifth Amendment.

Two related provisions of the Fifth Amendment, called the Due Process Clause and the Takings Clause, prohibit the government from arbitrarily depriving us of our most valuable assets. Together, they state: "No person shall be . . . deprived of life, liberty, or property without due process of law; nor shall private property be taken for public use, without just compensation." We will discuss the civil law aspects of these clauses, but due process also applies to criminal law. The reference to "life" refers to capital punishment. The criminal law issues of this subject are discussed in Chapter Seven, on crime.

PROCEDURAL DUE PROCESS

The government deprives citizens or corporations of their property in a variety of ways. The Internal Revenue Service may fine a corporation for late payment of taxes. The Customs Service may seize goods at the border. As to liberty, the government may take it by confining someone in a mental institution or by taking a child out of the home because of parental neglect. **The purpose of procedural due process is to ensure that before the government takes liberty or property, the affected person has a fair chance to oppose the action.**

The Due Process Clause protects Ralph because State University is part of the government. Ralph is entitled to due process. Does this mean that he gets a full court trial on the plagiarism charge? No. **The type of hearing the government must offer depends upon the importance of the property or liberty interest.** The more important the interest, the more formal the procedures must be. Regardless of how formal the hearing, one requirement is constant: The fact finder must be neutral.

In a criminal prosecution, the liberty interest is very great. A defendant can lose his freedom or even his life. The government must provide the defendant with a lawyer if he cannot afford one, adequate time to prepare, an unbiased jury, an opportunity to present his case and cross-examine all witnesses, and many other procedural rights.

A student faced with academic sanctions receives less due process, but still has rights. State University has failed to provide Ralph with due process. The school has accused the young man of a serious infraction. The school must promptly provide details of the charge, give Ralph all physical evidence, and allow him time to plan his response. The university must then offer Ralph a hearing, before a neutral person or group, who will listen to Ralph (as well as Dr. Watson) and examine any evidence the student offers. Ralph is not, however, entitled to a lawyer or a jury.

THE TAKINGS CLAUSE

Kabrina owns a 10-acre parcel of undeveloped land on Lake Halcyon. She plans to build a 20-bedroom inn of about 35,000 square feet—until the state environmental agency abruptly halts the work. The agency informs Kabrina that, to protect the lake from further harm, it will allow no shoreline development except single-family houses of 2,000 square feet or less. Kabrina is furious. Does the state have the power to wreck Kabrina's plans? To learn the answer, we look to another section of the Fifth Amendment.

The Takings Clause prohibits a state from taking private property for public use without just compensation. A town wishing to build a new football field *does* have the right to boot you out of your house. But the town must compensate you. The government takes your land through the power of eminent domain. Officials must notify you of their intentions and give you an opportunity to oppose the project and to challenge the amount the town offers to pay. When the hearings are done, though, the town may write you a check and grind your house into goalposts, whether you like it or not.

If the state actually wanted to take Kabrina's land and turn it into a park, the Takings Clause would force it to pay the fair market value. However, the state is not trying to seize the land—it merely wants to prevent large development.

"My land is worthless," Kabrina replies. "You might just as well kick me off my own property!" **A regulation that denies** *all beneficial use* **of property is a taking, and requires compensation.** Has the government denied Kabrina all beneficial use? No, it has not. Kabrina retains the right to build a private house. The environmental agency has decreased the value of the land, but owes her nothing. Had the state forbidden *any construction* on her land, it would have been obligated to pay Kabrina.

Fourteenth Amendment: Equal Protection Clause

Shannon Faulkner wanted to attend The Citadel, a state-supported military college in South Carolina. She was a fine student who met every admission requirement that The Citadel set except one: She was not a male. The Citadel argued that its long and distinguished history demanded that it remain all male. Faulkner responded that she was a citizen of the state and ought to receive the benefits that others got, including the right to a military education. Could the school exclude her on the basis of gender?

The Fourteenth Amendment provides that "No State shall . . . deny to any person within its jurisdiction the equal protection of the laws." This is the **Equal Protection Clause,** and it means that, generally speaking, all levels of government must treat people equally. Unfair classifications among people or corporations will not be permitted. **Regulations based on gender, race, or fundamental rights are generally void.** Shannon Faulkner won her case and was admitted to The Citadel. The Court found no justification for discriminating against women. Any regulation based on race or ethnicity is *certain* to be void. Similarly, all citizens enjoy the *fundamental right* to travel between states. If Kentucky limited government jobs to those who had lived in the state for two years, it would be discriminating against a fundamental right, and the restriction would be struck down.

ETHICS

Today over 800 high school girls wrestle competitively. Some join female clubs but others have no such opportunity and compete with boys—or seek to. Some schools allow girls to join the boys' wrestling team, but others refuse, citing moral reasons, concern for the girls' safety, and the possibility of sexual harassment. If a particular school has no female team, should girls be permitted to wrestle boys? Do they have an equal protection right to do so? ▪

STATUTORY LAW

Most new law is statutory law. Statutes affect each of us every day, in our business, professional, and personal lives. When the system works correctly, this is the one part of the law over which we the people have control. We elect the local legislators who pass state statutes; we vote for the senators and representatives who create federal statutes. If we understand the system, we can affect the largest source of contemporary law. If we live in ignorance of its strengths and pitfalls, we delude ourselves that we participate in a democracy.

As we saw in Chapter 1, there are many systems of government operating in the United States: a national government and 50 state governments. Each level of government has a legislative body. In Washington, D.C., Congress is our national legislature. Congress passes the statutes that govern the nation. In addition, each state has a legislature, which passes statutes for that state only. In this section we look at how Congress does its work creating statutes. State legislatures operate similarly, but the work of Congress is better documented and obviously of national importance.

COMMITTEE WORK

Congress is organized into two houses, the House of Representatives and the Senate. Either house may originate a proposed statute, which is called a **bill.** After a bill has been proposed, it is sent to an appropriate committee.[1]

If you visit either house of Congress, you will probably find half a dozen legislators on the floor, with one person talking and no one listening. This is because most of the work is done in committees. Both houses are organized into dozens of committees, each with special functions. The House currently has about 27 committees (further divided into about 150 subcommittees) and the Senate has approximately 20 committees (with about 86 subcommittees). For example, the armed services committee of each house oversees the huge defense budget and the workings of the armed forces. Labor committees handle legislation concerning organized labor and working conditions. Banking committees develop expertise on financial institutions. Judiciary committees review nominees to the federal courts. There are dozens of other committees, some very powerful, because they control vast amounts of money, and some relatively weak.

When a bill is proposed in either house, it is referred to the committee that specializes in that subject. Why are bills proposed in the first place? For any of several reasons:

- *New Issue, New Worry.* During the early years of this millennium, voters were increasingly irate about abuses in campaign financing, and, after years of hearings, Congress finally passed legislation designed to reduce excessive political donations.

- *Unpopular Judicial Ruling.* If Congress disagrees with a judicial interpretation of a statute, the legislators may pass a new statute to modify or "undo" the court decision. For example, if the Supreme Court misinterprets a statute about musical copyrights, Congress may pass a new law correcting the Court's error.

- *Criminal Law.* When legislators perceive that social changes have led to new criminal acts, they may respond with new statutes. The rise of Internet fraud has led to many new statutes outlawing such things as computer trespass and espionage, fraud in the use of cell phones, identity theft, and so on.

Congressional committees hold hearings to investigate the need for new legislation and consider the alternatives. Suppose a congressman believes that a growing number of American corporations locate their headquarters offshore to escape taxes. She requests committee hearings on the subject, hoping to discover the extent of the problem, its causes, and possible remedies. After hearings, if the committee votes in favor of the bill, it goes to the full body, meaning either the House of Representatives or the Senate. If the full body approves the bill, it goes to the other house.

---

[1] See the chart of state and federal governments in Chapter 1. A vast amount of information about Congress is available on the Internet. The House of Representatives has a Web page at **http://www.house.gov/**. The Senate's site appears at **http://www.senate.gov**. Each page provides links to current law, pending legislation, votes, committees, and more.

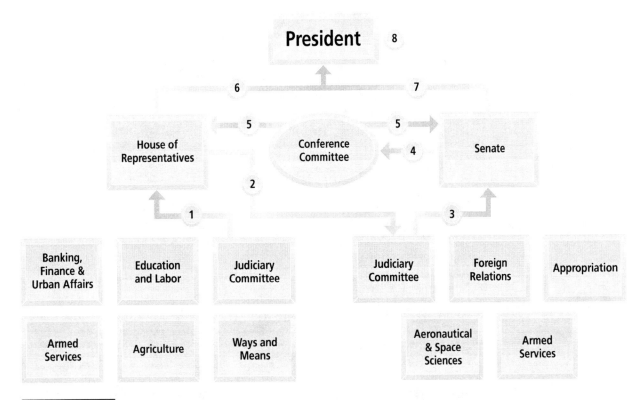

The two houses of Congress are organized into dozens of committees, a few of which are shown here. The path of the 1964 Civil Rights Act (somewhat simplified) was as follows: (1) The House Judiciary Committee approved the bill and sent it to the full House; (2) the full House passed the bill and sent it to the Senate, where it was assigned to the Senate Judiciary Committee; (3) the Senate Judiciary Committee passed an amended version of the bill and sent it to the full Senate; (4) the full Senate passed the bill with additional amendments. Since the Senate version was now different from the bill the House passed, the bill went to a Conference Committee. The Conference Committee (5) reached a compromise and sent the new version of the bill back to both houses. Each house passed the compromise bill (6 and 7) and sent it to the president, who signed it into law (8).

The bill must be voted on and approved by both branches of Congress. Assuming both houses pass it, the bill goes to the president. If the president signs the bill, it becomes law. If the president opposes the bill, he will veto it, in which case it is not law. When the president vetoes a bill, Congress has one last chance to make it law: an override. Should both houses re-pass the bill, each by a two thirds margin, it becomes law over the president's veto.

COMMON LAW

Jason observes a toddler wander onto the railroad tracks and hears a train approaching. He has plenty of time to pull the child from the tracks with no risk to himself, but chooses to do nothing. The youngster is killed. The child's family sues Jason for his callous behavior, and a court determines that Jason owes—nothing. How can that be?

Jason and the toddler present a classic legal puzzle: What, if anything, must a bystander do when he sees someone in danger? We will examine this issue to see how the common law works.

The common law is judge-made law. It is the sum total of all the cases decided by appellate courts. The common law of Pennsylvania consists of all cases decided by appellate courts in that state. The Illinois common law of bystander liability is all of the cases on that subject decided by Illinois appellate courts. Two hundred years ago, almost all of the law was common law. Today, most new law is statutory. But common law still predominates in tort, contract, and agency law, and it is very important in property, employment, and some other areas.

We focus on appellate courts because they are the only ones to make rulings of law, as discussed in Chapter 3. In a bystander case, it is the job of the state's highest court to say what legal obligations, if any, a bystander has. The trial court, on the other hand, must decide facts: Was this defendant able to see what was happening? Was the plaintiff really in trouble? Could the defendant have assisted without peril to himself?

STARE DECISIS

Nothing perks up a course like Latin. *Stare decisis* **means "let the decision stand."** It is the essence of the common law. The phrase indicates that once a court has decided a particular issue, it will generally apply the same rule in future cases. Suppose the highest court of Arizona must decide whether a contract for a new car, signed by a 16-year-old, can be enforced against him. The court will look to see if there is precedent, that is, whether the high court of Arizona has already decided a similar case. The Arizona court looks and finds several earlier cases, all holding that such contracts may not be enforced against a minor. The court will apply that precedent and refuse to enforce the contract in this case. Courts do not always follow precedent but they generally do: *Stare decisis.*

Two words explain why the common law is never as easy as we might like: *predictability* and *flexibility.* The law is trying to accommodate both goals. The need for predictability is apparent: People must know what the law is. If contract law changed daily, an entrepreneur who leased factory space and then started buying machinery would be uncertain if the factory would actually be available when she was ready to move in. Will the landlord slip out of the lease? Will the machinery be ready on time? The need for predictability created the doctrine of *stare decisis.*

Yet there must also be flexibility in the law, some means to respond to new problems and changing social mores. In this new millennium, we cannot be encumbered by ironclad rules established before electricity was discovered. These two ideas may be obvious but they also conflict: The more flexibility we permit, the less predictability we enjoy. We will watch the conflict play out in the bystander cases.

BYSTANDER CASES

This country inherited from England a simple rule about a bystander's obligations: You have no duty to assist someone in peril unless you created the danger. In *Union Pacific Railway Co. v. Cappier,*[2] through no fault of the railroad, a train struck a man, severing an arm and a leg. Railroad employees saw the incident

---

[2] 66 Kan. 649, 72 P. 281 (1903).

happen but did nothing to assist him. By the time help arrived, the victim had died. In this 1903 case the court held that the railroad had no duty to help the injured man. The court declared that it was legally irrelevant whether the railroad's conduct was inhumane.

As harsh as this judgment might seem, it was an accurate statement of the law at that time in both England and the United States: Bystanders need do nothing. With a rule this old and well established, no court was willing to scuttle it. What courts did do was seek openings for small changes.

Eighteen years after the Kansas case of Cappier, the court in nearby Iowa found the basis for one exception. Ed Carey was a farm laborer, working for Frank Davis. While in the fields, Carey fainted from sunstroke and remained unconscious. Davis simply hauled him to a nearby wagon and left him in the sun for an additional four hours, causing serious permanent injury. The judges said that was not good enough. Creating a modest exception in the bystander rule, the court ruled that when an employee suffers a serious injury *on the job*, the employer must take reasonable measures to help him. Leaving a stricken worker in the hot sun was not reasonable, and Davis was liable.[3]

And this is how the common law changes: bit by tiny bit. In the 1970s, changes came more quickly.

CASE SUMMARY

TARASOFF v. REGENTS OF THE UNIVERSITY OF CALIFORNIA

17 Cal. 3d 425, 551 P.2d 334, 131 Cal. Rptr. 14
Supreme Court of California, 1976

FACTS: On October 27, 1969, Prosenjit Poddar killed Tatiana Tarasoff. Tatiana's parents claimed that two months earlier Poddar had confided his intention to kill Tatiana to Dr. Lawrence Moore, a psychologist employed by the University of California at Berkeley. They sued the university, claiming that Dr. Moore should have warned Tatiana and/or should have arranged for Poddar's confinement.

ISSUE: Did Dr. Moore have a duty to Tatiana Tarasoff?

DECISION: Yes, Dr. Moore had a duty to Tatiana Tarasoff.

REASONING: Under the common law, one person generally owes no duty to control the conduct of another or to warn anyone who is in danger. However, courts make an exception when the defendant has a special relationship to a dangerous person or potential victim. A therapist is someone who has just such a special relationship with a patient.

No one can be expected to do a perfect job. A therapist must only exercise the reasonable degree of skill, knowledge, and care ordinarily possessed by others in the field. In this case, however, there is no dispute about whether Dr. Moore could have foreseen violence. He actually predicted Poddar would kill Tatiana. Once a therapist determines that a patient poses a serious danger of violence, he must make reasonable efforts to protect the victim. The Tarasoffs have stated a legitimate claim against Dr. Moore.

---

[3] *Carey v. Davis*, 190 Iowa 720, 180 N.W. 889 (1921).

The Tarasoff exception applies in the limited circumstance of a special relationship, such as therapist–patient. Does the decision mean an end to the bystander rule? By no means. Ernesto Parra was a customer at the Jiminez Restaurant when food became lodged in his throat. The employees did not use the Heimlich maneuver or any other method to try to save him. Parra choked to death. Was the restaurant liable? No, said the Illinois Appeals Court. The restaurant had no obligation to do anything.[4] The bystander rule, that hardy oak, is alive and well.

Administrative Law

Before beginning this section, please return your seat to its upright position. Stow the tray firmly in the seat back in front of you. Turn off any radios, CD players, or other electronic equipment. Sound familiar? Administrative agencies affect each of us every day in hundreds of ways. They have become the fourth branch of government. Supporters believe that they provide unique expertise in complex areas; detractors regard them as unelected government run amok.

Many administrative agencies are familiar. The Federal Aviation Administration, which requires all airlines to ensure that your seats are upright before takeoff and landing, is an administrative agency. The Internal Revenue Service haunts us every April 15. The Environmental Protection Agency regulates the water quality of the river in your town. The Federal Trade Commission oversees the commercials that shout at you from your television set.

Other agencies are less familiar. You may never have heard of the Bureau of Land Management, but if you go into the oil and gas industry, you will learn that this powerful agency has more control over your land than you do. If you develop real estate in Palos Hills, Illinois, you will tremble every time the Appearance Commission of the City of Palos Hills speaks, since you cannot construct a new building without its approval. If your software corporation wants to hire an Argentine expert on databases, you will get to know the complex workings of the Immigration and Naturalization Service: No one lawfully enters this country without its nod of approval.

Administrative agencies use three kinds of power to do the work assigned to them: they make rules, investigate, and adjudicate.

Rule Making

One of the most important functions of an administrative agency is to make rules. In doing this, the agency attempts, prospectively, to establish fair and uniform behavior for all businesses in the affected area. **To create a new rule is to promulgate it.** Agencies promulgate two types of rules: legislative and interpretive.

Legislative Rules

These are the most important agency rules, and they are much like statutes. Here, an agency is changing the law by requiring businesses or private citizens to act in

---

[4] 230 Ill. App. 3d 819, 595 N.E.2d 1186, 1992 Ill. App. LEXIS 935 (1992).

a certain way. For example, the Federal Communications Commission (FCC) promulgated a rule requiring all cable television systems with more than 3,500 subscribers to develop the capacity to carry at least 20 channels and to make some of those channels available to local community stations. This legislative rule has a heavy financial impact on many cable systems. As far as a cable company is concerned, it is more important than most statutes passed by Congress. Legislative rules have the full effect of a statute.

Interpretive Rules

These rules do not change the law. They are the agency's interpretation of what the law already requires. But they can still affect all of us.

In 1977, Congress passed the Clean Air Act in an attempt to reduce pollution from factories. The act required the Environmental Protection Agency (EPA) to impose emission standards on "stationary sources" of pollution. But what did "stationary source" mean? It was the EPA's job to define that term. Obscure work, to be sure, yet the results could be seen and even smelled, because the EPA's definition would determine the quality of air entering our lungs every time we breathe. Environmentalists wanted the term defined to include every smokestack in a factory so that the EPA could regulate each one. The EPA, however, developed the "bubble concept," ruling that "stationary source" meant an entire factory, but not the individual smokestacks. As a result, polluters could shift emission among smokestacks in a single factory to avoid EPA regulation. Environmentalists howled that this gutted the purpose of the statute, but to no avail. The agency had spoken, merely by interpreting a statute.

Investigation

Agencies do an infinite variety of work, but they all need broad factual knowledge of the field they govern. Some companies cooperate with an agency, furnishing information and even voluntarily accepting agency recommendations. For example, the United States Product Safety Commission investigates hundreds of consumer products every year and frequently urges companies to recall goods that the agency considers defective. Many firms comply. (For an up-to-the-minute report on dangerous products and company compliance, proceed carefully to **http://www.cpsc.gov/index.html**.)

Other companies, however, jealously guard information, often because corporate officers believe that disclosure would lead to adverse rules. To force disclosure, agencies use subpoenas and searches. **A subpoena is an order to appear at a particular time and place to provide evidence.** A subpoena *duces tecum* requires the person to appear and bring specified documents. Businesses and other organizations intensely dislike subpoenas and resent government agents plowing through records and questioning employees. Nonetheless, a subpoena is generally lawful if it is *relevant* to a valid investigation, does not create an *unreasonable burden* on the company, and does not seek *privileged material,* such as a document in which an executive admits committing a crime.

ADJUDICATION

To **adjudicate** a case is to hold a hearing about an issue and then decide it. Agencies adjudicate countless cases. The FCC adjudicates which applicant for a new television license is best qualified. The Occupational Safety and Health Administration (OSHA) holds adversarial hearings to determine whether a manufacturing plant is dangerous.

Most adjudications begin with a hearing before an **administrative law judge (ALJ)**. There is no jury. An ALJ is an employee of the agency but is expected to be impartial in her rulings. All parties are represented by counsel. The rules of evidence are informal, and an ALJ may receive any testimony or documents that will help resolve the dispute.

After all evidence is taken, the ALJ makes a decision. The losing party has a right to appeal to an appellate board within the agency. The appellate board has the power to make a *de novo* decision, meaning it may ignore the ALJ's decision. A party unhappy with that decision may appeal to federal court.

Chapter Conclusion

The legal battle over power never stops. When may a state outlaw waterfront development? Prohibit symbolic speech? Other issues are just as thorny, such as when a bystander is liable to assist someone in peril, or whether a government agency may subpoena corporate documents. Some of the questions will be answered by that extraordinary document, the Constitution, while others require statutory, common law or administrative responses. There are no easy answers to any of the questions, because there has never been a democracy so large, so diverse, or so powerful.

Chapter Review

1. The Constitution is a series of compromises about power.

2. Article I of the Constitution creates the Congress and grants all legislative power to it. Article II establishes the office of president and defines executive powers. Article III creates the Supreme Court and permits lower federal courts; the article also outlines the powers of the federal judiciary.

3. Under the Commerce Clause, Congress may regulate interstate trade. A state law that interferes with interstate commerce is void.

4. The president's key powers include making agency appointments, proposing legislation, conducting foreign policy, and acting as commander in chief of the armed forces.

5. The federal courts adjudicate cases and also exercise judicial review, which is the right to declare a statute or governmental action unconstitutional and void.

6. The First Amendment protects most freedom of speech, although the government may regulate the time, place, and manner of speech.

7. Procedural due process is required whenever the government attempts to take liberty or property.

8. The Takings Clause prohibits a state from taking private property for public use without just compensation.

9. The Equal Protection Clause generally requires the government to treat people equally.

10. Bills originate in congressional committees and go from there to the full House of Representatives or Senate. If both houses pass the bill, the legislation normally must go to a conference committee to resolve differences between the two versions. If the president signs the bill, it becomes a statute; if he vetoes it, Congress can pass it over his veto with a two thirds majority in each house.

11. *Stare decisis* means "let the decision stand," and indicates that once a court has decided a particular issue, it will generally apply the same rule in future cases.

12. The common law evolves in awkward fits and starts, because courts attempt to achieve two contradictory purposes: predictability and flexibility.

13. The common-law bystander rule holds that, generally, no one has a duty to assist someone in peril unless the bystander himself created the danger. Courts have carved some exceptions during the last 100 years, but the basic rule still stands.

14. Congress creates federal administrative agencies to supervise many industries. Agencies promulgate rules and investigate and adjudicate cases.

PRACTICE TEST

Matching Questions

Match the following terms with their definitions:

___ **A.** Statute

___ **B.** Equal Protection Clause

___ **C.** Judicial review

___ **D.** Takings Clause

___ **E.** Stare decisis

___ **F.** Promulgate

1. The power of federal courts to examine the constitutionality of statutes and acts of government.

2. Part of the Constitution that requires compensation in eminent domain cases.

3. The rule that requires courts to rule based on precedent.

4. The act of an administrative agency creating a new rule.

5. A law passed by a legislative body.

6. Generally prohibits regulations based on gender, race, or fundamental rights.

True/False Questions

Circle true or false:

1. T F The government may not prohibit a political rally, but it may restrict when and where the demonstrators meet.

2. T F The Due Process Clause requires that any citizen is entitled to a jury trial before any right or property interest is taken.

3. T F The government has the right to take a homeowner's property for a public purpose.

4. T F A subpoena is an order punishing a defendant who has violated a court ruling.

5. T F A bystander who sees someone in peril must come to that person's assistance, but only if he can do so without endangering himself or others.

6. T F Administrative agencies play an advisory role in the life of many industries but do not have the legal authority to enforce their opinions.

Multiple-Choice Questions

7. Colorado passes a hotel tax of 8% for Colorado residents and 15% for out-of-state visitors. The new law

(a) Is valid, based on the Supremacy Clause.

(b) Is void, based on the Supremacy Clause.

(c) Is valid, based on the Commerce Clause.

(d) Is void, based on the Commerce Clause.

(e) Is void, based on the Takings Clause.

8. Suppose a state legislature approves an education plan for the next year budgets $35 million for boys' athletics and $25 million for girls' athletics. Legislators explain the difference by saying, "In our experience, boys simply care more about sports than girls do." The new plan is

   (a) Valid.

   (b) Void.

   (c) Permissible, based on the legislator's statutory research.

   (d) Permissible, though unwise.

   (e) Subject to the Takings Clause.

9. Congress has passed a new bill but the president does not like the law. What could happen next?

   (a) The president must sign the bill whether he likes it or not.

   (b) The president may veto the bill, in which case it is dead.

   (c) The president may veto the bill, but Congress may attempt to override the veto.

   (d) The president may ask the citizens to vote directly on the proposed law.

   (e) The president may discharge the Congress and order new elections.

10. Which of these is an example of judicial review?

   (a) A trial court finds a criminal defendant guilty.

   (b) An appeals court reverses a lower court's ruling.

   (c) An appeals court affirms a lower court's ruling.

   (d) A federal court declares a statute unconstitutional.

   (e) A Congressional committee interviews a potential Supreme Court justice.

11. Martine, a psychiatrist, is convinced that Lance, her patient, intends to kill his own father.

   (a) Martine may not contact the father, because she is obligated to protect patient–therapist confidentiality.

   (b) Martine *may* contact the father, but she is *not obligated* to take any steps at all.

   (c) Martine must warn the father.

   (d) Martine may seek judicial review of the case.

   (e) Martine may warn Lance not to do anything but she herself may not become involved.

12. What is an example of a subpoena?

   (a) A court order to a company to stop polluting the air.

   (b) A court order requiring a deponent to answer questions.

   (c) A federal agency demands various internal documents from a corporation.

   (d) The president orders troops called up in the national defense.

   (e) The president orders Congress to pass a bill on an expedited schedule.

Short-Answer Questions

13. In the early 1970s, President Nixon became embroiled in the Watergate dispute. He was accused of covering up a criminal break-in at the national headquarters of the Democratic Party. Nixon denied any wrongdoing. A United States District Court judge ordered the president to produce tapes of conversations held in his office. Nixon knew that complying with the order would produce damaging evidence, probably destroying his presidency. He refused, claiming executive privilege. The case went to the Supreme Court. Nixon strongly implied that even if the Supreme Court ordered him to produce the tapes, he would refuse. What major constitutional issue did this raise?

14. Gilleo opposed American participation in the war in the Persian Gulf. She displayed a large sign on her front lawn that read, "Say No to War in the Persian Gulf, Call Congress Now." The city of Ladue prohibited signs on front lawns, and Gilleo sued. The city claimed that it was regulating "time, place, and manner." Explain that statement, and decide who should win.

15. Hiller Systems, Inc. was performing a safety inspection on board the M/V *Cape Diamond*, an oceangoing

vessel, when an accident occurred involving the fire extinguishing equipment. Two men were killed. The Occupational Safety and Health Administration (OSHA), a federal agency, attempted to investigate, but Hiller refused to permit any of its employees to speak to OSHA investigators. What could OSHA do to pursue the investigation? What limits were there on what OSHA could do?

16. Federal antitrust statutes are complex, but the basic goal is straightforward: to prevent a major industry from being so dominated by a small group of corporations that they destroy competition and injure consumers. Does Major League Baseball violate the antitrust laws? Many observers say that it does. A small group of owners not only dominate the industry, but actually own it, controlling the entry of new owners into the game. This issue went to the United States Supreme Court in 1922. Justice Holmes ruled, perhaps surprisingly, that baseball is exempt from the antitrust laws, holding that baseball is not "trade or commerce." Suppose that a congressman dislikes this ruling and dislikes the current condition of baseball. What could he do?

17. ETHICS: Suppose you were on a state supreme court and faced with a restaurant choking case. Should you require restaurant employees to know and employ the Heimlich maneuver to assist a choking victim? If they do a bad job, they could cause additional injury. Should you permit them to do nothing at all? Is there a compromise position? What social policies are most important?

18. ROLE REVERSAL: Write an exam question that involves any two of these important Fifth Amendment protections: procedural due process, the Takings Clause, and the Equal Protection Clause.

Internet Research Problem

Research some pending legislation in Congress. Go to **http://www.senate.gov**, and click on bills. Choose some key words that interest you, and see what your government is doing. Read the summary of the bill, if one is provided, or go to the text of the bill, and scan the introduction. What do the sponsors of this bill hope to accomplish? Do you agree or disagree with their goals?

You can find further practice problems in the Online Quiz at **http://beatty.westbuslaw.com** or in the Study Guide that accompanies this text.

5

Intentional Torts and Business Torts

In a small Louisiana town, Don Mashburn ran a restaurant called Maison de Mashburn. *The New Orleans States-Item* newspaper reviewed his eatery, and here is what the article said:

"'Tain't Creole, 'tain't Cajun, 'tain't French, 'tain't country American, 'tain't good. I don't know how much real talent in cooking is hidden under the mélange of hideous sauces which make this food and the menu a travesty of pretentious amateurism but I find it all quite depressing. Put a yellow flour sauce on top of the duck, flame it for drama and serve it with some horrible multi-flavored rice in hollowed-out fruit and what have you got? A well-cooked duck with an ugly sauce that tastes too sweet and thick and makes you want to scrape off the glop to eat the plain duck. [The stuffed eggplant was prepared by emptying] a shaker full (more or less) of paprika on top of it. [One sauce created] trout à la green plague [while another should have been called] yellow death on duck."

Mashburn sued, claiming that the newspaper had committed libel, damaging his reputation and hurting his business.[1] Trout à la green plague will be the first course on our menu of tort law. Mashburn learned, as you will, why filing such a lawsuit is easier than winning it.

This odd word "tort" is borrowed from the French, meaning "wrong." And that is what it means in law: A tort is a wrong. More precisely, **a tort is a violation of a duty imposed by the civil law.** When a person breaks one of those duties and injures another, it is a tort. The injury could be to a person or her property. Libel is one example of a tort where, for example, a newspaper columnist falsely accuses someone of being an alcoholic. A surgeon who removes the wrong kidney from a patient commits a different kind of tort, called negligence. A business executive who deliberately steals a client away from a competitor, interfering with a valid contract, commits a tort called interference with a contract. A con artist who tricks money out of you with a phony offer to sell you a boat commits fraud, yet another tort.

Because tort law is so broad, it takes a while to understand its boundaries. To start with, we must distinguish torts from criminal law.

It is a crime to steal a car, to embezzle money from a bank, to sell cocaine. As discussed in Chapter 1, society considers such behavior so threatening that the government itself will prosecute the wrongdoer, whether or not the car owner or bank president wants the case to go forward. A district attorney, who is paid by the government, will bring the case to court, seeking to send the defendant to prison and/or to fine him. If there is a fine, the money goes to the state, not to the victim.

In a tort case, it is up to the injured party, the plaintiff, to seek compensation. She must hire her own lawyer, who will file a lawsuit. Her lawyer must convince the court that the defendant breached some legal duty and ought to pay money damages to the plaintiff. The plaintiff has no power to send the defendant to jail. Bear in mind that a defendant's action might be both a crime *and* a tort. The con artist who tricks money out of you with a fake offer to sell you a boat has committed the tort of fraud. You may file a civil suit against him and will collect money damages if you can prove your case. The con artist has also committed the crime of fraud. The state will prosecute, seeking to imprison and fine him.

Tort law is divided into categories. In this chapter we consider **intentional torts,** that is, harm caused by a deliberate action. The newspaper columnist who wrongly accuses someone of being a drunk has committed the intentional tort of libel. The con artist who tricks money from you has committed the intentional tort of fraud. In the next chapter we examine **negligence and strict liability,** which are injuries caused by neglect and oversight rather than by deliberate conduct.

---

[1] *Mashburn v. Collins*, 355 So.2d 879 (La. 1977).

Intentional Torts

DEFAMATION

The First Amendment guarantees the right to free speech, a vital freedom that enables us to protect other rights. But that freedom is not absolute. Courts have long recognized that we cannot permit irresponsible speech to harm another's reputation. Free speech should not include the right to falsely accuse your neighbor of selling drugs. That sounds sensible enough, yet once we say that free speech and personal reputation both deserve protection, we have guaranteed perpetual conflict.

The law of defamation concerns false statements that harm someone's reputation. Defamatory statements can be written or spoken. Written defamation is **libel.** Suppose a newspaper accuses a local retail store of programming its cash registers to overcharge customers, when the store has never done so. That is libel. Oral defamation is **slander.** If Professor Wilson, in class, refers to Sally Student as a drug dealer, and Sally has never sold anything stronger than Arm & Hammer, he has slandered her. (Defamatory comments made on television and radio are considered libel, because the vast audiences mean that the damage is similar to that done by newspapers.)

There are four elements to a defamation case. **An element is a fact that a plaintiff must prove to win a lawsuit.** The plaintiff in any kind of lawsuit must prove all of the elements to prevail. The elements in a defamation case are:

- *Defamatory statement.* This is a statement likely to harm another person's reputation. When Professor Wisdom accuses Sally of dealing drugs, that will clearly harm her reputation.

- *Falseness.* The statement must be false to be defamatory. If Sally Student actually sold marijuana to a classmate, then Professor Wisdom has a defense to slander.

- *Communicated.* The statement must be communicated to at least one person other than the plaintiff. If Wisdom speaks only to Sally and accuses her of dealing drugs, there is no slander. But there is if he shouts the accusation in a crowded hall.

- *Injury.* In slander cases, the plaintiff generally must show some injury. Sally's injury would be lower reputation in the school, embarrassment, and humiliation. But in libel cases, the law is willing to assume injury. Since libel is written, and more permanent, courts award damages even without proof of injury.

Opinion

Remember that the plaintiff must demonstrate a "false" statement. Opinions, though, cannot be proven true or false. For that reason, **opinion is generally a valid defense in a defamation suit.**

Mr. Mashburn, who opened the chapter suing over his restaurant review, lost his case. The court held that a reasonable reader would have understood the statements to be opinion only. "A shaker full of paprika" and "yellow death on duck" were not to be taken literally but were merely the author's expression of his personal dislike. What about a crude description of a college official, appearing in the school's newspaper? You be the judge.

YOU BE THE JUDGE

YEAGLE v. COLLEGIATE TIMES

255 Va. 293, 497 S.E.2d 136, 1998 Va. LEXIS 32
Virginia Supreme Court, 1998

FACTS: Sharon Yeagle was assistant to the vice-president of student affairs at the Virginia Polytechnic Institute and State University. The state had an academic honors program called the Governor's Fellows Program, and one of Yeagle's duties was to help students apply. The school newspaper, the *Collegiate Times*, published an article describing the university's success at placing students in the Fellows Program. The article included a block quotation in larger print, attributed to Yeagle. Underneath Yeagle's name was the phrase "Director of Butt Licking."

Yeagle sued the *Collegiate Times*, alleging that the vulgar phrase defamed her. The trial court dismissed the case, ruling that no reasonable person would take the words literally, and that the phrase conveyed no factual information. Yeagle appealed to the Virginia Supreme Court.

YOU BE THE JUDGE: Was the phrase defamatory, or was it deliberate exaggeration that no reasonable person would take literally?

ARGUMENT FOR YEAGLE: The disgusting phrase that the *Collegiate Times* used to describe Ms. Yeagle is defamatory for several reasons. The conduct described by the words happens to be a crime in Virginia, a violation of the state sodomy statute. Thus the paper is accusing her of criminal offenses that she has never committed. That is defamation, and in itself entitles Ms. Yeagle to damages.

If, however, defendants argue that the phrase must be interpreted figuratively, then the newspaper has accused Ms. Yeagle of currying favor, or directing others to do so, in a uniquely degrading fashion. The *Collegiate Times* is informing its readers that she performs her job in a sleazy, unprofessional manner evidently because she cannot succeed by merit. The paper is suggesting that she is devoid of integrity and capable of achieving goals only by devious, deviant methods.

ARGUMENT FOR COLLEGIATE TIMES: Statements are only defamatory if a reasonable reader would understand them as asserting facts that can be proven true or false. There is no such statement in this case, and no defamation. No reasonable reader, after finishing an article about the Fellows Program, would believe that Ms. Yeagle was actually the director as described, or even that there is such a job.

The paper chose to inject humor into its coverage of a mundane issue, for the entertainment of its readers. The great majority of the paper's readers appreciate lively language that is at times irreverent. For anyone who is quick to take offense, the proper recourse is not to file suit, but to put down the paper.

Public Personalities

The rules of the game change for those who play in the open. Public officials and public figures receive less protection from defamation. An example of a public official is a police chief. A public figure is a movie star, for example, or a multimillionaire playboy constantly in the news. In the landmark case *New York Times Co. v. Sullivan*, the Supreme Court ruled that the free exchange of information is vital in a democracy and is protected by the First Amendment to the Constitution. If the information wounds public people, that may just be tough luck.

The rule from the *New York Times v. Sullivan* case is that a public official or public figure can win a defamation case only by proving actual malice by the defendant. **Actual malice means that the defendant knew the statement was false or acted with reckless disregard of the truth.** If the plaintiff merely shows that the defendant newspaper printed incorrect statements, even very damaging ones, that will not suffice to win the suit. In the *New York Times v. Sullivan* case, the police chief of Birmingham, Alabama claimed that the *Times* falsely accused him of racial violence in his job. He lost because he could not prove that the *Times* had acted with actual malice. If he had shown that the *Times* knew the accusation was false, he would have won.

FALSE IMPRISONMENT

False imprisonment is the intentional restraint of another person without reasonable cause and without consent. False imprisonment cases most commonly arise in retail stores, which sometimes detain employees or customers for suspected theft. Most states now have statutes governing the detention of suspected shoplifters. **Generally, a store may detain a customer or worker for alleged shoplifting provided there is a reasonable basis for the suspicion and the detention is done reasonably.** To detain a customer in the manager's office for 20 minutes and question him about where he got an item is lawful. To chain that customer to a display counter for three hours and humiliate him in front of other customers is unreasonable, and false imprisonment.

Assume that you are a junior vice-president of a chain of 15 retail clothing stores, all located in your state. The president has asked you to outline a sensible plan, to be given to all employees, for dealing with suspected shoplifters. Here are some ideas to consider:

- There are competing social values. Shoplifting is very costly to our society, causing businesses to lose anywhere from $5 billion to $25 billion annually. On the other hand, no one wants to shop in a "police state" environment.

- What is a "reasonable" suspicion of shoplifting? What if a clerk sees a customer hurry out, wearing a sweater identical to those on display? Must the clerk have seen the customer pick up the sweater? Put it on?

- What is "reasonable" detention? Can you tackle someone running through the parking lot? Can you shoot him?

Some people in our society are biased against others, based on race or gender, while others are entirely free of such prejudices. How do you take that into account?

BATTERY AND ASSAULT

These two torts are related, but not identical. **Battery is an intentional touching of another person in a way that is unwanted or offensive.** There need be no intention to hurt the plaintiff. If the defendant intended to do the physical act, and a reasonable plaintiff would be offended by it, battery has occurred.

Suppose an irate parent throws a chair at a referee during his daughter's basketball game, breaking the man's jaw. It is irrelevant that the father did not intend to injure the referee. But a parent who cheerfully slaps the winning coach on the back has not committed battery, because a reasonable coach would not be offended.

Assault occurs when a defendant does some act that makes a plaintiff fear an imminent battery. It is assault even though the battery never occurs. Suppose Ms. Wilson shouts "Think fast!" at her husband and hurls a toaster at him. He turns and sees it flying at him. His fear of being struck is enough to win a case of assault, even if the toaster misses. If the toaster happens to strike him, Ms. Wilson has also committed battery.

FRAUD

Fraud is injuring another person by deliberate deception. It is fraud to sell real estate knowing that there is a large toxic waste deposit underground, of which the buyer is ignorant. Fraud is a tort, but it typically occurs during the negotiation or performance of a contract, and it is discussed in detail in Unit 2, on contracts.

INTENTIONAL INFLICTION OF EMOTIONAL DISTRESS

A credit officer was struggling in vain to locate Sheehan, who owed money on his car. The officer finally phoned Sheehan's mother, falsely identified herself as a hospital employee, and said she needed to find Sheehan because his children had been in a serious auto accident. The horrified mother provided Sheehan's whereabouts, which enabled the company to seize his car. But Sheehan himself spent seven hours frantically trying to locate his supposedly injured children, who in fact were fine. He was not injured physically, but he sued for his emotional distress—and won. **The intentional infliction of emotional distress results from extreme and outrageous conduct that causes serious emotional harm.** The credit company was liable for the intentional infliction of emotional distress.[2] The following case arose in a setting that guarantees controversy—an abortion clinic.

CASE SUMMARY

JANE DOE AND NANCY ROE v. LYNN MILLS

212 Mich. App. 73, 536 N.W.2d 824, 1995 Mich. App. LEXIS 313
Michigan Court of Appeals, 1995

FACTS: Late one night, an antiabortion protestor named Robert Thomas climbed into a Dumpster located behind the Women's Advisory Center, an abortion clinic. He found documents indicating that the plaintiffs were soon to have abortions at the clinic. Thomas gave the information to Lynn Mills. The next day, Mills and Sister Lois Mitoraj created signs, using the women's names, indicating that they were about to undergo abortions, and urging them not to "kill their babies."

Doe and Roe (not their real names) sued, claiming intentional infliction of emotional distress (as well as breach of privacy, discussed later in this chapter). The trial court dismissed the lawsuit, ruling that the defendants' conduct was not extreme and outrageous. The plaintiffs appealed.

ISSUE: Have the plaintiffs made a valid claim of intentional infliction of emotional distress?

DECISION: The plaintiffs have made a valid claim of intentional infliction of emotional distress.

REASONING: A defendant is liable for the intentional infliction of emotional distress only when his conduct is outrageous in character, extreme in degree, and utterly intolerable in a civilized community. A good test is whether the average member of the community would respond to the defendant's conduct by exclaiming, "Outrageous!"

These defendants have a constitutional right to protest against abortions, but they have no such right to publicize private matters. Their behavior here might well cause the average person to say, "Outrageous!" The plaintiffs are entitled to a trial, so that a jury can decide whether the defendants have inflicted emotional distress.

---

[2] *Ford Motor Credit Co. v. Sheehan*, 373 So. 2d 956, 1979 Fla. App. LEXIS 15416 (Fla. Dist. Ct. App. 1979).

Damages

COMPENSATORY DAMAGES

Mitchel Bien, a deaf mute, enters the George Grubbs Nissan dealership, where folks sell cars aggressively. Very aggressively. Maturelli, a salesman, and Bien communicate by writing messages back and forth. Maturelli takes Bien's own car keys, and the two then test drive a 300ZX. Bien says he does not want the car, but Maturelli escorts him back inside and fills out a sales sheet. Bien repeatedly asks for his keys, but Maturelli only laughs, pressuring him to buy the new car. Minutes pass. Hours pass. Bien becomes frantic, writing a dozen notes, begging to leave, threatening to call the police. Maturelli mocks Bien and his physical disabilities. Finally, after four hours, the customer escapes.

Bien sues for the intentional infliction of emotional distress. Two former salesmen from Grubbs testify that they have witnessed customers cry, yell, and curse as a result of the aggressive tactics. Doctors state that the incident has traumatized Bien, dramatically reducing his confidence and self-esteem and preventing his return to work even three years later.

The jury awards Bien damages. But how does a jury calculate the money? For that matter, why should a jury even try? Money can never erase pain or undo a permanent injury. The answer is simple: Money, however inexact and ineffective, is the only thing a court has to give. A successful plaintiff generally receives **compensatory damages, meaning an amount of money that the court believes will restore him to the position he was in before the defendant's conduct caused an injury.** Here is how damages are figured.

First, a plaintiff receives money for medical expenses that he has proven by producing bills from doctors, hospitals, physical therapists, and psychotherapists. If a doctor testifies that he needs future treatment, Bien will offer evidence of how much that will cost. The **single recovery principle** requires a court to settle the matter once and for all, by awarding a lump sum for past and future expenses.

Second, the defendants are liable for lost wages, past and future. The court takes the number of days or months that Bien has missed (and will miss) work and multiplies that times his salary.

Third, a plaintiff is paid for pain and suffering. Bien testifies about how traumatic the four hours were and how the experience has affected his life. He may state that he now fears shopping, suffers nightmares, and seldom socializes. To bolster the case, a plaintiff uses expert testimony, such as the psychiatrists who testified for Bien. In this case, the jury awarded Bien $573,815, calculated as in the following table.[3]

---

[3] The compensatory damages are described in *George Grubbs Enterprises v. Bien*, 881 S.W.2d 843, 1994 Tex. App. LEXIS 1870 (Tex. Ct. App. 1994). In addition to the compensatory damages described, the jury awarded $5 million in punitive damages. The Texas Supreme Court reversed the award of punitive damages, but not the compensatory. Id., 900 S.W.2d 337, 1995 Tex. LEXIS 91 (Tex. 1995). The high court did not dispute the appropriateness of punitive damages, but reversed because the trial court failed to instruct the jury properly as to how it should determine the assets actually under the defendants' control, an issue essential to punitive damages but not compensatory damages.

Past medical	$ 70.00
Future medical	6,000.00
Past rehabilitation	3,205.00
Past lost earning capacity	112,910.00
Future lost earning capacity	34,650.00
Past physical symptoms and discomfort	50,000.00
Future physical symptoms and discomfort	50,000.00
Past emotional injury and mental anguish	101,980.00
Future emotional injury and mental anguish	200,000.00
Past loss of society and reduced ability to socially interact with family, former fiancee, and friends, and hearing (i.e., nondeaf) people in general	10,000.00
Future loss of society and reduced ability to socially interact with family, former fiancee, and friends, and hearing people	5,000.00
TOTAL	$573,815.00

PUNITIVE DAMAGES

The Ford Bronco II that Pamela Ammerman was riding in rolled over. Pamela suffered a crushed pelvis, skull fractures, and brain damage that left her with manic depression and suicidal tendencies. She sued Ford. The jury concluded that the car rolled over because it was defectively designed, and that the company knew of the dangers but recklessly hurried the car into production, against the advice of its own engineers, in order to maximize profits. They awarded Pamela $4 million in compensatory damages plus a larger sum in punitive damages.

Punitive damages are not designed to compensate the plaintiff for harm, because compensatory damages will have done that. **Punitive damages are intended to punish the defendant for conduct that is extreme and outrageous.** Courts award these damages in relatively few cases. When an award of punitive damages is made, it is generally in a case of intentional tort, although as the Ammerman case illustrates, they also occur in negligence suits. The idea behind punitive damages is that certain behavior is so unacceptable that society must make an example of it. A large award of money should deter the defendant from repeating the mistake and others from ever making it.

The jury awarded Pamela Ammerman $13.8 million in punitive damages (beyond the compensatory damages). Ford appealed—and lost. The court concluded that the jury reasonably concluded that the company had acted with callous indifference to the lives of its customers.

Although a jury has wide discretion in awarding punitive damages, the U.S. Supreme Court has ruled that a verdict must be reasonable. In awarding punitive damages, a court must consider three "guideposts":

- The reprehensibility of the defendant's conduct.

- The ratio between the harm suffered and the award. Generally, the punitive award should not be more than nine times the compensatory award.

- The difference between the punitive award and any civil penalties used in similar cases.

Business Torts

TORTIOUS INTERFERENCE WITH A CONTRACT

Competition is the essence of business. Successful corporations compete aggressively, and the law permits and expects them to. But there are times when healthy competition becomes illegal interference. This is called **tortious interference with a contract.** To win such a case, a plaintiff must establish four elements:

- There was a contract between the plaintiff and a third party.

- The defendant knew of the contract.

- The defendant improperly induced the third party to breach the contract or made performance of the contract impossible; and

- There was injury to the plaintiff.

Because businesses routinely compete for customers, employees, and market share, it is not always easy to identify tortious interference. There is nothing wrong with two companies bidding against each other to buy a parcel of land, and nothing wrong with one corporation doing everything possible to convince the seller to ignore all competitors. But once a company has signed a contract to buy the land, it is improper to induce the seller to break the deal. The most commonly disputed issues in these cases concern elements one and three: Was there a contract between the plaintiff and another party? Did the defendant improperly induce a party to breach it? Defendants will try to show that the plaintiff had no contract.

INTRUSION

Intrusion into someone's private life is a tort if a reasonable person would find it offensive. Peeping through someone's windows or wiretapping his telephone are obvious examples of intrusion. In a famous case involving a "paparazzo" photographer and Jacqueline Kennedy Onassis, the court found that the photographer had invaded her privacy by making a career out of photographing her. He had bribed doormen to gain access to hotels and restaurants she visited, had jumped out of bushes to photograph her young children, and had driven powerboats dangerously close to her. The court ordered him to stop.[4] Nine years later the paparazzo was found in contempt of court for again taking photographs too close to Ms. Onassis. He agreed to stop once and for all—in exchange for a suspended contempt sentence.

Robert Konop, a pilot for Hawaiian Airlines, was distressed with the demands his company was making on employees, and also with his union's response. On a private Web site, he criticized both parties and urged fellow pilots to switch to a different union. Konop gave his colleagues passwords to the site, while denying access to management and union officials. Hawaiian Airlines Vice-President James Davis surreptitiously visited the site by using the name and password of two pilots, with their consent. Davis entered the site at least 20 times in this fashion. Konop sued, claiming

---

[4] *Galella v. Onassis*, 487 F. 2d 986, 1973 U.S.App.LEXIS 7901 (2d Cir. 1973).

a violation of two important statutes:

- The Electronic Communications Privacy Act, which prohibits the unauthorized interception or disclosure of wire and electronic communications;[5] and

- The Stored Communications Act, which prohibits unauthorized access to a facility through which an electronic service is provided.[6]

The district court dismissed the claims, but the appellate court reversed, holding that Konop had raised legitimate—and novel—issues under both statutes. He deserved a trial to demonstrate that Davis had in fact violated these two laws.[7]

The explosive growth of electronic commerce inevitably fosters a burgeoning docket of novel litigation. For a more detailed look at the statutes and issues involved, see Chapter 42 on cyberlaw. ▪

COMMERCIAL EXPLOITATION

This right prohibits the unauthorized use of another person's likeness or voice for commercial purposes. For example, it would be illegal to run a magazine ad showing actress Gwyneth Paltrow holding a can of soda, without her permission. The ad would imply that she endorses the product. Someone's identity is her own, and it cannot be exploited unless she permits it. Ford Motor Company hired a singer to imitate Bette Midler's version of a popular song. The imitation was so good that most listeners were fooled into believing that Ms. Midler was endorsing the product. That, ruled a court, violated her right to commercial exploitation.

Chapter Conclusion

This chapter has been a potpourri of sin, a bubbling cauldron of conduct best avoided. Although tortious acts and their consequences are diverse, two generalities apply. First, the boundaries of intentional torts are imprecise, the outcome of a particular case depending to a considerable extent upon the fact finder who analyzes it. Second, the thoughtful executive and the careful citizen, aware of the shifting standards and potentially vast liability, will strive to ensure that his or her conduct never provides that fact finder an opportunity to give judgment.

Chapter Review

1. A tort is a violation of a duty imposed by the civil law.

2. Defamation involves a defamatory statement that is false, uttered to a third person, and causes an injury.

3. False imprisonment is the intentional restraint of another person without reasonable cause and without consent.

4. Battery is an intentional touching of another person in a way that is unwanted or offensive. Assault involves an act that makes the plaintiff fear an imminent battery.

5. The intentional infliction of emotional distress involves extreme and outrageous conduct that causes serious emotional harm.

---

[5] 18 U.S.C. §2511.

[6] 18 U.S.C. §2701.

[7] *Konop v. Hawaiian Airlines, Inc.*, 236 F.3d 1035, 2001 U.S. App. LEXIS 191 (9th Cir. 2001).

6. Compensatory damages are the normal remedy in a tort case. In unusual cases, the court may award punitive damages, not to compensate the plaintiff but to punish the defendant.

7. Tortious interference with a contract involves the defendant unfairly harming an existing contract.

8. The Electronic Communications Privacy Act prohibits the unauthorized interception or disclosure of wire and electronic communications, and the Stored Communications Act bars unauthorized access to a facility through which an electronic service is provided.

9. Commercial exploitation means the exclusive right to use one's own name, likeness, or voice.

PRACTICE TEST

Matching Questions

Match the following terms with their definitions:

___ A. Interference with a contract

___ B. Fraud

___ C. Defamation

___ D. False imprisonment

___ E. Punitive damages

___ F. Intentional infliction of emotional distress

___ G. Commercial exploitation

1. Money awarded to punish the wrongdoer.

2. Intentionally restraining another person without reasonable cause.

3. Intentional deception, frequently used to obtain a contract with another party.

4. Deliberately stealing a client who has a contract with another.

5. Violation of the exclusive right to use one's own name, likeness, or voice.

6. Using a false statement to damage someone's reputation.

7. An act so extreme that an average person would say, "Outrageous!"

True/False Questions

Circle true or false:

1. T   F   A store manager who believes a customer has stolen something may question him but not restrain him.

2. T   F   Becky punches Kelly in the nose. Becky has committed the tort of assault.

3. T   F   A defendant cannot be liable for defamation if the statement, no matter how harmful, is true.

4. T   F   In most cases, a winning plaintiff receives compensatory and punitive damages.

5. T   F   A beer company that wishes to include a celebrity's picture in its magazine ads must first obtain the celebrity's permission.

Multiple-Choice Questions

6. A valid defense in a defamation suit is

(a) Falseness.

(b) Honest error.

(c) Improbability.

(d) Opinion.

(e) Third-party reliance.

7. Joe Student, irate that on an exam he received a B- rather than a B, stands up in class and throws his laptop at the professor. The professor sees it coming and ducks just in time; the laptop smashes against the chalkboard. Joe has committed

(a) Assault.

(b) Battery.

(c) Negligence.

(d) Slander.

(e) No tort, because the laptop missed the professor.

8. Marsha, a supervisor, furiously berates Ted in front of 14 other employees, calling him "a loser, an incompetent, a failure as an employee and as a person." She hands around copies of Ted's work and for twenty minutes mocks his efforts. If Ted sues Marsha, his best claim will be

(a) Assault.

(b) Battery.

(c) Intentional infliction of emotional distress.

(d) Negligence.

(e) Interference with a contract.

9. Rodney is a star player on the Los Angeles Lakers basketball team. He has two years remaining on his four-year contract. The Wildcats, a new team in the league, try to lure Rodney away from the Lakers by offering him more money, and Rodney agrees to leave Los Angeles. The Lakers sue. The Lakers will

(a) Win a case of defamation.

(b) Win a case of commercial exploitation.

(c) Win a case of intentional interference with a contract.

(d) win a case of negligence.

(e) Lose.

10. While Mark is driving, he drinks from a bottle of whiskey, becoming intoxicated. Because he is drunk, he swerves into the wrong lane, causing an accident and seriously injuring Janet. Which statement is true?

(a) Janet could sue Mark, who might be found guilty in her suit.

(b) Janet and the state could start separate criminal cases against Mark.

(c) Janet could sue Mark, and the state could prosecute Mark for drunk driving.

(d) The state could sue Mark but only with Janet's consent.

(e) The state could prosecute Mark and sue him at the same time, for drunk driving.

Short-Answer Questions

11. Benzaquin had a radio talk show in Boston. On the program, he complained about an incident earlier in the day, in which state trooper Fleming had stopped his car, apparently for lack of a proper license plate and safety sticker. Even though Benzaquin explained that the license plate had been stolen and the sticker had fallen onto the dashboard, Fleming refused to let him drive the car away, and Benzaquin and his daughter and two young grandsons had to find other transportation. On the show, Benzaquin angrily recounted the incident, then made the following statements about Fleming and troopers generally: "arrogants wearing trooper's uniforms like tights"; "little monkey, you wind him up and he does his thing"; "we're not paying them to be dictators and Nazis"; "this man is an absolute barbarian, a lunkhead, a meathead." Fleming sued Benzaquin for defamation. Comment.

12. Caldwell was shopping in a K-Mart store, carrying a large purse. A security guard observed her look at various small items such as stain, hinges, and antenna wire. On occasion she bent down out of sight of the guard. The guard thought he saw Caldwell put something in her purse. Caldwell removed her glasses from her purse and returned them a few times. After she left, the guard approached her in the parking lot and said that he believed she had store merchandise in her pocketbook, but was unable to say what he thought was put there. Caldwell opened the purse, and the guard testified that he saw no K-Mart merchandise in it. The guard then told Caldwell to return to the store with him. They walked around the store for approximately 15 minutes, while the guard said six or seven times that he saw her put something in her purse. Caldwell left the store after another store employee indicated she

could go. Caldwell sued. What kind of suit did she file, and what should the outcome be?

13. Tata Consultancy of Bombay, India is an international computer consulting firm. It spends considerable time and effort recruiting the best personnel from India's leading technical schools. Tata employees sign an initial three-year employment commitment, often work overseas, and agree to work for a specified additional time when they return to India. Desai worked for Tata, but then quit and formed a competing company, which he called Syntel. His new company contacted Tata employees by phone, offering more money to come work for Syntel, bonuses, and assistance in obtaining permanent resident visas in the United States. At least 16 former Tata employees left their work without completing their contractual obligations and went to work for Syntel. Tata sued. What did it claim, and what should be the result?

14. Johnny Carson was for many years the star of a well-known television show, The Tonight Show. For about 20 years, he was introduced nightly on the show with the phrase, "Here's Johnny!" A large segment of the television-watching public associated the phrase with Carson. A Michigan corporation was in the business of renting and selling portable toilets. The company chose the name "Here's Johnny Portable Toilets," and coupled the company name with the marketing phrase, "The World's Foremost Commodian." Carson sued. What claim is he making? Who should win, and why?

15. ETHICS: Fifteen-year-old Terri Stubblefield was riding in the backseat of a Ford Mustang II when the car was hit from behind. The Mustang was engulfed in a ball of fire, and Terri was severely burned. She died. Terri's family sued Ford, alleging that the car was badly designed—and that Ford knew it. At trial, Terri's family introduced evidence that Ford knew the fuel tank was dangerous and that it could have taken measures to make the tank safe. There was evidence that Ford consciously decided not to remedy the fuel tanks in order to save money. The jury awarded $8 million in punitive damages to the family. Ford appealed. Should the punitive damages be affirmed? What are the obligations of a corporation when it knows that one of its products may be dangerous? Should we require a manufacturer to improve the safety of its cars if doing so will make them too expensive for many drivers? What would you do if you were a midlevel executive and saw evidence that your company was endangering the lives of consumers to save money? What would you do if you were on a jury and saw such evidence?

16. ROLE REVERSAL: Write a multiple-choice question about defamation in which one and only one element is missing from the plaintiff's case. Choose a set of answers that forces the student to isolate the missing element.

Internet Research Problem

Using the Internet, find a recent case in which a court awarded punitive damages for the intentional tort of assault, battery, intentional infliction of emotional distress, or false imprisonment. What facts led to the punitive damages award? Make your own award of punitive damages, and then compare your judgment with the court's.

You can find further practice problems in the Online Quiz at **http://beatty.westbuslaw.com** or in the Study Guide that accompanies this text.

6

Negligence and Strict Liability

Party time! A fraternity at the University of Arizona welcomed new members, and the alcohol flowed freely. Several hundred people danced and shrieked and drank, and no one checked for proof of age. A common occurrence—but one that ended tragically. A minor student drove away, intoxicated, and slammed into another car. The other driver was gravely injured. The drunken student was obviously liable, but his insurance did not cover the huge medical bills. The injured man also sued the fraternity. Should the organization be legally responsible? The issue is one of negligence law. In this contentious area, courts continually face one question: When someone is injured, how far should responsibility extend?

Negligence

We might call negligence the "unintentional" tort because it concerns harm that arises by accident. A person, or perhaps an organization, does some act, not expecting to hurt anyone, yet someone is harmed. Should a court impose liability? The fraternity members who gave the party never wanted—or thought—that an innocent man would suffer terrible damage. But he did. Is it in society's interest to hold the fraternity responsible?

Before we can answer this question, we need some guidance. Things go wrong all the time, and people are hurt in large ways and small. Society needs a method of analyzing negligence cases consistently and fairly. One of America's greatest judges, Benjamin Cardozo, offered his thoughts more than 75 years ago. His decision still dominates negligence thinking today, so we will let him introduce us to Helen Palsgraf.

CASE SUMMARY

PALSGRAF v. LONG ISLAND RAILROAD CO.

248 N.Y. 339, 162 N.E. 99, 1928 N.Y. LEXIS 1269
New York Court of Appeals, 1928

FACTS: Helen Palsgraf was waiting on a railroad platform. As a train began to leave the station, a man carrying a package ran to catch it. He jumped aboard but looked unsteady, so a guard on the car reached out to help him as another guard, on the platform, pushed from behind. The man dropped the package, which struck the tracks and exploded—since it was packed with fireworks. The shock knocked over some heavy scales at the far end of the platform, and one of them struck Palsgraf. She sued the railroad. The jury found that the guards had acted negligently, and held the railroad liable. The company appealed.

ISSUE: Assuming the guards did a bad job assisting the passenger, was the railroad liable for the injuries to Ms. Palsgraf?

DECISION: No, the railroad was not liable because it had no duty to Palsgraf. Reversed.

REASONING: To win a negligence suit, an injured plaintiff must show that the defendant had a duty *specifically to her,* not to anyone else. There is no such thing as responsibility to society in general.

The guard's conduct was not a wrong to Palsgraf, even though it might have been a wrong to the man holding the package. The guard could not realize that the package might injure a passenger at the far end of the platform. If the guard had grabbed the package and deliberately hurled it to the ground, he would never have expected to hurt a distant passenger. Here, where his act was *un*intentional, he obviously cannot be liable.

To win a negligence case, the plaintiff must prove *all five* of these elements:

- *Duty of due care.* The defendant had a duty of due care *to this plaintiff.* This is Judge Cardozo's point in the Palsgraf case.

- *Breach.* The defendant breached her duty.

- *Factual cause.* The defendant's conduct actually caused the injury.

- *Foreseeable harm.* It was foreseeable that conduct like the defendant's might cause this type of harm.

- *Injury.* The plaintiff has actually been hurt.

DUTY OF DUE CARE

The first issue may be the most difficult in all of tort law: Did the defendant have a duty of due care to the injured person? Judges draw an imaginary line around the defendant and say that she owes a duty to the people within this circle, but not to those outside it. The test is generally "foreseeability." **If a defendant can foresee injury to a particular person, she has a duty to him.** If she cannot foresee the harm, there is usually no duty.

Some cases are easy. Suppose Glorious University operates a cafeteria. Does the school have a duty of due care to its diners? Absolutely. Management can foresee that a grimy kitchen will cause serious illness, so the university has a duty to each of its patrons. On the other hand, assume the school bookstore sells a road map of Greece to a student. During spring break, the student drives recklessly along a narrow country lane in Greece, injuring a farmer. The university could never have foreseen harm to a Greek farmer merely from selling a map, so it had no duty to the man.

Let us apply these principles to the fraternity case.

CASE SUMMARY

HERNANDEZ v. ARIZONA BOARD OF REGENTS

177 Ariz. 244, 866 P.2d 1330, 1994 Ariz. LEXIS 6
Arizona Supreme Court, 1994

FACTS: At the University of Arizona, the Epsilon Epsilon chapter of Delta Tau Delta fraternity gave a welcoming party for new members. The fraternity's officers knew that the majority of its members were under the legal drinking age, but permitted everyone to consume alcohol. John Rayner, who was under 21 years of age, left the party. He drove negligently and caused a collision with an auto driven by Ruben Hernandez. At the time of the accident, Rayner's blood alcohol level was 0.15, exceeding the legal limit. The crash left Hernandez blind, severely brain damaged, and quadriplegic.

Hernandez sued Rayner, who settled the case, based on the amount of his insurance coverage. The victim also sued the fraternity, its officers and national organization, all fraternity members who contributed money to buy alcohol, the university, and

others. The trial court granted summary judgment for all defendants and the court of appeals affirmed. Hernandez appealed to the Arizona Supreme Court.

ISSUE: Did the fraternity and the other defendants have a duty of due care to Hernandez?

DECISION: Yes, the defendants did have a duty of due care to Hernandez. Reversed and remanded.

REASONING: Historically, Arizona and most states have considered that *consuming* alcohol led to liability, but not *furnishing* it. However, the common law also has had a long-standing rule that a defendant could be liable for supplying some object to a person who is likely to endanger others. Giving a car to an intoxicated youth is an example of such behavior.

The youth might easily use the object (the car) to injure other people.

There is no difference between giving a car to an intoxicated youth and giving alcohol to a young person with a car. Both acts involve minors who, because of their age and inexperience, are likely to endanger third parties. Furthermore, furnishing alcohol to a minor violates several state statutes. The defendants did have a duty of due care to Hernandez and to the public in general. ◢

ETHICS | In most states, anyone serving alcohol to a minor is liable for injuries that result to a third party. One of the intriguing aspects of the common law is that every answer prompts another question. Should a homeowner who serves alcohol to an *adult* friend be liable for resulting harm? New Jersey has answered this question "Yes." In that state, if an adult pours drinks for a friend, aware that he is becoming drunk, and the friend injures a third party, the host is fully liable. However, the great majority of states to consider this issue have reached the opposite conclusion, holding that a social host is not liable for harm caused by an adult drinker. Why do most states distinguish between adult and underage guests, holding a social host liable only for serving minors? Using the ethics checklist, ask yourself: What are the consequences of serving alcohol to an adult guest? Which values are in conflict? Which of those values are most important to you? ▪

UPDATE | Online, find a recent case of social host liability. How did the accident occur? What was the outcome? In your view, was the outcome fair? ▪

Landowner's Duty

The common law applies special rules to a landowner for injuries occurring on her property. In most states, the owner's duty depends on why the injured person came onto the property.

- *Lowest Liability: Trespasser.* A **trespasser** is anyone on the property without consent. A landowner is only liable to a trespasser for intentionally injuring him or for some other gross misconduct. The landowner has no liability to a trespasser for mere negligence. Jake is not liable if a vagrant wanders onto his land and is burned by defective electrical wires.

- *Higher Liability: Licensee.* A **licensee** is anyone on the land for her own purposes but with the owner's permission. A social guest is a typical licensee. A licensee is entitled to a warning of hidden dangers that the owner knows about. If Juliet invites Romeo for a late supper on the balcony and fails to mention that the wooden railing is rotted, she is liable when her hero plunges to the courtyard.

- *Highest Liability: Invitee.* An **invitee** is someone on the property as of right because it is a public place or a business open to the public. The owner has a duty of reasonable care to an invitee. Perry is an invitee when he goes to the town beach. If riptides have existed for years and the town fails to post a warning, it is liable if Perry drowns. Perry is also an invitee when he shops at Daphne's Boutique. Daphne is liable if she ignores spilled coffee that causes Perry to slip.

CRIME AND TORT: LANDOWNER'S LIABILITY

Law shows us trends in social issues. Regrettably, a major concern of tort law today is how to respond to injury caused by criminals. If a criminal assaults and robs a pedestrian in a shopping mall, that act is a crime and may be prosecuted by the state. But prosecution leaves the victim uncompensated. The assault is also an intentional tort (discussed in Chapter 5), and the victim could file a civil lawsuit against the criminal. But most violent criminals have no assets. Given this economic frustration and the flexibility of the common law, it is inevitable that victims of violence look elsewhere for compensation. Because crimes now occur in offices, shopping malls, and parking lots, plaintiffs increasingly seek compensation from the owners of these facilities.

CASE SUMMARY

ANN M. v. PACIFIC PLAZA SHOPPING CENTER

6 Cal. 4th 666, 863 P.2d 207, 1993 Cal. LEXIS 6127
Supreme Court of California, 1994

FACTS: Ann M. worked at the Original 60 Minute Photo Company in the Pacific Plaza Shopping Center, a strip mall in San Diego. About 25 commercial tenants occupied the center. She was the only employee on duty one day when a man walked in "just like a customer," pulled a knife, went behind the counter, and raped her. He robbed the store, fled, and was never caught.

Ann M. sued Pacific Plaza, claiming that it negligently failed to provide security patrols in the common areas of the shopping center. Under the terms of the lease, Pacific Plaza had exclusive control of these areas, and the right to police them if it chose.

ISSUE: Did Pacific Plaza have a duty to Ann M. to provide security patrols?

DECISION: No, Pacific Plaza did not have a duty to Ann M. to provide security patrols.

REASONING: Deciding the scope of a landlord's duty involves a balancing act. The law must weigh any potential harm to tenants against the burden imposed on the landlord. Hiring security guards is very expensive. Violent criminal acts must be clearly foreseeable before the courts impose such an expensive obligation.

Before Ann M. was raped, tenants and employees of the shopping center had been concerned about their safety. Some evidence indicated that criminals had robbed banks, snatched purses, and pulled down women's pants in the shopping center. However, Pacific Plaza's own records revealed no criminal activity at all. As a result, violent criminal assaults were not foreseeable, and the landlord had no duty to provide security guards.

 AT RISK

The court found Pacific Plaza not liable, because it could not have foreseen the harm. If this brutal crime occurred again at the same mall, would it be foreseeable? What advice would you give to Pacific Plaza? Now consider some other retail store or office with which you are familiar. What steps could the employer take to diminish the likelihood of workplace violence?

BREACH OF DUTY

The second element of a plaintiff's negligence case is **breach of duty.** Courts apply the *reasonable person* standard: **A defendant breaches his duty of due care by failing to behave the way a reasonable person would under similar circumstances.** Reasonable "person" means someone of the defendant's occupation. A taxi driver must drive as a reasonable taxi driver would. An architect who designs a skyscraper's safety features must bring to the task far greater knowledge than the average person possesses.

Two medical cases illustrate the reasonable person standard. A doctor prescribes a powerful drug without asking his 21-year-old patient about other medicines she is currently taking. The patient suffers a serious drug reaction from the combined medications. The physician is liable for the harm. A reasonable doctor always checks current medicines before prescribing new ones.

On the other hand, assume that an 84-year-old patient dies on the operating table in an emergency room. While the surgeon was repairing heart damage, the man had a fatal stroke. If the physician followed normal medical procedures, and acted with reasonable speed, he is not liable. A doctor must do a reasonable professional job, but cannot guarantee a happy outcome.

FACTUAL CAUSE AND FORESEEABLE HARM

A plaintiff must also show that the defendant's breach of duty *caused* the plaintiff's harm. Courts look at two issues to settle causation: Was the defendant's behavior the *factual cause* of the harm? Was *this type of harm foreseeable?*[1]

Factual Cause

Nothing mysterious here. **If the defendant's breach physically led to the ultimate harm, it is the factual cause.** Suppose that Dom's Brake Shop tells Customer his brakes are now working fine, even though Dom knows that is false. Customer drives out of the shop, cannot stop at a red light, and hits Bicyclist crossing at the intersection. Dom is liable to Bicyclist. Dom's unreasonable behavior was the *factual cause* of the harm. Think of it as a row of dominoes. The first domino (Dom's behavior) knocked over the next one (failing brakes), which toppled the last one (the cyclist's injury).

Suppose, alternatively, that just as Customer is exiting the repair shop, Bicyclist hits a pothole and tumbles off her cycle, avoiding Customer's auto. Bicyclist's injuries stem from her fall, not from the auto. Customer's brakes still fail, and Dom has breached his duty to Customer, but Dom is not liable to Bicyclist. She would have been hurt anyway. No factual causation.

Foreseeable Type of Harm

For the defendant to be liable, the *type of harm* must have been reasonably foreseeable. In the case above, Dom could easily foresee that bad brakes would cause an automobile accident. He need not have foreseen exactly what happened. He did not know there would be a cyclist nearby. What he could foresee was this general type of harm involving defective brakes. Because the accident that occurred was of the type he could foresee, he is liable.

By contrast, assume the collision of car and bicycle produces a loud crash. Two blocks away, a pet pig, asleep on the window ledge of a 12th-story apartment, is startled by the noise, awakens with a start, and plunges to the sidewalk, killing a

---

[1] Courts often refer to these two elements, grouped together, as *proximate cause* or *legal cause*. However, as many judges have acknowledged, those terms have created legal confusion, so we use *factual cause* and *foreseeable type of harm*, the issues on which most decisions ultimately focus.

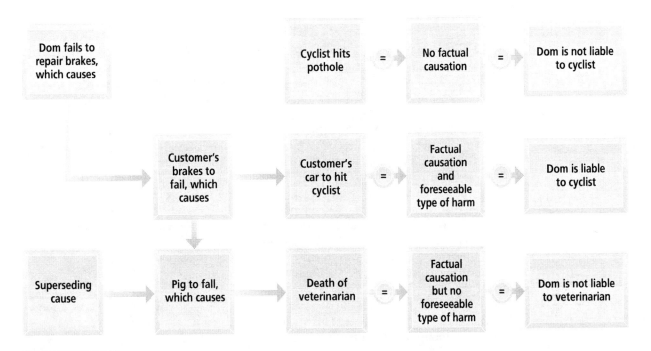

Exhibit 6.1

veterinarian who was making a house call. If the vet's family sues Dom, should it win? Dom's negligence was the factual cause: It led to the collision, which startled the pig, which flattened the vet. Most courts would rule, though, that Dom is not liable. The *type of harm* is too bizarre. Dom could not reasonably foresee such an extraordinary chain of events, and it would be unfair to make him pay for it. See Exhibit 6.1.

Res Ipsa Loquitur

Normally, a plaintiff must prove factual cause and foreseeable type of harm in order to establish negligence. But in a few cases, a court may be willing to infer that the defendant caused the harm, under the doctrine of *res ipsa loquitur* ("the thing speaks for itself"). Suppose a pedestrian is walking along a sidewalk when an air conditioning unit falls on his head from a third-story window. The defendant, who owns the third-story apartment, denies any wrongdoing, and it may be difficult or impossible for the plaintiff to prove why the air conditioner fell. In such cases, many courts will apply *res ipsa loquitur* and declare that the facts imply that the defendant's negligence caused the accident. If a court uses this doctrine, then the defendant must come forward with evidence establishing that it did not cause the harm.

Because *res ipsa loquitur* dramatically shifts the burden of proof from plaintiff to defendant, it applies only when (1) the defendant had exclusive control of the thing that caused the harm; (2) the harm normally would not have occurred without negligence; and (3) the plaintiff had no role in causing the harm. In the air conditioner example, most states would apply the doctrine and force the defendant to prove she did nothing wrong.

INJURY

Finally, a plaintiff must prove that he has been injured. In some cases, injury is obvious. For example, Ruben Hernandez suffered grievous harm when struck by a drunk driver. But in other cases, injury is unclear. **The plaintiff must persuade the court that he has suffered a harm that is genuine, not one that is merely speculative.**

UPDATE

A federal judge awarded $4 million to a California man who suffered severe brain damage after merchandise fell on him at a Wal-Mart store. Todd Caranto, a former Air Force medical corpsman, was Christmas shopping when more than a dozen heavy boxes of toys tumbled off high shelves and knocked him to the floor. The accident resulted in permanent brain damage and left the 26-year-old father of two unable to take care of himself. Caranto will require total care, 24 hours a day, for the rest of his life. He can walk but is unable to speak or communicate with anyone around him.

Find a current personal injury case that resulted in a jury verdict. How large was the award? What factors do you think most affected the jury's decision. How could the harm have been avoided? Are there lessons that a business can take from the case?

The following lawsuit concerns a woman's fear of developing AIDS, a worry that can be overwhelming. The court must still decide, however, whether the cause of the unhappiness is genuine injury or mere speculation.

CASE SUMMARY

REYNOLDS v. HIGHLAND MANOR, INC.

24 Kan. App. 2d 859, 954 P.2d 11, 1998 Kan. App. LEXIS 20
Kansas Court of Appeals, 1998

FACTS: Angelina Reynolds and her family checked into a Holiday Inn, but since the air conditioner did not work they requested a room change. As they were repacking their luggage, Reynolds felt for items left under the bed, and picked up what she thought was a candy wrapper. Reynolds felt a "gush" as she retrieved the item, which unfortunately turned out to be a wet condom. She screamed and quickly washed her hands. There was a second condom under the bed. Reynolds and her husband rushed to an emergency room, taking the condoms with them. Hospital staff said that they were unable to test the contents of the condoms. A doctor examined Reynolds's hand, which had a burn on the middle finger and bloody cuticles, but told her that there was nothing he could do if she had been exposed to infectious diseases.

The condom was never tested. Reynolds sued the motel, claiming among other things that she feared she would die of AIDS. The trial court dismissed the case, ruling that there was no showing of injury. Reynolds appealed.

ISSUE: Has Reynolds demonstrated injury?

DECISION: No, Reynolds has not demonstrated injury. Affirmed.

REASONING: A plaintiff may win a suit based on fear of a future disease or condition, but only if her anxiety is reasonable. She must show a substantial probability that her present injury will develop into a future ailment. If the medical evidence indicates that will not happen, the plaintiff loses.

Reynolds tested HIV-negative four times, including one result obtained more than a year after the incident at the motel. The condom never tested positive. It is more than 99% probable that Reynolds will never become HIV-positive. As a result, her fear of contracting AIDS is legally unreasonable, and she may not recover damages.

DAMAGES

The plaintiff's damages in a negligence case are generally **compensatory damages,** meaning an amount of money that the court believes will restore him to the position he was in before the defendant's conduct caused an injury. In unusual cases, a court may award **punitive damages,** that is, money intended not to compensate the plaintiff but to punish the defendant. We discussed both forms of damages in Chapter 5.

Defenses

ASSUMPTION OF THE RISK

Quick, duck! Close call—that baseball nearly knocked your ear off. If it had, the home team would owe you . . . nothing. Here at the ballpark, there is always a slight chance of injury, and you are expected to realize it. Wherever there is an obvious hazard, a special rule applies. **Assumption of the risk: A person who voluntarily enters a situation that has an obvious danger cannot complain if she is injured.** If you are not willing to tolerate the risk of being hurt by a batted ball, stay home and watch the game on television. And while you are here—pay attention, will you?

Suppose that Good Guys, a restaurant, holds an ice-fishing contest on a frozen lake, to raise money for accident victims. Margie grabs a can full of worms and strolls to the middle of the lake to try her luck, but slips on the ice and suffers a concussion. When she returns to consciousness, Margie should not bother filing suit—she assumed the risk.

CONTRIBUTORY AND COMPARATIVE NEGLIGENCE

Sixteen-year-old Michelle Wightman was out driving at night, with her friend Karrie Wieber in the passenger seat. They came to a railroad crossing, where the mechanical arm had descended and warning bells were sounding, in fact, had been sounding for a long time. A Conrail train, SEEL-7, had suffered mechanical problems and was stopped 200 feet from the crossing, where it had stalled for roughly an hour. Michelle and Karrie saw several cars ahead of them go around the barrier and cross the tracks. Michelle had to decide whether she would do the same.

Long before Michelle made her decision, the train's engineer had seen the heavy Saturday night traffic crossing the tracks, and realized the danger. A second train had passed the crossing at 70 miles per hour, without incident. SEEL-7's conductor and brakeman also understood the peril, but rather than posting a flagman, who could have stopped traffic when a train approached, they walked to the far end of their train to repair the mechanical problem. A police officer had come upon the scene, told his dispatcher to notify Conrail of the danger, and left.

Michelle decided to cross the tracks. She slowly followed the cars ahead of her. TV-9, a freight train traveling at 60 miles per hour, struck the car broadside, killing both girls instantly.

Michelle's mother sued Conrail for negligence. The company claimed that it was Michelle's foolish risk that led to her death. Who wins when both parties are partly responsible? It depends on whether the state uses a legal theory called contributory negligence. **Under contributory negligence, if the plaintiff is even**

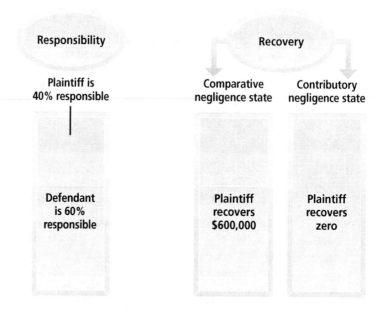

Exhibit 6.2
Defendant's negligence injures plaintiff, who suffers $1 million in damages.

slightly **negligent she recovers nothing.** If Michelle's death occurred in a contributory negligence state, and the jury considered her even minimally responsible, her estate would receive no money.

Critics attacked this rule as unreasonable. A plaintiff who was 1% negligent could not recover from a defendant who was 99% responsible. So most states threw out the contributory negligence rule, replacing it with comparative negligence. **In a comparative negligence state, a plaintiff may generally recover even if she is partially responsible.** The jury will be asked to assess the relative negligence of the two parties.

Michelle died in Ohio, which is a comparative negligence state. The jury concluded that reasonable compensatory damages were $1 million. It also concluded that Conrail was 60% responsible for the tragedy and Michelle 40%. See Exhibit 6.2. The girl's mother received $600,000 in compensatory damages.[2]

Strict Liability

Some activities are so naturally dangerous that the law places an especially high burden on anyone who engages in them. A corporation that produces toxic waste can foresee dire consequences from its business that a stationery store cannot. This higher burden is **strict liability.** There are two main areas of business that incur strict liability: ultrahazardous activity and defective products. We discuss **defective products** in Chapter 20, on product liability.

[2] *Wightman v. Consolidated Rail Corporation*, 86 Ohio St. 3d 431, 715 N.E.2d 546 (Ohio, 1999).

ULTRAHAZARDOUS ACTIVITY

Ultrahazardous activities include using harmful chemicals, operating explosives, keeping wild animals, bringing dangerous substances onto property, and a few similar activities where the danger to the general public is especially great. **A defendant engaging in an ultrahazardous activity is virtually always liable for any harm that results.** Plaintiffs do not have to prove duty or breach or foreseeable harm. Recall the deliberately bizarre case we posed earlier of the pig falling from a window ledge and killing a veterinarian. Dom, the mechanic whose negligence caused the car crash, could not be liable for the veterinarian's death because the plunging pig was not foreseeable. But if the pig had been jolted off the window ledge by Sam's Blasting Company doing perfectly lawful blasting for a new building down the street, Sam would be liable. Even if Sam had taken extraordinary care, he would lose. The "reasonable person" rule is irrelevant in a strict liability case.

YOU BE THE JUDGE

NEW JERSEY DEPARTMENT OF ENVIRONMENTAL PROTECTION v. ALDEN LEEDS, INC.

153 N.J. 272; 708 A.2d 1161; 1998 N.J. LEXIS 212; 46 ERC(BNA) 1447
Supreme Court of New Jersey, 1998

FACTS: The Alden Leeds company packages, stores, and ships swimming pool chemicals. The firm does most of its work at its facility in Kearns, New Jersey. At any given time, about 21 different hazardous chemicals are present.

The day before Easter, a fire of unknown origin broke out in "Building One" of the company's site, releasing chlorine gas and other potentially dangerous by-products into the air. There were no guards or other personnel on duty. The fire caused $9 million in damage to company property. Because of the danger, the Department of Environmental Protection (DEP) closed the New Jersey Turnpike along with half a dozen other major highways, halted all commuter rail and train service in the area, and urged residents to stay indoors with windows closed. An unspecified number of residents went to local hospitals with respiratory problems.

Based on New Jersey's air pollution laws, the DEP fined Alden Leeds for releasing the toxic chemicals. The appellate court reversed, declaring that there was no evidence the company had caused the fire or the harm. The case reached the state's high court.

YOU BE THE JUDGE: Is the company responsible for the harm?

ARGUMENT FOR ALDEN LEEDS: Alden Leeds did nothing wrong. Why should the company pay a fine? The firm was licensed to use these chemicals, and did so in a safe manner. There is no evidence the company caused the fire. Sometimes accidents just happen. Do not penalize a responsible business simply to make somebody pay. The state should go after careless firms that knowingly injure the public. Leave good companies alone so they can get on with business and provide jobs.

ARGUMENT FOR THE DEPARTMENT OF ENVIRONMENTAL PROTECTION: This accident made innocent people sick and caused massive difficulties for tens of thousands. It makes no difference why the accident happened. That is the whole point of strict liability. When a company chooses to participate in an ultrahazardous activity, it accepts full liability for anything that goes wrong, regardless of the cause. If you want the profits, you accept the responsibility. Alden Leeds must pay.

Chapter Conclusion

Negligence issues necessarily remain in flux, based on changing social values and concerns. There is no final word on what is an ultrahazardous activity, or how much security a shop owner must provide, or whether a social host can be liable for the destruction caused by a guest. What is clear is that a working knowledge of these issues and pitfalls can help everyone—business executive and ordinary citizen alike.

Chapter Review

1. The five elements of negligence are duty of due care, breach, factual causation, foreseeable type of harm, and injury.

2. If the defendant could foresee that misconduct would injure a particular person, he probably has a duty to her.

3. In most states, a landowner's duty of due care is lowest to trespassers; higher to a licensee (anyone on the land for her own purposes but with the owner's permission); and highest of all to an invitee (someone on the property as of right).

4. A defendant breaches his duty of due care by failing to behave the way a reasonable person would under similar circumstances.

5. If an event physically led to the ultimate harm, it is the factual cause.

6. For the defendant to be liable, the type of harm must have been reasonably foreseeable.

7. The plaintiff must persuade the court that he has suffered a harm that is genuine, not speculative.

8. In a contributory negligence state, a plaintiff who is even slightly responsible for his own injury recovers nothing; in a comparative negligence state, the jury may apportion liability between plaintiff and defendant.

9. A defendant is strictly liable for harm caused by an ultrahazardous activity or a defective product. Ultrahazardous activities include using harmful chemicals, blasting, and keeping wild animals. Strict liability means that if the defendant's conduct led to the harm, the defendant is liable, even if she exercises extraordinary care.

PRACTICE TEST

Matching Questions

Match the following terms with their definitions:

___ **A.** Breach.

___ **B.** Strict liability.

___ **C.** Compensatory damages.

___ **D.** Invitee.

___ **E.** Negligence.

1. Money awarded to an injured plaintiff.

2. Someone who has a legal right to enter upon land.

3. A defendant's failure to perform a legal duty.

4. A tort caused accidentally.

5. Legal responsibility that comes from performing ultrahazardous acts.

True/False Questions

Circle true or false:

1. **T**   F   There are five elements in a negligence case, and a plaintiff wins who proves at least three of them.

2. **T**   F   Max, a 19-year-old sophomore, gets drunk at a fraternity party and then causes a serious car accident. Max can be found liable and so can the fraternity.

3. **T**   F   Some states are comparative negligence states but the majority are contributory negligence states.

4. **T**   F   A landowner might be liable if a dinner guest fell on a broken porch step, but not liable if a trespasser fell on the same place.

5. **T**   F   A defendant can be liable for negligence even if he never intended to cause harm.

6. **T**   F   When Ms. Palsgraf sued the railroad, the court found that the railroad should have foreseen what might go wrong.

Multiple-Choice Questions

7. In which case is a plaintiff most likely to sue based on strict liability?

   (a) Defamation.

   (b) Injury caused on the job.

   (c) Injury caused by a tiger that escapes from a zoo.

   (d) Injury caused by defendant's careless driving.

   (e) Injury caused partially by plaintiff and partially by defendant.

8. Martha signs up for a dinner cruise on a large commercial yacht. While the customers are eating dinner, the yacht bangs into another boat. Martha is thrown to the deck, breaking her wrist. She sues. At trial, which of these issues is likely to be the most important?

   (a) Whether the yacht company had permission to take Martha on the cruise.

   (b) Whether the yacht company improperly restrained Martha.

   (c) Whether Martha feared an imminent injury.

   (d) Whether the yacht's captain did a reasonable job of driving the yacht.

   (e) Whether Martha has filed similar suits in the past.

9. Dolly, an architect, lives in Pennsylvania, which is a comparative negligence state. While she is inspecting a construction site for a large building she designed, she is injured when a worker drops a hammer from two stories up. Dolly was not wearing a safety helmet at the time. Dolly sues the construction company. The jury concludes that Dolly has suffered $100,000 in damages. The jury also believes that Dolly was 30% liable for the accident, and the construction company was 70% liable. Outcome?

   (a) Dolly wins nothing.

   (b) Dolly wins $30,000.

   (c) Dolly wins $50,000.

   (d) Dolly wins $70,000.

   (e) Dolly wins $100,000.

10. A taxi driver, hurrying to pick up a customer at the airport, races through a 20 mph hospital zone at 45 mph, and strikes May, who is crossing the street in a pedestrian crosswalk. May sues the driver and the taxi company. What kind of suit is this?

   (a) Contract.

   (b) Remedy.

   (c) Negligence.

   (d) Assault.

   (e) Battery.

Short-Answer Questions

11. At approximately 7:50 p.m., bells at the train station rang and red lights flashed, signaling an express train's approach. David Harris walked onto the tracks, ignoring a yellow line painted on the platform instructing people to stand back. Two men shouted to Harris, warning him to get off the tracks. The train's engineer saw him too late to stop the train, which was traveling at approximately 99 mph. The train struck and killed Harris as it passed through the station. Harris's widow sued the railroad, arguing that the railroad's negligence caused her husband's death. Evaluate the widow's argument.

12. A new truck, manufactured by General Motors Corp., stalled in rush hour traffic on a busy interstate highway because of a defective alternator, which caused a complete failure of the truck's electrical system. The driver stood nearby and waved traffic around his stalled truck. A panel truck approached the GMC truck. Immediately behind the panel truck, Davis was driving a Volkswagen fastback. Because of the panel truck, Davis was unable to see the stalled GMC truck. The panel truck swerved out of the way of the GMC truck, and Davis drove straight into it. The accident killed him. Davis's widow sued GMC. GMC moved for summary judgment, alleging (1) no duty to Davis; (2) no factual causation; and (3) no foreseeable harm. Comment on the three defenses that GMC has raised.

13. A prison inmate bit a hospital employee. The employee sued the state for negligence and lack of supervision, claiming a fear of AIDS. The plaintiff had tested negative for the AIDS virus three times, and there was no proof that the inmate had the virus. Comment on the probable outcome.

14. Van Houten owned a cat and allowed it to roam freely outside. In the three years he had owned it, it had never bitten anyone. The cat entered Pritchard's garage. Pritchard attempted to move it outside his garage, and the cat bit him. As a direct result of the bite, Pritchard underwent four surgeries, was fitted with a plastic finger joint, and spent more than $39,000 in medical bills. He sued Van Houten, claiming both strict liability and ordinary negligence. Please evaluate his claims.

15. ETHICS: Koby, age 16, works after school at Fast-Food, from 4 p.m. until 11 p.m. On Friday night, the restaurant manager sees that Koby is exhausted, but insists that he remain until 4:30 a.m., cleaning up, then demands that he work Saturday morning from 8 a.m. until 4 p.m. On Saturday afternoon, as Koby drives home, he falls asleep at the wheel and causes a fatal car accident. Should FastFood be liable? What important values are involved in this issue? How does the Golden Rule apply?

16. ROLE REVERSAL: Create a short-answer question that focuses on either factual cause, foreseeable type of harm, or *res ipsa loquitur*.

Internet Research Problem

Everyone knows that drunk driving is bad, but many people still do it. Proceed to **http://www.madd.org/**. Find something that you did not know about drunk driving. What role should the law play in this problem, and what role should parents, students, and schools play?

You can find further practice problems in the Online Quiz at **http://beatty.westbuslaw.com** or in the Study Guide that accompanies this text.

7

Criminal Law
and Procedure

Crime can take us by surprise. Stacey tucks her nine-year-old daughter, Beth, into bed. Promising her husband, Mark, that she will be home by 11 p.m., she jumps into her car and heads back to Be Patient, Inc. She puts a compact disk in the player of her $85,000 sedan and tries to relax. Be Patient is a health care organization that owns five geriatric hospitals. Most of its patients use Medicare, and Stacey supervises all billing to their largest client, the federal government.

She parks in a well-lighted spot on the street and walks to her building, failing to notice two men, collars turned up, watching from a parked truck. Once in her office, she goes straight to her computer and works on billing issues. Tonight's work goes more quickly than she expected, thanks to new software she helped develop. At 10:30 p.m., she emerges from the building with a quick step and a light heart, walks to her car—and finds it missing.

A major crime has occurred during the 90 minutes Stacey was at her desk, but she will never report it to the police. It is a crime that costs Americans countless dollars each year, yet Stacey will not even mention it to friends or family. Stacey is the criminal. ◾

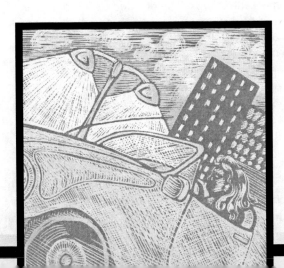

When we think of crime, we imagine the drug dealers and bank robbers endlessly portrayed on television. We do not picture corporate executives sitting at polished desks. "Street crimes" are indeed serious threats to our security and happiness. But when measured only in dollars, street crime takes second place to white-collar crime, which costs society tens of billions of dollars annually.

The hypothetical about Stacey is based on many real cases and is used to illustrate that crime does not always dress the way we expect. Her car was never stolen; it was simply towed. Two parking bureau employees, watching from their truck, saw Stacey park illegally and did their job. It is Stacey who committed a crime—Medicare fraud. Stacey has learned the simple but useful lesson that company profits rise when she charges the government for work that Be Patient has never done. For months she billed the government for imaginary patients. Then she hired a computer hacker to worm into the Medicare computer system and plant a "Trojan horse," a program that seemed useful to Medicare employees but actually contained a series of codes opening the computer to Stacey. Stacey simply entered the Medicare system and altered the calculations for payments owed to Be Patient. Every month, the government paid Be Patient about $10 million for imaginary work. Stacey's scheme was quick and profitable—and a distressingly common crime.

Crime, Society, and Law

CIVIL LAW/CRIMINAL LAW

Conduct is criminal when society outlaws it. When a state legislature or Congress concludes that certain behavior threatens the population generally, it passes a statute forbidding that behavior, in other words, declaring it criminal. Medicare fraud, which Stacey committed, is a crime because Congress has outlawed it.

Prosecution

Suppose the police arrest Roger and accuse him of breaking into a video store and stealing 25 video cameras, videos, and other equipment. The owner of the video store is the one harmed, but it is the government that prosecutes crimes. The local prosecutor will decide whether or not to charge Roger and bring him to trial.

Jury Right

The facts of the case will be decided by a judge or jury. A criminal defendant has a right to a trial by jury for any charge that could result in a sentence of six months or longer. The defendant may demand a jury trial or may waive that right, in which case the judge will be the fact finder.

Punishment

In a civil lawsuit, the plaintiff seeks a verdict that the defendant is liable for harm caused to her. But in a criminal case, the government asks the court to find the defendant guilty of the crime. If the judge or jury finds the defendant guilty, the court will punish him with a fine and/or a prison sentence. The fine is paid to the government, not to the injured person (although the court will sometimes order restitution, meaning that the defendant must reimburse the victim for harm suffered). It is generally the judge who imposes the sentence. If the jury is not persuaded of the defendant's guilt, it will acquit him, that is, find him not guilty.

Felony/Misdemeanor

A felony is a serious crime, for which a defendant can be sentenced to one year or more in prison. Murder, robbery, rape, drug dealing, wire fraud, and embezzlement are felonies. A misdemeanor is a less serious crime, often punishable by a year or less in a county jail. Driving without a license and simple possession of one marijuana cigarette are considered misdemeanors in most states.

THE PROSECUTION'S CASE

In all criminal cases, the prosecution faces several basic issues.

Conduct Outlawed

Virtually all crimes are created by statute. The prosecution must demonstrate to the court that the defendant's alleged conduct is indeed outlawed by a statute. Returning to Roger, the alleged video thief, the state charges that he stole video cameras from a store, a crime clearly defined by statute as burglary.

Burden of Proof

In a civil case, the plaintiff must prove her case by a preponderance of the evidence. But in a criminal case, the government must prove its case beyond a reasonable doubt. This is because the potential harm to a criminal defendant is far greater. The stigma of a criminal conviction will stay with him, making it more difficult to obtain work and housing.

Actus Reus

Actus reus means the "guilty act." The prosecution must prove that the defendant voluntarily committed a prohibited act. Suppose Mary Jo files an insurance claim for a stolen car, knowing that her car was not stolen. That is insurance fraud. Filing the claim is the *actus reus:* Mary Jo voluntarily filled out the insurance claim and mailed it. At a bar, Mary Jo describes the claim to her friend, Chi Ling, who laughs and replies, "That's great. It'll serve the company right." Has Chi Ling committed a crime? No. She may be cynical, but Chi Ling has committed no *actus reus*.

Mens Rea

The prosecution must also show *mens rea,* a "guilty state of mind," on the defendant's part. This is harder to prove than *actus reus*—it requires convincing evidence about something that is essentially psychological. Precisely what "state of mind" the prosecution must prove varies, depending on the crime. Most crimes require a showing of **general intent,** meaning that the defendant intended to do the prohibited physical action (the *actus reus*). Suppose Miller, a customer in a bar, picks up a bottle and smashes it over the head of Bud. In a trial for criminal assault, the *mens rea* would simply be the intention to hit Bud. The prosecution need not show that Miller intended serious harm, only that he intended the blow.

Some crimes require **specific intent.** The prosecution must prove that the defendant willfully intended to do something beyond the physical act. For example, burglary requires proof that the defendant entered a building at night and intended to commit a felony inside, such as stealing property.

DEFENSES

A criminal defendant will frequently dispute the facts that link her to the crime. For example, she might claim mistaken identity (that she merely resembles the real criminal) or offer an alibi (that she can prove she was elsewhere when the crime was committed). In addition, a defendant may offer legal defenses. One of the most controversial is the insanity defense.

Insanity

In most states, a defendant who can prove that he was insane at the time of the criminal act will be declared not guilty. This reflects the moral basis of our criminal law. Insane people, though capable of great harm, historically have not been considered responsible for their acts. A defendant found to be insane will generally be committed to a mental institution. If and when that hospital determines that he is no longer a danger to society, he will, in theory, be released.

States use different rules to gauge sanity. The most common test is the M'Naghten Rule. The defendant must show (1) that he suffered a serious, identifiable mental disease and that because of it (2) he did not understand the nature of his act or did not know that it was wrong. Suppose Jerry, a homeless man, stabs Phil. At trial, a psychiatrist testifies that Jerry suffers from chronic schizophrenia, that he does not know where he is or what he is doing, and that when he stabbed Phil he believed he was sponging down his pet giraffe. If the jury believes the psychiatrist, it may find Jerry not guilty by reason of insanity.

What if the alleged mental defect is a result of the defendant's own behavior? You be the judge.

YOU BE THE JUDGE

BIEBER v. PEOPLE

856 P.2d 811, 1993 Colo. LEXIS 630 Supreme Court of Colorado, 1993

FACTS: Donald Bieber walked up to a truck in which William Ellis was sitting and shot Ellis, whom he did not know, in the back of his head. He threw Ellis's body from the truck and drove away. Shortly before and after the killing, Bieber encountered various people in different places. He sang "God Bless America" and the "Marine Hymn" to them and told them he was a prisoner of war and was being followed by communists. He told people he had killed a Communist on "War Memorial Highway." The police arrested him.

Bieber had a long history of drug abuse. Several years before the homicide, Bieber voluntarily sought treatment for mental impairment, entering a hospital and saying he thought he was going to hurt someone. He was later released into a long-term drug program.

Bieber was charged with first-degree murder. He pleaded not guilty by reason of insanity. An expert witness testified that he was insane, suffering from "amphetamine delusional disorder" (ADD), a recognized psychiatric illness resulting from long-term use of amphetamines and characterized by delusions. At trial, Bieber's attorney argued that he was not intoxicated at the time of the crime but that he was insane due to ADD. The trial court refused to instruct that Bieber could be legally insane due to ADD, and the jury found Bieber guilty of first-degree murder. He appealed.

YOU BE THE JUDGE: May a jury find that a defendant with ADD is legally insane?

ARGUMENT FOR BIEBER: It is morally and legally proper to distinguish between people who commit a crime out of viciousness and those who suffer serious mental illness. Mr. Bieber suffered from a serious psychotic illness recognized by the American Psychiatric Association. There was overwhelming evidence that he was out of control and did not know what he was doing at the time of the homicide. The fact that ADD is brought about by years of amphetamine use should make no difference in an insanity case. This man's reason was destroyed by a serious illness. He should not be treated the same as a cold-blooded killer.

ARGUMENT FOR THE STATE: Your honors, there is no qualitative difference between a person who drinks or takes drugs knowing that he or she will be momentarily "mentally defective" as an immediate result and one who drinks or takes drugs knowing that he or she may be "mentally defective" as an eventual, long-term result. In both cases, the person is aware of the possible consequences of his or her actions.

As a matter of public policy, we must not excuse a defendant's actions, which endanger others, based upon a mental disturbance or illness that he or she actively and voluntarily contracted. If anything, the moral blameworthiness would seem to be even greater with respect to the long-term effects of many, repeated instances of voluntary intoxication occurring over an extended period of time. We ask that you affirm.

Crimes That Harm Business

LARCENY

It is holiday season at the mall, the period of greatest profits—and the most crime. At the Foot Forum, a teenager limps in wearing ragged sneakers and sneaks out wearing Super Rags, valued at $195. Down the aisle at a home furnishing store, a man is so taken by a $375 power saw that he takes it.

Larceny is the trespassory taking of personal property with the intent to steal it. "Trespassory taking" means that someone else originally had the property. The Super Rags are personal property (not real estate), they were in the possession of the Foot Forum, and the teenager deliberately left without paying, intending never to return the goods. That is larceny. By contrast, suppose Fast Eddie leaves Bloomingdale's in New York, descends to the subway system, and jumps over a turnstile without paying. Larceny? No. He has "taken" a service—the train ride—but not personal property.

FRAUD

Robert Dorsey owned Bob's Chrysler in Highland, Illinois. He ordered cars from the manufacturer, the First National Bank of Highland paid Chrysler, and Dorsey—supposedly—repaid the loans as he sold autos. Dorsey, though, began to suffer financial problems, and the bank suspected he was selling cars without repaying his loans. A state investigator notified Dorsey that he planned to review all dealership records. One week later a fire engulfed the dealership. An arson investigator discovered that an electric iron, connected to a timer, had been placed on a pile of financial papers doused with accelerant.

The saddest part of this true story is that it is only too common. Some experts suggest that 1% of corporate revenues are wasted on fraud alone. Dorsey was convicted and imprisoned for committing two crimes that cost business billions of dollars annually—fraud and arson.[1]

Fraud refers to various crimes, all of which have a common element: the deception of another person for the purpose of obtaining money or property from him. Robert Dorsey's precise violation was bank fraud, a federal crime. It is **bank fraud** to use deceit to obtain money, assets, securities, or other property under the control of any financial institution.

Wire fraud and **mail fraud** are additional federal crimes, involving the use of interstate mail, telegram, telephone, radio, or television to obtain property by deceit. For example, if Marsha makes an interstate phone call to sell land that she does not own, that is wire fraud.

Finally, Stacey, the hospital executive described in the chapter's introduction, committed a fourth type of fraud. **Medicare fraud** includes using false statements, bribes, or kickbacks to obtain Medicare payments from the federal or state government.

Arson

Robert Dorsey, the Chrysler dealer, committed a second serious crime. Arson is the malicious use of fire or explosives to damage or destroy any real estate or personal property. It is both a federal and a state crime. Dorsey used arson to conceal his bank fraud. Most arsonists hope to collect on insurance policies. Every year thousands of buildings burn, particularly in economically depressed neighborhoods, as owners try to make a quick kill or extricate themselves from financial difficulties. We involuntarily subsidize their immorality by paying higher insurance premiums.

EMBEZZLEMENT

This crime also involves illegally obtaining property, but with one big difference: The culprit begins with legal possession. **Embezzlement is the fraudulent conversion of property already in the defendant's possession.** A bank teller is expected to handle thousands of bills every day. But when she decides to tidy her cash drawer by putting all the wrinkled hundred-dollar bills in her pocket, she has embezzled.

COMPUTER CRIME

A 29-year-old computer whiz stole a car—using his keyboard. The man infiltrated a telephone company network and rigged a radio station's call-in promotion, winning himself a splendid new Porsche. He also damaged court-ordered wiretaps of alleged gangsters and may even have jammed the phones on an Unsolved Mysteries television episode in which he was the featured fugitive! The ascent of the Internet

---

[1] *United States v. Dorsey,* 27 F.3d 285 (7th Cir. 1994).

inevitably brings with it new forms of crime. Various federal statutes criminalize this behavior.

- The **Computer Fraud and Abuse Act** prohibits using a computer to commit theft, espionage, trespass, fraud, and damage to another computer. An angry employee who hacks into his company's central computer system and damages the billing system has violated this law.

- The **Access Device Fraud Act** outlaws the fraudulent use of cards, codes, account numbers, and other devices to obtain money, goods, or services. For example, it is a violation of this act to reprogram a cellular telephone so that calls are charged to an improper account.

- The **Identity Theft and Assumption Deterrence Act** bars the use of false identification to commit fraud or other crime. A waiter who uses stolen credit card numbers to buy airline tickets has violated this act. The Federal Trade Commission receives about 100,000 complaints of identity theft every year, so you should guard identifying data carefully.

- The **Wire and Electronic Communications Interception Act** makes it a crime to intercept most wire, oral, and electronic communications. (This law does not prohibit recording your own conversations.) We warned you not to tape your roommate's conversations!

Crimes Committed by Business

A corporation can be found guilty of a crime based on the conduct of any of its agents, who include anyone undertaking work on behalf of the corporation. An agent can be a corporate officer, an accountant hired to audit a statement, a sales clerk, or almost any other person performing a job at the company's request.

If an agent commits a criminal act within the scope of his employment and with the intent to benefit the corporation, the company is liable. This means that the agent himself must first be guilty. The normal requirements of *actus reus* and *mens rea* apply. If the agent is guilty, the corporation is, too. The most common punishment for a corporation is a fine. This makes sense in that the purpose of a business is to earn a profit, and a fine, if large enough, hurts.

CASE SUMMARY

WISCONSIN v. KNUTSON, INC.

196 Wis. 2d 86, 537 N.W.2d 420, 1995 Wis. App. LEXIS 1223
Wisconsin Court of Appeals, 1995

FACTS: Richard Knutson, Inc. (RKI) was constructing a sanitary sewer line for the city of Oconomowoc. An RKI crew attempted to place a section of corrugated metal pipe in a trench in order to remove groundwater. The backhoe operator misjudged the distance from the backhoe's boom to the overhead power lines and failed to realize that he had placed the the boom in contact with the wires. A crew member attempted to attach a chain to the backhoe's bucket and was instantly electrocuted.

The state charged RKI with negligent vehicular homicide under a statute that says: "Whoever causes the death of another human being by the negligent operation or handling of a vehicle is guilty of a Class E felony." The jury convicted, and RKI appealed, claiming that a corporation could not be held guilty under the statute.

ISSUE: May a corporation be guilty of vehicular homicide under the statute?

DECISION: Yes, a corporation can be found guilty of vehicular homicide. Affirmed.

REASONING: Corporations are a dominant part of life in the United States, and criminal responsibility is one of the primary ways we regulate our affairs. It would be unfair to assign guilt to a group of people within a company while ignoring the corporate culture that may have prompted the illegal conduct. Because crime can be profitable, firms may pressure workers to break the law. Corporations must be held responsible for the harm they cause. Furthermore, because many corporations are so large, identifying guilty employees within a company may be impossible.

Here, if RKI had enforced OSHA's written safety regulations, or if the company had complied with the procedures outlined in its contract, the victim would never have died. RKI's failure to take elementary precautions for its employees was a substantial cause of this electrocution. ◢

COMPLIANCE PROGRAMS

The Federal Sentencing Guidelines are the detailed rules that judges must follow when sentencing defendants convicted of crimes in federal court. The guidelines instruct judges to determine whether, at the time of the crime, the corporation had in place a serious compliance program, that is, a plan to prevent and detect criminal conduct at all levels of the company. A company that can point to a detailed, functioning compliance program may benefit from a dramatic reduction in the fine or other punishment meted out. Indeed, a tough compliance program may even convince federal investigators to curtail an investigation and to limit any prosecution to those directly involved, rather than attempting to get a conviction against high-ranking officers or the company itself.

WORKPLACE CRIMES

The workplace can be dangerous. Working on an assembly line exposes factory employees to fast-moving machinery. For a roofer, the first slip may be the last. The invisible radiation in a nuclear power plant can be deadlier than a bullet. The most important statute regulating the workplace is the federal Occupational Safety and Health Act of 1970 (OSHA), which sets safety standards for many industries. May a state government go beyond standards set by OSHA and use the criminal law to punish dangerous conditions? The courts of Illinois answered that question with a potent "yes," permitting a *murder prosecution* against corporate executives who had caused the death of a worker by forcing him to work with life-threatening chemicals, including bubbling vats of sodium cyanide.

RICO

The Racketeer Influenced and Corrupt Organizations Act (RICO) is one of the most powerful and controversial statutes ever written. Congress passed the law primarily to prevent gangsters from taking money they earned illegally and investing it in legitimate businesses. But RICO has expanded far beyond the original intentions of Congress and is now used more often against ordinary businesses than against organized criminals.

The government may prosecute both individuals and organizations for violating RICO. For example, the government may prosecute a mobster, claiming that he has run a heroin ring for years. It may also prosecute an accounting firm, claiming that it lied about corporate assets in a stock sale to make the shares appear more valuable than they really were. If the government proves its case, the defendant can be hit with large fines and a prison sentence of up to 20 years.

What is a violation of this law? RICO prohibits using two or more racketeering acts to accomplish any of these goals: (1) investing in or acquiring legitimate businesses with criminal money; (2) maintaining or acquiring businesses through criminal activity; or (3) operating businesses through criminal activity.

What does that mean in English? It is a two-step process to prove that a person or an organization has violated RICO.

- The prosecutor must show that the defendant committed two or more racketeering acts, which are any of a long list of specified crimes: embezzlement, arson, mail fraud, wire fraud, and so forth. If a stockbroker told two customers that Bronx Gold Mines was a promising stock, when she knew that it was worthless, that would be two racketeering acts.

- The prosecutor must show that the defendant used these racketeering acts to accomplish one of the three purposes listed above. If the stockbroker gave fraudulent advice and used the commissions to buy advertising for her firm, that would violate RICO.

ENVIRONMENTAL CRIMES

Federal and state statutes prohibit many forms of air and water pollution. Some of the laws create criminal liability. For example, the Clean Water Act (CWA), a federal statute, is designed to protect the waters that we use for recreation and commerce, including lakes, rivers and oceans. The CWA prohibits discharging raw sewage without a permit, an issue in the following case.

CASE SUMMARY

UNITED STATES v. WEITZENHOFF

35 F.3d 1275 (9th Cir. 1994)
Ninth Circuit Court of Appeals

FACTS: Michael Weitzenhoff and Thomas Mariani managed the East Honolulu Community Services Sewage Treatment Plant, located near Sandy Beach, a popular playground on the island of Oahu. The plant treats four million gallons of residential wastewater each day by removing solids and other harmful pollutants from the sewage, so that the resulting effluent can be safely discharged into the ocean. During treatment, sludge accumulates in the bottom of the tanks. The sludge is supposed to be re-treated, or else shipped to a separate facility.

When the sludge levels became unmanageable, Weitzenhoff and Mariani ordered workers to discharge the untreated matter directly into the ocean. Lifeguards promptly complained about foul odors coming from the ocean water; swimmers became sick. During an FBI investigation, Weitzenhoff and Mariani admitted authorizing the discharge. They were convicted of "knowingly violating" the discharge provisions, and sentenced to several years in prison. On appeal, they argued that they could not be found guilty because they were unaware that their conduct was illegal.

ISSUE: Can the defendants be guilty of "knowingly violating" a CWA provision they knew nothing about?

DECISION: Yes, the defendants can be guilty of violating the CWA whether or not they knew of its criminal provisions. Affirmed.

REASONING: The term *knowingly* requires only that the defendants knew they were discharging the pollutants, not that they were aware of the legal consequences. Weitzenhoff and Mariani personally authorized the discharge. Congress included the term *knowingly* in the CWA so that those who realized they were polluting the water would receive harsher penalties than those who accidentally caused pollution. ◢

Weitzenhoff and Mariani knew what they were doing. Other cases have found corporate officers guilty of *unintended* water pollution, that is, for their mere negligence in allowing harmful substances to enter the water.[2] Anyone involved in an industry that could potentially cause pollution must beware of the criminal law.

The Criminal Process

How does the government investigate and prosecute criminal cases? The steps vary from case to case, but the summary in Exhibit 7.1 highlights the important steps.

Informant

Yasmin is a secretary to Stacey, the Be Patient executive who opened this chapter. She speaks to Moe, an FBI. She reports that Stacey routinely charges the government for patients who do not exist. Moe prepares an affidavit for Yasmin to sign, detailing everything she told him. An affidavit is simply a written statement signed under oath.

WARRANT

Moe takes Yasmin's affidavit to a United States magistrate, an employee of the federal courts who is similar to a judge. Moe asks the magistrate to issue search warrants for Be Patient's patient records. A search warrant is written permission from a neutral official, such as the magistrate, to conduct a search. A warrant must specify with reasonable certainty the place to be searched and the items to be seized.

Probable Cause

The magistrate will issue a warrant only if there is probable cause. Probable cause means that, based on all of the information presented, it is likely that evidence of crime will be found in the place mentioned. The magistrate will look at Yasmin's affidavit to determine (1) whether the informant (Yasmin) is reliable and (2) whether she has a sound basis for the information. The magistrate issues the warrant.

---

[2] *United States v. Hanousek,* 176 F.3d 1116 (9th Cir. 1999).

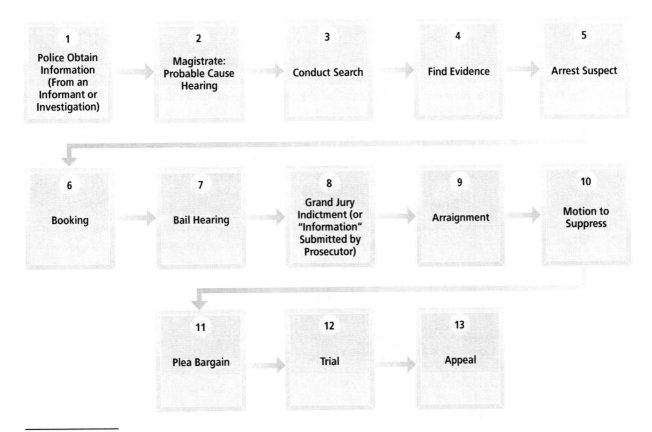

Exhibit 7.1

SEARCH AND SEIZURE

Armed with the warrants, Moe and other agents arrive at Be Patient hospitals, show the warrants, and take away the appropriate records. The search may not exceed what is described in the warrant. The agents cart the records back to headquarters and enter the data into a computer. The computer compares the records of actual patients with the bills submitted to the government and indicates that 10% of all bills are for fictional patients. Moe summarizes the new data on additional affidavits and presents the affidavits to the magistrate, who issues arrest warrants.

Fourth Amendment

The Fourth Amendment prohibits the government from making illegal searches and seizures. This amendment protects individuals, corporations, partnerships, and other organizations. In general, the police must obtain a warrant before conducting a search. If the police search without one, they have probably violated the Fourth Amendment.

Exclusionary Rule

Under the exclusionary rule, evidence obtained illegally may not be used at trial against the victim of the search. Suppose when Yasmin called the FBI, Moe simply drove straight to one of Be Patient's hospitals and grabbed patient records. Moe lacked a warrant, the search was illegal, and the evidence would be excluded from trial.

ARREST

Moe arrives at Be Patient and informs Stacey that she is under arrest. He informs her of her right to remain silent. He drives Stacey to FBI headquarters, where she is booked; that is, her name, photograph, and fingerprints are entered in a log. She is entitled to a prompt bail hearing. A judge or magistrate will set an amount of bail that she must pay in order to go free pending the trial. The purpose of bail is to ensure that Stacey will appear for all future court hearings.

Self-Incrimination

The Fifth Amendment bars the government from forcing any person to testify against himself. In other words, the police may not use mental or physical coercion to force a confession out of someone. Society does not want a government that engages in torture. Such abuse might occasionally catch a criminal, but it would grievously injure innocent people and make all citizens fearful of the government that is supposed to represent them. Before the police obtain a confession, the defendant must be told that he has the right to remain silent; that anything he says can be used against him at trial; that he has the right to a lawyer; and that if he cannot afford a lawyer, the court will appoint one for him.

INDICTMENT

Moe turns all of his evidence over to Larry, the local prosecutor for the United States. Larry presents the evidence to a grand jury. It is the grand jury's job to determine whether there is probable cause that this defendant committed the crime with which she is charged. The grand jury votes to indict Stacey. An indictment is the government's formal charge that the defendant has committed a crime and must stand trial. The grand jury is persuaded that there is probable cause that Stacey billed for 1,550 nonexistent patients, charging the government for $290 million worth of services that were never performed. The grand jury indicts her for (1) Medicare fraud, (2) mail fraud, (3) computer crimes, and (4) RICO violations. It also indicts Be Patient, Inc., and other employees.

ARRAIGNMENT

Stacey is ordered back to court. A clerk reads her the formal charges of the indictment. The judge asks whether Stacey has a lawyer, and of course she does. If she did not, the judge would urge her to get one quickly. If a defendant cannot afford a lawyer, the court will appoint one to represent her free of charge. The judge now asks the lawyer how Stacey pleads to the charges. Her lawyer answers that she pleads not guilty to all charges.

Plea Bargaining

Sometime before trial, the two attorneys will meet to consider a plea bargain. A plea bargain is an agreement between prosecution and defense that the defendant will plead guilty to a reduced charge, and the prosecution will recommend to the judge a relatively lenient sentence. Based on the RICO violations alone, Stacey faces a possible 20-year prison sentence, along with a large fine and a devastating forfeiture order. The government makes this offer: Stacey will plead guilty to 100 counts of mail fraud; Be Patient will repay all $290 million and an additional $150 million in fines; the government will drop the RICO and computer crime charges and recommend to the judge that Stacey be fined only $1 million and sentenced to three years in prison. In the federal court system, about 75% of all prosecutions end in a plea bargain. In state court systems the number is often higher.

Stacey agrees to the government's offer. The judge accepts the plea, and Stacey is fined and sentenced accordingly. A judge need not accept the bargain, but usually does.

TRIAL AND APPEAL

When there is no plea bargain, the case must go to trial. The mechanics of a criminal trial are similar to those for a civil trial, described in Chapter 3, on dispute resolution. It is the prosecution's job to convince the jury beyond a reasonable doubt that the defendant committed every element of the crime charged.

THE PATRIOT ACT OF 2001

In response to the devastating attacks of September 11, 2001, Congress passed a sweeping antiterrorist law known as the Patriot Act. The statute was designed to give law enforcement officials greater power to investigate and prevent potential terrorist assaults. The bill raced through Congress nearly unopposed. Proponents hailed it as a vital weapon for use against continuing lethal threats. Opponents argued that the law was passed in haste and threatened the liberties of the very people it purported to shield. They urged that the statute gave law officers too much power, permitting them to conduct searches, intercept private Internet communications, and examine financial and academic records—all with little or no judicial oversight. Supporters of the law responded that its most controversial sections were scheduled to expire in four years. In the meantime, they said, constitutional protections governed the law as they did all others.

As this book goes to press, it is difficult to assess the full impact of the Patriot Act. In an early legal test, a federal judge permitted the government to use secret evidence in its effort to freeze the assets of Global Relief Foundation, a religious organization suspected of terrorist activity. The group, which claimed to be purely humanitarian, asserted that it could hardly defend itself against unseen evidence. Finding "acute national security concerns," the judge allowed the government to introduce the evidence in private, without the foundation ever seeing it.

Chapter Conclusion

Business crime appears in unexpected places, with surprising suspects. A corporate executive aware of its protean nature is in the best position to prevent it. Classic fraud and embezzlement schemes are often foiled with commonsense preventive measures. Federal sentencing guidelines make it eminently worthwhile for corporations to establish aggressive compliance programs. Sophisticated computer and money laundering crimes can be thwarted only with determination and the cooperation of citizens and police agencies. We can defeat business crime if we have the knowledge and the will.

UPDATE | Find a recent case involving the Patriot Act. What were the precise issues? How did the court rule and why? ▗

Chapter Review

1. The rationales for punishment include restraint, deterrence and retribution.

2. In all prosecutions, the government must establish that the defendant's conduct was outlawed, that the defendant committed the actus reus, and that he had the necessary mens rea.

3. In addition to factual defenses, such as mistaken identity or alibi, a defendant may offer various legal defenses, such as insanity, entrapment.

4. Larceny is the trespassory taking of personal property with the intent to steal.

5. Fraud refers to a variety of crimes, all of which involve the deception of another person for the purpose of obtaining money or property.

6. Arson is the malicious use of fire or explosives to damage or destroy real estate or personal property.

7. Embezzlement is the fraudulent conversion of property already in the defendant's possession.

8. Computer crime statutes prohibit computer trespass and fraud; wrongful use of cards, codes, and identification; and most intercepting or taping of conversations.

9. If a company's agent commits a criminal act within the scope of her employment and with the intent to benefit the corporation, the company is liable.

10. RICO prohibits using two or more racketeering acts to invest in legitimate business or carry on certain other criminal acts. RICO permits civil lawsuits as well as criminal prosecutions.

PRACTICE TEST

Matching Questions

Match the following terms with their definitions:

___ **A.** Larceny

___ **B.** RICO

___ **C.** Felony

___ **D.** *Mens rea*

___ **E.** M'Naughten Rule

___ **F.** Embezzlement

1. A statute designed to prevent the use of criminal proceeds in legitimate businesses.

2. Fraudulently keeping property already in defendant's possession.

3. A test used to gauge a defendant's sanity.

4. The most serious type of crime, usually punishable by a year or more in prison.

5. The trespassory taking of personal property.

6. A guilty state of mind.

True/False Questions

Circle true or false:

1. T   F   Both the government and the victim are entitled to prosecute a crime.

2. T   F   A misdemeanor is a less serious crime, punishable by less than a year in jail.

3. T   F   In all criminal cases, the prosecution must prove *actus reus.*

4. T   F   Corporate officers can be convicted of crimes; corporations themselves cannot be.

5. T   F   An affidavit is the government's formal charge of criminal wrongdoing.

Multiple-Choice Questions

6. The insanity defense

(a) is available in less than 5 states nationwide.

(b) means that if the jury finds that a defendant was insane at the time of the crime, the defendant goes free.

(c) means that if the jury finds that a defendant was insane at the time of the crime, the defendant is locked in prison for the same time period as if he had been found guilty.

(d) means that if the jury finds that a defendant was insane at the time of the crime, the defendant will be locked in a mental hospital until he is no longer a danger to society.

(e) used to be the law in all states, but has now been outlawed by court rulings.

7. Probable cause means

(a) substantial evidence that the person signing the affidavit has legitimate reasons for requesting the warrant.

(b) substantial similarity between the items sought and the items found.

(c) substantial likelihood that a crime has taken place or is about to take place.

(d) trustworthy evidence that the victim of the search is known to have criminal tendencies.

(e) that based on all of the information presented it is likely that evidence of crime will be found in the place mentioned.

8. Police believe that Jay is dealing drugs from his apartment. They search his apartment without a warrant and find 3 kilos of cocaine. The cocaine

(a) Will be excluded from Jay's trial.

(b) Is valid evidence provided the police reasonably believed Jay was a drug dealer.

(c) Is valid evidence provided the police had spoken to neighbors before searching.

(d) Was improperly obtained but may be used in Jay's trial.

(e) May not be used in Jay's trial but may be used during his sentencing.

9. A prosecutor concerned that he may lack sufficient evidence to obtain a conviction may agree to

(a) An affidavit.

(b) A warrant.

(c) An appeal.

(d) An indictment.

(e) A plea bargain.

10. Professor asks Janice, his teaching assistant, to please drive the professor's car to the repair shop. Janice gets in and drives, not to the garage, but 1,400 miles further west, to Las Vegas. Janice has committed

(a) Fraud

(b) Embezzlement

(c) Larceny

(d) RICO violation

(e) Access Device Fraud

Short-Answer Questions

11. Arnie owns a two-family house in a poor section of the city. A fire breaks out, destroying the building and causing $150,000 damage to an adjacent store. The state charges Arnie with arson. Simultaneously, Vickie, the store owner, sues Arnie for the damage to her property. Both cases are tried to juries, and the two juries hear identical evidence of Arnie's actions. But the criminal jury acquits Arnie, while the civil jury awards Vickie $150,000. How did that happen?

12. ETHICS: Nineteen-year-old David Lee Nagel viciously murdered his grandparents, stabbing them repeatedly and slitting their throats, all because they denied him use of the family car. He was tried for murder and found not guilty by reason of insanity. He has lived ever since in mental hospitals. In 1994 he applied for release. The two psychiatrists who examined him stated that he was no longer mentally ill and was a danger neither to society nor to himself. Yet the Georgia Supreme Court refused to release him, seemingly because of the brutality of the killings. Comment on the court's ruling. What is the rationale for treating an insane defendant differently from others? Do you find the theory persuasive? If you do, what result must logically follow when psychiatrists testify that the defendant is no longer a danger? Should the brutality of the crime be a factor in deciding whether to prolong the detention? If you do not accept the rationale for treating such defendants differently, explain why not.

13. Federal law requires that all banks file reports with the IRS anytime a customer engages in a cash transaction in an amount over $10,000. It is a crime for a bank to "structure" a cash transaction, that is, to break up a single transaction of more than $10,000 into two or more smaller transactions (and thus avoid the filing requirement). In *Ratzlaf v. United States*, 510 U.S. 135, 114 S. Ct. 655 (1994), the Supreme Court held that in order to find a defendant guilty of structuring, the government must prove that he specifically intended to break the law, that is, that he knew that what he was doing was a crime and meant to commit it. Congress promptly passed a law "undoing" Ratzlaf. A bank official can now be convicted on evidence that he structured a payment, even with no evidence that he knew it was a crime. The penalties are harsh. (1) Why is structuring so serious? (2) Why did Congress change the law about the defendant's intent?

14. Northwest Telco Corp. (Telco) provides long-distance telephone service. Customers dial a general access number, then enter a six-digit access code and then the phone number they want to call. A computer places the call and charges the account. On January 10, 1990, Cal Edwards, a Telco engineer, noticed that Telco's general access number was being dialed exactly every 40 seconds. After each dialing, a different six-digit number was entered, followed by a particular long-distance number. This continued from 10 p.m. to 6 a.m. Why was Edwards concerned?

15. Kathy Hathcoat was a teller at a Pendleton, Indiana bank. In 1990 she began taking home money that belonged in her cash drawer. Her branch manager, Mary Jane Cooper, caught her. But rather than reporting Hathcoat, Cooper joined in. The two helped cover for each other by verifying that their cash drawers were in balance. They took nearly $200,000 before bank officials found them out. What criminal charge did the government bring against Hathcoat?

16. ROLE REVERSAL: Write a short-answer question that focuses on the elements of a RICO violation.

Internet Research Problem

A Web site devoted to Internet crime is **http://www.digitalcentury.com/encyclo/update/crime.html**. Find a current crime that might victimize you. What steps should you take to avoid harm?

You can find further practice problems in the Online Quiz at **http://beatty.westbuslaw.com** or in the Study Guide that accompanies this text.

8

Introduction to Contracts

In Marina del Rey, California, Cassandra sits on the sunny deck of her waterside condominium, sipping a mocha latte while watching spinnakers fill with the warm Pacific wind. She has just received an offer of $1.7 million to buy her condominium. Cassandra has decided to counteroffer for $1.9 million. She is in high spirits because she assumes that at the very worst she has $1.7 million guaranteed, and that represents a huge profit to her. Cassandra plans to buy a cheaper house in North Carolina and invest her profits so that she can retire early. She opens the newspaper, notices a headline "Hard Body Threatens Suit," and turns the page, thinking that a corporate lawsuit in Ohio is of no concern to her. She is mistaken and may learn some hard lessons about contract law.

A year earlier, Jerusalem Steel had signed a contract with Hard Body, a manufacturer of truck and bus bodies. Jerusalem was to deliver 20,000 tons of steel to Hard Body's plant in Joy, Ohio. Hard Body relied on the contract, hiring 300 additional workers even before the steel was delivered, so that the plant would be geared up and ready to produce buses when the metal arrived. To help deal with the new workers, Hard Body offered a midlevel personnel job to Nicole. Hard Body told Nicole, "Don't worry, we expect your job to last forever." Nicole, in turn, relied on that statement to quit her old job in Minneapolis, move to Joy, and sign an agreement with Jasper to purchase his house for $450,000. Based on that sales contract, Jasper phoned his offer to Cassandra's real estate agent for $1.7 million. See Exhibit 9.1.

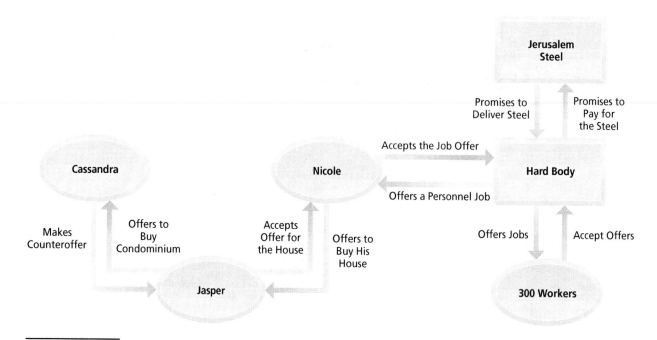

Exhibit 9.1
Contracts are intended to make business matters more predictable. Frequently, a series of contracts becomes mutually dependent.

But in the year since Jerusalem signed its contract, the price of the specified steel has gone up 60%. Jerusalem now refuses to deliver the steel unless the price is renegotiated. Hard Body has insisted on the original contract price. Hard Body cannot afford to buy steel at the current price, which would make its deal to produce buses unprofitable. If Hard Body receives no steel, does it have a valid lawsuit against Jerusalem? May the company force Jerusalem to deliver the steel? If it cannot get steel, may Hard Body lay off the newly hired workers? May it fire Nicole, or does she have a job for life? If Nicole loses her paycheck, will the law force her to buy a house she no longer wants? Jasper will never get such a good price from anyone else, because with no work at Hard Body property prices in Joy will plummet. May Jasper refuse to buy Cassandra's condo, or is he committed for $1.7 million?

Contracts

Throughout this unit on contracts, we will consider issues like those raised in the Cassandra–Hard Body story. Parties enter into contracts attempting to control their future. **Contracts exist to make business matters more predictable.**

JUDICIAL ACTIVISM VERSUS JUDICIAL RESTRAINT

We will see that courts generally, but not always, do what we expect. In most contract cases, judges do their best simply to enforce whatever terms the parties have agreed to. This is judicial restraint—a court taking a passive role and requiring the parties to fulfill whatever obligations they agreed to, whether the deal was wise or foolish. For example, if a real estate developer contracts with a builder to erect 10 expensive homes, but the housing market collapses before construction begins, a judge will order the developer to pay for the houses, even though the expense will cause him devastating losses. **Judicial restraint makes the law less flexible but more predictable.**

On the other hand, courts sometimes practice judicial activism. In contract law, this means that a court will ignore certain provisions of a contract, or an entire agreement, if the judge believes that enforcing the deal would be unjust. Since judicial activism is always phrased in terms of "doing justice," it has an initial appeal. For example, when one party deceives the other with a misleading contract, it may be appropriate for a court to rewrite the agreement. But when a court practices judicial activism, it may diminish our ability to control our own future—which is the whole point of creating a contract. **Judicial activism makes the law more flexible but less predictable.**

ISSUES (AND ANSWERS)

The chain of contracts connecting Jerusalem Steel and Cassandra illustrates various contract problems. We consider each problem in detail in this unit, but here we briefly identify the issues and summarize the answers. A contract has four elements:

- **Agreement.** One party must make a valid offer, and the other party must accept it.

- **Consideration.** There has to be bargaining that leads to an exchange between the parties.

- **Legality.** The contract must be for a lawful purpose.

- **Capacity.** The parties must be adults of sound mind.

The chapters that follow cover each of the elements in sequence. Contract cases often raise several other important issues, which we examine in later chapters:

- **Consent.** Neither party may trick or force the other into the agreement.

- **Written contracts.** Some contracts must be in writing to be enforceable.

- **Third party interests.** Some contracts affect people other than the parties themselves.

- **Performance and discharge.** If a party fully accomplishes what the contract requires, his duties are discharged.

- **Remedies.** A court will award money or other relief to a party injured by a breach of contract.

When we apply these principles to the problem at this chapter's beginning, we see that Jerusalem Steel is almost certainly bound by its agreement. A rise in price is generally no excuse to walk away from a contract. Hard Body has made the bargain precisely to protect itself in case of a price rise. These are issues of offer and acceptance, consideration, and discharge, discussed in later chapters. Can Hard Body force Jerusalem to deliver the steel? Probably not, as we learn in Chapter 17, on remedies. Hard Body is entitled to money damages if it is forced to buy steel at higher prices. If Hard Body is unable to obtain steel in the rising market, may it lay off its workers? Very likely, as Chapter 10, on agreement, indicates. Can it fire Nicole? The statement about expecting her job to last forever almost certainly creates no lifetime employment. What about the fact that she quit her job in reliance on this one? That raises an issue called promissory estoppel, which we discuss later in this chapter.

Must Nicole go through with her purchase of Jasper's house? Probably, as Chapter 14, on written contracts, demonstrates. Do Jasper and Cassandra have a contract? No, because the agreement must be in writing to be enforceable. Even if there is no settled price, is Cassandra safe in assuming she has $1.7 million guaranteed? Not at all, as the chapter on agreement explains. If Cassandra had read this unit, she would be faxing a written contract to Jasper rather than waiting for her latte to cool.

CONTRACTS DEFINED

Contract law is a study in promises. Is Nicole entitled to a lifetime job at Hard Body? Is Jasper obligated to buy Cassandra's condominium? Contract law determines which promises to enforce. **A contract is a promise that the law will enforce.**

As we look more closely at the elements of contract law, we will encounter some intricate issues. This is partly because we live in a complex society, which conducts its business in an infinite variety of ways. It is also due to the constant tug between predictability and fairness, described above. Remember, though, that we are usually interested in answering three basic questions of common sense, all relating to promises:

* Is it certain that the defendant promised to do something?

* If she did promise, is it fair to make her honor her word?

* If she did not promise, are there unusual reasons to hold her liable anyway?

Types of Contracts

BILATERAL AND UNILATERAL CONTRACTS

In a bilateral contract, both parties make a promise. Suppose a producer says to Gloria, "I'll pay you $2 million to star in my new romantic comedy, *A Promise for a Promise,* which we are shooting three months from now in Santa Fe." Gloria says, "It's a deal." That is a bilateral contract: one promise in exchange for another promise. The producer is now bound to pay Gloria $2 million, and Gloria is obligated to show up on time and act in the movie. The vast majority of contracts are bilateral contracts.

In a unilateral contract, one party makes a promise that the other party can accept only by doing something. These contracts are less common. Suppose the movie producer says to Leo, "I'll give you a hundred bucks if you mow my lawn this weekend." Leo is not promising to do it. If he mows the lawn, he has accepted the offer and is entitled to his hundred dollars. If he spends the weekend at the beach, neither he nor the producer owes anything.

Express and Implied Contracts

In an express contract, the two parties explicitly state all important terms of their agreement. Most contracts are express contracts. The contract between the producer and Gloria is an express contract, because the parties explicitly state what Gloria will do and how much she will be paid. Some express contracts are oral, as that one was, and some are written. Obviously, it is good business sense always to make express contracts, and wise to put them in writing. We emphasize, however, that *many oral contracts are fully enforceable.*

In an implied contract, the words and conduct of the parties indicate that they intended an agreement. Suppose every Friday, for two months, the producer asks Leo to mow his lawn, and loyal Leo does so each weekend. Then for three more weekends, Leo simply shows up without the producer asking, and the producer continues to pay for the work done. But on the 12th weekend, when Leo rings the doorbell to collect, the producer suddenly says, "I never asked you to mow it. Scram." The producer is correct that there was no express contract, because the parties had not spoken for several weeks. But a court will probably rule that the conduct of the parties has implied a contract. Not only did Leo mow the lawn every weekend, but the producer even paid on three weekends when they had not spoken. It was reasonable for Leo to assume that he had a weekly deal to mow and be paid. Naturally, there is no implied contract thereafter.

Today, the hottest disputes about implied contracts continue to arise in the employment setting. Many corporate employees have **at-will contracts** with their companies. This means that the employees are free to quit at any time and the company has the right to fire them at any time, for virtually any reason. But often a company provides its workers with personnel manuals that guarantee certain rights. The manual may assure all workers that they will have a hearing and a chance to present evidence on their behalf before being fired. Is that a binding promise? You decide.

YOU BE THE JUDGE

FEDERAL EXPRESS CORP. v. DUTSCHMANN

846 S.W.2d 282, 1993 Tex. LEXIS 9
Supreme Court of Texas, 1993

FACTS: When Marcie Dutschmann began working as a courier at Federal Express, she received an *Employment Handbook and Personnel Manual* stating that her employment was at will and "would continue as long as it was mutually satisfactory to both parties." The manual specified that it created no contractual rights. But it also described a "Guaranteed Fair Treatment Policy" (GFTP). According to the GFTP, any employee who was terminated would have a hearing at a board of review, at which he could appear and present evidence.

Federal Express fired Dutschmann in October 1987, claiming that she had falsified delivery records. She responded that her termination was in retaliation for her complaints of sexual harassment. She attempted to appeal her termination through the GFTP, but Federal Express did not allow her the kind of hearing that the handbook described. Dutschmann sued. At trial, Federal Express argued that Dutschmann was an employee at will and that the company was free to fire her at any time without a hearing. Dutschmann contended that the employee handbook and manual created an implied contract giving her the right to present witnesses and evidence. The jury found that the handbooks did create an implied contract and that Federal Express had not given her a fair hearing. The court of appeals affirmed. Federal Express appealed to the Texas Supreme Court.

YOU BE THE JUDGE: Did the employee handbook and manual create an implied contract guaranteeing a fair hearing?

ARGUMENT FOR FEDERAL EXPRESS: Your honors, when Federal Express created its employee manuals, it was well aware that some state courts have ruled that these handbooks may create an implied contract. And that is why Federal Express wrote employee manuals including the following statements: "The employee's employment is at will and will continue as long as it is mutually satisfactory to both parties. This manual does not create any contractual rights. Its use is intended only as a reference." That manual states that it is intended "solely as a guide for management and employees and is not a contract of employment and that no such contract may be implied from its provisions." We think that language is about as clear as it is possible to be, but we didn't stop there. At the inception of Ms. Dutschmann's employment, she signed an agreement stating that she understood the employee manuals did not constitute a contract.

Freedom to contract means freedom, among other things, to create at-will employment. Ms. Dutschmann signed an agreement saying she understood her position. It is time for her to keep her word.

ARGUMENT FOR Ms. DUTSCHMANN: Your honors, the manuals do state that the employment is at will. But those manuals then go on to say that all employees are guaranteed certain rights, including the rights to a fair, thorough termination hearing. The company refused to hear her evidence and refused to see her documents, because they knew she could prove sexual harassment. So they just fired her, pretending that there was no booklet and no guarantee of a hearing.

Federal Express is trying to have it both ways. The company creates these handsome, glossy booklets, filled with assurances of fair dealing. The booklets describe reasonable, sensible ways of treating employees and guarantee those rights to all employees. But then Federal Express comes into court and argues that a guarantee is not a guarantee, and a hearing is not a hearing.

Federal Express knew that guaranteeing fair treatment was a proven way to attract and retain good employees. Would Ms. Dutschmann have gone to work for Federal Express if she had been told she might be sexually harassed and then fired without a fair hearing? Of course not. Federal Express created an implied contract and the company should honor its promise.

UPDATE Besides Dutschmann and the company, who are their other stakeholders? What alternatives were available to Federal Express? What are the most important values involved in this dispute? If there are conflicting values, which are most important?

EXECUTORY AND EXECUTED CONTRACTS

A contract is executory when one or more parties has not fulfilled its obligations. Recall Gloria, who agrees to act in the producer's film beginning in three months. The moment Gloria and the producer strike their bargain, they have an executory bilateral express contract. A contract is executed when all parties have fulfilled their obligations. When Gloria finishes acting in the movie and the producer pays her final fee, their contract will be fully executed.

Remedies Created by Judicial Activism

Now we turn away from true contracts and consider two remedies created by judicial activism: promissory estoppel and quasi-contract. We emphasize that these remedies are exceptions. Most of the agreements that courts enforce are the express contracts that we have already studied. Nonetheless, the next two remedies have grown in importance over the last 100 years. In each case, a sympathetic plaintiff can demonstrate an injury. The harm has occurred in a setting where a contract might well have been made. But the crux of the matter is this: There is no contract. The plaintiff cannot claim that the defendant breached the agreement, because none ever existed. The plaintiff must hope for more "creative" relief.

The two remedies can be confusingly similar. The best way to distinguish them is this:

- In promissory estoppel cases, the defendant made a promise that the plaintiff relied on.

- In quasi-contract cases, the defendant did not make any promise, but did receive a benefit from the plaintiff.

PROMISSORY ESTOPPEL

A fierce fire swept through Dana and Derek Andreason's house in Utah, seriously damaging it. The good news was that agents for Aetna Casualty promptly visited the Andreasons and helped them through the crisis. The agents reassured the couple that all of the damage was covered by their insurance, instructed them on which things to throw out and replace, and helped them choose materials for repairing other items. The bad news was that the agents were wrong: The Andreasons' policy had expired six weeks before the fire. When Derek Andreason presented a bill for $41,957 worth of meticulously itemized work that he had done under the agents' supervision, Aetna refused to pay.

The Andreasons sued—but not for breach of contract. There was no contract; that was exactly the problem. So they sued Aetna under the legal theory of **promissory estoppel: Even when there is no contract, a plaintiff may use promissory estoppel to enforce the defendant's promise if he can show that:**

- The defendant made a promise knowing that the plaintiff would likely rely on it.

- The plaintiff did rely on the promise; and

- The only way to avoid injustice is to enforce the promise.

Aetna made a promise to the Andreasons, namely, its assurance that all the damage was covered by insurance. The company knew that the Andreasons would rely on that promise, which they did by ripping up a floor that might have been salvaged, throwing out some furniture, and buying materials to repair the house.

Is enforcing the promise the only way to avoid injustice? Yes, ruled the Utah Court of Appeals. The Andreasons' conduct was reasonable and based entirely on what the Aetna agents told them. Under promissory estoppel, the Andreasons received virtually the same amount they would have obtained had the insurance contract been valid.[1]

Promissory estoppel is an important development of 20th-century law. This is judicial activism, helping people by crafting new remedies. But, as is true whenever the rules are "bent," it means that the outcome of a particular case is less predictable.

QUASI-CONTRACT

Don Easterwood leased over 5,000 acres of farmland in Jackson County, Texas from PIC Realty for one year. The next year he obtained a second one-year lease. Each year, Easterwood farmed the land, harvested the crops, and prepared the land for the following year's planting. Toward the end of the second lease, he and PIC began discussing the terms of another lease. While they negotiated, Easterwood prepared the land for the following year, cutting, plowing, and disking the soil. But the negotiations for a new lease failed, and Easterwood moved off the land. He sued PIC Realty for the value of his work preparing the soil.

Easterwood had neither an express nor an implied contract for the value of his work. How could he make any legal claim? By relying on the legal theory of a quasi-contract: **Even when there is no contract, a court may use quasi-contract to compensate a plaintiff who can show that:**

* The plaintiff gave some benefit to the defendant

* The plaintiff reasonably expected to be paid for the benefit and the defendant knew this; and

* The defendant would be unjustly enriched if he did not pay.

If a court finds all these elements present, it will generally award the value of the goods or services that the plaintiff has conferred. The damages awarded are called *quantum meruit*, meaning that the plaintiff gets "as much as he deserved." The court is awarding money that it believes the plaintiff morally ought to have, even though there was no valid contract entitling her to it. This again is judicial activism, with the courts inventing a "quasi" contract where no true contract exists.

Don Easterwood testified that in Jackson County, it was quite common for a tenant farmer to prepare the soil for the following year but then be unable to farm the land. In those cases, he claimed, the landowner compensated the farmer for the work done. Other witnesses agreed that this was the local custom. The court ruled that all elements of quasi-contract had been satisfied. Easterwood gave a benefit to PIC because the land was ready for planting. Jackson County custom caused Easterwood to assume he would be paid, and PIC Realty knew it. Finally, said the court, it would be unjust to let PIC benefit without paying anything. The court ordered PIC to pay the fair market value of Easterwood's labors.

---

[1] *Andreason v. Aetna Casualty & Surety Co.*, 848 P.2d 171 (Utah App. 1993).

Four Theories of Recovery

Theory	Did the Defendant Make a Promise?	Is There a Contract?	Description
Express Contract	Yes	Yes	The parties intend to contract and agree on explicit terms.
Implied Contract	Not explicitly	Yes	The parties do not formally agree, but their words and conduct indicate an intention to create a contract.
Promissory Estoppel	Yes	No	There is no contract, but the defendant makes a promise that she can foresee will induce reliance; the plaintiff relies on it; and it would be unjust not to enforce the promise.
Quasi-Contract	No	No	There is no intention to contract, but the plaintiff gives some benefit to the defendant, who knows that the plaintiff expects compensation; it would be unjust not to award the plaintiff damages.

Sources of Contract Law

COMMON LAW

Express and implied contracts, promissory estoppel, and quasi-contract were all crafted, over centuries, by appellate courts deciding one contract lawsuit at a time. In this country, the basic principles are similar from one state to another, but there have been significant differences concerning most important contract doctrines.

In part because of these differences, the 20th century saw the rise of two major new sources of contract law: the Uniform Commercial Code and the Restatement of Contracts.

UNIFORM COMMERCIAL CODE

Business methods changed quickly during the first half of the 20th century. Executives used new forms of communication, such as telephone and wire, to make deals. Corporations conducted business across state borders and around the world. Executives, lawyers, and judges wanted a body of law for commercial transactions that reflected modern business methods and provided uniformity throughout the United States. That desire gave birth to the Uniform Commercial Code (UCC), created in 1952. The drafters intended the UCC to facilitate the easy formation and enforcement of contracts in a fast-paced world. The Code governs many aspects of commerce, including the sale of goods, negotiable instruments, and secured transactions. Every state has adopted at least part of the UCC to govern commercial transactions within that state. For our purposes in studying contracts, the most important part of the Code is Article 2. The entire UCC is available online at **http://www.law.cornell.edu/ucc/ucc.table.html**.

UCC Article 2 governs the sale of goods. "Goods" means anything movable, except for money and securities. Goods include pencils, commercial aircraft, books, and Christmas trees. Goods do not include land or a house, because neither is movable, nor do they include a stock certificate. A contract for the sale of 10,000 sneakers is governed by the UCC; a contract for the sale of a condominium in

Marina del Rey is governed by the California common law and its statute of frauds. Thus, when analyzing any contract problem as a student or business executive, you must note whether the agreement concerns the sale of goods. Most of the time the answer is clear, and you will immediately know whether the UCC or the common law governs. In some cases, as in a mixed contract for goods and services, it is not so obvious. **In a mixed contract, Article 2 governs only if the primary purpose was the sale of goods.** In the following case, the court had to decide the primary purpose.

CASE SUMMARY

PASS v. SHELBY AVIATION, INC.

2000 Tenn. App. LEXIS 247
Tennessee Court of Appeals, 2000

FACTS: Max Pass was flying a single-engine Piper airplane that he owned when he encountered turbulence, lost control of the aircraft, and crashed, killing his wife and himself. Pass's parents filed suit against Shelby Aviation, which had serviced the Piper four months before the tragedy. Among other things, Shelby had replaced both rear wing attachpoint brackets. The parents asserted that the brackets were defective because they lacked the necessary bolts.

The primary claim in their suit was breach of warranty under the UCC. A warranty is an assurance that a product will work properly, and Article 2 of the Code establishes several warranties for goods. In other words, the Passes claimed that Shelby's use of faulty parts cost two lives. The company moved to dismiss, claiming that the UCC did not apply, because the contract had been one for services. If the common law governed the contract, there were no warranties and the parents had no valid claim. The trial court denied the motion and Shelby appealed.

ISSUE: Did the UCC or the common law govern this contract?

DECISION: The common law governed. Reversed and remanded.

REASONING: This contract, like many others, involved a mix of goods and services. To decide whether the UCC or the common law governs, we determine whether the predominant purpose of the agreement was for services or for the sale of goods.

Shelby's invoice states that "the following repair work" will be done, using necessary material. A box is checked indicating an "annual 100 hour periodic inspection." The document also includes a list of services performed and parts used. Only about 37% of the charges were for parts. Overall, the invoice emphasizes the inspection and repair of the airplane.

Shelby's business appears to be primarily service. All the parts sold to Pass were ordered specifically for his airplane except for one, which the customer himself supplied. If Shelby were in the business of selling parts, it would not have accepted one from Pass. The predominant purpose of this contract was services, and Shelby is entitled to judgment on the UCC warranty claims. ◢

The common law governs contracts for services, employment, real estate and certain other things, and so each chapter in this unit will analyze the relevant common law principles. But the sale of goods is obviously a major element in business nationwide, and therefore each chapter will also discuss appropriate aspects of the Code.

RESTATEMENT (SECOND) OF CONTRACTS

In 1932 the American Law Institute (ALI), a group of lawyers, scholars, and judges, drafted the Restatement of Contracts, attempting to codify what its members regarded as the best rulings of contract law. Where courts had disagreed, for example, about when to enforce promissory estoppel, the drafters of the Restatement chose what they considered the wisest decisions. The Restatement was a treatise and never became the law anywhere. But because of the eminence of those who wrote it, the Restatement influenced many courts as they decided contract cases.

In 1979, the ALI issued a new version, the Restatement (Second) of Contracts. Like its predecessor, the Restatement (Second) is not the law anywhere, and in this respect it differs from the common law and the UCC. But the Restatement (Second) influences lawyers as they draft contracts and judges as they decide cases; we, too, will seek its counsel throughout the chapters on contracts.

Chapter Conclusion

Contracts govern countless areas of our lives. Understanding contract principles is especially important, because courts no longer rubber-stamp any agreement that two parties have made. If we know the issues that courts scrutinize, the agreement we draft is likelier to be enforced. We thus achieve greater control over our affairs—the very purpose of a contract.

Chapter Review

A contract is a promise that the law will enforce. Contracts are intended to make business matters more predictable. Analyzing a contract generally involves inquiring into some or all of these issues:

1. What is the subject of the agreement?
   - If the contract is for the sale of goods, UCC Article 2 governs.
   - If the contract is for services, employment, or real estate, the common law governs.
2. Did the parties intend to contract?
   - If the parties formally agreed and stated explicit terms, there is probably an express contract.
   - If the parties did not formally agree but their conduct, words, or past dealings indicate that they intended a binding agreement, there may be an implied contract.

3. If there is an agreement, is there any reason to doubt its enforceability?
4. If there is no contract, are there other reasons to give the plaintiff damages?
   - A claim of promissory estoppel requires that the defendant made a promise knowing that the plaintiff would likely rely, and the plaintiff did so. It would be wrong to deny recovery.
   - A claim of quasi-contract requires that the defendant received a benefit, knowing that the plaintiff would expect compensation, and it would be unjust not to grant it.

PRACTICE TEST

Matching Questions

Match the following terms with their definitions:

___ **A.** Quasi-contract

___ **B.** Implied contract

___ **C.** Express contract

___ **D.** Promissory estoppel

___ **E.** Bilateral contract

1. An agreement with all terms stated explicitly

2. A judicial remedy based on a defendant's promise on which the plaintiff reasonably relied.

3. An agreement based on one promise in exchange for another.

4. A judicial remedy based on a benefit given by the plaintiff to the defendant.

5. An agreement based on the words and actions of the parties.

True/False Questions

Circle true or false:

1. T F An express contract is an example of judicial activism.

2. T F To be enforceable, all contracts must be in writing.

3. T F Maria agrees to photograph Caitlin's children, and Caitlin agrees to pay $800 for the pictures. This is a bilateral contract.

4. T F Abdul hires Sean to work in his store, and agrees to pay him $9 per hour. This agreement is governed by the UCC.

5. T F A principal purpose of contracts is to make business matters more predictable.

Multiple-Choice Questions

6. Which contract is governed by the Uniform Commercial Code?

(a) An agreement for an actor to appear in a movie for a $600,000 fee.

(b) An agreement for an actor to appear in a movie for a fee of $600,000 plus 2% of box office.

(c) An agreement for the sale of a house.

(d) An agreement for the sale of 22,000 picture frames.

(e) An agreement for the rental of an apartment.

7. Mark, a newspaper editor, walks into the newsroom and announces to a group of five reporters: "I'll pay a $2,000 bonus to the first reporter who finds definitive evidence that Senator Blue smoked marijuana at the celebrity party last Friday." Anna, the first reporter to produce the evidence, claims her bonus based on

(a) Unilateral contract.

(b) Promissory estoppel.

(c) Quasi-contract.

(d) Implied contract.

(e) Express contract.

8. What are the elements of a contract?

(a) Express, implied, quasi-contract, promissory estoppel.

(b) Agreement, consideration, legality, capacity.

(c) Common law, UCC, Restatement.

(d) Bilateral, unilateral, express, implied.

(e) The reasonable expectations of similarly placed parties.

9. Raul has finished the computer he promised to perform for Tanya, and she has paid him in full. This is

(a) An express contract.

(b) An implied contract.

(c) An executed contract.

(d) A bilateral contract.

(e) No contract.

10. Business affairs can be made less certain because of

(a) Restatement of Contracts.

(b) UCC.

(c) Judicial activism.

(d) Judicial restraint.

(e) Executory contracts.

Short-Answer Questions

11. Pennsylvania contracted with Envirotest Systems, Inc., an Arizona company, to build 86 automobile emissions inspection stations in 25 counties, and operate them for seven years. This contract is worth hundreds of millions of dollars to Envirotest. But suddenly, Pennsylvania legislators opposed the entire system, claiming that it would lead to long delays and high expenses for motorists. These lawmakers urged that Pennsylvania simply stop construction of the new system. Was Pennsylvania allowed to get out of the contract because its legislators concluded that the whole system is unwise?

12. Central Maine Power Company made a promotional offer in which it promised to pay a substantial sum to any homeowner or builder who constructed new housing heated with electricity. Motel Services, Inc., which was building a small housing project for the city of Waterville, Maine, decided to install electrical heat in the units in order to qualify for the offer. It built the units and requested payment for the full amount of the promotional offer. Is Central Maine obligated to pay? Why or why not?

13. Interactive Data Corp. hired Daniel Foley as an assistant product manager at a starting salary of $18,500. Over the next six years Interactive steadily promoted Foley until he became Los Angeles branch manager at a salary of $56,116. Interactive's officers repeatedly told Foley that he would have his job as long as his performance was adequate. In addition, Interactive distributed an employee handbook that specified "termination guidelines," including a mandatory seven-step, pretermination procedure. Two years later Foley learned that his recently hired supervisor, Robert Kuhne, was under investigation by the FBI for embezzlement at his previous job. Foley reported this to Interactive officers. Shortly thereafter, Interactive fired Foley. He sued, claiming that Interactive could only fire him for good cause, after the seven-step procedure. What kind of a claim is he making? Should he succeed?

14. The Hoffmans owned and operated a successful small bakery and grocery store. They spoke with Lukowitz, an agent of Red Owl Stores, who told them that for $18,000 Red Owl would build a store and fully stock it for them. The Hoffmans sold their bakery and grocery store and purchased a lot on which Red Owl was to build the store. Lukowitz then told Hoffman that the price had gone up to $26,000. The Hoffmans borrowed the extra money from relatives, but then Lukowitz informed them that the cost would be $34,000. Negotiations broke off and the Hoffmans sued. The court determined that there was no contract because too many details had not been worked out— the size of the store, its design, and the cost of constructing it. Can the Hoffmans recover any money?

15. ETHICS: John Stevens owned a dilapidated apartment that he rented to James and Cora Chesney for a low rent. The Chesneys began to remodel and rehabilitate the unit. Over a four-year period, they installed two new bathrooms, carpeted the floors, installed new septic and heating systems, and rewired, replumbed, and painted. Stevens periodically stopped by and saw the work in progress. The Chesneys transformed the unit into a respectable apartment. Three years after their work was done, Stevens served the Chesneys with an eviction notice. The Chesneys counterclaimed, seeking the value of the work they had done. Are they entitled to it? Comment on the law and the ethics.

16. ROLE REVERSAL: Write a multiple-choice question that requires use of the predominant factor test to determine whether a contract is one for goods or services.

Internet Research Problem

Visit **http://www.law.cornell.edu/states/listing.html**. Select a state. Then click on judicial opinions. Search for a case concerning "quasi-contract." What are the details of the quasi-contract dispute? Who won and why?

You can find further practice problems in the Online Quiz at **http://beatty.westbuslaw.com** or in the Study Guide that accompanies this text.

9

Agreement

Interior. A glitzy café, New York. Evening. Bob, a famous director, and Katrina, a glamorous actress, sit at a table, near a wall of glass looking onto a New York sidewalk that is filled with life and motion. Bob sips a margarita while carefully eying Katrina. Katrina stares at her wine glass.

BOB (smiling confidently): *Body Work* is going to be huge—for the right actress. I know a film that's gonna gross a hundred million when I'm holding one. I'm holding one.

KATRINA (perking up at the mention of money): It is quirky. It's fun. And she's very strong, very real.

BOB: She's you. That's why we're sitting here. We start shooting in seven months.

KATRINA (edging away from the table): I have a few questions. That nude scene.

BOB: The one on the toboggan run?

KATRINA: That one was OK. But the one in the poultry factory—very explicit. I don't work nude.

BOB: It's not really nude. Think of all those feathers fluttering around.

KATRINA: It's nude.

BOB: We'll work it out. This is a romantic comedy, not tawdry exploitation. Katrina, we're talking $2.5 million. A little accommodation, please. $600,000 up front, and the rest deferred, the usual percentages.

KATRINA: Bob, my fee is $3 million. As you know. That hasn't changed.

Katrina picks up her drink, doesn't sip it, places it on the coaster, using both hands to center it perfectly. He waits, as she stares silently at her glass.

BOB: We're shooting in Santa Fe, the weather will be perfect. You have a suite at the Excelsior plus a trailer on location.

KATRINA: I should talk with my agent. I'd need something in writing about the nude scene, the fee, percentages—all the business stuff. I never sign without talking to her.

Bob shrugs and sits back.

BOB: A *lot* of people love that role. (That jolts her.) I have to put this together fast. We can get you the details you want in writing.

Katrina looks at Bob. He nods reassuringly. Bob sticks out his hand, smiling. Katrina hesitates, lets go of her drink, and *shakes hands,* looking unsure. Bob signals for the check.

Do Bob and Katrina have a deal? They seem to think so. But is her fee $2.5 million or $3 million? What if Katrina demands that all nude scenes be taken out, and Bob refuses? Must she still act in the film? What if Bob auditions another actress the next day, likes her, and signs her? Does he owe Katrina her fee?

Bob and Katrina have acted out a classic problem in agreement, one of the basic issues in contract law. Their lack of clarity means that disputes are likely and lawsuits possible. Similar bargaining goes on every day around the country and around the world. Some of the negotiating is done in person; more is done by phone, fax, and e-mail. This chapter highlights the most common sources of misunderstanding and litigation so that you can avoid making deals you never intended—or "deals" that you cannot enforce.

There almost certainly is no contract between Bob and Katrina. Bob's offer was unclear. Even if it was valid, Katrina counteroffered. When they shook hands, it is impossible to know what terms each had in mind.

Meeting of the Minds

As courts dissect a negotiation that has gone awry, they examine the intent of the parties. **The parties can form a contract only if they had a meeting of the minds.** This requires that they (1) understood each other and (2) intended to reach an agreement.

Keep in mind that judges must make objective assessments of the respective intent of each party. A court will not try to get inside Katrina's head and decide what she was thinking as she shook hands. It will look at the handshake objectively, deciding how a reasonable person would interpret the words and conduct. Katrina may honestly have meant to conclude a deal for $3 million with no nude scenes, while Bob might in good faith have believed he was committing himself to $2.5 million and absolute control of the script. Neither belief will control the outcome. A reasonable person observing their discussion would not have known what terms they agreed to, and hence there is no agreement.

Offer

Bargaining begins with an offer. **An offer is an act or statement that proposes definite terms and permits the other party to create a contract by accepting those terms.**

The person who makes an offer is the **offeror.** The person to whom he makes that offer is the **offeree.** The terms are annoying but inescapable because, like handcuffs, all courts use them. In most contract negotiations, two parties bargain back and forth, maybe for minutes, perhaps for months. Each may make several offers, revoke some proposals, suggest counteroffers, and so forth. For our purposes, the offeror remains the one who made the first offer, and the offeree is the one who received it.

Two questions determine whether a statement is an offer:

- Did the offeror intend to make a bargain?

- Are the terms of the offer definite?

PROBLEMS WITH INTENT

Zachary says to Sharon, "Come work in my English language center as a teacher. I'll pay you $500 per week for a 35-hour week, for nine months starting Monday." This is a valid offer. Zachary intends to make a bargain and his offer is definite. If Sharon accepts, the parties have a contract that either one can enforce. By contrast, we will consider several categories of statements that are generally not valid offers.

Invitations to Bargain

An invitation to bargain is not an offer. Suppose Martha telephones Joe and leaves a message on his answering machine, asking if Joe would consider selling his vacation condo on Lake Michigan. Joe faxes a signed letter to Martha saying, "There is no way I could sell the condo for less than $150,000." Martha promptly sends Joe a cashier's check for that amount. Does she own the condo? No. Joe's fax was not an offer. It is merely an invitation to bargain. Joe is indicating that he would be happy to receive an offer from Martha. He is not promising to sell the condo for $150,000 or for any amount.

Letters of Intent

In complex business negotiations, the parties may spend months bargaining over dozens of interrelated issues. It may be tempting during the negotiations to draft a **letter of intent,** summarizing the progress made thus far. But is such a letter binding? As the following case illustrates, an ambiguous letter of intent is often an invitation to court.

CASE SUMMARY

QUAKE CONSTRUCTION v. AMERICAN AIRLINES

141 Ill. 2d 281, 565 N.E.2d 990 1990 Ill. LEXIS 151
Supreme Court of Illinois, 1990

FACTS: Jones Brothers Construction was the general contractor on a job to expand American Airlines' facilities at O'Hare International Airport. Jones Brothers invited Quake Construction to bid on the employee facilities and automotive maintenance shop ("the project"). Quake bid, and Jones Brothers sent a letter of intent that stated, among other things:

"We have elected to award the contract for the subject project to your firm as we discussed on April 15, 1985. A contract agreement outlining the detailed terms and conditions is being prepared and will be available for your signature shortly. Your scope of work includes the complete installation of expanded lunchroom, restroom and locker facilities for

American Airlines employees as well as an expansion of American Airlines' existing Automotive Maintenance Shop. The entire project shall be complete by August 15, 1985.

"This notice of award authorizes the work set forth in the [attached] documents at a lump sum price of $1,060,568.00. Jones Brothers Construction Corporation reserves the right to cancel this letter of intent if the parties cannot agree on a fully executed subcontract agreement."

The parties never signed the fully written contract, and ultimately Jones Brothers hired another company. Quake sued, seeking to recover the money it spent in preparation and its loss of anticipated profit.

ISSUE: Was Jones Brothers' letter of intent a valid offer?

DECISION: The letter is ambiguous, and the case is remanded for the trial court to determine what the parties intended.

REASONING: Whether a letter of intent creates a binding contract depends on what the parties meant when they wrote it. If the parties intended the letter to create an enforceable agreement, then it does. However, if the letter says that the parties will *not* be bound until a more formal document is signed, then the letter is unenforceable. In deciding what the parties intended, a court should consider the normal practice in the industry, the amount of detail in the letter, and whether the letter states that a more formal contract is essential.

This letter of intent is ambiguous. The document states that Jones was awarding the project to Quake, and that work could begin within just a few days. Even the cancellation clause suggests a binding agreement, since otherwise there would be nothing to cancel. On the other hand, the letter refers several times to the signing of a more formal contract, and this indicates that the parties did not consider this document binding. It is impossible to tell what the parties meant. In the trial court, the parties must use other evidence to demonstrate their intentions. ◢

So after several years of litigation, Jones Brothers and Quake had to go back to court to prove their intent. At times, ambiguity in a letter of intent is deliberate, because one party is hoping to obtain the other side's commitment while leaving itself an escape hatch. As the interminable Quake litigation demonstrates, that is a dangerous game.

Advertisements

Mary Mesaros received a notice from the United States Bureau of the Mint, announcing a new $5 gold coin to commemorate the Statue of Liberty. The notice contained an order form stating:

"VERY IMPORTANT—PLEASE READ: YES, Please accept my order for the U.S. Liberty Coins I have indicated. I understand that all sales are final and not subject to refund. Verification of my order will be made by the Department of the Treasury, U.S. Mint. If my order is received by December 31, 1985, I will be entitled to purchase the coins at the Pre-Issue Discount price shown."

Mesaros ordered almost $2,000 worth of the coins. But the Mint was inundated with so many requests for the coin that the supply was soon exhausted. Mesaros and thousands of others never got their coins. This was particularly disappointing because the market value of the coins doubled shortly after their issue. Mesaros sued on behalf of the entire class of disappointed purchasers. Like most who sue based on an advertisement, she lost.

An advertisement is generally not an offer. An advertisement is merely a request for offers. The consumer makes the offer, whether by mail, as above, or by arriving at a merchant's store ready to buy. The seller is free to reject the offer.

Note that while the common law regards advertisements as mere solicitations, consumers do have protection from those shopkeepers intent upon deceit. Almost every state has some form of **consumer protection statute.** These statutes outlaw false advertising. For example, an automobile dealer who advertises a remarkably low price but then has only one automobile at that price has probably violated a consumer protection statute because the ad was published in bad faith, to trick consumers into coming to the dealership. The United States Mint did not violate any consumer protection statute because it acted in good faith and simply ran out of coins.

PROBLEMS WITH DEFINITENESS

It is not enough that the offeror intends to enter into an agreement. **The terms of the offer must be definite.** If they are vague, then even if the offeree "accepts" the deal, a court does not have enough information to enforce it and there is no contract.

You want a friend to work in your store for the holiday season. This is a definite offer: "I offer you a job as a sales clerk in the store from November 1 through December 29, 40 hours per week at $10 per hour." But suppose, by contrast, you say: "I offer you a job as a sales clerk in the store from November 1 through December 29, 40 hours per week. We will work out a fair wage once we see how busy things get." Your friend replies, "That's fine with me." This offer is indefinite and there is no contract. What is a fair wage? $6 per hour? $15 per hour? How will the determination be made? There is no binding agreement.

The following case presents a problem with definiteness. You be the judge.

YOU BE THE JUDGE

LEMMING v. MORGAN

228 Ga. App. 763, 492 S.E.2d 742, 1997 Ga. App. LEXIS 1264
Georgia Court of Appeals, 1997

FACTS: Larry Lemming and Jackson Morgan were good friends who became business associates—and then ex-friends. According to Lemming, he and Morgan orally agreed to form a partnership. Lemming would use his business connections and influence to locate real estate that was ripe for development. He would help Morgan obtain financing and then assist in developing and reselling the property. Morgan would temporarily hold the property in his name alone because Lemming was going through a divorce and also had tax problems. The two men agreed that, "if and when Lemming's divorce and tax problems subsided," Morgan would transfer to Lemming one half of all property and one half of all profits.

Lemming claims that over a five-year period, he located five properties, which he helped Morgan develop and resell. Then Morgan refused to give Lemming his one half stake. Lemming leaped into court. Morgan denied that the parties had ever formed a partnership. The trial court granted summary judgment for Morgan, ruling that even if the parties had made the agreement Lemming described, it was too indefinite to enforce. Lemming appealed.

YOU BE THE JUDGE: Assuming the parties reached the agreement Lemming described, was it sufficiently definite to create a contract?

ARGUMENT FOR LEMMING: Both parties understood exactly what the deal was. Mr. Lemming was temporarily unable to hold property in his name. But he was willing to help run the business, and Morgan eagerly exploited his friend's expertise. For five years Mr. Lemming did everything he could to make the business a success, and that is what has caused the problem: The business succeeded. Now the trial court says that Morgan can keep 100% of the profits. In other words, even if both parties *intended* to split the money, and Mr. Lemming *did his share* to create the profit, he earns nothing because of some technical contract rule. Surely, the law is not designed to encourage such deceit.

ARGUMENT FOR MORGAN: The rule requiring definite terms is more than a technicality. To be enforceable, a promise must be sufficiently definite that a court can determine who was supposed to do what. Even if Mr. Morgan made the agreement Lemming describes, it is so vague that no court could possibly enforce it. Exactly when was Mr. Morgan supposed to transfer the property to Lemming? How was the division to be made? Would one person receive certain properties? Which ones? If there were profits, how were they to be calculated, and when paid? Mr. Morgan was the only one who borrowed money, bought the land, paid all interest and taxes, and assumed full liability. Why should Lemming be entitled to half, when Mr. Morgan bore all the risk?

ETHICS: Why did Lemming want all property listed in Morgan's name? Analyze the agreement by using the ethics checklist from Chapter 2. Was the agreement legal? How would it look in the light of day? Generally, vague terms creep into negotiations unobserved, because the parties want to conclude the deal and get to work. What happens when ambiguity is deliberate?

UCC and Open Terms

Throughout this unit, we witness how the Uniform Commercial Code makes the law of sales more flexible. There are several areas of contract law where imperfect negotiations may still create a binding agreement under the Code, even though the same negotiations under the common law would have yielded no contract. "Open terms" is one such area.

Yuma County Corp. produced natural gas. Yuma wanted a long-term contract to sell its gas so that it could be certain of recouping the expenses of exploration and drilling. Northwest Central Pipeline, which operated an interstate pipeline, also wanted a deal for 10 or more years so it could make its own distribution contracts, knowing it would have a steady supply of natural gas in a competitive market. But neither Yuma nor Northwest wanted to make a long-term price commitment, because over a period of years the price of natural gas could double—or crash. Each party wanted a binding agreement without a definitive price. If their negotiations had been governed by the common law, they would have run smack into the requirement of definiteness—no price, no contract. But because this was a sale of goods, it was governed by the UCC.

> *UCC §2-204(3): Even though one or more terms are left open, a contract for sale does not fail for indefiniteness if the parties have intended to make a contract and there is a reasonably certain basis for giving an appropriate remedy.*

Yuma County and Northwest drafted a contract with alternative methods of determining the price. In the event that the price of natural gas was regulated by the Federal Energy Regulatory Commission (FERC), the price would be the highest allowed by the FERC. If the FERC deregulated the price (as it ultimately did), the contract price would be the average of the two highest prices paid by different gas producers in a specified geographic area. Under the UCC, this was an enforceable agreement.

If the contract lacks a method for determining missing terms, the Code itself contains gap-filler provisions, which are rules for supplying missing terms. Some of the most important gap-filler provisions of the Code are these:

- If the parties do not settle on a price, the Code establishes a **reasonable price.** This will usually be the market value or a price established by a neutral expert or agency (UCC §2-305).

- Delivery, time, and payment. The place of delivery is the seller's business. The time for shipping goods is usually a reasonable time, based on the normal trade practice. And payment is normally due when and where the buyer receives the goods (UCC §§2-308 through 2-310).

- Warranties. The Code includes a **warranty of merchantability,** which means that the goods must be of at least average, passable quality in the trade. Ten thousand pairs of sneakers must be such that a typical shoe store would accept them (UCC §§2-312 through 2-317).

TERMINATION OF OFFERS

As we have seen, the great power that an offeree has is to form a contract by accepting an offer. But this power is lost when the offer is revoked or rejected.

Termination by Revocation

In general, the offeror may revoke the offer any time before it has been accepted. **Revocation is effective when the offeree receives it.** Douglas County, Oregon sought bids on a construction job involving large quantities of rock. The Taggart Company discovered a local source of supply with cheap rock and put in a bid. Shortly thereafter, Taggart discovered that the local rock was no longer for sale. Taggart hand-delivered a written revocation of its bid. Later, the county opened all bids and accepted Taggart's low offer—but lost the case. By delivering its revocation, Taggart terminated the county's power to accept.

Termination by Rejection

If an offeree rejects an offer, the rejection terminates the offer. Suppose a major accounting firm telephones you and offers a job, starting at $80,000. You respond, "Nah. I'm gonna work on my surfing for a year or two." The next day you come to your senses and write the firm, accepting its offer. No contract. Your rejection terminated the offer and ended your power to accept.

Counteroffer.   Frederick faxes Kim, offering to sell a 50% interest in the Fab Hotel in New York for only $335 million. Kim faxes back, offering to pay $285 million. Moments later, Kim's business partner convinces her that Frederick's offer was a bargain, and she faxes an acceptance of his $335 million offer. Does Kim have a binding deal? No. **A counteroffer is a rejection.** When Kim offered $285 million, she rejected Frederick's offer. Her original fax created a new offer, for $285 million, which Frederick never accepted. The parties have no contract at any price.

Acceptance

As we have seen, when there is a valid offer outstanding, the offeree can create a contract by accepting. **The offeree must say or do something to accept.** Silence, though golden, is not acceptance. Marge telephones Vick and leaves a message on his answering machine: "I'll pay $75 for your law textbook from last semester. I'm desperate to get a copy, so I will assume you agree unless I hear from you by 6 o'clock tonight." Marge hears nothing by the deadline and assumes she has a deal. She is mistaken. Vick neither said nor did anything to indicate that he accepted.

Mirror Image Rule

If only he had known! A splendid university, an excellent position as department chair—gone. And all because of the mirror image rule.

Ohio State University wrote to Philip Foster offering him an appointment as a professor and chair of the art history department. His position was to begin July 1, and he had until June 2 to accept the job. On June 2, Foster telephoned the Dean and left a message accepting the position, effective July 15. Later, Foster thought better of it and wrote the university, accepting the school's starting date of July 1. Too late! Professor Foster never did occupy that chair at Ohio State. The court held that since his acceptance varied the starting date, it was a counteroffer. And a counteroffer, as we know, is a rejection.

Was it sensible to deny the professor a job over a mere 14-day difference? Sensible or not, that is the law. **The common-law mirror image rule requires that acceptance be on precisely the same terms as the offer.** If the acceptance contains terms that add or contradict the offer, even in minor ways, courts generally consider it a counteroffer. The rule worked reasonably well 100 years ago, when parties would write an original contract and exchange it, penciling in any changes. But now that businesses use standardized forms to purchase most goods and services, the rule creates enormous difficulties. Sellers use forms they have prepared, with all conditions stated to their advantage, and buyers employ their own forms, with terms they prefer. The forms are exchanged in the mail or electronically, with neither side clearly agreeing to the other party's terms.

The problem is known as the "battle of forms." Once again, the UCC has entered the fray, attempting to provide flexibility and common sense for those contracts involving the sale of goods.

UCC and the Battle of Forms

UCC §2-207 dramatically modifies the mirror image rule for the sale of goods. Under this provision, an acceptance that adds additional or different terms will often create a contract. The full rule is beyond the scope of this chapter, but it is important to understand its basic features because most goods are bought and sold with standardized forms. One thing we see is that the Code gives different treatment to merchants than consumers. **A merchant is anyone who routinely deals in the goods involved,** such as a wholesaler or retailer.

Additional or Different Terms

One basic principle of the common law of contracts remains unchanged: The key to creation of a contract is a valid offer that the offeree intends to accept. If there is no intent to accept, there is no contract. The big change brought about by UCC §2-207 is this: **For the sale of goods, the mirror image rule does not apply. The acceptance may include new terms.**

Additional terms are those that bring up new issues not contained in the original offer. Additional terms in the acceptance are considered proposals to add to the contract. Assuming that both parties are merchants, the additional terms will generally become part of the contract unless the other side rejects them.

Example A.   Wholesaler writes to Manufacturer, offering to buy "10,000 wheelbarrows at $50 per unit. Payable on delivery, 30 days from today's date." Manufacturer writes back, "We accept your offer of 10,000 wheelbarrows at $50 per unit, payable on delivery. Interest at normal trade rates for unpaid balances." Manufacturer clearly intends to form a contract. The company has added a new term about interest rates, but there is still a valid agreement. If Wholesaler is late in paying, it owes interest at the current rate.

Example B.   Same offer and acceptance. This time, though, when Wholesaler receives the form mentioning interest rates, it rejects the added term. Wholesaler sends an e-mail, saying, "We do not accept that interest rate." There is no contract.

Different terms are those that contradict terms in the offer. For example, if the seller's form clearly states that no warranty is included, and the buyer's form insists that the seller warrants all goods for three years, the acceptance contains *different* terms. An acceptance may contain different terms and still create a contract. **The majority of states hold that different (contradictory) terms cancel each other out.** Neither term is included in the contract. Instead, the neutral terms from the Code itself are "read into" the contract. These are the gap-filler terms discussed above. Suppose the forms have contradictory clauses about where the goods will be delivered. The different terms cancel each other out, and the gap-filler clause from the UCC is substituted. The place of delivery is the seller's business.

CYBERLAW

Clickwraps and Shrinkwraps. You want to purchase Attila brand software and download it to your computer. You type in your credit card number and other information, agreeing to pay $99. Attila also requires that you "read and agree to" all of the company's terms. You click "I agree," without having read one word of the terms. Three frustrating weeks later, tired of trying to operate defective Attilaware, you demand a refund and threaten to sue. The company breezily replies that you are barred from suing, because the terms you agreed to included an arbitration clause. To resolve any disputes, you must travel to Attila's hometown, halfway across the nation, use an arbitrator that the company chooses, pay one half the arbitrator's fee, and also pay Attila's legal bills if you should lose. The agreement makes it financially impossible for you to get your money back. Is that contract enforceable?

You have entered into a "clickwrap" agreement. Similar agreements, called "shrinkwraps," are packaged inside many electronic products. A shrinkwrap notice might require that before inserting a purchased CD into your computer, you must read and agree to all terms in the brochure. Clickwraps and shrinkwraps often include arbitration clauses. They frequently limit the seller's liability if anything goes wrong, saying that the manufacturer's maximum responsibility is to refund the purchase price (even if the software destroys your hard drive).

Most of the courts that have analyzed these issues have ruled that clickwrap and shrinkwrap agreements are indeed binding, even against consumers. Some of the judges have relied on §2-207 to reach that conclusion, while others have used different UCC provisions. The courts have emphasized that sellers are entitled to offer a product on any terms they wish, and that shrinkwrap and clickwrap are the most efficient methods of including complicated terms in a small space. At least one court has refused to enforce such contracts against a consumer, stating that the buyer never understood or agreed to the shrinkwrapped terms. However, the trend is toward enforcement of these agreements. Think before you click!

COMMUNICATION OF ACCEPTANCE

The offeree must communicate his acceptance for it to be effective. Generally acceptance may be made in person or by mail, telephone, e-mail, or fax. If Masako e-mails Eric an offer to sell 20,000 pairs of jeans for $20 each, he may mail, fax, or e-mail his acceptance. However, if Masako's offer demands one method of acceptance (such as in writing, by mail) then the acceptance must comply.

Acceptance is generally effective upon dispatch, meaning the moment it is out of the offeree's control. Eric prints a copy of the offer that Masako e-mailed. He writes "I accept" on the document, signs it, and mails it back to Masako. The moment he places the envelope in the mailbox, he has accepted. Suppose he mails his acceptance at 2:05 p.m. and then, at 2:15 p.m., Masako telephones to revoke her offer. Result? A binding contract, created the moment the envelope fell into the mailbox.

Chapter Conclusion

The law of offer and acceptance can be complex. Yet for all its fault, the law is not the principal source of dispute between parties unhappy with negotiations. Most litigation concerning offer and acceptance comes from lack of clarity on the part of the people negotiating. Letters of intent are often an effort to "have it both ways," that is, to ensure the other side's commitment without accepting a corresponding obligation. Similarly, the "battle of the forms" is caused by corporate officers seeking to make a deal and hurry things forward without settling details. These, and the many other examples discussed, are all understandable given the speed and fluidity of the real world of business. But the executive who insists on clarity is likelier in the long run to spend more time doing business and less time in court.

Chapter Review

1. The parties can form a contract only if they have a meeting of the minds, which requires that they understand each other and intend to reach an agreement.

2. An offer is an act or statement that proposes definite terms and permits the other party to create a contract by accepting those terms.

3. Invitations to bargain and advertisements are generally not offers. A letter of intent may or may not be an offer, depending upon the exact language and whether it indicates that the parties have reached an agreement.

4. The terms of the offer must be definite, although under the UCC the parties may create a contract that has open terms.

5. An offer may be terminated by revocation or rejection.

6. The offeree must say or do something to accept. Silence is not acceptance.

7. The common-law mirror image rule requires acceptance on precisely the same terms as the offer. Under the UCC, an offeree may often create a contract even when the acceptance includes terms that are additional to or different from those in the offer.

8. Clickwrap and shrinkwrap agreements are generally enforceable.

9. If the offer does not specify a type of acceptance, the offeree may accept in any reasonable method.

PRACTICE TEST

Matching Questions

Match the following terms with their definitions:

___ **A.** Mirror image rule.

___ **B.** Letter of intent.

___ **C.** Gap-filler.

___ **D.** Counteroffer.

___ **E.** Clickwrap.

1. A communication between negotiating parties that summarizes their progress and may imply a binding agreement.

2. An agreement made online by a consumer who may not understand its terms.

3. One method of rejecting an offer.

4. A common law principle requiring the acceptance to be on exactly the terms of the offer.

5. Terms supplied by the UCC for use in sale-of-goods contracts.

True/False Questions

Circle true or false:

1. T   F   Shrinkwraps are typically enforceable even if the buyer does not bother to read them.

2. T   F   An acceptance must be made in the same manner as the offer, that is, in writing, by phone, etc.

3. T   F   If an offer demands a reply within a stated period, the absence of a reply indicates acceptance.

4. T   F   An offer may generally be revoked at any time before it is accepted.

5. T   F   Without a meeting of the minds there cannot be a contract.

Multiple-Choice Questions

6. Alejandro sees an ad in the newspaper, with a beautiful sweater pictured: "Versace sweaters, normally $600, today only: $300." He phones the store and says that he wants two sweaters, a black one and a gray one. When he arrives at the store, the sweaters are sold out. He sues. Alejandro will

   (a) Win, because the store never revoked its offer.

   (b) Win, because he accepted within a reasonable time.

   (c) Win, because there was a meeting of the minds.

   (d) Lose, because he needed to accept in person.

   (e) Lose, because the store never made an offer.

7. On Monday night, Louise is talking on her cell phone with Bill. "I'm desperate for a manager in my store," says Louise. "I'll pay you $45,000 per year, if you can start tomorrow morning. What do you say?"

"It's a deal," says Bill. "I can start tomorrow at 8 a.m. I'll take $45,000 and I also want 10% of any profits you make above last year's." Just then Bill loses his cell phone signal. The next morning he shows up at the store, but Louise refuses to hire him. Bill sues. Bill will

(a) Win, because there was a valid offer and acceptance.

(b) Win, based on promissory estoppel.

(c) Lose, because he rejected the offer.

(d) Lose, because the agreement was not put in writing.

(e) Lose, because Louise revoked the offer.

8. Tanya is having lunch with three friends. "I am going to sell my Ferrari," she says. "I expect to get between $125,000 and $150,000." An hour later, Mike emails Tanya: "I agree to buy your Ferrari for $150,000." He promptly arrives at Tanya's house with a cashier's check for the full amount, but she refuses to sell. Mike sues. Mike will

(a) Win.

(b) Lose, because Tanya never made a definite offer.

(c) Lose, because he should have accepted in person.

(d) Lose, because Tanya revoked her offer.

(e) Lose, because Tanya owns the car.

9. Reggie is hiring an accountant for his firm. During any negotiations that take place

(a) The UCC governs.

(b) The Restatement of Contracts governs.

(c) The mirror image rule applies.

(d) A letter of intent is mandatory.

(e) Either party may accept while making a counteroffer.

10. A wholesaler sells a retailer 25 parrots. Both sides use preprinted forms. The wholesaler's form says, "No warranty of any kind." The retailer's form says, "All birds fully warranted." Result?

(a) There is no contract.

(b) There is a contract with no warranty.

(c) There is a contract with full warranty.

(d) There is a contract and the birds must be of average quality in the trade.

(e) There is a contract and the parties must re-negotiate the warranty issue.

Short-Answer Questions

11. Arnold owned a Pontiac dealership and wanted to expand by obtaining a Buick outlet. He spoke with Patricia Roberts and other Buick executives on several occasions. He now claims that those discussions resulted in an oral contract that requires Buick to grant him a franchise, but the company disagrees. His strongest evidence of a contract is the fact that Roberts gave him forms on which to order Buicks. Roberts answered that it was her standard practice to give such forms to prospective dealers, so that if the franchise were approved, car orders could be processed quickly. Is there a contract?

12. The Tufte family leased a 260-acre farm from the Travelers Insurance Co. Toward the end of the lease, Travelers mailed the Tuftes an option to renew the lease. The option arrived at the Tuftes' house on March 30, and gave them until April 14 to accept. On April 13, the Tuftes signed and mailed their acceptance, which Travelers received on April 19. Travelers claimed there was no lease and attempted to evict the Tuftes from the farm. May they stay?

13. Northrop is a huge defense firm, and Litronic manufactures electronic components such as printed wire boards. Northrop requested Litronic to submit an offer on certain printed boards. Litronic sent its offer form, stating a price and including its preprinted warranty clause, which limited its liability to 90 days. Northrop orally accepted the offer, then sent its own purchase order form, which contained a warranty clause holding the seller liable with no time limit. Six months after the goods were delivered, Northrop discovered they were defective. Northrop sued, but Litronic claimed it had no liability. Was there a contract? If not, why not? If there was a contract, what were its warranty terms?

14. The Dukes leased land from Lillian Whatley. Toward the end of their lease, they sent Ms. Whatley a new

contract, renewing the lease for three years and giving themselves the option to buy the land at any time during the lease for $50,000. Ms. Whatley crossed out the clause giving them an option to buy. She added a sentence at the bottom, saying, "Should I, Lillian Whatley, decide to sell at end [sic] of three years, I will give the Dukes the first chance to buy." Then she signed the lease, which the Dukes accepted in the changed form. They continued to pay the rent until Ms. Whatley sold the land to another couple for $35,000. The Dukes sued. Are the Dukes entitled to the land at $50,000? At $35,000?

15. Academy Chicago Publishers (Academy) approached the widow of author John Cheever about printing some of his unpublished stories. She signed a contract, which stated:

"The Author will deliver to the Publisher on a mutually agreeable date one copy of the manuscript of the Work as finally arranged by the editor and satisfactory to the Publisher in form and content . . . .

"Within a reasonable time and a mutually agreeable date after delivery of the final revised manuscript, the Publisher will publish the Work at its own expense, in such style and manner and at such price as it deems best, and will keep the Work in print as long as it deems it expedient."

Within a year, Academy had located and delivered to Mrs. Cheever more than 60 unpublished stories. But she refused to go ahead with the project. Academy sued for the right to publish the book. The trial court ruled that the agreement was valid; the appeals court affirmed; and the case went to the Illinois Supreme Court. Was Academy's offer valid, and was the contract enforceable?

16. ROLE REVERSAL: Write a multiple-choice question focusing on UCC 2-207.

Internet Research Problem

Search the Internet for an auction with a ring selling for over $500. Is the site reliable? Who is actually selling the item? If you were to pay for the ring, would you receive it? If you were unhappy with your purchase, what remedies would you have? How can you ascertain the Web site's reliability?

You can find further practice problems in the Online Quiz at **http://beatty.westbuslaw.com** or in the Study Guide that accompanies this text.

10

Consideration

We have all made promises that we soon regretted. Mercifully, the law does not hold us accountable for everything we say. Yet some promises must be enforced. Which ones? The doctrine of consideration exists for one purpose: to distinguish promises that are binding from those that are not. Which of these four promises should a court enforce?

PROMISE ONE. In a delirious burst of affection, Professor Parsley says to a class of 50 students, "You've been a great class all semester. Next week I'm going to mail each of you a check for $1,000." But that night, the professor reconsiders and decides that her class is actually a patch full of cabbage heads whose idea of work is getting out of bed before noon. The following day, in class, Parsley announces that she has changed her mind. Mike, a student, sues for his $1,000. Should a court enforce the professor's promise?

PROMISE TWO. After class, Parsley promises a student, Daisy, a part-time job as a researcher for the rest of the semester. "You can start on Monday," she says, "and we'll work out pay and all the details then." "You mean I can give up my job at Burger Bucket?" asks an elated Daisy. "Sure thing," chirps the prof. But on Monday, Parsley informs Daisy that she has lost the funding for her research and can offer no job. Daisy is unable to get back her position at Burger Bucket and sues Parsley.

PROMISE THREE. Professor Parsley announces in class that she will be selling her skis at the end of the semester for $450. After class, Arabella says she would like to buy the skis but can only afford to pay $250. Parsley frowns and mutters, "They're worth a lot more than that." But Arabella looks so heartbroken that Parsley adds, "OK, what the heck. You can have them May 15." On that date Arabella shows up with the cash, but Parsley explains that another student offered her the full $450 for the skis and she sold them. Arabella purchases a nearly identical pair for $475 and sues Parsley.

PROMISE FOUR. The professor makes no promise at all. In fact, she announces in class that she will be unable to attend the next session because her favorite racehorse, Preexisting Duty, is running in the third race at the local track and she wants to be there. The students are crushed at the idea of missing a class. Sam wails, "Don't do this to us, Professor! I'll pay you 20 bucks if you'll be here to teach us." Other students chime in, and in a groundswell of tears and emotion, the students promise a total of $1,000 if Parsley will do her job. She agrees. When she arrives to teach the next class, 50 suddenly sullen students refuse to pay, and she sues.

Society could enforce *all* promises in the interests of simple morality. Or should it enforce only those where the two sides engaged in some bargaining? Does it matter whether someone relied on a promise? Should the outcome be different if someone is promising to do what she is already obligated to do? These are important policy questions, affecting promises for a hundred dollars and deals for a billion; their answers lie in the law of consideration.

A Bargain and an Exchange

Consideration is a required element of any contract. **Consideration means that there must be bargaining that leads to an exchange between the parties.** "Bargaining" indicates that each side is obligating itself in some way to induce the other side to agree. Generally, a court will enforce one party's promise only if the other party did something or promised something in exchange. Without an exchange of mutual obligations, there is usually no deal.

How would the four Parsley examples in the introduction work out? In the first case, Mike loses. There is no consideration because the students neither bargained for Parsley's promise nor gave anything in exchange for it. In the second case, there is also no contract because none of the terms were definite. What were Daisy's hours, her salary, her duties? Daisy cannot sue on a contract, but she does have a claim of promissory estoppel, the one major exception to the rule of consideration. Because Daisy relied on Parsley's promise, a court may give her some compensation. In case three, Arabella should win. A bargain and an exchange occurred. The professor promised to sell the skis at a given price, then broke her promise. Arabella will probably recover $225, the difference between the contract price and what she was forced to pay for substitute skis. Finally, in the fourth case, the professor loses. Clearly, bargaining and an exchange took place, but the professor only promised to do something that she was already obligated to do. The law does not respect such a promise.

When trying to enforce a defendant's promise, the plaintiff must show that she did something or promised something in exchange for that promise. What sort of action or promise is good enough? It need not be much. **Consideration can be anything that someone might want to bargain for.** As we explore this idea, we need to use two more legal terms: promisor, meaning the person who makes the promise, and promisee, the person to whom the promise is made. In consideration cases, a court is typically trying to determine whether the promisee should be able to enforce the promise, and the decision will depend upon whether the promisee gave consideration.

The thing bargained for can be another promise or action. Usually, the thing bargained for is another promise. Suppose an employer says to a valued computer technician, "I will give you 1% of the company's stock, effective in 60 days, if you promise to be on-call 24/7." The technician agrees. Two months later, the employer is obligated to hand over the stock, regardless of whether he has taken advantage of his worker's availability. The pair had a typical bilateral contract. See Exhibit 11.1.

The thing bargained for can be an action, rather than a promise. Suppose Professor Parsley says to Wade, "If you plow my driveway by tonight, I'll pay you $150." Her offer seeks an action, not a promise. If Wade plows the driveway, his work is consideration and the parties have a binding contract.

The thing bargained for can be a benefit to the promisor or a detriment to the promisee. Suppose Professor Parsley says to the class, "You're all in terrible shape. I offer $25 to anyone who enters next week's marathon and finishes the race." "No way," shouts Joanne. "But I'll do it for $100." Parsley agrees and Joanne completes the entire race. Her running was of no particular benefit to Parsley, but it was clearly a detriment to Joanne, so Parsley owes her $100.

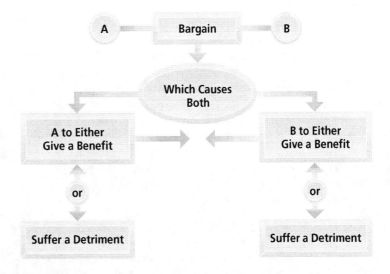

Exhibit 11.1
There is consideration to support a contract when A and B bargain, and their bargaining causes both A and B either to give a benefit to the other or to suffer a detriment.

The thing bargained for can be a promise to do something, but it can also be a promise to refrain from doing something. Leroy, who runs a beauty parlor, offers Chloe $75,000 not to open a beauty parlor within 30 miles. Chloe's promise not to compete is consideration.

The most famous of all consideration lawsuits began in 1869, when a well-meaning uncle made a promise to his nephew. Ever since *Hamer v. Sidway* appeared, generations of American law students have dutifully inhaled the facts and sworn by its wisdom; now you, too, may drink it in.

CASE SUMMARY

HAMER v. SIDWAY

124 N.Y. 538, 27 N.E. 256, 1891 N.Y. LEXIS 1396
New York Court of Appeals, 1891

FACTS: This is a story with two Stories. William Story wanted his nephew to grow up healthy and prosperous. In 1869, he promised the 15-year-old boy (also William Story) $5,000 if the lad would refrain from drinking liquor, using tobacco, swearing, and playing cards or billiards for money until his 21st birthday. (In that wild era—can you believe it?—the nephew had a legal right to do all those things.) The nephew agreed and, what is more, he kept his word. When he reached his 21st birthday, the nephew notified his uncle that he had honored the agreement. The uncle congratulated the young man and promised to give him the money, but said he would wait a few more years before handing over the cash, until the nephew was mature enough to handle such a large sum. The uncle died in 1887 without having paid, and his estate refused to honor the promise. Because the nephew had transferred his rights in the money, it was a man named Hamer who eventually sought to collect from the uncle's estate. The estate argued that since the nephew had given no consideration for the uncle's promise, there was no enforceable contract. The trial court found for the plaintiff, and the uncle's estate appealed.

ISSUE: Did the nephew give consideration for the uncle's promise?

DECISION: Yes, the nephew's conduct was valid consideration and the contract must be enforced.

REASONING: The uncle's estate argues that the conduct, far from harming the boy, actually aided him. Because it is wise to avoid tobacco, alcohol, and gambling, the nephew's decision to give up those vices could never be consideration. But the estate's argument is unpersuasive. What matters is simply this: Did one party do something or refrain from doing something at the request of the other party? If so, that conduct or forbearance is consideration.

Before making the agreement, the nephew had lawfully used alcohol and tobacco. When his uncle promised him $5,000, the nephew gave up the activities, restricting his freedom for several years. The contract must be enforced, whether or not anyone benefited. ◢

ADEQUACY OF CONSIDERATION

John Tuppela was a gold prospector in Alaska, but mental problems overwhelmed him and a court ordered him institutionalized in Oregon. Four years later, Tuppela emerged (with a court-appointed guardian supervising his assets) and learned two things: The guardian had sold the mine for pennies, and shortly thereafter, gold had been discovered on his property, which was now valued at over half a million dollars. Tuppela turned to his lifelong friend, Embola, saying, "If you will give me $50 so I can go to Alaska and get my property back, I will pay you $10,000 when I win the property." Embola advanced the $50.

Tuppela won back his mine, and asked the guardian to pay the full $10,000 to Embola, but the guardian refused, saying the $50 advance was too small to support such a huge payment. Embola sued.

Courts seldom inquire into the adequacy of consideration. The question of adequacy is for the parties as they bargain, not for the courts. Embola won, and the guardian paid him the full $10,000.

Mutuality of Obligations

Generally, both sides must be committed to the agreement to make it enforceable. Though courts will not inquire into the adequacy of consideration, they will insist that it be genuine. In some cases a party appears to make a commitment but actually does not. The result: no contract. Here we examine the major issues concerning mutuality.

ILLUSORY PROMISE

Annabel calls Jim and says, "I'll sell you my bicycle for 325 bucks. Interested?" Jim says, "I'll look at it tonight in the bike rack. If I like what I see, I'll pay you three and a quarter in the morning." At sunrise, Jim shows up with the $325 but Annabel refuses to sell. Can Jim enforce their deal? No. He said he would buy the bicycle if he liked it, keeping for himself the power to get out of the agreement for any reason at all. He is not committing himself to do anything, and the law considers his promise illusory, that is, not really a promise at all. **An illusory promise is not consideration.** Because he has given no consideration, there is no contract and neither party can enforce the deal. Is the promise in the following case illusory?

YOU BE THE JUDGE

CULBERTSON v. BRODSKY

788 S.W.2d 156, 1990 Tex. App. LEXIS 1008
Texas Court of Appeals, 1990

FACTS: Sam Culbertson had some Texas real estate to sell. He and Frederick Brodsky signed an option contract. Brodsky was to deliver a check for $5,000, representing "earnest money," to a bank. The bank would hold the check in escrow for 60 days. During that period, the bank would not cash it. Brodsky could inspect the property and perform engineering studies to determine whether the real estate could be used for his purposes. If he decided that the land was of no use to him, he could terminate the agreement and demand return of his earnest money. Ultimately, Brodsky decided that he did want to buy the land, but Culbertson refused to sell, claiming that Brodsky gave no consideration to support their contract. The trial court gave judgment for Brodsky, ordering Culbertson to convey the land. Culbertson appealed.

YOU BE THE JUDGE: Did Brodsky give valid consideration that makes Culbertson's promise enforceable?

ARGUMENT FOR CULBERTSON: Your honors, Mr. Brodsky made a very sly promise, since it was in fact no promise at all. Brodsky insisted on keeping the right to terminate this phony agreement at any time, for any reason. Mr. Culbertson was expected to leave the property off the market for 60 valuable days while Brodsky took his own sweet time to inspect the land. Please note that he didn't even lose the use of the $5,000. The bank was not permitted to cash the check until Brodsky made up his mind. Brodsky had no obligation at all, and thus never formed a contract.

ARGUMENT FOR BRODSKY: Your honors, it is rather disingenuous of Mr. Culbertson to pose as an injured party here. He is, in fact, a sophisticated property owner. He voluntarily entered into a contract with Mr. Brodsky for one reason: It was in his own interest. He concluded that the best way to "land" Mr. Brodsky was first to "hook" him with an option contract. He wanted Mr. Brodsky to show serious interest, and demanded earnest money. He got it. He insisted that Mr. Brodsky's check be held in escrow. He got it. Culbertson hoped that Mr. Brodsky would perform the necessary tests and conclude he wanted to buy it. And that is precisely what happened. This is a binding deal.

SALES LAW: REQUIREMENTS AND OUTPUT CONTRACTS

You decide to open a "novelty T-shirt" business. You will buy plain white T-shirts from a wholesaler and then arrange for them to be printed with funny pictures and quotes. Your single biggest expense will be the wholesale cost of the T-shirts. How many will you need? You have no idea whether sales will soar or slide. Your solution may be a requirements contract.

In a requirements contract, the buyer agrees to purchase 100% of her goods from one seller. The seller agrees to sell the buyer whatever quantity she reasonably needs. The quantity is not stated in the contract, though it may be estimated, based on previous years or best calculations.

The common law regarded requirements contracts as void because the buyer could purchase a vast quantity or none at all. She was making no commitment, and hence, giving no consideration. Common-law courts refused to enforce requirements contracts, as well as their counterpart, output contracts. **In an output contract, the seller guarantees to sell 100% of its output to one buyer, and the buyer agrees to accept the entire quantity.** For example, a timber company might agree to sell all of its wood products to a lumber wholesaler. The common law frowned because now it was the seller who was making no real commitment.

The problem with the common-law rule was that many merchants valued these contracts. From the buyer's viewpoint, a requirements contract provides flexibility. The buyer can adjust purchases based on consumer demands. For a seller, the requirements agreement will ensure him at least this one outlet and will prevent competitors from selling to this buyer. Output contracts have similar value.

The UCC responded in a forthright fashion: **Section §2-306 expressly allows output and requirements contracts in the sale of goods.** However, the Code places one limitation on how much the buyer may demand (or the seller may offer):

"A term which measures the quantity by the output of the seller or the requirements of the buyer means such actual output or requirements as may occur in good faith . . ."

The "good faith" phrase is critical. A buyer must make its requirement demands in good faith, based on the expectations the parties had when they signed the deal. A seller has the same obligation in an output contract.

PAST CONSIDERATION

Past consideration is generally no consideration. If one party makes a promise based on what the other party has already done, there is no exchange, and there will usually be no enforceable contract. It all goes back to our basic definition of consideration, which requires bargaining and an exchange of obligations.

CASE SUMMARY

DEMENTAS v. ESTATE OF TALLAS

95 Utah Adv. Rep. 28, 764 P.2d 628, 1988 Utah App. LEXIS 174
Utah Court of Appeals, 1988

FACTS: Jack Tallas came to the United States from Greece in 1914. He lived in Salt Lake City for nearly 70 years, achieving great success in insurance and real estate. When he died, he left a large estate. During the last 14 years of his life, Tallas was a close friend of Peter Dementas, who helped him with numerous personal and business chores. Two months before his death, Tallas met with Dementas and dictated a memorandum to him, in Greek, stating:

"PETER K. DEMENTAS, is my best friend I have in this country and since he came to the United States he treats me like a father and I think of him as my own son. He takes me in his car grocery shopping. He drives me to the doctor and also takes me every week to Bingham to pick up my mail, collect the rents and manage my properties. For all the services Peter has given me all these years, I owe to him the amount of $50,000 (Fifty Thousand Dollars.) I will shortly change my will to include him as my heir."

Tallas signed the memorandum, but he did not in fact alter his will to include Dementas. The estate refused to pay, and Dementas sued. The trial was entertaining, thanks to Judge Dee, whose remarks included: "It's hearsay, I agree, but its damn good hearsay, and I want to hear it." Urging a lawyer to hurry up, the judge snapped, "Go on to your next

question. This witness—who is supposed to be one witness for 15 minutes—is now into the second day, and we've still got the same witness . . . At the rate we're going, I will have long retired and been happily fishing in Wyoming." Finally hearing something worthwhile from the witness, he interrupted, "Wait a minute. Wait. Wait. Wait. Now, the fact finder has finally got a fact. He said, 'I did it a lot of times.' I've identified a fact in a day and a half. Let's go to the next witness and see if we can find another one in this case."

Unfortunately for Dementas, when the testimony ground to a halt, Judge Dee ruled that there was no consideration to support Tallas's promise. Dementas appealed.

ISSUE: Was there consideration to make Tallas's promise enforceable?

DECISION: There was no consideration to support the promise. Affirmed.

REASONING: Consideration refers to a legal detriment that has been bargained for and exchanged for a promise. Any detriment, no matter how economically inadequate, will support a promise. The trial judge correctly stated: "If Tallas thought it was worth 50,000 bucks to get one ride to Bingham, that's Tallas's decision. The only thing you can't do is take it with you."

On the other hand, services performed *before* the promise is made, with no intention of inducing that promise, are not consideration. This is so because no bargaining has taken place. No one has said if you will do this for me, I will do that for you. Dementas gave no consideration for Tallas's statement, so the promise may not be enforced. ◢

PROMISSORY ESTOPPEL

You enjoy your job in human resources at a major company in Minnesota, although the pay is disappointing. Then an old college friend, Ralph, phones and invites you to come to his glitzy new company in Miami. "Come on down. The weather is better and you'll make much more than you're making now." You ask Ralph if he's serious and he replies, "Darn right I am. See you in two weeks." A fortnight later you quit your job and hustle to Miami, only to learn that Ralph has hired someone else.

Do you have an enforceable contract? No. You and Ralph never exchanged promises. You gave no consideration. Ralph never asked you for a promise and you have done nothing to benefit him. Furthermore, there are no definite terms, or indeed any agreement at all. Your only hope is *promissory estoppel*. This doctrine is a result of judicial activism and requires a plaintiff to prove that:

* The offeror made a promise knowing the offeree was likely to rely.

* The offeree did in fact rely; and

* The only way to avoid injustice is to enforce the promise.

A court *may* award you some damages because Ralph made a promise knowing you were likely to rely, and that you did in fact rely, with serious consequences to your career. Remember, though, that promissory estoppel is very much the exception to the rule. Courts use it only to avoid serious injustice, and it is never a remedy you can count on.

PREEXISTING DUTY

You are building your dream house, a shingle and glass mansion nestled on a hillside overlooking 300 acres of postcard-perfect wilderness. The builder has agreed to finish the project by September 1, and you have already sold your current house, scheduled the moving company, and committed yourself at a new job. But in July, the builder announces he cannot finish the job. You're furious. He replies that transporting material has proven more expensive than he anticipated, and also that his carpenters and electricians have raised their rates. He can complete the work only if you agree to pay an extra $90,000, on top of the $850,000 you have already promised. You cannot afford the extra money and bitterly resent paying. But you desperately need the house finished, so you agree. On September 1 you move in, and the builder arrives to collect the final $90,000. Must you pay?

No. The builder gave no consideration to support your promise to pay the extra $90,000. It is true that the builder promised to finish by September 1, and true that a promise to do something is normally valid consideration. But the builder was already obligated to finish on September 1. He has not taken on any increased burden. **A promise to do something the promisor is already obligated to do is not valid consideration.**

Of course, exceptions are the spice of law, and the preexisting obligation rule provides us with a rack full. Courts have created these exceptions because a rigid application of the rule may interfere with legitimate business goals.

Exception: Additional Work

When a promisor agrees to do something above and beyond what he is obligated to do, his promise is valid consideration. Thus, if the builder asked for $90,000 extra but agreed that he would landscape the two acres surrounding the house, his promise is consideration. If you agree to pay the extra $90,000, you have created a binding contract.

Exception: Unforeseen Circumstances

Hugo has a deal to repair major highways. Hugo hires Hal's Hauling to cart soil and debris. Hal's trucks begin work, but after crossing the work site several times they sink to their axles in sinister, sucking slime. Hal demands an additional 35% payment from Hugo to complete the job, pointing out that the surface was dry and cracked and that neither Hal nor Hugo was aware of the subsurface water. Hal howls that he must use different trucks with different tires and work more slowly to permit the soil to dry. Hugo hems and haws and finally agrees. But when the hauling is finished, Hugo refuses to pay the extra money. Is Hugo liable?

Yes. **When *unforeseeable changes* cause one party to make a promise regarding an unfinished project, that promise is often valid consideration.** Even though Hal is only promising to finish what he was already obligated to do, many courts will declare his promise to be valid consideration, because neither party knew of the subsoil mud. Hal was facing a situation quite different from what the parties anticipated. Hal has given consideration and Hugo is bound by *his* promise to pay extra money. Because this is an exception to the rule, some courts will refuse to apply it. Others will use this exception only when unforeseeable *physical* circumstances change the very nature of the work to be done, and dramatically increase one party's expenses. Recall from the earlier example that a contractor who merely discovers that some of his costs are higher than he expected is *not* entitled to extra payment for doing the work he promised to perform. Any party seeking additional money for work already due faces a tough battle.

AT RISK

Unexpected problems such as subsoil water often arise in construction cases. A well-drafted contract will reduce the chances of a dispute. The parties should state in their agreement what conditions they expect to find, how they anticipate the work to proceed, and how they will compensate a party that encounters unexpected problems. For example, in the hauling contract, Hugo and Hal should have agreed on the following:

- A description of the surface and subsurface conditions that they anticipated.

- The type of equipment necessary to haul it and the approximate time needed to transport a given quantity, such as "two hours per hundred cubic yards."

- A provision for periodic review of the conditions actually encountered; and

- A summary of how they will adjust the price—if at all—in the event the hauler encounters unexpected hardship.

Exception: Modification

If both parties agree that a modification is necessary, the surest way to accomplish that is to rescind the original contract and draft a new one. **To rescind means to cancel.** Thus, if neither party has completed its obligations, the agreement to rescind will terminate each party's rights and obligations under the old contract. This should be done in writing. Then the parties sign the new agreement. Most courts will enforce a rescission and modification unless it appears that one party unfairly coerced the other into the changes.

Once again the UCC has changed the common law, making it easier for merchants to modify agreements for the sale of goods. UCC §2-209 provides:

* An agreement modifying a contract for the sale of goods needs no consideration to be binding.

* A signed agreement which excludes modification or rescission except by a signed writing cannot be otherwise modified or rescinded.

Here is how these two provisions work together. Mike's Magic Mania agrees to deliver 500 rabbits and 500 top hats to State University, for the school's Sleight of Hand 101 course. The goods, including 100 cages and 1,000 pounds of rabbit food, are to arrive no later than September 1, in time for the new semester, with payment on delivery. By September 20 no rabbits have appeared, in or out of hats. The university buys similar products from another supply house at a 25% steeper price, and sues MMM for the difference. Mike claims that in early September the dean had orally agreed to permit delivery in October. The dean is on sabbatical in Tahiti and cannot be reached for comment. Is the alleged modification valid?

Under the common law, the modification would have been void, because MMM gave no consideration for the extended delivery date. However, this is a sale of goods, and under UCC §2-209, an oral modification may be valid even without consideration. Unfortunately for Mike, though, the original agreement included a clause forbidding oral modification. Any changes had to be in writing, signed by both parties. Mike never obtained such a document. Even if the dean did make the oral agreement, the university wins.

Settlement of Debts

You claim that your friend Felicity owes you $90,000, but she refuses to pay. Finally, when you are desperate, Felicity offers you a cashier's check for $60,000—provided you accept it as full settlement. To get your hands on some money, you agree and cash the check. The next day you sue Felicity for $30,000. Who wins? First, an ethical question.

ETHICS

Even if you think you have a chance of winning, is it right to accept the money as full settlement and then sue for the balance? From the Chapter 2 ethics checklist: Which values are in conflict? Which of these values are most important? Under what circumstances would you feel ethically correct in suing for the balance? When would you consider it wrong?

As to the legal outcome, it will depend principally upon one major issue: Was Felicity's debt liquidated or unliquidated?

LIQUIDATED DEBT

A **liquidated debt** is one in which there is no dispute about the amount owed. A loan is a typical example. If a bank lends you $10,000, and the note obligates you to repay that amount on June 1 of the following year, you clearly owe that sum. The debt is liquidated.

In cases of liquidated debt, if the creditor agrees to take less than the full amount as full payment, her agreement is not binding. The debtor has given no consideration to support the creditor's promise to accept a reduced payment, and therefore the creditor is not bound by her word. The reasoning is simply that the debtor is already obligated to pay the full amount, so no bargaining could reasonably cause the creditor to accept less. If Felicity's debt to you is liquidated, your agreement to accept $60,000 is not binding, and you will successfully sue for the balance.

UNLIQUIDATED DEBT: ACCORD AND SATISFACTION

A debt is **unliquidated** for either of two reasons: (1) the parties dispute whether any money is owed, or (2) the parties agree that some money is owed but dispute how much. When a debt is unliquidated, for either reason, the parties may enter into a binding agreement to settle for less than what the creditor demands.

Such a compromise will be enforced if:

- The debt is unliquidated and;

- The parties agree that the creditor will accept as full payment a sum less than she has claimed; and;

- The debtor pays the amount agreed upon.

This agreement is called an **accord and satisfaction.** The accord is the agreement to settle for less than the creditor claims. The satisfaction is the actual payment of that compromised sum. An accord and satisfaction is valid consideration to support the creditor's agreement to drop all claims. Each party is giving up something: the creditor gives up her full claim, and the debtor gives up his assertion that he owed little or nothing.

Chapter Conclusion

This old doctrine of consideration is simple to state but subtle to apply. The parties must bargain and enter into an exchange of promises or actions. If they do not, there is no consideration and the courts are unlikely to enforce any promise made. A variety of exceptions modify the law, but a party wishing to render its future more predictable—the purpose of a contract—will rely on a solid bargain and exchange.

Chapter Review

1. A promise is normally binding only if it is supported by consideration, which requires a bargaining and exchange between the parties.

2. The "thing" bargained for can be another promise or an action—virtually anything that a party might seek.

It can create a benefit to the promisor or a detriment to the promisee.

3. The courts will seldom inquire into the adequacy of consideration.

4. An illusory promise is not consideration.

5. Past consideration is generally no consideration.

6. Under the doctrine of promissory estoppel, reliance may permit a party to enforce a promise even when there is no consideration; but this is an exception and courts are reluctant to grant it.

7. Under the doctrine of preexisting duty, a promise to do something that the promisor is already legally obligated to perform is generally not consideration.

8. A liquidated debt is one in which there is no dispute about the amount owed.

9. For a liquidated debt, a creditor's promise to accept less than the full amount is not binding.

10. For an unliquidated debt, if the parties agree that the creditor will accept less than the full amount claimed and the debtor performs, there is an accord and satisfaction and the creditor may not claim any balance.

PRACTICE TEST

Matching Questions

Match the following terms with their definitions:

___ **A.** Liquidated debt

___ **B.** Consideration

___ **C.** Accord and satisfaction

___ **D.** Illusory promise

___ **E.** Preexisting duty

1. A promise made by one party which in reality obligates him to do nothing.

2. Something the promisor is already obligated to do.

3. A debt in which the amount is undisputed.

4. Payment of an agreed upon sum that is less than what the creditor originally claimed.

5. Bargaining that leads to an exchange between the parties.

True/False Questions

Circle true or false:

1. T   F   As long as one party gives consideration, there is a binding contract.

2. T   F   Valid consideration requires that each party suffer a detriment and give a benefit to the other.

3. T   F   An illusory promise is no consideration.

4. T   F   Promising to do something that one is already obligated to do is generally not consideration.

5. T   F   A creditor who agrees to take less than the full amount of a liquidated debt is not bound by her agreement.

Multiple-Choice Questions

6. Terrance admits that he owes Natasha money, but the two disagree over the size of his debt. This is

   (a) An accord and satisfaction.

   (b) A preexisting duty.

   (c) A liquidated debt.

   (d) An unliquidated debt.

   (e) An unforeseen circumstance.

7. Rollo is building a swimming pool for Tatiana for $65,000. When the job is half finished, he tells her that he needs an extra $15,000 (a total of $80,000) to finish the pool. She agrees to pay, but when the pool is finished, Tatiana refuses to pay more than $65,000.

   (a) Tatiana is obligated to pay the full $80,000.

   (b) Tatiana is only obligated to pay $65,000.

   (c) Tatiana is obligated to pay $80,000 if Rollo performed additional work.

   (d) Tatiana is obligated to pay only if she had a preexisting duty to do so.

   (e) Tatiana is not obligated to pay anything, because Rollo has committed fraud.

8. At Lorenza's 90th birthday party, she gives a speech to the 25 guests, praising her maid, Anna. "Anna has worked faithfully for me for 55 years. In appreciation, next week I am going to give Anna $100,000." Anna is ecstatic, but next week, Lorenza changes her mind. Is Anna entitled to the money?

   (a) Yes, provided the witnesses agree she made the promise.

   (b) Yes, provided Lorenza *intended* to make the gift.

   (c) Yes, because there is adequate consideration: Anna's work and Lorenza's promise.

   (d) Yes, provided Lorenza actually has the money.

   (e) No.

9. At 10 p.m., Professor suddenly realizes that he has forgotten to write the final exam, to be given at 8 a.m. He calls a former student and says, "I'm desperate. Help me out tonight. We'll work from 11 until 7 a.m. I'll pay you $100." Student, realizing professor is desperate, demands $1,000. "That's absurd," Professor responds—but ends up paying it because he has no choice. When the exam is written, Professor pays student $100. Student sues. Student

   (a) Wins $900.

   (b) Wins $900 provided the agreement was in writing.

   (c) Wins nothing because Student gave insufficient consideration.

   (d) Wins nothing because Professor gave insufficient consideration.

   (e) Wins nothing because he knowingly took advantage of the dire circumstances.

10. Two merchants have a two-year contract for the sale of 500,000 gallons of gasoline. One now wishes to modify the agreement. The original contract says nothing about modification. This contract

   (a) May not be modified.

   (b) May only be modified in writing.

   (c) May only be modified if the side requesting the change gives new consideration.

   (d) May be modified without new consideration.

   (e) May only be modified by accord and satisfaction.

Short-Answer Questions

11. An aunt saw her eight-year-old nephew enter the room, remarked what a nice boy he was, and said, "I would like to take care of him now." She promptly wrote a note, promising to pay the boy $3,000 upon her death. Her estate refused to pay. Is it obligated to do so?

12. Elio Pino took out a health insurance policy with the Union Bankers Insurance Company Eighteen months later he became ill, suffered medical expenses, and filed a claim for benefits. Union Bankers wrote Pino this letter:

    "Dear Mr. Pino:
    While servicing your claim, we learned that the medical facts on the application for this policy were not complete. If we had known the complete health history, we couldn't have issued this insurance. We must place you and ourselves back where we were when you applied for the policy and consider that the insurance was never in effect. (We are refunding the premiums you've paid us.)"

    Pino deposited the refund check, which was much less than his claim, and then sued for the full claim. Bankers Insurance argued that Pino had entered into an accord and satisfaction. The trial court gave summary judgment for the insurer, and Pino appealed. Did Pino enter into an accord and satisfaction by cashing the insurance company check?

13. Tindall operated a general contracting business in Montana. He and Konitz entered into negotiations for Konitz to buy the business. The parties realized that Konitz could succeed with the business only if Tindall gave support and assistance for a year or so after the purchase, especially by helping with the process of bidding for jobs and obtaining bonds to guarantee performance. Konitz bought the business and Tindall helped with the bidding and bonding. Two years later, Tindall presented Konitz with a contract for his services up to that point. Konitz did not want to sign but Tindall insisted. Konitz signed the agreement, which said: "Whereas Tindall sold his contracting business to Konitz and thereafter assisted Konitz in bidding and bonding without which Konitz would have been unable to operate, NOW THEREFORE Konitz agrees to pay Tindall $138,629." Konitz later refused to pay. Comment.

14. Eagle ran convenience stores. He entered into an agreement with Commercial Movie in which Commercial would provide Eagle with videotape cassettes for rental. Eagle would pay Commercial 50% of the rental revenues. If Eagle stopped using Commercial's service, Eagle could not use a competitor's services for 18 months. The agreement also provided: "Commercial shall not be liable for compensation or damages of any kind, whether on account of the loss by Eagle of profits, sales or expenditures, or on account of any other event or cause whatsoever." Eagle complied with the agreement for two years but then began using a competitor's service, and Commercial sued. Eagle claimed that the agreement was unenforceable for lack of consideration. Did Eagle's argument fly?

15. ETHICS: Melnick built a house for Gintzler, but the foundation was defective. Gintzler agreed to accept the foundation if Melnick guaranteed to make future repairs caused by the defects. Melnick agreed but later refused to make any repairs. Melnick argued that his promise to make future repairs was unsupported by consideration. Who will win the suit? Is either party acting unethically? Which one, and why?

16. ROLE REVERSAL: Write a short-answer question that focuses on one of these consideration issues: illusory promise, preexisting duty, or accord and satisfaction.

Internet Research Problem

Go to **http://www.law.cornell.edu/ucc/ucc.table.html** and click on Article 2. Find your way to §2-209, concerning contract modification. Write a clear, one- or two-paragraph explanation of subsections (1) and (2). Explain what these subsections mean (in English) and how they work together.

You can find further practice problems in the Online Quiz at **http://beatty.westbuslaw.com** or in the Study Guide that accompanies this text.

11

Legality

Soheil Sadri, a California resident, did some serious gambling at Caesar's Tahoe casino in Nevada. And lost. To keep gambling, he wrote checks to Caesar's and then signed two memoranda pledging to repay money advanced. After two days, with his losses totaling more than $22,000, he went home. Back in California, Sadri stopped payment on the checks and refused to pay any of the money he owed Caesar's. The casino sued. In defense, Sadri claimed that California law considered his agreements illegal and unenforceable. He was unquestionably correct about one thing: **A contract that is illegal is void and unenforceable.**

In this chapter we examine a variety of contracts that may be void. Illegal agreements fall into two groups: those that violate a statute, and those that violate public policy.

Contracts That Violate a Statute

WAGERS

Gambling is big business. Almost all states now permit some form of wagering, from casinos to racetracks to lotteries, but some people disapprove. With citizens and states divided over the ethics of gambling, it is inevitable that we have conflicts such as the dispute between Sadri and Caesar's. The basic rule, however, is clear: **A gambling contract is illegal unless it is specifically authorized by state statute.**

In California, as in many states, gambling on credit is not allowed. In other words, it is illegal to lend money to help someone wager. A contract based on a gambling debt is unenforceable. But in Nevada, gambling on credit is legal, and debt memoranda such as Sadri's are enforceable contracts. Caesar's sued Sadri in California (where he lived). The result? Here is what the court said:

> *"There is a special reason for treating gambling on credit differently from gambling itself. Gambling debts are characteristic of pathological gambling, a mental disorder which is recognized by the American Psychiatric Association and whose prevalence is estimated at 2 to 3 percent of the adult population. Characteristic problems include extensive indebtedness and consequent default on debts and other financial responsibilities . . . and financially motivated illegal activities to pay for gambling. In our view, this is why enforcement of gambling debts has always been against public policy in California and should remain so, regardless of shifting public attitudes about gambling itself. If Californians want to play, so be it. But the law should not invite them to play themselves into debt."*[1]

Caesar's lost and Sadri kept his money. The dispute is a useful starting place from which to examine contract legality because it illustrates two important themes. First, morality is a significant part of contract legality. In refusing to enforce an obligation that Sadri undeniably had made, the California court relied on the human and social consequences of gambling and on the ethics of judicial enforcement of gambling debts. Second, "void" really means just that: A court will not intercede to assist either party to an illegal agreement, even if its refusal leaves one party obviously shortchanged.

INSURANCE

Another market in which "wagering" unexpectedly pops up is that of insurance. You may certainly insure your own life for any sum you choose. But may you insure someone else's life? **Anyone taking out a policy on the life of another must have an insurable interest in that person,** meaning some legitimate reason for

---

[1] *Metropolitan Creditors Service of Sacramento v. Sadri,* 15 Cal.App. 4th 1821, 19 Ca. Rptr. 2d 646 (Cal.Ct.App.1993).

fearing his death. A common reason for insuring someone else is that the other person owes you money. You want to be sure you are paid if something happens to her.

Juanita, a college student, has never met Joe Loony, a movie star, but she knows two things: He is a distinguished actor, and he is prone to reckless behavior. Juanita takes out a $300,000 life insurance policy on Joe's life, with herself as the beneficiary (the person who gets the money if the insured dies). Six months later, Joe is killed in a car accident. Dutiful Juanita is briefly sad, then sprints to the insurance office, where she collects . . . nothing. She had no insurable interest in Joe, and the law considers her policy nothing but an unenforceable gambling contract.

LICENSING STATUTES

You sue your next-door neighbor in small claims court, charging that he keeps a kangaroo in his backyard and that the beast has disrupted your family barbecues by leaping over the fence, demanding salad, and even punching your cousin in the ear. Your friend Foster, a graduate student from Melbourne, offers to help you prepare the case, and you agree to pay him 10% of anything you recover. Foster proves surprisingly adept at organizing documents and arguments. You win $1,200 and Foster demands $120. Must you pay? The answer is determined by the law of licensing.

States require licenses for anyone who practices a profession, such as law or medicine, works as a contractor or plumber, and for many other kinds of work. These licenses are required in order to protect the public. **When a licensing requirement is designed to protect the public, any contract made by an unlicensed worker is unenforceable.** Foster cannot enforce his contract for $120.

States use other licenses simply to raise money. For example, most states require a license to open certain kinds of retail stores. This requirement does not protect the public, because the state will not investigate the store owner the way it will examine a prospective lawyer or electrician. The state is simply raising revenue. **When a licensing requirement is designed merely to raise revenue, a contract made by an unlicensed person is generally enforceable.**

Many cases, such as the following one, involve contractors seeking to recover money for work they did without a license.

CASE SUMMARY

CEVERN, INC. v. FERBISH

666 A.2d 17, 1995 D.C. App. LEXIS 183
District of Columbia Court of Appeals, 1995

FACTS: Cevern, Inc. was a small contractor. The company was bonded and insured, as local law required, but it did not have a license to do home improvement work. Cevern applied for such a license, and this is what then happened:

- August 24: The District of Columbia regulatory agency certified that Cevern met all of the

requirements for a license (but it did not yet grant the license).

- August 27: Cevern's agents met with Robert Ferbish and Viola Stanton, and the parties signed a contract for Cevern to do extensive work on the Ferbish-Stanton home (to re-Ferbish it).

- August 31: The owners made an advance payment of $7,000 for the work. Cevern immediately began work on the project, digging a ditch and perhaps erecting a wall.

- September 5: Cevern paid its licensing fee and received the home improvement license.

Ferbish and Stanton later paid an additional $7,000 for Cevern's work but claimed that it was defective. When the owners refused to make a final payment of $10,295, the company sued. Ferbish counterclaimed for the $14,000 already paid, alleging that he and Stanton had spent an additional $43,000 to repair poor-quality work.

The trial court gave summary judgment for Ferbish and Stanton, ruling that Cevern's contract was void and unenforceable because the company had been unlicensed when the parties made the agreement. The judge ordered restitution (repayment) of the $14,000 the owners had paid. Cevern appealed.

ISSUE: Was the contract void because Cevern was unlicensed when the parties reached agreement?

ARGUMENT FOR CEVERN: We concede that unlicensed contractors generally may not enforce contracts. That rule makes sense, to discourage unqualified companies from doing work that might endanger the public. This is no such case. The District's regulatory agency had already declared that Cevern met all licensing requirements. Cevern had only to pay the fee and collect its license. The company promptly did this and had the license in hand when it performed the bulk of the work.

It is the homeowners who seek to pull a fast one: They wish to take advantage of a technical licensing rule to obtain first-rate work for free. Unfair! Even if the court refuses to enforce the contract, we urge alternatively that it permit Cevern to collect quasi-contract damages. The owners have benefited and know that Cevern expected payment.

ARGUMENT FOR THE OWNERS: An unlicensed contractor may never enforce contracts. This old rule is designed to protect the public from shoddy work, and it should be enforced for two reasons. First, a contractor may easily comply. All the company needs to do is demonstrate its competence, fill out certain forms, and pay a fee. Second, to permit this builder to recover for unlicensed work would encourage other unqualified contractors to try the same ruse: begin the work with glib assurances of a pending license, then hope for the best. The court should deny quasi-contract damages for the same reason: A void contract deserves no reward. ◢

USURY

Henry Paper and Anthony Pugliese were real estate developers. They bought a $1.7 million property in West Palm Beach, Florida, intending to erect an office building. They needed $1 million to start construction but were able to raise only $800,000. Walter Gross, another developer, agreed to lend them the final $200,000 for 18 months at 15% interest. Gross knew the partners were desperate for the money, so at the loan closing, he demanded 15% equity (ownership) in the partnership, in addition to the interest. Paper and Pugliese had no choice but to sign the agreement. The two partners never repaid the loan, and when Gross sued, the court ruled they need never pay a cent. It pays to understand usury.

Usury laws prohibit charging excess interest on loans. A lender who charges a usurious rate of interest may forfeit the illegal interest, or all interest, or, in some states, the entire loan. Florida permits interest rates of up to 18% on loans such as Gross's. A lender who charges more than 18% loses the right to collect any interest. A lender who exceeds 25% interest forfeits the entire debt. Where was the usury? Just here: When Gross insisted on a 15% share of the partnership, he was simply extracting additional interest and disguising it as partnership equity. The Paper-Pugliese partnership had equity assets of $600,000. A 15% equity, plus interest payments of 15% over 18 months, was the equivalent of a per annum interest rate of

45%. Gross probably thought he had made a deal that was too good to be true. And in the state of Florida, it was. He lost the entire debt.

ETHICS | Is it fair for Paper and Pugliese to sign a deal and then walk away from it? Analyze the issue by using these items from the checklist in the ethics chapter: Who are the *stakeholders?* Has the process been *fair?*

Contracts That Violate Public Policy

In the preceding section, we saw that courts refuse to enforce contracts that violate a statute. In this section we examine cases in which no statute applies but where a *public policy* prohibits certain contracts. In other words, we focus primarily on the common law.

RESTRAINT OF TRADE

Free trade is the basis of the American economy, and any bargain not to compete is suspect. The two most common settings for legitimate noncompetition agreements are the sale of a business and an employment relationship.

Sale of a Business

Kory has operated a real estate office, Hearth Attack, in a small city for 35 years, building an excellent reputation and many ties with the community. She offers to sell you the business and its goodwill for $300,000. But you need assurance that Kory will not take your money and promptly open a competing office across the street. With her reputation and connections, she would ruin your chances of success. You insist on a noncompete clause in the sale contract. In this clause, Kory promises that for one year she will not open a new real estate office or go to work for a competing company within a 10-mile radius of Hearth Attack. Suppose, six months after selling you the business, Kory goes to work for a competing realtor, two blocks away. You seek an injunction to prevent her from working. Who wins?

When a noncompete agreement relates to the sale of a business, it is enforceable if reasonable in time, geographic area, and scope of activity. In other words, a court will not enforce a noncompete agreement that lasts an unreasonably long time, covers an unfairly large area, or prohibits the seller of the business from doing a type of work that she never had done before. Measured by this test, Kory is almost certainly bound by her agreement.

If, on the other hand, the noncompetition agreement had prevented Kory from working anywhere within 200 miles of Hearth Attack, and she started working 50 miles away, a court would refuse to enforce the contract. The geographic restriction is unreasonable, since Kory never previously did business 50 miles distant.

Employment

When you sign an employment contract, the document may well contain a noncompete clause. Employers have legitimate worries that employees might go to a competitor and take with them trade secrets or other proprietary information. Some employers, though, attempt to place harsh restrictions on their employees, perhaps demanding a blanket agreement that the employee will never go to work for a competitor. Once again, courts look at the reasonableness of restrictions placed on an employee's future work. Because the agreement now involves the very livelihood of the worker, a court scrutinizes the agreement more closely.

A noncompete clause in an employment contract is generally enforceable only if it is essential to the employer, fair to the employee, and harmless to the general public. Judges invariably enforce these agreements to protect trade secrets and confidential information. They may protect customer lists that have been expensive to produce. Courts rarely restrain an employee simply because he wants to work for a competitor, and they disfavor agreements that last too long or apply in a very wide area. The following chart summarizes the factors that courts look at in all types of noncompetition agreements.

The Legality of Noncompetition Clauses ("Noncompetes")

Type of Noncompetition Agreement	When Enforceable	
Not ancillary to a sale of business or employment	Never	
Ancillary to a sale of business	If reasonable in time, geography, and scope of activity	
Ancillary to employment	Contract is *more* likely to be enforced when it involves: • Trade secrets or confidential information: these are almost always protected • Customer lists developed over extended period of time and carefully protected • Limited time and geographical scope • Vital to protect the employer's business	Contract is *less* likely to be enforced when it involves: • Employee who already had the skills when he arrived, or merely developed general skills on the job • Customer lists that can be derived from public sources • Excessive time or geographical scope • Unduly harsh on the employee or contrary to public interest

Suppose that Gina, an engineer, goes to work for Fission Chips, a silicon chip manufacturer that specializes in defense work. She signs a noncompete agreement promising never to work for a competitor. Over a period of three years, Gina learns some of Fission's proprietary methods of etching information onto the chips. She acquires a great deal of new expertise about chips generally. And she periodically deals with Fission Chips's customers, all of whom are well-known software and hardware manufacturers. Gina accepts an offer from WriteSmall, a competitor. Fission Chips races into court, seeking an injunction that would prevent Gina from (1) working for WriteSmall; (2) working for any other competitor; (3) revealing any of Fission's trade secrets; (4) using any of the general expertise she acquired at Fission Chips; and (5) contacting any of Fission's customers.

This injunction threatens Gina's career, and no court will grant such a broad order. The court will allow Gina to work for competitors, including WriteSmall. It will order her not to use or reveal any trade secrets belonging to Fission. She will, however, be permitted to use the general expertise she has acquired, and she may contact former customers, since anyone could get their names from the yellow pages.

More law in a minute, but first, how about something to eat?

CASE SUMMARY

LIAUTAUD v. LIAUTAUD

221 F.3d 981
United States Court of Appeals for the Seventh Circuit, 2000

FACTS: Jim Liautaud owned and operated a chain of gourmet submarine sandwich shops in Illinois called Jimmy John's, Inc. When his cousin, Michael, inquired about opening his own sandwich shop in Madison, Wisconsin, Jim agreed to provide his "secrets of success." Jim sent Michael this letter, outlining their agreement:

"I want to confirm at this time exactly what we agreed on so that it is clear and understood by both parties. The agreement:

1. Mike will open up a sub shop in Madison using Jimmy John's products and systems.

2. Mike can open up as many shops [as] he would like in Madison only.

3. If you want to expand the sub/club business beyond Madison you will do so using Jimmy John's sub shops as a partner or franchisee. This is subject to 100% agreement on both parties. If you don't use Jimmy John's Inc. you will not expand the sub/club business beyond Madison.

4. You will not disclose to anyone: recipes, products, or systems that are given to you. (Except your managers who run your store).

I believe thats [sic] what we agreed on. If I have made any misrepresentations of our agreement please correct them in the margin of this letter and return a copy to me. If I don't receive a copy I'll assume this letter to be the agreement."

Jim then helped Michael open the shop in Madison. A few years later, Michael opened a sandwich shop outside that city, in LaCrosse, Wisconsin. Jim sued to enforce their agreement. The district court found the agreement unreasonable and void, and Jim appealed.

ISSUE: Was the noncompetition agreement valid?

DECISION: The noncompetition agreement was void. Affirmed.

REASONING: For the contract to be valid, its terms may not restrict Michael more than necessary, and may not injure the public. Jim asserts that his trade secrets are the fundamental element of his success, and deserve protection. It does seem fair that he receive some compensation for sharing his methods. However, this agreement is far too broad to be enforced.

The noncompetition clause prevents Michael from expanding anywhere in the world outside of Madison. The prohibition lasts for the rest of his life, and applies even if Michael makes no use of Jim's secrets, even if he enters areas where Jim has no plans to do business. This is too harsh. The agreement permanently stifles Michael's development, and injures the public by limiting competition. Because the restrictions are unnecessary and oppressive, the agreement is void.

EXCULPATORY CLAUSES

You decide to capitalize on your expert ability as a skier and open a ski school in Colorado, "Pike's Pique." But you realize that skiing sometimes causes injuries, so you require anyone signing up for lessons to sign this form:

> *I agree to hold Pike's Pique and its employees entirely harmless in the event that I am injured in any way or for any reason or cause, including but not limited to any acts, whether negligent or otherwise, of Pike's Pique or any employee or agent thereof.*

The day your school opens, Sara Beth, an instructor, deliberately pushes Toby over a cliff because Toby criticized her color combinations. Eddie, a beginning student, "blows out" his knee attempting an advanced racing turn. And Maureen, another student, reaches the bottom of a steep run and slams into a snowmobile that Sara Beth parked there. Maureen, Eddie, and Toby's family all sue Pike's Pique. You defend based on the form you had them sign. Does it save the day?

The form on which you are relying is an **exculpatory clause,** that is, one that attempts to release you from liability in the event of injury to another party. Exculpatory clauses are common. Ski schools use them and so do parking lots, landlords, warehouses, and daycare centers. All manner of businesses hope to avoid large tort judgments by requiring their customers to give up any right to recover. Is such a clause valid? Sometimes. Courts frequently—but not always—ignore exculpatory clauses, finding that one party was forcing the other party to give up legal rights that no one should be forced to surrender.

An exculpatory clause is generally unenforceable when it attempts to exclude an intentional tort or gross negligence. When Sara Beth pushes Toby over a cliff, that is the intentional tort of battery. A court will not enforce the exculpatory clause. Sara Beth is clearly liable. As to the snowmobile at the bottom of the run, if a court determines that was gross negligence (carelessness far greater than ordinary negligence), then the exculpatory clause will again be ignored. If, however, it was ordinary negligence, then we must continue the analysis.

An exculpatory clause is generally unenforceable when the affected activity is in the public interest, such as medical care, public transportation, or some essential service. Suppose Eddie goes to a doctor for surgery on his damaged knee, and the doctor requires him to sign an exculpatory clause. The doctor negligently performs the surgery, accidentally leaving his cuff links in Eddie's left knee. The exculpatory clause will not protect the doctor. Medical care is an essential service, and the public cannot give up its right to demand reasonable work.

But what about Eddie's suit against Pike's Pique? Eddie claims that he should never have been allowed to attempt an advanced maneuver. His suit is for ordinary negligence, and the exculpatory clause probably *does* bar him from recovery. Skiing is a recreational activity. No one is obligated to do it, and there is no strong public interest in ensuring that we have access to ski slopes.

An exculpatory clause is generally unenforceable when the parties have greatly unequal bargaining power. When Maureen flies to Colorado, suppose that the airline requires her to sign a form contract with an exculpatory clause. Because the airline almost certainly has much greater bargaining power, it can afford to offer a "take-it-or-leave-it" contract. The bargaining power is so unequal, though, that the clause is probably unenforceable.

An exculpatory clause is generally unenforceable unless the clause is clearly written and readily visible. Thus, if Pike's Pique gave all ski students an eight-page contract, and the exculpatory clause was at the bottom of page seven in small print, the average customer would never notice it. The clause would be void.

Bailment Cases

Exculpatory clauses are very common in bailment cases. **Bailment means giving possession and control of personal property to another person.** The person giving up possession is the bailor, and the one accepting possession is the bailee. When you leave your laptop computer with a dealer to be repaired, you create a bailment. The same is true when you check your coat at a restaurant or lend your Matisse to a museum. Bailees often try to limit their liability for damage to property by using an exculpatory clause.

Judges are slightly more apt to enforce an exculpatory clause in a bailment case, because the harm is to property and not person. But courts will still look at many of the same criteria we have just examined to decide whether a bailment contract is enforceable. In particular, when the bailee is engaged in an important public service, a court is once again likely to ignore the exculpatory clause. The following contrasting cases illustrate this.

In *Weiss v. Freeman*,[2] Weiss stored personal goods in Freeman's self-storage facility. Freeman's contract included an exculpatory clause relieving it of any and all liability. Weiss's goods were damaged by mildew and she sued. The court held the exculpatory clause valid. The court considered self-storage to be a significant business, but not as vital as medical care or housing. It pointed out that a storage facility would not know what each customer stored and therefore could not anticipate the harm that might occur. Freedom of contract should prevail, the clause was enforceable, and Weiss got no money.

In *Gardner v. Downtown Porsche Audi*,[3] Gardner left his Porsche 911 at Downtown for repairs. He signed an exculpatory clause saying that Downtown was "Not Responsible for Loss or Damage to Cars or Articles Left in Cars in Case of Fire, Theft, or Any Other Cause Beyond Our Control." Due to Downtown's negligence, Gardner's Porsche was stolen. The court held the exculpatory clause void. It ruled that contemporary society is utterly dependent upon automobile transportation, and Downtown was therefore in a business of great public importance. No repair shop should be able to contract away liability, and Gardner won. (This case also illustrates that using 17 uppercase letters in one sentence does not guarantee legal victory.)

UNCONSCIONABLE CONTRACTS

Gail Waters was young, naive, and insecure. A serious injury when she was 12 years old left her with an annuity, that is, a guaranteed annual payment for many years. When Gail was 21, she became involved with Thomas Beauchemin, an ex-convict, who introduced her to drugs. Beauchemin suggested that Gail sell her annuity to some friends of his, and she agreed. Beauchemin arranged for a lawyer to draw up a contract, and Gail signed it. She received $50,000 for her annuity, which at that time had a cash value of $189,000 and was worth, over its remaining 25 years, $694,000. Gail later decided this was not a wise bargain. Was the contract enforceable? That depends on the law of unconscionability.

An unconscionable contract is one that a court refuses to enforce because of fundamental unfairness. Historically, a contract was considered unconscionable

---

[2] 1994 Tenn.App. LEXIS 393 (Tenn. Ct. App. 1993).

[3] 180 Cal. App. 3d, 713, 225 Cal. Rptr. 757 (Cal. Ct. App. 1986).

if it was "such as no man in his senses and not under delusion would make on the one hand, and as no honest and fair man would accept on the other." The two factors that most often led a court to find unconscionability were (1) oppression, meaning that one party used its superior power to force a contract on the weaker party; and (2) surprise, meaning that the weaker party did not fully understand the consequences of its agreement.

Gail Waters won her case. The Massachusetts high court ruled:

> *"Beauchemin introduced the plaintiff to drugs, exhausted her credit card accounts, unduly influenced her, suggested that the plaintiff sell her annuity contract, initiated the contract negotiations, and benefited from the contract between the plaintiff and the defendants. For payment of not more than $50,000 the defendants were to receive an asset that could be immediately exchanged for $189,000, or they could elect to hold it for its guaranteed term and receive $694,000. The defendants assumed no risk and the plaintiff gained no advantage. We are satisfied that the disparity of interests in this contract is so gross that the court cannot resist the inference that it was improperly obtained and is unconscionable."[4]*

Adhesion Contracts

A related issue concerns **adhesion contracts, which are standard form contracts prepared by one party and given to the other on a "take-it-or-leave-it" basis.** We have all encountered them many times when purchasing goods or services. When a form contract is vigorously negotiated between equally powerful corporations, the resulting bargain is generally enforced. However, when the contract is simply presented to a consumer, who has no ability to bargain, it is an adhesion contract and subject to an unconscionability challenge.

CASE SUMMARY

WORLDWIDE INSURANCE v. KLOPP

603 A.2d 788, 1992 Del. LEXIS 13
Supreme Court of Delaware, 1992

FACTS: Ruth Klopp had auto insurance with Worldwide. She was injured in a serious accident that left her with permanent neck and back injuries. The other driver was uninsured, so Klopp filed a claim with Worldwide under her "uninsured motorist" coverage. Her policy required arbitration of such a claim, and the arbitrators awarded Klopp $90,000. But the policy also stated that if the arbitrators awarded more than the statutory minimum amount of insurance ($15,000), either side could appeal the award and request a full trial. Worldwide appealed and demanded a trial.

In the trial court, Klopp claimed that the appeal provision was unconscionable and void. The trial court agreed and entered judgment for the full $90,000. Worldwide appealed.

ISSUE: Is the provision that requires arbitration and then permits appeal by either party void as unconscionable?

---

[4] *Waters v. Min Ltd.,* 412 Mass. 64, 587 N.E.2d 231, 1992 Mass. LEXIS 66 (1992).

DECISION: The contract provision is unconscionable. Affirmed.

REASONING: Worldwide contends that the arbitration provision is clear and unambiguous, but Klopp argues that it is grossly unfair. This contract binds both parties to a low award, one that an insurance company would be unlikely to appeal anyway. Either party may appeal a high award, but common sense suggests that only the insurer would do so. The policy enables the insurer to avoid a high arbitration award that may have been perfectly fair. This "escape hatch" favors the insurance company. The provision is unconscionable and void.

Chapter Conclusion

It is not enough to bargain effectively and obtain a contract that gives you exactly what you want. You must also be sure that the contract is legal. Accidentally forgetting to obtain a state license to perform a certain job could mean you will never be paid for it. Bargaining a contract with a non-compete or exculpatory clause that is too one-sided may lead a court to ignore it. Legality is many-faceted, sometimes subtle, and always important.

Chapter Review

Illegal contracts are void and unenforceable. Illegality most often arises in these settings:

1. *Wagering.* A purely speculative contract—whether for gambling or insurance—is likely to be unenforceable.

2. *Licensing.* When the licensing statute is designed to protect the public, a contract by an unlicensed plaintiff is generally unenforceable. When such a statute is designed merely to raise revenue, a contract by an unlicensed plaintiff is generally enforceable.

3. *Usury.* Excessive interest is generally unenforceable and may be fatal to the entire debt.

4. *Noncompete.* A noncompete clause in the sale of a business must be limited to a reasonable time, geographic area, and scope of activity. In an employment contract, such a clause is considered reasonable—and enforceable—only to protect trade secrets, confidential information, and customer lists.

5. *Exculpatory clauses.* These clauses are generally void if the activity involved is in the public interest, the parties are greatly unequal in bargaining power, or the clause is unclear. In other cases they are generally enforced.

6. *Unconscionability.* Oppression and surprise may create an unconscionable bargain. An adhesion contract is especially suspect when it is imposed by a corporation on a consumer.

PRACTICE TEST

Matching Questions

Match the following terms with their definitions:

___ **A.** Usury

___ **B.** Unconscionable

___ **C.** Exculpatory

1. A contract clause intended to relieve one party from potential tort liability.

2. A contract clause designed to prevent, among other things, an employee from working for a competitor.

___ **D.** Licensing statute   **3.** A contract provision that no one who understood it would sign.

___ **E.** Noncompete   **4.** Illegally high interest rates.

                                   5. A law designed to protect the public from incompetent professionals and trades people.

True/False Questions

Circle true or false:

1.   T   F   A merchant who fails to obtain a license to operate a retail store cannot enforce a commercial contract.

2.   T   F   Noncompete clauses are suspect because they tend to restrain free trade.

3.   T   F   An unconscionable contract clause is immoral but legal.

4.   T   F   A court is unlikely to enforce an exculpatory clause included in a contract for surgery.

5.   T   F   Giving possession and control of personal property is called personal domain.

Multiple-Choice Questions

6. Ernie attends a political rally where for the first time he meets Senator Smiles. Ernie thinks that Smiles looks unhealthy, and that same day purchases a $100,000 life insurance contract on Smiles, with himself as the beneficiary. A month later, Smiles dies of a heart attack. Ernie is entitled to

   (a) $33,333.   (d) $100,000.

   (b) $50,000.   (e) Nothing.

   (c) $66,666.

7. In which case is a court most likely to enforce an exculpatory clause?

   (a) Dentistry.   (d) Public transportation.

   (b) Hang gliding.   (e) Accounting.

   (c) Parking lot.

8. Molly is a graduate student in architecture. Her uncle, Shelby, asks her to design a lakefront cottage for him, and offers a fee of $20,000. Molly says, "I'd love to do it, but you have to understand I'm still just a student. I don't have a license." Shelby says, "I know that, but I've seen your work and you're far better than most of the professionals." Molly designs a splendid house, which is built to Shelby's satisfaction. He then refuses to pay and she sues. Molly wins

   (a) $10,000 because she is not licensed.   (d) $20,000 because the work is finished and there is no risk of harm to anyone.

   (b) $20,000 because she did the work.

   (c) $20,000 because she told Shelby about her lack of license and he did not mind.   (e) Nothing.

9. You drive up to a fancy restaurant and hand your car keys to the valet. You have created

   (a) An exculpatory clause.   (d) An illusory contract.

   (b) A noncompete clause.   (e) An adhesion contract.

   (c) A bailment.

10. One policy reason that courts dislike noncompete clauses is their desire to protect

   (a) Job mobility.   (d) Lower interest rates.

   (b) Employer satisfaction.   (e) The public from unlicensed professionals.

   (c) A valid contract.

Short-Answer Questions

11. For 20 years, Art's Flower Shop relied almost exclusively on advertising in the Yellow Pages to bring business to its shop in a small West Virginia town. One year the Yellow Pages printer accidentally omitted to print Art's ad, and Art's suffered an enormous drop in business. Art's sued for negligence and won a judgment of $50,000 from the jury, but the printing company appealed, claiming that under an exculpatory clause in the contract, the company could not be liable to Art's for more than the cost of the ad, about $910. Art's claimed that the exculpatory clause was unconscionable. Please rule.

12. Oasis Waterpark, located in Palm Springs, California, sought out Hydrotech Systems, Inc., a New York corporation, to design and construct a surfing pool. Hydrotech replied that it could design the pool and sell all the necessary equipment to Oasis, but could not build the pool because it was not licensed in California. Oasis insisted that Hydrotech do the construction work, because Hydrotech had unique expertise in these pools. Oasis promised to arrange for a licensed California contractor to "work with" Hydrotech on the construction; Oasis also assured Hydrotech that it would pay the full contract price of $850,000, regardless of any licensing issues. Hydrotech designed and installed the pool as ordered. But Oasis failed to make the final payment of $110,000. Hydrotech sued. Can Hydrotech sue for either breach of contract or fraud (trickery)?

13. Guyan Machinery, a West Virginia manufacturing corporation, hired Albert Voorhees as a salesman and required him to sign a contract stating that if he left Guyan he would not work for a competing corporation anywhere within 250 miles of West Virginia for a two-year period. Later, Voorhees left Guyan and began working at Polydeck Corp., another West Virginia manufacturer. The only product Polydeck made was urethane screens, which comprised half of 1% of Guyan's business. Is Guyan entitled to enforce its noncompete clause?

14. McElroy owned 104 acres worth about $230,000. He got into financial difficulties and approached Grisham, asking to borrow $100,000. Grisham refused, but ultimately the two reached this agreement: McElroy would sell Grisham his property for $80,000, and the contract would include a clause allowing McElroy to repurchase the land within two years for $120,000. McElroy later claimed the contract was void. Is he right?

15. ETHICS: Richard and Michelle Kommit traveled to New Jersey to have fun in the casinos. While in Atlantic City, they used their MasterCard to withdraw cash from an ATM conveniently located in the "pit," which is the gambling area of a casino. They ran up debts of $5,500 on the credit card and did not pay. The Connecticut National Bank sued for the money. What argument should the Kommits make? Which party, if any, has the moral high ground here? Should a casino offer ATM services in the gambling pit? If a credit card company allows customers to withdraw cash in a casino, is it encouraging them to lose money? Do the Kommits have any ethical right to use the ATM, attempt to win money by gambling, and then seek to avoid liability?

16. ROLE REVERSAL: Write one multiple-choice question with two noncompete clauses, one of which is valid and the other void.

Internet Research Problem

Go to **http://www.law.cornell.edu/topics/state_statutes.html#criminal_code** and choose any state, and then search for that state's law on Internet gambling. Is it legal in that state? Has the state attempted to regulate this activity in any way? Do you believe the state will succeed? Conduct the same search in a second state and compare the results of the two searches.

You can find further practice problems in the Online Quiz at **http://beatty.westbuslaw.com** or in the Study Guide that accompanies this text.

12

Capacity and Consent

For Kevin Green, it was love at first sight. She was sleek, as quick as a cat, and a beautiful deep blue. He paid $4,600 cash for the used Camaro. The car soon blew a gasket, and Kevin demanded his money back. But the Camaro came with no guarantee, and the dealer refused. Kevin repaired the car himself. Next, some unpleasantness on the highway left the car a worthless wreck. Kevin received the full value of the car from his insurance company. Then he sued the dealer, seeking a refund of his purchase price. The dealer pointed out that it was not responsible for the accident, and that the car had no warranty of any kind. Yet the trial court awarded Kevin the full $4,600.

Kevin Green was only 16 years old when he bought the car, and a minor, said the court, has the right to cancel any agreement he has made. We will see how the appellate court resolved the case, as we examine two related issues: capacity and consent.

Capacity

Capacity is the legal ability to enter into a contract. An adult of sound mind has the legal capacity to contract. Generally, any deal she enters into will be enforced if all elements we have seen—agreement, consideration, and so forth—are present. But two groups of people usually lack legal capacity: minors and those with a mental impairment.

MINORS

A minor is someone under the age of 18. Because a minor lacks legal capacity, she normally can create only a voidable contract. **A voidable contract may be canceled by the party who lacks capacity.** Notice that only the party lacking capacity may cancel the agreement. So a minor who enters into a contract generally may choose between enforcing the agreement or negating it. The other party, however, has no such right.

Disaffirmance

A minor who wishes to escape from a contract generally may **disaffirm** it; that is, he may notify the other party that he refuses to be bound by the agreement. He also may file a suit seeking to **rescind** the contract, that is, to have a court formally cancel it.

Kevin Green was 16 when he signed a contract with Star Chevrolet. Since he was a minor, the deal was voidable. When the Camaro blew a gasket and Kevin informed Star Chevrolet that he wanted his money back, he was disaffirming the contract. He happened to do it because the car suddenly seemed a poor buy, but notice that he could have disaffirmed for any reason at all, such as deciding that he no longer liked Camaros. When Kevin disaffirmed, he was entitled to his money back. If Star Chevrolet had understood the law of capacity, it would have towed the Camaro away and returned Kevin's $4,600. At least Star would have had a repairable automobile.

Restitution

A minor who disaffirms a contract must return the consideration he has received, to the extent he is able. Restoring the other party to its original position is called restitution. The consideration that Kevin Green received in the contract was, of course, the Camaro. If Star Chevrolet had delivered a check for $4,600, Kevin would have been obligated to return the car.

What happens if the minor is not able to return the consideration because he no longer has it or it has been destroyed? Most states hold that the minor is still entitled to his money back. Star Chevrolet hoped that Mississippi would prove to be an exception.

CASE SUMMARY

STAR CHEVROLET CO. v. GREEN

473 So. 2d 157, 1985 Miss. LEXIS 2141
Supreme Court of Mississippi, 1985

FACTS: The facts are summarized in the opening paragraph of this chapter.

ISSUE: Is Kevin Green entitled to disaffirm the contract with Star Chevrolet even though the Camaro has been destroyed?

DECISION: Green is entitled to disaffirm the contract. Affirmed.

REASONING: Sound public policy permits a minor to disaffirm a contract. The goal is to protect a young person from her own impetuous conduct and to discourage aggressive adults from taking advantage of youthful inexperience. The simple way for an adult to avoid the harsh consequences of this rule is to refrain from contracts with those under 18.

When a minor disaffirms an agreement, she must return any portion of the property still in her possession. However, the young person need not return or pay for anything she has sold, destroyed, or otherwise lost.

Kevin Green had the automobile when he notified Star Chevrolet that he was disaffirming the contract. If Star had offered Kevin the full purchase price, as the law required, the young man would have been obligated to return the vehicle. The car dealer failed to do that, though, and the auto was demolished. Kevin need not return the auto or pay for it.[1]

AT RISK   As the Mississippi court tells us, the rule permitting a minor to disaffirm a contract is designed to discourage adults from making deals with innocent children. The rule is centuries old. But is this rule workable in our consumer society? There are entire industries devoted to (and dependent upon) minors. Think of children's films, and music, and sneakers, and toys. Does this rule imperil retailers? How should a retailer protect himself? An automobile dealer?

Timing of Disaffirmance/Ratification

A minor may disaffirm a contract anytime before she reaches age 18. She also may disaffirm within a reasonable time after turning 18. Suppose that Betsy is 17 when she buys her stereo. Four months later she turns 18, and two months after that she disaffirms the contract. Her disaffirmance is effective. In most states, she gets 100% of her money back. In some cases, minors have been entitled to disaffirm a contract several years after turning 18.

Exception: Necessaries

There is one exception on which all states agree, and that is a contract for necessaries. Food, clothing, housing, and medical care are **necessaries.** On a contract for

---

[1] The court awarded Kevin $3,100, representing the $4,600 purchase price minus $1,500, which was the salvage value of the car when he delivered it to his insurance company. You may wonder why Kevin Green is permitted to keep the insurance money and his original purchase price, thus putting him in a better position than he was in before buying the Camaro. The reason is the collateral source rule, which states that a defendant (Star Chevrolet) that is found to owe the plaintiff (Green) money may not have its liability reduced because the plaintiff will be compensated by another source (the insurance company). The rule is routinely applied in tort cases. Many courts refuse to use it in contract cases, but the Mississippi court applied it, and as a result, Kevin was in the green.

necessaries, a minor must pay for the value of the benefit received. In other words, the minor may still disaffirm the contract and return whatever is unused. But he is liable to pay for whatever benefit he obtained from the goods while he had them. The Mississippi court followed the general rule and held that an automobile was not a necessary.

MENTALLY IMPAIRED PERSONS

A person suffers from a mental impairment if by reason of mental illness or defect he is unable to understand the nature and consequences of the transaction. The mental impairment can be insanity that has been formally declared by a court, or mental illness that has never been ruled on but is now evident. The impairment may also be due to other mental health problems, such as mental retardation or senility.

A party suffering a mental impairment generally creates only a voidable contract. The impaired person has the right to disaffirm the contract just as a minor does. But again, the contract is voidable, not void. The mentally impaired party generally has the right to full performance if she wishes.

The law presumes that an adult is mentally competent. As always, courts respect the freedom to contract. Anyone seeking to avoid a contract because of mental impairment has the burden of proving the infirmity, since "mental incompetence" could be a very handy way out of a deal gone sour. **A mentally infirm party who seeks to void a contract must make restitution.** If a party succeeds with a claim of mental impairment, the court will normally void the contract but will require the impaired party to give back whatever she got.

Intoxication

Similar rules apply in cases of drug or alcohol intoxication. When one party is so intoxicated that he cannot understand the nature and consequences of the transaction, the contract is voidable. Toby's father gives him a new Jaguar sports car for his birthday, and foolish Toby celebrates by getting drunk. Amy, realizing how intoxicated he is, induces Toby to promise in writing that he will sell his car to her the next day for $1,000. Toby may void the contract and keep his auto.

Reality of Consent

Smiley offers to sell you his house for $300,000, and you agree in writing to buy. After you move in, you discover that the house is sinking into the earth at the rate of 6 inches per week. In 12 months, your only access to the house will be through the chimney. You sue, asking to rescind. You argue that when you signed the contract you did not truly consent because you lacked essential information. In this section we look at claims parties make in an effort to rescind a contract based on lack of valid consent: (1) misrepresentation or fraud; (2) mistake; and (3) undue influence.

MISREPRESENTATION AND FRAUD

Misrepresentation occurs when a party to a contract says something that is factually wrong. "This house has no termites," says a homeowner to a prospective buyer. If the house is swarming with the nasty pests, the statement is a misrepresentation.

The misrepresentation might be innocent or fraudulent. If the owner believes the statement to be true and has a good reason for that belief, he has made an innocent misrepresentation. If the owner knows that it is false, the statement is **fraudulent misrepresentation.** To explain these concepts, we will assume that two people are discussing a possible deal. One is the "maker," that is, the person who makes the statement that is later disputed. The other is the "injured person," the one who eventually claims to have been injured by the statement. **In order to rescind the contract, the injured person must show that the maker's false statement was fraudulent or a material misrepresentation, and that she relied on it.**

Element One: False Statement of Fact

The injured party must show a false statement of fact. Notice that this does not mean the statement was a lie. If a homeowner says that the famous architect Stanford White designed his house, but Bozo Loco actually did the work, it is a false statement. The owner might have a good reason for the error. Perhaps a local history book identifies the house as a Stanford White. Or his words might be an intentional lie. In either case, it is a false statement of fact.

An opinion, though, is not a statement of fact. A realtor says, "I think land values around here will be going up 20% or 30% for the foreseeable future." That statement is pretty enticing to a buyer, but it is not a false statement of fact. The maker is clearly stating her own opinion, and the buyer who relies on it does so at his peril.

Puffery. **A statement is puffery when a reasonable person would realize that it is a sales pitch, representing the exaggerated opinion of the seller.** Puffery is not a statement of fact. Because puffery is not factual, it is never a basis for rescission.

Marie Rodio purchased auto insurance from Allstate and then, after she was involved in a serious accident, received from the company less money than she thought fair. She sued, arguing that the company had committed fraud by advertising that customers would be in "good hands." She lost when the state supreme court ruled that, even if she could prove the company did not treat her well, the ad was mere puffery and not fraud.

Element Two: Fraud or Materiality

This is the heart of the case. The injured party must demonstrate that the statement was fraudulent or material:

* The statement was *fraudulent* if the maker intended to induce the other party to contract, either knowing that her words were false or uncertain that they were true.

* The statement was *material* if the maker expected the other party to rely on her words in reaching an agreement.

Consider the examples in the following chart. In case 1, the homeowner tells a prospective buyer that the heating system works perfectly, when he knows that it barely functions, leaving some rooms suitable only for penguins. The words are fraudulent.

In case 2, the homeowner is not lying when he says his cliff house is built on solid bedrock, but he is making a statement without being certain of its truth. This is also fraud.

By contrast, in case 3 there is no fraud because the homeowner is acting in good faith. He says that the roof is six years old because half a dozen years ago the previous owner said it was new. In fact, the roof is 25 years old and will soon need replacement. The homeowner's statement is a *material misrepresentation* because it is incorrect and the owner expects the buyer to rely on it.

Finally, in case 4 the homeowner says that the swimming pool is 30 feet long because he measured it himself. But he did the job incorrectly, and the pool is only 29 feet. This is another misrepresentation, but is it material? No. An error of a foot or so would not influence a reasonable purchaser, and this buyer has failed to prove her case.

The Difference between Fraud and Misrepresentation

Statement. In each case, the words are false.	Owner's Belief	Legal Result	Explanation
1. "The heating system is perfect."	Owner knows this is false.	Fraud.	Owner knew the statement was false and intended to induce the buyer to enter into a contract.
2. "The house is built on solid bedrock."	Owner has no idea what is under the surface.	Fraud.	Owner was not certain the statement was true and intended to induce the buyer to enter into a contract.
3. "The roof is only six years old."	Owner has a good reason to believe the statement is true.	Material misrepresentation.	Owner acted in good faith, but the statement is material because owner expects the buyer to rely on it.
4. "The pool is 30 feet long."	Owner has a good reason to believe the statement is true.	Not a material misrepresentation.	Although this is a misrepresentation, it is not material, since a reasonable buyer would not make a decision based on a one-foot error in the pool length.

Element Three: Justifiable Reliance

The injured party must also show that she reasonably relied on the false statement. Suppose the seller of a gas station lies through his teeth about the structural soundness of the building. The buyer believes what he hears but does not much care, because he plans to demolish the building and construct a daycare center. There was fraud but no reliance, and the buyer may not rescind.

Plaintiff's Remedy for Misrepresentation or Fraud

Both innocent and fraudulent misrepresentation permit the injured party to rescind the contract. In other words, the injured party who proves all three elements will get her money back. She will, of course, have to make restitution to the other party. If she bought land and now wants to rescind, she will get her money back but must return the property to the seller. She often has the option of simply suing for damages.

ETHICS

Lilly is a good person. She runs a nonprofit center in Los Angeles that teaches adoptive parents to care for troubled children. Yet major airlines believe that people such as Lilly routinely commit fraud. Here is why.

Lilly needs to fly to Chicago to attend a fundraising conference on Wednesday. She would like to travel on Tuesday and return two days later, but an economy-class ticket would cost her agency a crushing $1,650. So Lilly buys a pair of "back-to-back" tickets. The first is for a flight leaving Los Angeles on Tuesday, with a return date a week later. Because the travel includes a Saturday stayover, this ticket costs a mere $325. The second ticket, also for $325, allows travel leaving Chicago on Thursday and returning one week later. Lilly uses only the first half of each ticket. She flies to Chicago on Tuesday and returns to Los Angeles 48 hours later, having avoided a Saturday stayover while saving her agency $1,000. Clever? "No," respond the airlines, "fraud!"

What are the consequences of Lilly's behavior? What values are involved?

Special Problem: Silence

We know that a party negotiating a contract may not misrepresent a material fact. What about silence? Suppose the seller knows the roof is in dreadful condition but the buyer never asks. Does the seller have an affirmative obligation to disclose what she knows?

A seller who knows something that the buyer does not know is often required to divulge it. The Restatement (Second) of Contracts offers guidance: **Nondisclosure of a fact is misrepresentation when disclosure is necessary to correct a *previous assertion* or a *basic mistake*.**

To Correct a Previous Assertion.   During the course of negotiations, one party's perception of the facts may change. When an earlier statement later appears inaccurate, the change generally must be reported.

W. R. Grace & Company wanted to buy a natural-gas field in Mississippi. An engineer's report indicated large gas reserves. On the basis of the engineering report, the Continental Illinois National Bank committed to a $75 million nonrecourse production loan, meaning that Continental would be repaid only with revenues from the gas field. After Continental committed but before it had closed on the loan, Grace had an exploratory well drilled and struck it rich—with water. The land would never produce any gas. Without informing Continental of the news, Grace closed the $75 million loan. When Grace failed to repay, Continental sued and won. A party who learns new information indicating that a previous statement is inaccurate must disclose the bad news.

To Correct a Basic Mistake.   When one party knows that the other is negotiating with a mistaken assumption about an important fact, the party who knows of the error must correct it. Jeffrey Stambovsky agreed to buy Helen Ackley's house in Nyack, New York for $650,000. Stambovsky signed a contract and made a $32,500 down payment. Before completing the deal, he learned that in several newspaper articles Ackley had publicized the house as being haunted. Ackley had also permitted the house to be featured in a walking tour of the neighborhood as "a riverfront Victorian (with ghost)." Stambovsky refused to go through with the deal and sued to rescind. He won. The court ruled that Ackley sold the house knowing Stambovsky was ignorant of the alleged ghosts. She also knew that a reasonable buyer might avoid a haunted house, fearing grisly events—or diminished resale value. Stambovsky could not have discovered the apparitions himself, and Ackley's failure to warn permitted him to rescind the deal.

A seller generally must report any latent defect he knows about that the buyer should not be expected to discover himself. The judge in the following case states the rule somewhat differently, but the outcome is the same.

CASE SUMMARY

FIMBEL v. DECLARK

695 N.E.2d 125
Indiana Court of Appeals, 1998

FACTS: Ronald and Patricia Fimbel bought two lake-front lots on Lake Latonka in Indiana, intending to build a summer cottage. However, they discovered that the soil was not suitable for a septic system. They would have to hire an engineer at a substantial expense to determine if it was even possible to construct an alternative system. They decided to sell the land.

The Fimbels met with several interested buyers, including Thomas and Joan DeClark. The Fimbels said nothing about the septic problems. The DeClarks bought the property and, one week later, learned that the property was unbuildable. They sued, and the trial court granted them rescission. The Fimbels appealed.

ISSUE: Did the Fimbels have a duty to disclose the septic problems?

DECISION: Yes, the Fimbels had a duty to disclose. Affirmed.

REASONING: If a buyer questions the condition or quality of property, a seller is obligated to disclose what he knows. When asked if he had ever planned to construct a house on the lots, Fimbel replied that he had considered doing so but decided instead to build on land he owned in Minnesota, near a friend's residence. DeClark mentioned that he did in fact want to erect a house on the property. That conversation obligated Fimbel to inform DeClark about the septic problem.

Fimbel argues that he never misrepresented the soil's condition. Although that is technically accurate, Fimbel's statement as to why he preferred to build in Minnesota was only partially correct, at best. He concealed what he knew about the land he was selling. Creating a false impression by partially disclosing facts is misrepresentation. The Fimbels' silence, together with their misrepresentation, makes them liable for fraud. ◢

ETHICS

There are various disclosure rules that a state could adopt:

- Caveat emptor—let the buyer beware.

- Seller has a duty to disclose only if asked.

- Seller has a duty to disclose regardless of whether asked.

- Seller's only duty is to notify buyer of important considerations that buyer may wish to investigate (soil condition, building laws, problems with neighboring property, etc.).

Which rule do you prefer, and why? As you answer this question, apply these concepts from the Chapter 2 ethics checklist: What are the alternatives? What outcome does the Golden Rule require? ▪

MISTAKE

Most contract principles come from appellate courts, but in the area of "legal mistake" a cow wrote much of the law. The cow was Rose 2d of Aberlone, a gentle animal that lived in Michigan in 1886. Rose's owner, Hiram Walker & Sons, had bought her for $850. After a few years, the company concluded that Rose could have no calves. As a barren cow she was worth much less, so Walker contracted to sell her to T. C. Sherwood for $80. But when Sherwood came to collect Rose, the parties realized she was pregnant. Walker refused to part with the happy mother, and Sherwood sued. Walker defended, claiming that both parties had made a mistake and that the contract was voidable.

Mistake can occur in many ways. The first distinction is between bilateral and unilateral mistakes.

Bilateral Mistake

A **bilateral mistake** occurs when both parties negotiate based on the same factual error. Sherwood and Walker both thought Rose was barren, both negotiated accordingly, and both were wrong. The Michigan Supreme Court gave judgment for Walker, the seller, permitting him to rescind the contract because the parties were both wrong about the essence of what they were bargaining for.

If the parties contract based on an important factual error, the contract is voidable by the injured party. Sherwood and Walker were both wrong about Rose's reproductive ability, and the error was basic enough to cause a tenfold difference in price. Walker, the injured party, was entitled to rescind the contract. Note that the error must be *factual*. Suppose Walker sold Rose thinking that the price of beef was going to drop, when in fact the price rose 60% in five months. He made a mistake, but it was simply a business prediction that proved wrong. Walker would have no right to rescind.

Conscious Uncertainty. No rescission is permitted where one of the parties knows he is taking on a risk, that is, he realizes there is uncertainty about the quality of the thing being exchanged. Rufus offers 10 acres of mountainous land to Priscilla. "I can't promise you anything about this land," he says, "but they've found gold on every adjoining parcel." Priscilla, panting with gold lust, buys the land, digs long and hard, and discovers—mud. She may not rescind the contract because she understood the risk.

Unilateral Mistake

Sometimes only one party enters a contract under a mistaken assumption, a situation called **unilateral mistake.** In these cases it is more difficult for the injured party to rescind a contract. To rescind for unilateral mistake, a party must demonstrate that she entered the contract because of a basic factual error and that either (1) enforcing the contract would be unconscionable; or (2) the nonmistaken party knew of the error.

UNDUE INFLUENCE

She was single and pregnant. A shy young woman in a large city with no family nearby, she needed help and support. She went to the Methodist Mission Home of Texas, where she found room and board, support, and a lot of counseling. Her discussions with a minister and a private counselor stressed one point: that she should give up her baby for adoption. She signed the adoption papers, but days later she decided she wanted the baby after all. Was there any ground to rescind? She claimed undue influence, in other words, that the Mission Home so dominated her thinking that she never truly consented. Where one party has used undue influence, the contract is voidable at the option of the injured party. There are two elements to the plaintiff's case. **To prove undue influence, the injured party must demonstrate:**

- A relationship between the two parties either of trust or of domination, and

- Improper persuasion by the stronger party.

In other words, a party seeking to rescind based on undue influence must first show that the parties had some close bond, either because one would normally have trusted and relied on the other or because one was able to dominate the other. Second, the party seeking to rescind must show improper persuasion, which is an effort by the stronger party to coerce the weaker one into a decision that she otherwise would not have made.

Keeping those two factors in mind, what should be the outcome of the Methodist Mission case? The court held that the plaintiff had been young and extremely vulnerable during the emotional days following the birth of her child. The mission's counselor, to whom she turned for support, had spent day after day forcefully insisting that the young woman had no moral or legal right to keep her child. The harangue amounted to undue influence. The court voided the adoption agreement.[2]

Chapter Conclusion

An agreement between two parties may not be enough to make a contract enforceable. A minor or a mentally impaired person may generally disaffirm contracts. Even if both parties are adults of sound mind, courts will insist that consent be genuine. Misrepresentation, mistake, and undue influence all indicate that at least one party did not truly consent. As the law evolves, it imposes an increasingly greater burden of good-faith negotiating on the party in the stronger position. Do not bargain for a contract that is too good to be true.

Chapter Review

1. Capacity and consent are different contract issues that can lead to the same result: a voidable contract. A voidable agreement is one that can be canceled by a party who lacks legal capacity or who did not give true consent.

2. A minor (someone under the age of 18) generally may disaffirm any contract while she is still a minor or within a reasonable time after reaching age 18.

3. A minor who disaffirms must make restitution; that is, she must return to the other party whatever consideration she received, such as goods that she purchased. If she cannot make restitution because the goods are damaged or destroyed, in most states the minor is still entitled to disaffirm and receive her money.

---

[2] *Methodist Mission Home of Texas v. N A B*, 451 S.W.2nd 539, 1970 Tex. App. LEXIS 2055 (Tex. Civ. App. 1970).

4. A mentally impaired person may generally disaffirm a contract. In this case, though, he generally must make restitution.

5. Fraud and misrepresentation. Both fraud and material misrepresentation are grounds for disaffirming a contract. The injured party must prove:

    (a) A false statement of fact; and

    (b) Fraud *or* materiality; and

    (c) Justifiable reliance.

6. Silence amounts to misrepresentation when disclosure is necessary to correct a previous assertion or to correct a basic mistake.

7. *Mistake.* In a case of bilateral mistake, either party may rescind the contract. In a case of unilateral mistake, the injured party may rescind only upon a showing that enforcement would be unconscionable or that the other party knew of her mistake.

8. *Undue Influence.* Once again the injured party may rescind a contract, but only upon a showing of a special relationship and improper persuasion.

PRACTICE TEST

Matching Questions

Match the following terms with their definitions:

___ **A.** Undue influence

___ **B.** Disaffirm

___ **C.** Restitution

___ **D.** Fraud

___ **E.** Misrepresentation

1. Misstatement of fact.

2. The intention to deceive the other party.

3. One party to a contract notifies the other that he refuses to go through with the agreement.

4. Restoring the other party to its original position.

5. A dominant relationship together with improper persuasion.

True/False Questions

Circle true or false:

1. T   F   A minor may disaffirm a contract for any reason at all.

2. T   F   A mentally ill person may not disaffirm a contract, but may request restitution.

3. T   F   A contract may not be rescinded based on puffery.

4. T   F   A fraudulent statement permits rescission, regardless of whether there was reliance.

5. T   F   A seller of property must generally disclose latent defects that he knows about.

Multiple-Choice Questions

6. Sarah, age 17, uses $850 of her hard-earned, summer-job money to pay cash for a diamond pendant for the senior prom. She has a wonderful time at the dance but decides the pendant was an extravagance, returns it, and demands a refund. The store has a "no refund" policy that is clearly stated, on a sign on the wall. There was no defect in the pendent. The store refuses the refund. When Sarah sues, she will

    (a) Win $850.

    (b) Win $425.

    (c) Win, but only if she did not notice the "no refund" policy.

    (d) Win, but only if she did not think the "no refund" policy applied to her.

    (e) Lose.

7. Miles is selling his used Corvette for $35,000. "The brakes have less than 1,000 miles on them," he says, knowing that in fact the brakes are old and need replacement. Kody buys the car, takes it to his mechanic, and instructs the man to install new, larger racing brakes. When the mechanic informs Kody that the existing brakes had at least 40,000 miles on them, Kody sues Miles.

   (a) Kody will win because Miles committed fraud.

   (b) Kody will win because Miles committed misrepresentation.

   (c) Kody will win because Miles expected him to rely on a false statement.

   (d) Kody will win because Miles has shown deliberate bad faith.

   (e) Kody will lose because he did not rely on the statement.

8. Tobias is selling a Surrealist painting. He tells Maud that the picture is by the famous French artist Magritte, although in fact Tobias has no idea whether that is true or not. Tobias's statement is

   (a) Bilateral mistake.

   (b) Unilateral mistake.

   (c) Fraud.

   (d) Misrepresentation.

   (e) Legal, as long as he acted in good faith.

9. Beverly, a sales clerk, sells a $6,000 stereo to Samantha. The next day, Samantha's brother comes to the store and presents a doctor's letter indicating that Samantha is mentally disabled. The store refuses to refund the money.

   (a) Samantha is not entitled to her money back unless the clerk suspected she had mental health problems.

   (b) Samantha would only be entitled to her money if the clerk had seen the doctor's letter before selling the stereo.

   (c) Samantha is entitled to her money back, but she must return the stereo.

   (d) Samantha is entitled to her money back, and she does not have to return the stereo.

   (e) Samantha is not entitled to her money back.

10. Marty, a college student, finds a pretty ring on the way to class. He shows it to Felicia. "Gorgeous," she says. "Is that a real emerald?" "I have no idea what it is," Marty answers truthfully. "I'll sell it to you for a hundred bucks." Felicia buys it. When she discovers that the colored stone is glass, she sues for her $100. Felicia

   (a) Wins, based on fraud.

   (b) Wins, based on misrepresentation.

   (c) Wins, based on mutual mistake.

   (d) Wins, based on unilateral mistake.

   (e) Loses.

Short-Answer Questions

11. On television and in magazines, Maurine and Mamie Mason saw numerous advertisements for Chrysler Fifth Avenue automobiles. The ads described the car as "luxurious," "quality-engineered," and "reliable." When they went to inspect the car, the salesman told them the warranty was "the best . . . comparable to Cadillacs and Lincolns." After the Masons bought a Fifth Avenue, they began to have many problems with it. Even after numerous repairs, the car was unsatisfactory and required more work. The Masons sued, seeking to rescind the contract based on the ads and the dealer's statement. Will they win?

12. John Marshall and Kirsten Fletcher decided to live together. They leased an apartment, each agreeing to pay one half of the rent. When he signed the lease, Marshall was 17. Shortly after signing the lease, Marshall turned 18, and two weeks later he moved into the apartment. He paid his half of the rent for two months and then moved out because he and Fletcher were not getting along. Fletcher sued Marshall for one half of the monthly rent for the remainder of the lease. Who wins?

13. The McAllisters had several serious problems with their house, including leaks in the ceiling, a buckling wall, and dampness throughout. They repaired the buckling wall by installing I-beams to support it. They never resolved the leaks and the dampness. When they decided to sell the house, they said nothing to prospective buyers about the problems. They stated that the I-beam had been added for reinforcement.

The Silvas bought the house for $60,000. Soon afterwards, they began to have problems with leaks, mildew, and dampness. Are the Silvas entitled to any money damages? Why or why not?

14. **ETHICS:** Sixteen-year-old Travis Mitchell brought his 19-year-old Pontiac GTO into M&M Precision Body and Paint for body work and a paint job. M&M did the work and charged $1,900, which Travis paid. Travis later complained about the quality of the work and M&M did some touching up, but Travis was still dissatisfied. Travis demanded his $1,900 back, but M&M refused to give it back since all of the work was "in" the car and Travis could not return it to the shop. The state of Nebraska, where this occurred, follows the majority rule on this issue. Does Travis get his money? What is the common-law rule? Who ought to win? Is the common-law rule fair? What is the rationale for the rule?

15. Susan Gould was appointed to a three-year probationary position as a teacher at Sewanhaka High School. Normally, after three years, the school board either grants tenure or dismisses the teacher. The Sewanhaka school board notified Gould she would not be rehired. To keep the termination out of her file, Gould agreed to resign. In fact, because Gould had previously taught at a different New York school, state law required that she be given a tenure decision after only two years. If the board failed to do that, the teacher was automatically tenured. When she learned this, Gould sued to rescind her agreement to resign. Is Gould entitled to rescind the contract (i.e., her agreement to resign)?

16. **ROLE REVERSAL:** Write a short-essay question that includes one instance each of puffery, misrepresentation, and fraud.

Internet Research Problem

Visit **http://www.tobaccofreekids.org** and find the link that focuses on marketing to children. Use the ethics checklist from Chapter 9 to analyze the conduct described. Should society limit tobacco marketing? If not, why not? If so, should it be done by legislation, regulation, litigation, or some other means?

You can find further practice problems in the Online Quiz at **http://beatty.westbuslaw.com** or in the Study Guide that accompanies this text.

13

Written Contracts

Oliver and Perry were college roommates, two sophomores with contrasting personalities. They were sitting in the cafeteria with some friends. Oliver suggested that they buy a lottery ticket, as the prize for that week's drawing was $13 million. Perry muttered, "Nah. You never win if you buy just one ticket." Oliver bubbled up, "OK, we'll buy a ticket every week. We'll keep buying them from now until we graduate. This month, I'll buy the tickets. Next month, you will, and so on." Other students urged Perry to do it and, finally, grudgingly, he agreed. The two friends carefully reviewed their deal. Each party was providing consideration, namely, the responsibility for purchasing tickets during his month. The amount of each purchase was clearly defined at one dollar. They would start that week and continue until graduation day, two and a half years down the road. Finally, they would share equally any money won. As three witnesses looked on, they shook hands on the bargain. That month, Oliver bought a ticket every week, randomly choosing numbers, and won nothing. The next month, Perry bought a ticket with equally random numbers—and won $52 million. Perry moved out of their dorm room into a suite at the Ritz and refused to give Oliver one red cent. Oliver sued, seeking $26 million, and the return of an Eric Clapton compact disk that he had loaned Perry. If the former friends had understood the statute of frauds, they would never have slid into this mess. ▪

The rule we examine in this chapter is not exactly news. The British Parliament passed the original statute of frauds in 1677. The purpose was to prevent lying (fraud) in contracts that historically were the most important. The law required that in six types of cases, a contract would be enforced only if it were in writing. Almost all states in this country later passed their own statutes making the same requirements. It is important to remember, as we examine the rules and exceptions, that Parliament and the state legislatures all wanted to provide a court with the best possible evidence of whether the parties intended to make a contract.

The statute of frauds: A plaintiff may not enforce any of the following agreements, unless the agreement, or some memorandum of it, is in writing and signed by the defendant. The agreements that must be in writing are those:

- For any interest in **land.**
- That cannot be performed within **one year.**
- To pay the **debt of another.**
- Made by an executor of an **estate.**
- Made in consideration of **marriage**; and
- For the sale of **goods worth $500 or more.**

Unenforceable

In other words, when two parties make an agreement covered by any one of these six topics, it must be in writing to be enforceable. Oliver and Perry agreed to share the cost—and proceeds—of lottery tickets for two and one half years. But a contract must be in writing if it cannot be performed within one year. The good news is, Oliver gets back his Eric Clapton disk. The bad news is he gets none of the lottery money. Perry the pessimist will walk away with all $52 million.

Contracts That Must Be in Writing

AGREEMENTS FOR AN INTEREST IN LAND

A contract for the sale of any interest in land must be in writing to be enforceable. Notice the phrase "interest in land." This means any legal right regarding land. A house on a lot is an interest in land. A mortgage, an easement, and a leased apartment are all interests in land.

Kary Presten and Ken Sailer were roommates in a rental apartment in New Jersey, with a view of the Manhattan skyline. The lease was in Sailer's name, but the two split all expenses. Then the building became a "cooperative," meaning that each tenant would have the option of buying the apartment. Sailer learned he could buy his unit for only $55,800 if he promptly paid a $1,000 fee to maintain his rights. He mentioned to Presten that he planned to buy the unit, and Presten asked if he could become half owner. Sailer agreed and borrowed the $1,000 from Presten to pay his initial fee. But as the time for closing on the purchase came nearer, Sailer realized that he could sell the apartment for a substantial profit. He placed an ad in a paper, and promptly received a firm offer for $125,000. Sailer then told Presten that their deal was off, and that he, Sailer, would be buying the unit alone. He did exactly that, and Presten filed suit. Regrettably, the outcome of Presten's suit was only too easy to predict.

A cooperative apartment is an interest in land, said the court. This agreement could be enforced only if put in writing and signed by Sailer. The parties had put nothing in writing, and therefore Presten was out of luck. He was entitled to his $1,000 back, but nothing more. The apartment belonged to Sailer, who could live in it or sell it for a large, quick profit.

Exception: Full Performance by the Seller

If the seller completely performs her side of a contract for an interest in land, a court is likely to enforce the agreement even if it was oral. Adam orally agrees to sell his condominium to Maggie for $150,000. Adam delivers the deed to Maggie and expects his money a week later, but Maggie fails to pay. Most courts will allow Adam to enforce the oral contract and collect the full purchase price from Maggie.

Exception: Part Performance by the Buyer

The buyer of land may be able to enforce an oral contract if she paid part of the purchase price and either entered upon the land *or* made improvements to it. Suppose that Eloise sues Grover to enforce an alleged oral contract to sell a lot in Happydale. She claims they struck a bargain in January. Grover defends based on the statute of frauds, saying that even if the two did reach an oral agreement, it is unenforceable. Eloise proves that she paid 10% of the purchase price and that in February she began excavating on the lot, to build a house, and that Grover knew of the work. Eloise has established part performance and will be allowed to enforce her contract.

This exception makes sense if we recall the purpose of the statute of frauds: to provide the best possible evidence of the parties' intentions. The fact that Grover permitted Eloise to enter upon the land and begin building on it is compelling evidence that the two parties had reached an agreement.

Exception: Promissory Estoppel

The other exception to the writing requirement is our old friend promissory estoppel. **If a promisor makes an oral promise that should reasonably cause the promisee to rely on it, and the promisee does rely, the promisee *may* be able to enforce the promise,** despite the statute of frauds, if that is the only way to avoid injustice. This exception potentially applies to any contract that must be written (not only to agreements concerning land).

Maureen Sullivan and James Rooney lived together for seven years, although they never married. They decided to buy a house. The parties agreed that they would be equal owners, but Rooney told Sullivan that in order to obtain Veterans Affairs financing he would have to be the sole owner on the deed. They each contributed to the purchase and maintenance of the house, and Rooney repeatedly told Sullivan that he would change the deed to joint ownership. He never did. When the couple split up, Sullivan sued, seeking a 50% interest in the house. She won. The agreement was for an interest in land and should have been in writing, said the court. But Rooney had clearly promised Sullivan that she would be a half owner, and she had relied by contributing to the purchase and maintenance. The statute of frauds was passed to prevent fraud, not to enable one person to mislead another and benefit at her expense.

In the following case, the plaintiffs make three valiant efforts to evade the piercing grasp of the statute of frauds.

CASE SUMMARY

HERSHON v. CANNON

1993 U.S. Dist. LEXIS 689
United States District Court, District of Maryland, 1993

FACTS: Mary Drysdale and her husband, Simon Hershon, wanted to buy Tulip Hill, an 18th-century mansion located on 54 acres in Anne Arundel County, Maryland. Drysdale and Hershon orally agreed with Cannon on a purchase price of $1.2 million. Cannon promised that while the lawyers were drafting the written purchase agreement, he would not seek offers from anyone else. Also, if he received an unsolicited offer, he agreed to give Drysdale and Hershon the opportunity to match it.

Drysdale and Hershon applied for a mortgage to buy Tulip Hill. They also met with the Maryland Historical Commission to discuss improvements to the property. Meanwhile, Cannon sold Tulip Hill to someone else. Drysdale and Hershon sued.

ISSUE: Did Drysdale and Hershon have an enforceable contract for Tulip Hill?

DECISION: No, the plaintiffs have no enforceable contract. Case dismissed.

REASONING: The buyers admit that they have no written contract but make three arguments for enforcement of an oral agreement. First, they claim that they are only trying to enforce Cannon's agreement not to sell elsewhere. Wrong. What they are really trying to do is enforce an oral contract for the sale of real estate, and they may not do it.

Next, they urge part performance. The buyers did meet with an historical commission, apply for mortgages, and liquidate assets. They might, however, have taken these steps in anticipation of an agreement; the actions are too ambiguous to demonstrate a contract.

Finally, the buyers suggest that promissory estoppel entitles them to complete the purchase. The problem is that even if they relied on Cannon's promises, the actions they took were very modest. They will suffer no great injustice if denied Tulip Hill. Their claims must be dismissed. ◢

AGREEMENTS THAT CANNOT BE PERFORMED WITHIN ONE YEAR

Contracts that cannot be performed within one year are unenforceable unless they are in writing. This one-year period begins on the date the parties make the agreement. The critical phrase here is "*cannot* be performed within one year." If a contract *could* be completed within one year, it need not be in writing. Betty gets a job at Burger Brain, throwing fries in oil. Her boss tells her she can have Fridays off for as long as she works there. That oral contract is enforceable, whether Betty stays one week or five years. It could have been performed within one year if, say, Betty quit the job after six months. Therefore it does not need to be in writing.

If the agreement will necessarily take longer than one year to finish, it must be in writing to be enforceable. If Betty is hired for three years as manager of Burger Brain, the agreement is unenforceable unless put in writing. She cannot perform three years of work in one year.

Type of Agreement	Enforceability
Cannot be performed within one year. *Example:* An offer of employment for three years.	Must be in writing to be enforceable.
Might be performed within one year, although could take many years to perform. *Example:* "As long as you work here at Burger Brain you may have Fridays off."	Enforceable whether it is oral or written, since the employee might quit working a month later.

PROMISE TO PAY THE DEBT OF ANOTHER

When one person agrees to pay the debt of another as a favor to that debtor, it is called a collateral promise, and it must be in writing to be enforceable. D. R. Kemp was a young entrepreneur who wanted to build housing in Tuscaloosa, Alabama. He needed $25,000 to complete a project he was working on, so he went to his old college professor, Jim Hanks, for help. Professor Hanks spoke with his good friend Travis Chandler, telling him that Kemp was highly responsible and would be certain to repay any money loaned. The professor assured Chandler that if for any reason Kemp did not repay the loan, he, Hanks, would pay in full. With that assurance, Chandler wrote out a check for $25,000, payable to Kemp, never having met the young man.

Kemp, of course, never repaid the loan. (Thank goodness he did not; this textbook has no use for people who do what they are supposed to.) Kemp exhausted the cash trying to sustain his business, which failed anyway, so he had nothing to give his creditor. Chandler approached Professor Hanks, who refused to pay (some professor!), and Chandler sued. The outcome was only too predictable. Chandler had nothing in writing, and that is exactly what he got from his lawsuit—nothing.

PROMISE MADE BY AN EXECUTOR OF AN ESTATE

This rule is merely a special application of the previous one, concerning the debt of another person. An executor is the person who is in charge of an estate after someone dies. The executor's job is to pay debts of the deceased, obtain money owed to him, and disburse the assets according to the will. In most cases, the executor will use only the estate's assets to pay those debts. The statute of frauds comes into play only when an executor promises to pay an estate's debts with her own funds. **An executor's promise to use her own funds to pay a debt of the deceased must be in writing to be enforceable.** Suppose Esmeralda dies penniless, owing Tina $35,000. Emeralda's daughter, Sapphire, is the executor of her estate. Tina comes to Sapphire and demands her $35,000. Sapphire responds, "There is no money in mama's estate, but don't worry, I'll make it up to you with my own money." Sapphire's oral promise is unenforceable. Tina should get it in writing while Sapphire is feeling generous.

PROMISE MADE IN CONSIDERATION OF MARRIAGE

Barney is a multimillionaire with the integrity of a gangster and the charm of a tax collector. He proposes to Li-Tsing, who promptly rejects him. Barney then pleads that if Li-Tsing will be his bride, he will give her an island he owns off the coast of California. Li-Tsing begins to see his good qualities and accepts. After they are married, Barney refuses to deliver the deed. Li-Tsing will get nothing from a court either, since **a promise made in consideration of marriage must be in writing to be enforceable.**

What the Writing Must Contain

Each of the five types of contract described above must be in writing in order to be enforceable. What must the writing contain? It may be a carefully typed contract, using precise legal terminology, or an informal memorandum scrawled on the back of a paper napkin at a business lunch. The writing may consist of more than one document, written at different times, with each document making a piece of the puzzle. But there are some general requirements: **The contract or memorandum**

- **Must be signed by the defendant;** and

- **Must state with reasonable certainty the name of each party, the subject matter of the agreement, and all of the essential terms and promises.**

SIGNATURE

A statute of frauds typically states that the writing must be "signed by the party to be charged therewith," that is, the party who is resisting enforcement of the contract. Throughout this chapter we refer to that person as the defendant, since when these cases go to court, it is the defendant who is disputing the existence of a contract.

Judges define "signature" very broadly. Using a pen to write one's name, though sufficient, is not required. A secretary who stamps an executive's signature on a letter fulfills this requirement. Any other mark or logo placed on a document to indicate acceptance, even an "X," will likely satisfy the statute of frauds. Electronic commerce creates new methods of signing—and new controversies, discussed in the Cyberlaw feature later in the chapter.

REASONABLE CERTAINTY

Suppose Garfield and Hayes are having lunch, discussing the sale of Garfield's vacation condominium. They agree on a price and want to make some notation of the agreement even before their lawyers work out a detailed purchase and sales agreement. A perfectly adequate memorandum might say, "Garfield agrees to sell Hayes his condominium at 234 Baron Boulevard, apartment 18, for $350,000 cash, payable on June 18, 2005, and Hayes promises to pay the sum on that day." They should make two copies of their agreement and sign both. Notice that although Garfield's memo is short, it is certain and complete.

Sale of Goods

The UCC requires a writing for the sale of goods worth $500 or more. This is the sixth and final contract that must be in writing, although the Code's requirements are easier to meet than those of the common law.

UCC §2-201(1)—THE BASIC RULE

A contract for the sale of goods worth $500 or more is not enforceable unless there is some writing, signed by the defendant, indicating that the parties reached an agreement. The key difference between the common-law rule and the UCC rule is that the Code does not require all of the terms of the agreement to be in writing. The Code looks for something simpler: an indication that the parties reached an agreement. The two things that *are* essential are the signature of the defendant and the quantity of goods being sold. The quantity of goods is required because this is the one term for which there will be no objective evidence. Suppose a short memorandum between textile dealers indicates that Seller will sell to Buyer "grade AA 100% cotton, white athletic socks." If the writing does not state the price, the parties can testify at court about what the market price was at the time of the deal. But how many socks were to be delivered? One hundred pairs, or 100,000? The quantity must be written. (A basic sale-of-goods contract appears at **http://www.lectlaw.com/form.html**.)

Writing	Result
"Confirming phone conversation today, I will send you 1,000 reams of paper for laser printing, usual quality & price. [Signed,] Seller."	This memorandum satisfies UCC §2-201(1), and the contract may be enforced against the seller. The buyer may testify as to the "usual" quality and price between the two parties, and both sides may rely on normal trade usage.
"Confirming phone conversation today, I will send you best quality paper for laser printing, $3.25 per ream, delivery date next Thursday. [Signed,] Seller."	This memorandum is not enforceable because it states no quantity.

UCC §2-201(2)—THE MERCHANTS' EXCEPTION

When both parties are "merchants," that is, businesspeople who routinely deal in the goods being sold, the Code will accept an even more informal writing. **Within a reasonable time of making an oral contract, if one merchant sends a written confirmation to the other, and the confirmation is definite enough to bind the sender herself, then the merchant who receives the confirmation will also be bound by it unless he objects in writing within 10 days.**

Madge manufactures "beanies," that is, silly caps with plastic propellers on top. Rachel, a retailer, telephones her and they discuss the price of the beanies, shipping time, and other details. Madge then faxes Rachel a memo: "This confirms your order for 2,500 beanies at $12.25 per beanie. Colors: blue, green, black, orange, red. Delivery date: 10 days. [Signed] Madge." Rachel receives the fax and throws it in the wastebasket. She buys her beanies elsewhere and Madge sues. Rachel claims there is no written contract because she never signed anything. Madge wins, under UCC §2-201(2). Both parties were merchants, because they routinely dealt in these goods. Madge signed and sent a confirming memo that could have been used to hold her, Madge, to the deal. When Rachel received it, she was not free to disregard it. Obviously, the intelligent business practice would have been promptly to fax a reply saying, "I disagree. We do not have any deal for beanies." Since Rachel failed to respond within 10 days, Madge has an enforceable contract. In the following case, the merchant's confirmation contained a troubling ambiguity.

CASE SUMMARY

GPL TREATMENT, LTD. v. LOUISIANA-PACIFIC CORP.

323 Or. 116, 914 P.2d 682, 1996 Ore. LEXIS 34
Oregon Supreme Court, 1996

FACTS: GPL manufactures and sells cedar shakes, which are wooden shingles that many homeowners use for their roofs. Louisiana-Pacific (L-P) often purchased shakes from GPL. Executives of the two companies negotiated over the telephone and allegedly agreed that L-P would buy 88 truckloads of shakes. GPL sent an "Order Confirmation" form that included this language:

> "CONDITIONS OF SALES: GPL LTD.
> "All orders accepted subject to strikes, labor troubles, car shortages or other contingencies beyond our power to control. Any freight rate increases, sales, or use taxes is for buyers account.
> "SIGN CONFIRMATION COPY AND RETURN BY: _____ THANK YOU."

L-P neither signed nor rejected the form. The company accepted 13 truckloads of shakes but about that time the market price of shakes dropped, and L-P refused to accept any more. GPL sued. A jury awarded the company its lost profits, and the court of appeals affirmed. L-P appealed, arguing that, because GPL's form required the buyer to sign, no acceptance was valid without a signature.

ISSUE: Was GPL's form sufficient to satisfy the merchants' exception to the statute of frauds?

DECISION: Yes, GPL's form satisfied the merchant's exception. Affirmed.

REASONING: GPL's confirmation form clearly identified the parties, price, and quantity of goods. After GPL signed the document, L-P received it and did not object within 10 days. The order form would have been sufficient against GPL, the sender, if the price of shakes suddenly increased and the company tried to get out of the deal. Therefore, it would normally be valid against the buyer, too.

L-P argues that the phrase "sign confirmation copy and return" indicates that GPL did not expect either party to be bound by the agreement until L-P signed and returned a copy. That is not, however, what those words indicate. The phrase simply asks the recipient to acknowledge receipt of the form. This was nothing more than GPL's method of record keeping. The form satisfied the merchant exception of UCC §2-201 (2). ◢

AT RISK | Assume that you work for GPL. What change in the form should you make? ▪

CYBERLAW | **Electronic Contracts and Signatures.** E-commerce has grown at a dazzling rate, and U.S. enterprises buy and sell tens of billions of dollars worth of goods and services over the Internet. What happens to the writing requirement, though, when there is no paper? The present statute of frauds requires some sort of "signing" to ensure that the defendant committed to the deal. Today, an "electronic signature" could mean a name typed (or automatically included) at the bottom of an e-mail message, a retinal or vocal scan, or a name signed by electronic pen on a writing tablet, among others.

Are electronic signatures valid? Yes. State legislatures and Congress are struggling to craft a cohesive law, and the job is incomplete, but here are the rules so far:

- The **Uniform Electronic Transaction Act** (UETA). This proposed legislation was drafted by the National Conference of Commissioners on Uniform State Laws, who also draft the UCC. As this book goes to press, UETA is the law in about 48 states and territories, with more likely to adopt it soon. UETA declares that a contract or signature may not be denied enforceability simply because it is in electronic form. In other words, the normal rules of contract law apply, but one party may not avoid such a deal simply because it originated in cyberspace.

- The **Electronic Signatures in Global and National Commerce Act** (E-Sign). This federal statute, which applies in any state that has not adopted UETA, also states that contracts will not be denied enforcement simply because they are in electronic form, or signed electronically.

With cyberlaw in its early stages, how can an executive take advantage of the Internet's commercial opportunities while protecting his company against losses unique to the field?

First, acknowledge the risks, which include lost or intercepted communications, fraudulently altered documents, and difficulties authenticating the source of an offer or acceptance. Second, be cautious about "electronic signatures." Assume that any commitments you make electronically can be enforced against you. Paradoxically, if the contract is important, do not assume that the other party's promises, if made electronically, are enforceable unless your lawyer has given you assurance.

Parol Evidence

Tyrone agrees to buy Martha's house for $800,000. The contract obligates Tyrone to make a 10% down payment immediately and pay the remaining $720,000 in 45 days. As the two parties sign the deal, Tyrone discusses his need for financing. Unfortunately, at the end of 45 days, he has failed to get a mortgage. He claims that the parties orally agreed that he would get his deposit back if he could not obtain financing. But the written agreement says no such thing, and Martha disputes the claim. Who will win? Martha, because of the parol evidence rule. To understand this rule, you need to know two terms. **Parol evidence** refers to anything (apart from the written contract itself) that was said, done, or written before the parties signed the agreement or as they signed it. Martha's conversation with Tyrone about financing the house was parol evidence. The other important term is **integrated contract,** which means a writing that the parties intend as the final, complete expression of their agreement. Now for the rule.

The parol evidence rule: When two parties make an integrated contract, neither one may use parol evidence to contradict, vary, or add to its terms. Negotiations may last for hours or years. Almost no contract includes everything that the parties said. When parties consider their agreement integrated, any statements they made before or while signing are irrelevant. If a court determines that Martha and Tyrone intended their agreement to be integrated, it will prohibit testimony about Martha's oral promises.

EXCEPTION: AN INCOMPLETE OR AMBIGUOUS CONTRACT

If a court determines that a written contract is incomplete or ambiguous, it will permit parol evidence. Suppose that an employment contract states that the company will provide "full health coverage for Robert Watson and his family." Three years later, Watson divorces and remarries, acquiring three stepchildren, and a year later his second wife has a baby. Watson now has two children by his first marriage, and four by the second. The company refuses to ensure Watson's first wife or his stepchildren. A court will probably find that the health care clause is ambiguous. A judge cannot determine exactly what the clause means from the contract itself, so the parties will be permitted to introduce parol evidence to prove whether or not the company must insure Watson's extended family.

One way to avoid parol evidence disputes is to include an **integration clause.** That is a statement clearly proclaiming that this writing is the full and final expression of the parties' agreement, and that anything said before signing or while signing is irrelevant.

Chapter Conclusion

Some contracts must be in writing to be enforceable. Drafting the contract need not be arduous. The disputes illustrated in this chapter could all have been prevented with a few carefully crafted sentences. It is worth the time and effort to write them.

Chapter Review

1. Contracts that must be in writing to be enforceable concern:

    - The sale of any interest in land.
    - Agreements that cannot be performed within one year.
    - Promises to pay the debt of another.
    - Promises made by an executor of an estate.
    - Promises made in consideration of marriage; and
    - The sale of goods for $500 or more.

2. The writing must be signed by the defendant and must state the names of all parties, the subject matter of the agreement, and all essential terms and promises.

3. A contract or memorandum for the sale of goods may be less complete than those required by the common law.

4. Between merchants, even less is required. If one merchant sends written confirmation of a contract, the merchant who receives the document must object within 10 days or be bound by the writing.

5. When an integrated contract exists, neither party may generally use parol evidence to contradict, vary, or add to its terms.

PRACTICE TEST

Matching Questions

Match the following terms with their definitions:

___ **A.** Executor

___ **B.** Parol evidence

___ **C.** Merchant exception

___ **D.** Integration clause

___ **E.** Part performance

1. Entry onto land, or improvements made to it, by a buyer who has no written contract.

2. A rule permitting enforcement of certain oral contracts for the sale of goods.

3. A provision limiting a contract to the writing alone.

4. The person in charge of a deceased's estate.

5. Anything said or written before the parties sign a contract or as they do so.

True/False Questions

Circle true or false:

1. T F An agreement for the sale of a house does not need to be in writing if the deal will be completed within one year.

2. T F An agreement for the sale of 600 plastic cups, worth $.50 each, does not need to be in writing to be enforceable.

3. T F An agreement to lease an apartment for two years must be in writing to be enforceable.

4. T F To create an enforceable contract, the signatures must appear on a "hard copy," i.e., a piece of paper.

5. T F On Monday, two parties sign a written contract for the sale of 600 athletic jerseys. On Tuesday, the parties orally modify the deliver date. The oral modification is barred by the parol evidence rule.

Multiple-Choice Questions

6. Louise e-mails Sonya, "I will sell you my house at 129 Brittle Blvd. for $88,000, payable in one month. Best, Louise." Sonya e-mails back, "Louise, I accept the offer to buy your house at that price. Sonya." Neither party prints a copy of the two e-mails.

   (a) The parties have a binding contract for the sale of Louise's house.

   (b) Louise is bound by the agreement but Sonya is not.

   (c) Sonya is bound by the agreement but Louise is not.

   (d) Neither party is bound because the agreement was never put in writing.

   (e) Neither party is bound because the agreement was never signed.

7. Raul sends Barclay a fax: "Confirm our agreement; you buy 9,000 pounds of my Grade A peanuts; market price next September. Raul." Barclay spends two weeks negotiating with other peanut salesmen for a better price, but fails to find them cheaper. He e-mails Raul, "Accept.Barclay."

   (a) The parties have a binding contract for peanuts.

   (b) Raul is bound by his fax but Barclay is not bound.

   (c) Barclay is bound by his email, but Raul is not bound.

   (d) Neither party is bound because Barclay counteroffered.

   (e) Neither party is bound because this contract must be in writing.

8. In February, Chuck orally agrees to sell his hunting cabin, with 15 acres, to Kyle for $35,000, with the deal to be completed in July, when Kyle will have the money. In March, while Chuck is vacationing on his land, he permits

Kyle to enter the land and dig the foundation for a new cottage. In July, Kyle arrives with the money but Chuck refuses to sell. Kyle sues.

(a) Chuck wins because the contract was never put in writing.

(b) Chuck wins because the contract terms were unclear.

(c) Kyle wins because a contract for vacation property does not need to be written.

(d) Kyle wins because Chuck allowed him to dig the foundation.

(e) Kyle wins because Chuck has committed fraud.

9. Cathy hires Molly to work in her shop. "You will start as a sales clerk. After 18 months, I promise to make you store manager, at a 50% pay raise." Molly works for 18 months, and several times Cathy renews the promise about manager. After 18 months, Cathy says, "The store isn't doing well. I can't afford to make you manager." Molly sues. Her best argument is

(a) Statute of frauds.

(b) Part performance.

(c) Parol evidence.

(d) Promissory estoppel.

(e) Reasonable certainty.

10. Barney sells a sophisticated computer system to a large warehouse, for $320,000. Both parties sign a written contract. A month later, when the warehouse complains about the system, Barney states that there were no warranties included. The warehouse replies that as they were negotiating the agreement, Barney promised to fix any glitches that arose during the first six months. Barney's best defense is

(a) UETA.

(b) Part performance.

(c) The contract's integration clause.

(d) The contract's price.

(e) Fraud by the warehouse.

Short-Answer Questions

11. Richard Griffin and three other men owned a grain company called Bearhouse, Inc., which needed to borrow money. First National Bank was willing to loan $490,000, but insisted that the four men sign personal guaranties on the loan, committing themselves to repaying up to 25% of the loan each if Bearhouse defaulted. Bearhouse went bankrupt. The bank was able to collect some of its money from Bearhouse's assets, but it sued Griffin for the balance. At trial, Griffin wanted to testify that before he signed his guaranty, a bank officer assured him that he would only owe 25% of whatever balance was unpaid, not 25% of the total loan. How will the court decide whether Griffin is entitled to testify about the conversation?

12. Donald Waide had a contracting business. He bought most of his supplies from Paul Bingham's supply center. Waide fell behind on his bills, and Bingham told Waide that he would extend no more credit to him. That same day, Donald's father, Elmer Waide, came to Bingham's store, and said to Bingham that he would "stand good" for any sales to Donald made on credit. Based on Elmer's statement, Bingham again gave Donald credit, and Donald ran

up $10,000 in goods before Bingham sued Donald and Elmer. What defense did Elmer make and what was the outcome?

13. Lonnie Hippen moved to Long Island, Kansas to work in an insurance company owned by Griffiths. After he moved there, Griffiths offered to sell Hippen a house he owned, and Hippen agreed in writing to buy it. He did buy the house and moved in, but two years later Hippen left the insurance company. He then claimed that at the time of the sale, Griffiths had orally promised to buy back his house at the selling price if Hippen should happen to leave the company. Griffiths defended based on the statute of frauds. Hippen argued that the statute of frauds did not apply because the repurchase of the house was essentially part of his employment with Griffiths. Comment.

14. ETHICS: Jacob Deutsch owned commercial property. He orally agreed to rent it for six years to Budget Rent-A-Car. Budget took possession, began paying monthly rent, and over a period of several months expended about $6,000 in upgrading the property. Deutsch was aware of the repairs. After a year,

Deutsch attempted to evict Budget. Budget claimed it had a six-year oral lease, but Deutsch claimed that such a lease was worthless. Please rule. Is it ethical for Deutsch to use the statute of frauds in attempting to defeat the lease? Assume that, as landlord, you had orally agreed to rent premises to a tenant, but then for business reasons preferred not to carry out the deal. Would you evict a tenant if you thought the statute of frauds would enable you to do so? How should you analyze the problem? What values are most important to you?

15. Landlord owned a clothing store and agreed in writing to lease the store's basement to another retailer. The written lease, which both parties signed, (1) described the premises exactly; (2) identified the parties; and (3) stated the monthly rent clearly. But an appeals court held that the lease did not satisfy the statute of frauds. Why not?

16. Mast Industries and Bazak International were two textile firms. Mast orally offered to sell certain textiles to Bazak for $103,000. Mast promised to send documents confirming the agreement, but never did. Finally, Bazak sent a memorandum to Mast confirming the agreement, describing the goods, and specifying their quantity and the price. Bazak's officer signed the memo. Mast received the memo but never agreed to it in writing. When Mast failed to deliver the goods, Bazak sued. Who won?

17. ROLE REVERSAL: Write a multiple-choice question that focuses on the merchants' exception to the statute of frauds.

Internet Research Problem

Examine the lease shown at **http://www.kinseylaw.com/freestuff/leaseten/ResLease.html**. Is it important for a lease to be in writing? Who probably drafted the lease, a landlord or a tenant? How can you tell? Should any other provisions be included?

You can find further practice problems in the Online Quiz at **http://beatty.westbuslaw.com** or in the Study Guide that accompanies this text.

14

Third Parties

During television's formative days, Howdy Doody was one of the medium's biggest stars. His acting was wooden—as were his head and body—but for 13 years Howdy and an assorted group of puppets starred in one of the most popular children's programs of all time. Rufus Rose maintained and repaired the puppets. When Howdy took his last double-jointed bow (to a chorus of toddler wails), NBC permitted Rose temporarily to keep the various puppets. Six years later, NBC became concerned that Rose was inadequately maintaining them. The network wanted Howdy and friends moved to a safe, public location. Rose claimed the puppets were in good shape and wanted payment for the maintenance he had provided. The two parties agreed in writing that Rose would give Howdy and the other stars of the show (including Dilly Dally and Flub-A-Dub) to a puppet museum at the Detroit Institute of Arts (DIA). NBC agreed to pay the puppeteer for his work. The company permitted Rose to keep some of the minor puppets from the program, provided they were not used for commercial purposes.

When Rose died, his son Christopher took possession of the famous puppet. At about that time, a copy of Howdy sold at auction for $113,000. Christopher then claimed ownership

of Howdy Doody and refused to give him to the museum. The DIA wanted its famous puppet, but the museum had never been a party to the agreement between NBC and Rose. Did the DIA have any rights to Howdy? The museum filed suit, making a third party claim. ◾

The basic pattern in third party law is quite simple. Two parties make a contract, and their rights and obligations are subject to the rules that we have already studied: offer and acceptance, consideration, and so forth. However, sometimes their contract affects a *third party*, one who had no role in forming the agreement itself. The two contracting parties may intend to benefit a third person. Those are cases of *third party beneficiary*. In other cases, one of the contracting parties may actually transfer his rights or responsibilities to a third party, raising issues of *assignment* or *delegation*. We consider the issues one at a time.

Third Party Beneficiary

The two parties who make a contract always intend to benefit themselves. Oftentimes their bargain will also benefit someone else. **A third party beneficiary is someone who was not a party to the contract but stands to benefit from it.** Many contracts create third party beneficiaries. In the chapter's introduction, NBC and Rufus Rose contracted to give Howdy Doody to the Detroit Institute of Arts. The museum stood to benefit from this agreement.

As another example, suppose a city contracts to purchase from Seller 20 acres of an abandoned industrial site in a rundown neighborhood, to be used for a new domed stadium. The owner of a pizza parlor on the edge of Seller's land might benefit enormously. A once marginal operation could become a gold mine of cheese and pepperoni.

When the two contracting parties fulfill their obligations and the third party receives her benefit, there is no dispute to analyze. If Christopher Rose had walked Howdy Doody into the puppet museum, and if the city completed the stadium, there would be no unhappy third parties. Problems arise when one of the parties fails to perform the contract as expected. The issue is this: May the third party beneficiary enforce the contract? The museum had no contract with the Rose family. Is the museum entitled to the puppet? The pizza parlor owner was not a party to the contract for the sale of the stadium land. If the city breaks its agreement to buy the property, should the owner recover profits for unsold sausage and green pepper?

The outcome in cases like these depends upon the intentions of the two contracting parties. If they intended to benefit the third party, she will probably be permitted to enforce their contract. If they did not intend to benefit her, she probably has no power to enforce the agreement. The Restatement (Second) of Contracts uses more detail to analyze these cases. We must first recall the terms "promisor" and "promisee." The **promisor** is the one who makes the promise that the third party beneficiary is seeking to enforce. The **promisee** is the other party to the contract.

According to the Restatement §302: **A beneficiary of a promise is an intended beneficiary and may enforce a contract if the parties intended her to benefit and if either (A) enforcing the promise will satisfy a duty of the promisee to the beneficiary, or (B) the promisee intended to make a gift to the beneficiary.**

Any beneficiary who is not an intended beneficiary is an **incidental benefi-ciary,** and may not enforce the contract. In other words, a third party beneficiary must show two things. First, she must show that the two contracting parties were aware of her situation and knew that she would receive something of value from their deal. Second, she must show that the promisee wanted to benefit her for one of two reasons: either to satisfy some duty owed or to make her a gift.

We will apply this rule to the dispute over Howdy Doody. Like most contracts, the deal between NBC and Rufus Rose had two promises: Rose's agreement to give the puppet to the museum, and NBC's promise to pay for the work done on Howdy. The promise that interests us was the one concerning Howdy's destina-tion in Detroit. Rose was the promisor and NBC was the promisee.

Did the two parties intend to benefit the museum? Yes, they did. NBC wanted Howdy to be displayed to the general public, and in a noncommercial venue. Rose, who wanted payment for work already done, was happy to go along with the network's wishes. Did NBC owe a duty to the museum? No. Did the network intend to make a gift to the museum? Yes. The museum wins! The Detroit Institute of Arts was an intended third party beneficiary, and is entitled to Howdy Doody. See Exhibit 15.1.

By contrast, the pizza parlor owner will surely lose. A stadium is a multimillion-dollar investment, and it is most unlikely that the city and the seller of the land

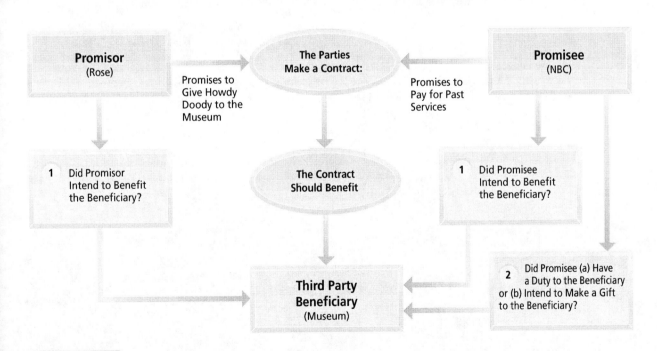

Exhibit 15.1
The issue: May a third party beneficiary enforce a contract to which it was not a party?
The answer: A third party beneficiary may enforce a contract if (1) the parties intended to benefit it *and either* (2)(a) enforcing the promise will satisfy a duty of the promisee to the beneficiary or (2)(b) the promisee intended to make a gift to the beneficiary.
In this case: Rose and NBC both intended to benefit the museum. The promisee (NBC) intended to make a *gift* to the museum. The museum is therefore an intended third party beneficiary, entitled to the puppet.

were even aware of the owner's existence, let alone that they intended to benefit him. He probably cannot prove either the first element or the second element, and certainly not both.

Real Estate Support Services (RESS) performed house inspections for potential buyers. RESS contracted with a realtor, Coldwell Banker Relocation Services, Inc., to inspect houses and furnish reports to Coldwell. The agreement stated that the purpose of the reports was:

> *"To provide the client [Coldwell] with a report of a relocating employee's home, which the client may, at its discretion, disclose to other interested parties."*

RESS inspected a house in Greencastle, Indiana and gave its report to Coldwell, which passed the document on to Paul and Norma Nauman. The Naumans relied on the report and bought the house, but later discovered defects RESS had not mentioned. They sued RESS, claiming to be third party beneficiaries of the company's contract with Coldwell. The court ruled for the Naumans. Coldwell obviously intended to use the reports as a sales tool, and RESS knew it, making buyers such as the Naumans intended beneficiaries.

Coldwell presented RESS with a contract that invited claims from third party beneficiaries. That was the time for RESS to decide, "Can we tolerate liability to all buyers who might see the report?" If the company was unwilling to assume such extensive liability, it should have proposed appropriate contract language, such as:

> *"RESS is preparing these reports exclusively for Coldwell's use. Coldwell will not disclose any report to a house purchaser or any other person without first obtaining written permission from RESS."*

If Coldwell had accepted the language, there would have been no lawsuit. If Coldwell had rejected the wording, RESS would have had two options: sign the contract, acknowledging the company's exposure to third parties, or walk away from the negotiations.

Although most third party cases arise in traditional business settings, contract law is a powerful tool that can be used in unexpected settings, as the criminal defendant in the following case demonstrates.

CASE SUMMARY

UNITED STATES v. EL-SADIG

133 F. Supp. 2d 600
Northern District of Ohio, 2001

FACTS: Prince Bander of Saudi Arabia came to the Cleveland Clinic, in Ohio, for medical treatment, accompanied by a large entourage that included his son, Prince Mansour. During their stay in Cleveland, the visitors employed Gabshawi El-Sadig, a lawful resident of the United States, as a driver and errand man. Two members of the Saudi entourage asked El-Sadig to buy guns for them. He bought more than 20 weapons for them at a local gun store, falsely indicating in the required forms that he himself was the true purchaser.

The Bureau of Alcohol, Tobacco and Firearms learned that the weapons had been purchased for the group and would be illegally exported when the

Saudi entourage left the country. In a series of rapid phone conversations among the Justice Department, the State Department, the Saudi Embassy, and others, it was agreed that if all of the weapons were turned over to the police chief of the Cleveland Clinic, the case would be dropped. The weapons were promptly delivered and the Saudi group left the United States.

The government prosecuted El-Sadig for illegally purchasing the weapons and assisting in an illegal attempt to export them, claiming that the agreement not to prosecute applied only to the Saudi nationals. El-Sadig moved to dismiss, arguing that he was a third party beneficiary of the agreement.

ISSUE: **Was El-Sadig a third party beneficiary of the agreement to avoid prosecution?**

DECISION: Motion to dismiss granted. El-Sadig was a third party beneficiary of the agreement. The government may not prosecute him.

REASONING: Prince Mansour was not involved in any of the illegal activity. He negotiated with the government on behalf of other people (third parties), hoping to protect the Saudi delegation and royal family from embarrassment. The Prince clearly wanted to benefit everybody associated with the Saudi group, because if anyone was prosecuted for the gun purchases, the full story would become public and the royal family implicated. The government, in turn, agreed that "the matter would be closed" if all weapons were given to the police.

If the parties to an agreement intend to benefit a third party, that person can enforce the contract. Although El-Sadig was never named by either party, he was a member of the group that the Prince intended to benefit, and the government consented to protect. He was a third party beneficiary of the contract not to prosecute. The government agreed to close the matter if all weapons were delivered, and it lost the right to prosecute El-Sadig the moment the guns were handed over. ◢

Assignment and Delegation

A contracting party may transfer his rights under the contract, which is called an **assignment of rights.** Or a party may transfer her duties pursuant to the contract, which is a **delegation of duties.** Frequently, a party will make an assignment and delegation simultaneously, transferring both rights and duties to a third party.

For our purposes, the Restatement (Second) of Contracts serves as a good summary of common-law provisions. (The UCC rules are similar but not identical.) Our first example is a sale-of-goods case, governed by the UCC, but the outcome would be the same under the Restatement.

Lydia needs 500 bottles of champagne. Bruno agrees to sell them to her for $10,000, payable 30 days after delivery. He transports the wine to her. Bruno happens to owe Doug $8,000 from a previous deal, so he says to Doug, "I don't have the money, but I'll give you my claim to Lydia's $10,000." Doug agrees. Bruno then assigns to Doug his rights to Lydia's money, and in exchange Doug gives up his claim for $8,000. Bruno is the **assignor, the one making an assignment,** and Doug is the **assignee, the one receiving an assignment.**

Why would Bruno offer $10,000 when he owed Doug only $8,000? Because all he has is a claim to Lydia's money. Cash in hand is often more valuable. Doug, however, is willing to assume some risk for a potential $2,000 gain.

Bruno notifies Lydia of the assignment. Lydia, who owes the money, is called the **obligor,** that is, the one obligated to do something. At the end of 30 days, Doug arrives at Lydia's doorstep, asks for his money, and gets it, since Lydia is obligated to him. Bruno has no claim to any payment. See Exhibit 15.2.

Lydia bought the champagne because she knew she could sell it at a profit. She promptly agrees to sell and deliver the 500 bottles to Coretta, at a mountaintop

Exhibit 15.2

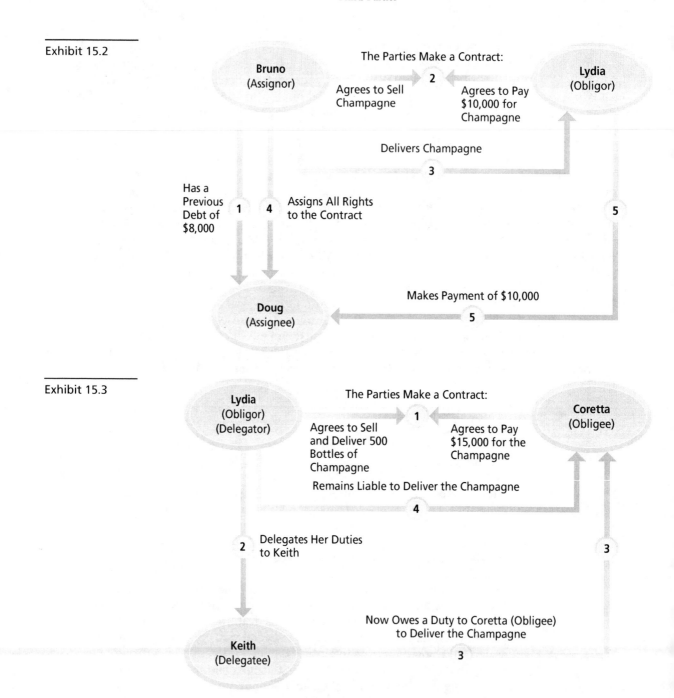

Exhibit 15.3

wilderness camp. Lydia has no four-wheel-drive cars, so she finds Keith, who is willing to deliver the bottles for $1,000. Lydia delegates her duty to Keith to deliver the bottles to Coretta. Keith is now obligated to deliver the bottles to Coretta, the obligee, that is, the one who has the obligation coming to her. As we see later, Lydia also remains obligated to Coretta, the **obligee,** to ensure that the bottles are delivered. See Exhibit 15.3.

Assignment and delegation can each create problems. We will examine the most common ones.

ASSIGNMENT

What Rights Are Assignable?

Any contractual right may be assigned unless assignment

(a) Would substantially change the obligor's rights or duties under the contract; or

(b) Is forbidden by law or public policy; or

(c) Is validly precluded by the contract itself.

Substantial Change.   Subsection A prohibits an assignment if it would substantially change the obligor's situation. For example, Bruno is permitted to assign to Doug his rights to payment from Lydia because it makes no difference to Lydia whether she writes a check to one or the other. But suppose Erica, who lives on a quarter-acre lot in Hardscrabble, hires Keith to mow her lawn once per week for the summer, for a total fee of $700. Erica pays up front, before she leaves for the summer. May she assign her right to weekly lawn care to Lloyd, who enjoys a 3-acre estate in Halcyon, 60 miles distant? No. The extra travel and far larger yard would dramatically change Keith's obligations.

Public Policy.   Some assignments are prohibited by public policy. For example, someone who has suffered a personal injury may not assign her claim to a third person.

Contract Prohibition.   Finally, one of the contracting parties may try to prohibit assignment in the agreement itself. For example, most landlords include in the written lease a clause prohibiting the tenant from assigning the tenancy without the landlord's written permission. Such clauses are generally, but not always, enforced by a court.

The following case begins with everyone's dream come true: a winning lottery ticket.

CASE SUMMARY

PETERSON v. DISTRICT OF COLUMBIA LOTTERY AND CHARITABLE GAMES CONTROL BOARD

673 A.2d 664, 1996 D.C. App. LEXIS 54
District of Columbia Court of Appeals, 1996

FACTS: In 1986, Eugene Peterson won $1,050,000 in the District of Columbia Lucky Lotto Game, payable in 20 installments. In 1993, he assigned his future payments to Stone Street Capital, Inc., in exchange for a present-value lump sum. The District's Lottery and Charitable Games Control Board (the Board) refused to honor the assignment, based on its regulations. Peterson and Stone Street sued, but the court ruled that the assignment was illegal. Peterson and Stone Street appealed.

ISSUE: Was Peterson entitled to assign his lottery winnings?

DECISION: Peterson was entitled to assign his lottery winnings.

REASONING: Courts generally protect a party's right to assign unless the contract contains a clear prohibition. The District of Columbia acknowledges that its lottery regulations do not expressly forbid a prize winner from assigning her winnings. However, the District points to a regulation that discharges the Board of liability once it pays the person named on the ticket. The District argues that this regulation was intended to prohibit assignments. A simpler interpretation, though, is that payment need be made only to the named winner, relieving the Board of any obligation to pay others claiming a stake in the prize. The Board's regulation is too ambiguous to prevent an assignment. Peterson had a right to assign his winnings. ▲

How Rights Are Assigned

An assignment may be written or oral, and no particular formalities are required. However, when someone wants to assign rights governed by the statute of frauds, she must do it in writing. Suppose City contracts with Seller to buy Seller's land for a domed stadium and then brings in Investor to complete the project. If City wants to assign to Investor its rights to the land, it must do so in writing.

Rights of the Parties after Assignment

Once the assignment is made and the obligor notified, the assignee may enforce her contractual rights against the obligor. If Lydia fails to pay Doug for the champagne she gets from Bruno, Doug may sue to enforce the agreement. The law will treat Doug as though he had entered into the contract with Lydia.

But the reverse is also true. **The obligor may generally raise all defenses against the assignee that she could have raised against the assignor.** Suppose Lydia opens the first bottle of champagne—silently. "Where's the pop?" she wonders. There is no pop because all 500 bottles have gone flat. Bruno has failed to perform his part of the contract, and Lydia may use Bruno's nonperformance as a defense against Doug. If the champagne was indeed worthless, Lydia owes Doug nothing.

DELEGATION OF DUTIES

Garret has always dreamed of racing stock cars. He borrows $250,000 from his sister, Maybelle, in order to buy a car and begin racing. He signs a promissory note in that amount, in other words, a document guaranteeing that he will repay Maybelle the full amount, plus interest, on a monthly basis over 10 years. Regrettably, during his first race, on a Saturday night, Garret discovers that he has a speed phobia. He finishes the race at noon on Sunday and quits the business. Garret transfers the car and all of his equipment to Brady, who agrees in writing to pay all money owed to Maybelle. For a few months Brady sends a check, but he is killed while watching bumper cars at a local carnival. Maybelle sues Garret, who defends based on the transfer to Brady. Will his defense work?

Garret has assigned his rights in the car and business to Brady, and that is entirely legal. But more important, he has *delegated his duties* to Brady. Garret was the **delegator** and Brady was the **delegatee**. In other words, the promissory note he signed was a contract, and the agreement imposed certain duties on Garret, primarily the obligation to pay Maybelle $250,000 plus interest. Garret had a right to delegate his duties to Brady, but delegating those duties did not relieve Garret of his own obligation to perform them. When Maybelle sues, she will win. Garret, like many debtors, would have preferred to wash his hands of his debt, but the law is not so obliging.

Most duties are delegable. But delegation does not by itself relieve the delegator of his own liability to perform the contract. See Exhibit 15.4.

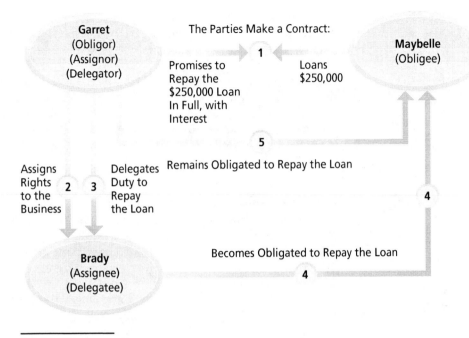

Exhibit 15.4

What Duties Are Delegable

The rules concerning what duties may be delegated mirror those about the assignment of rights.

An obligor may delegate his duties unless

1. Delegation would violate public policy; or

2. The contract prohibits delegation; or

3. The obligee has a substantial interest in personal performance by the obligor.

Public Policy. Delegation may violate public policy, for example, in a public works contract. If City hires Builder to construct a subway system, state law may prohibit Builder from delegating his duties to Beginner. The theory is that a public agency should not have to work with parties that it never agreed to hire.

Contract Prohibition. The parties may forbid almost any delegation, and the courts will enforce the agreement. Hammer, a contractor, is building a house and hires Spot as his painter, including in his contract a clause prohibiting delegation. Just before the house is ready for painting, Spot gets a better job elsewhere and wants to delegate his duties to Brush. Hammer may refuse the delegation even if Brush is equally qualified.

Substantial Interest in Personal Performance. Suppose Hammer had omitted the "nondelegation" clause from his contract with Spot. Could Hammer still refuse the delegation on the grounds that he has a substantial interest in having Spot do the work? No. Most duties are delegable. There is nothing so special about painting a house that one particular painter is required to do it. But some kinds of work do require personal performance, and obligors may not delegate these tasks. The services of lawyers, doctors, dentists, artists, and performers are considered too personal to be delegated. There is no single test that will perfectly define this group, but generally, when the work will test the character, skill, discretion, and good faith of the obligor, she may *not* delegate her job.

AT RISK

The law can be annoyingly vague, as it is with the test of "personal performance" contracts. But avoiding problems is not difficult. Before entering into a contract, briefly discuss delegation with the other party and decide what duties, if any, may be delegated. Then include an appropriate clause in the contract. As always, if there are differences over delegation, it is better to be aware of them early. ▪

Novation

As we have seen, a delegator does not get rid of his duties merely by delegating them. But there is one way a delegator can do so. **A novation is a three-way agreement in which the obligor transfers all rights and duties to a third party. The obligee agrees to look *only* to that third party for performance.**

Recall Garret, the forlorn race car driver. When he wanted to get out of his obligations to Maybelle, he should have proposed a novation. He would assign all rights and delegate all duties to Brady, and Maybelle would agree that *only Brady* was obligated by the promissory note, releasing Garret from his responsibility to repay. Why would Maybelle do this? She might conclude that Brady was a financially better bet than Garret and that this was the best way to get her money. Maybelle would prefer to have both people liable. But Garret might refuse to bring Brady into the deal until Maybelle permits a novation. In the example given, Garret failed to obtain a novation, and hence he and Brady (or Brady's estate) were *both* liable on the promissory note.

Since a novation has the critical effect of releasing the obligor from liability, you will not be surprised to learn that two parties to a contract sometimes fight over whether some event was a simple delegation of duties or a novation. In the following case, who pays for the ice cream?

YOU BE THE JUDGE

ROSENBERG v. SON, INC.

491 N.W.2d 71, 1992 N.D. LEXIS 202
Supreme Court of North Dakota, 1992

FACTS: The Rosenbergs owned a Dairy Queen in Grand Forks, North Dakota. They agreed in writing to sell the Dairy Queen to Mary Pratt. The contract required her to pay $10,000 down and $52,000 over 15 years, at 10% interest. Two years later, Pratt assigned her rights and delegated her duties under the sales contract to Son, Inc. The agreement between Pratt and Son contained a "Consent to Assignment" clause that the Rosenbergs signed. Pratt then moved to Arizona and had nothing further to do with the Dairy Queen. The Rosenbergs never received full payment for the Dairy Queen. They sued Mary Pratt.

The trial court gave summary judgment for Pratt, finding that she was no longer obligated on the original contract. The Rosenbergs appealed.

YOU BE THE JUDGE: Did Pratt obtain a novation relieving her of her duties under the original sales contract?

ARGUMENT FOR THE ROSENBERGS: Your honors, a party cannot escape contract liability merely by assigning its rights and delegating its duties to a third party. It is evident from the express language of the agreement between Pratt and Son, Inc. that the parties only intended an assignment, not a novation. The agreement made no mention of discharging Pratt from liability. It would be odd to write a novation and make no mention of discharge, which happens to be the primary point of a true novation. It is true that the Rosenbergs signed a consent to the assignment, but merely by permitting Son, Inc. to become involved they did not discharge their principal obligor—Pratt.

ARGUMENT FOR Ms. PRATT: Your honors, it is obvious from the contract that Ms. Pratt intended to rid herself entirely of this business. She planned to move out of state, and wanted to terminate all rights and responsibilities in the business. Why would she go to the trouble of assigning rights *and* delegating duties if she still expected to be involved in the business? If that weren't enough, she went one step further, by asking the Rosenbergs to acknowledge the new arrangement—which the Rosenbergs did. If Son, Inc. failed to keep its end of the bargain, then the Rosenbergs should sue that company—not an innocent woman who is long out of the business.

Chapter Conclusion

A moment's caution! That is what enables contracting parties to anticipate and realistically appraise any rights and responsibilities of third parties.

Chapter Review

1. A third party beneficiary is an intended beneficiary and may enforce a contract if the parties intended her to benefit from the agreement and if either (1) enforcing the promise will satisfy a debt of the promisee to the beneficiary; or (2) the promisee intended to make a gift to the beneficiary. Any beneficiary who meets neither description is an incidental beneficiary and has no right to enforce the contract.

2. An assignment transfers the assignor's contract rights to the assignee. A delegation transfers the delegator's duties to the delegatee.

3. A party generally may assign contract rights unless doing so would substantially change the obligor's rights or duties, is forbidden by law, or is validly precluded by the contract.

4. Once the assignment is made and the obligor notified, the assignee may enforce her contractual rights against the obligor. The obligor, in turn, may generally raise all defenses against the assignee that she could have raised against the assignor.

5. Duties are delegable unless delegation would violate public policy, the contract prohibits delegation, or the obligee has a substantial interest in personal performance by the obligor.

6. Unless the obligee agrees otherwise, delegation does not discharge the delegator's duty to perform.

7. A novation is a three-way agreement in which the obligor delegates all duties to the delegatee and the obligee agrees to hold only the delegatee responsible.

PRACTICE TEST

Matching Questions

Match the following terms:

___ **A.** Intended beneficiary   **1.** One way in which an obligor can get rid of his contractual obligations.

___ **B.** Personal performance   **2.** A type of contract in which assignment is typically prohibited.

___ **C.** Novation   **3.** A third party who should be able to enforce a contract between two others.

___ **D.** Lease   **4.** A type of contractual obligation that generally cannot be delegated.

___ **E.** Rights to real property   **5.** A type of assignment that must be in writing.

True/False Questions

Circle true or false:

1. T F   All parties must normally agree before a contract can be assigned.

2. T F   An incidental beneficiary has the same rights to enforce a contract as any other party.

3. T F   A party who delegates duties remains liable for contract performance.

4. T F   Assignment implies novation whereas delegation does not.

5. T F   Once an assignment has been made, the obligor may raise all defenses against the assignee that she could have raised against the assignor.

Multiple-Choice Questions

6. Bob, a mechanic, claims that Cathy owes him $1,500 on a repair job. Bob wants to assign his claim to Hardknuckle Bank. The likeliest reason that Bob wants to do this is

   (a) Cathy also owes Hardknuckle Bank money.

   (b) Hardknuckle Bank owes Bob money on a consumer claim.

   (c) Hardknuckle Bank owes Bob money on a repair job.

   (d) Bob owes Hardknuckle Bank money.

   (e) Bob and Cathy are close friends.

7. The agreement between Bob and Cathy says nothing about assignment. May Bob assign his claim to Hardknuckle?

   (a) Bob may assign his claim but only with Cathy's agreement.

   (b) Bob may assign his claim, but only if Cathy and Hardknuckle agree.

   (c) Bob may assign his claim without Cathy's agreement.

   (d) Bob may assign his claim but Cathy may nullify the assignment.

   (e) Bob may not assign his claim because it violates public policy.

8. Assuming that Bob successfully assigns his claim to the Hardknuckle Bank, which statement is true?

   (a) Hardknuckle could sue Cathy for the money, with or without Bob's consent.

   (b) Hardknuckle could sue Cathy for the money, but only with Bob's consent.

   (c) Hardknuckle could sue Cathy for the money, but only with Bob *and* Cathy's consent.

   (d) Hardknuckle could sue Bob *and* Cathy for the money.

   (e) Hardknuckle could sue only Bob for the money.

9. Assuming that Bob successfully assigns his claim to the Hardknuckle Bank, which statement is true?

   (a) Cathy remains obligated only to Bob.

   (b) Cathy is now obligated to Bob and Hardknuckle.

   (c) Cathy could raise any defenses against Hardknuckle that she could have raised against Bob.

   (d) Cathy may assign her rights to any party she wishes.

   (e) Cathy may delegate her duties to any party she wishes.

10. Cathy believes that her friend, Stephanie, owes her more money than she, Cathy, owes to Bob. Cathy wants Stephanie to take over her obligation to pay Bob. Cathy wants no further dealings with Bob. Cathy's best approach is

    (a) Intended beneficiary.

    (b) Incidental beneficiary

    (c) Delegation.

    (d) Assignment.

    (e) Novation.

Short-Answer Questions

11. Intercontinental Metals Corp. (IMC) contracted with the accounting firm of Cherry, Bekaert & Holland to perform an audit. Cherry issued its opinion about IMC, giving all copies of its report directly to the company. IMC later permitted Dun & Bradstreet to examine the statements, and Raritan River Steel Company saw a report published by Dun & Bradstreet. Relying on the audit, Raritan sold IMC $2.2 million worth of steel on credit, but IMC promptly went bankrupt. Raritan sued Cherry, claiming that IMC was not as sound as Cherry had reported, and that the accounting firm had breached its contract with IMC. Comment on Raritan's suit.

12. Angelo Zavarella and Yvette Rodrigues were injured in an automobile accident allegedly caused by a vehicle belonging to Truck Equipment of Boston. Travelers Insurance Company paid insurance benefits to Zavarella and Rodrigues, who then assigned to Travelers their claims against Truck Equipment. Travelers sued Truck Equipment, which moved to dismiss. What is Truck Equipment's claim that the case should be dismissed, and how would you rule?

13. Woodson Walker and Associates leased computer equipment from Park Ryan Leasing. The lease said nothing about assignment. Park Ryan then assigned the lease to TCB as security for a loan. Park Ryan defaulted on its loan, and Walker failed to make several payments on the lease. TCB sued Walker for the lease payments. Please rule on two issues:

    (a) Was the assignment valid, given the fact that the original lease made no mention of it?

    (b) If the assignment was valid, may Walker raise defenses against TCB that it could have raised against Park Ryan?

14. ETHICS: A century and a half ago an English judge stated: "All painters do not paint portraits like Sir Joshua Reynolds, nor landscapes like Claude Lorraine, nor do all writers write dramas like Shakespeare or fiction like Dickens. Rare genius and extraordinary skill are not transferable." What legal doctrine is the judge describing? What is the ethical basis of this rule?

15. Pizza of Gaithersburg, Maryland owned five pizza shops. Pizza arranged with Virginia Coffee Service to install soft drink machines in each of its stores and maintain them. The contract made no mention of the rights of either party to delegate. Virginia Coffee delegated its duties to the Macke Co., leading to litigation between Pizza and Macke. Pizza claimed that Virginia Coffee was barred from delegating because Pizza had a close working relationship with the president of Virginia Coffee, who personally kept the machines in working order. Was the delegation legal?

16. Judith and John Brooks hired Wayne Hayes to build a house. The contract required Hayes to "provide all necessary labor and materials and perform all work of every nature whatsoever to be done in the erection of the residence." Hayes hired subcontractors to do all of the work. One of Hayes's employees checked on the work site daily, but neither Hayes nor any of his employees actively supervised the building. The Brookses were aware of this working arrangement and consented to it. The mason negligently installed

the fireplace, ultimately leading to a serious fire. The Brookses sued Hayes for breach of contract. Hayes contended that when the Brookses approved of his hiring of subcontractors to do all work, that created a novation, relieving him of any liability. Discuss.

17. ROLE REVERSAL: Write a short-answer question that highlights the difference between an assignment and a novation.

Internet Research Problem

Go to **http://www.kinseylaw.com/freestuff/leaseten/ResLease.html** and read clause 5(b) of the lease. What does the clause mean, in English? Do leases commonly include such clauses? Suppose you intend to rent an apartment next year, live there during the school year, and then sublet over the summer. What legal issue will probably arise concerning a sublet?

You can find further practice problems in the Online Quiz at **http://beatty.westbuslaw.com** or in the Study Guide that accompanies this text.

15

Performance and Discharge

Polly was elated. It was the grand opening of her new restaurant, Polly's Folly, and everything was bubbling. The wait staff hustled and Caesar, the chef, churned out succulent dishes. Polly was determined that her Folly would be a glorious one. Her three-year lease would cost $6,000 per month, and she had signed an advertising deal with Billboard Bonanza for the same period. Polly had also promised Eddie, a publicity agent, a substantial monthly fee, to begin as soon as the restaurant was 80% booked for one month. Tonight, with candles flickering at packed tables, Polly beamed.

After a week, Polly's smiles were a bit forced. The restaurant was only 60% full, and the publicity agent yelled at Caesar for costing him money. Then troubles gushed forth—literally. A water main burst in front of Polly's restaurant, flooding the street. The city embarked on a two-month repair job that ultimately took four times that long. The street was closed to traffic, and no one could park within blocks of the Folly. For several months Polly bravely served food, but patronage dropped steadily, as hungry customers refused to deal with the bad parking and construction noise. Finally, behind on the rent and in debt to everyone, Polly closed her doors for good.

Discharge

Grimly, the court doors swung open, offering a full menu of litigation. Polly's landlord sued for three years' rent, and Billboard Bonanza demanded its money for the same period. Eddie, the agent, insisted on some money for his hard work.

Polly defended vigorously, seeking to be discharged from her various contracts. **A party is discharged when she has no more duties under a contract.** In each lawsuit, Polly asked a court to declare that her obligations were terminated and that she owed no money.

DEFENSES THAT DISCHARGE

Most contracts are discharged by full performance. In other words, the parties generally do what they promise. At times, though, a court may discharge a party who has not performed. When things have gone amiss, a judge must interpret the contract to determine who, in fairness, should suffer the loss. In the lawsuits brought by the landlord and Billboard Bonanza, Polly argued a defense called "commercial impracticability," claiming that she should not be forced to rent space that was useless to her or buy advertising for a restaurant that had closed. The claim was understandable, but we can also respect her opponents' argument, that they did not break the water main. Claims of commercial impracticability are difficult to win, and Polly lost against both of these opponents. Though she was making no money at all from the restaurant, the court found her liable in full for the lease and the advertising contract.

As to Eddie's suit, Polly raised a defense based on a "condition," meaning that some event had to occur before she was obligated to pay. Polly claimed that she owed Eddie money only if and when the restaurant was 80% full, and that had never happened. The court agreed and discharged Polly on Eddie's claim.

We will analyze each of these issues, and begin with a look at conditions.

Conditions

Parties often put conditions in a contract. **A condition is an event that must occur before a party becomes obligated under a contract.** Polly agreed to pay Eddie, the agent, a percentage of her profits, but with an important condition: 80% of the tables had to be booked for a month. Unless and until those tables were occupied, Polly owed Eddie nothing. That never happened, or, in contract language, the *condition failed*, and so Polly was discharged.

Conditions can take many forms. Alex would like to buy Kevin's empty lot and build a movie theater on it, but the city's zoning law will not permit such a business in that location. Alex signs a contract to buy Kevin's empty lot in 120 days, provided that within 100 days the city rezones the area to permit a movie theater. If the city fails to rezone the area by day 100, Alex is discharged and need not complete the deal.

HOW CONDITIONS ARE CREATED

No special language is necessary to create the condition. Contract phrases such as "provided that" frequently indicate a condition, but neither those nor any other words are essential. As long as the parties intended to create a condition, a court will enforce it.

Because informal language can create a condition, the parties may dispute whether they intended one or not. Sand Creek Country Club, in Indiana, was eager to expand its clubhouse and awarded the design work to CSO Architects. The club wanted the work done quickly but had not secured financing. The architects sent a letter confirming their agreement:

"It was our intent to allow Mr. Dan Moriarty of our office to start work on your project as early as possible in order to allow you to meet the goals that you have set. Also, it was the intent of CSO to begin work on your project and delay any billings to you until your financing is in place. As I explained to you earlier, we will continue on this course until we reach a point where we can no longer continue without receiving some payment."

The club gave CSO the go-ahead to begin design work, and the architects did their work and billed Sand Creek for $33,000. But the club, unable to obtain financing, refused to pay. Sand Creek claimed that CSO's letter created a condition in their agreement, namely, that the club would have to pay only if and when it obtained financing. The court was unpersuaded and ruled that the parties had never intended to create an express condition. The architects were merely delaying their billing as a convenience to the club. It would be absurd, said the court, to assume that CSO intended to perform $33,000 worth of work for free.

The Sand Creek case demonstrates the need for clarity in business dealings. The architect's letter should have emphasized that Sand Creek was obligated to pay the full amount, for example by saying: "CSO agrees to delay billing for a reasonable period but the Club remains liable for the full amount of the contract, whether or not it obtains financing." A one-sentence ambiguity meant that the firm could not obtain its money without a lawsuit and an appeal. ◾

Public Policy

At times a court will refuse to enforce an express condition on the grounds that it is unfair and harmful to the general public. In other words, a court might agree that the parties created a conditional clause but conclude that permitting its enforcement would hurt society. Did the insurance contract in the following case harm society? You be the judge.

YOU BE THE JUDGE

ANDERSON v. COUNTRY LIFE INS. CO.

180 Ariz. 625, 886 P.2d 1381, 1994 Ariz. App. LEXIS 240
Arizona Court of Appeals, 1994

FACTS: On November 26, a Country Life Insurance agent persuaded Donald and Anna Mae Anderson to buy a life insurance policy. He accepted a check for $1,600. The agent gave the Andersons a "conditional receipt for medical policy." The form stated that the Andersons would have a valid life insurance policy with Country Life, effective November 26, but only when all conditions were met. The most important of these conditions was that the Country Life home office accept the Andersons as medical risks. The Andersons were pleased with the new policy and glad it was effective that same day.

It was not. Donald Anderson died of a heart attack a few weeks later. Country Life declined the Andersons as medical risks and refused to issue a policy. Anna Mae Anderson sued. Country Life pointed out that medical approval was a contract condition. In other words, the policy would be effective as of November 26, but only if the company later gave medical approval. The trial court gave summary judgment for Country Life. Ms. Anderson appealed, claiming that the conditional clause was a violation of public policy.

YOU BE THE JUDGE: **Did the conditional clause violate public policy?**

ARGUMENT FOR Ms. ANDERSON: Your honors, this policy is a scam. This so-called "conditional receipt for medical policy" is designed to trick customers and steal their money. The company leads people to believe they are covered as of the day they write the check. But they aren't.

The company gets the customer's money right away and gives nothing in exchange. If the company, after taking its time, decides the applicant is not medically fit, it returns the money, having used it to earn interest. If the insurance company decides the applicant is a good bet, it then issues the policy effective for weeks or months in the *past*, when coverage is of no use. The company is being paid for a period during which it had no risk.

ARGUMENT FOR COUNTRY LIFE: Your honors, is Country Life supposed to issue life insurance policies without doing a medical check? Of course we do a medical inquiry, as quickly as possible. It's in our interest to get the policy decided one way or the other.

The policy clearly stated that coverage was effective only when approved by the home office, after all inquiries were made. The Andersons knew that as well as the agent. If they were covered immediately, why would the company do a medical check? Ms. Anderson is trying to profit from a tragedy that was not the company's fault.

Performance

Caitlin has an architect draw up plans for a monumental new house, and Daniel agrees to build it by September 1. Caitlin promises to pay $900,000 on that date. The house is ready on time but Caitlin has some complaints. The living room was supposed to be 18 feet high but it is only 17 feet; the pool was to be azure yet it is aquamarine; the maid's room was not supposed to be wired for cable television but it is. Caitlin refuses to pay anything for the house. Is she justified? Of course not, it would be absurd to give her a magnificent house for free when it has only tiny defects. And that is how a court would decide the case. But in this easy answer lurks a danger. Technically, Daniel did breach the contract, and yet the law allows him to recover the full contract price, or virtually all of it. Once that principle is established, how far will a court stretch it? Suppose the living room is only 14 feet high, or 10 feet, or 5 feet?

STRICT PERFORMANCE AND SUBSTANTIAL PERFORMANCE

Strict Performance

Caitlin argued that Daniel had not *strictly performed*. Caitlin was right, yet she lost anyway. Courts dislike strict performance because it enables one party to benefit without paying, and sends the other one home empty-handed. **A party is generally not required to give strict performance unless the contract expressly demands it *and* such a demand is reasonable.** Caitlin's contract never suggested that Daniel would forfeit all payment if there were minor problems.

There are cases where strict performance does make sense. Marshall agrees to deliver 500 sweaters to Leo's store, and Leo promises to pay $20,000 cash on delivery. If Leo has only $19,000 cash and a promissory note for $1,000, he has failed to perform, and Marshall need not give him the sweaters. Leo's payment represents 95% of what he promised, but there is a big difference between cash and a promissory note.

Substantial Performance

Daniel, the house builder, won his case against Caitlin because he fulfilled most of his obligations, even though he did an imperfect job. **In a contract for services, a party that substantially performs its obligations will receive the full contract price, minus the value of any defects.** Daniel receives $900,000, the contract price, minus the value of a ceiling that is one foot too low, a pool the wrong color, and so forth. It will be for the trial court to decide how much those defects are worth. If the court decides the low ceiling is a $10,000 damage, the pool color worth $5,000, and the cable television worth $500, then Daniel receives $884,500.

On the other hand, **a party that fails to give substantial performance receives nothing on the contract itself and will only recover the value of the work, if any.** If the foundation cracks in Caitlin's house and the walls collapse, Daniel will not receive his $900,000. In such a case he collects only the market value of the work he has done, which is probably zero.

To analyze substantial performance, courts look at these issues:

- How much benefit has the promisee received?

- If it is a construction contract, can the owner use the thing for its intended purpose?

- Can the promisee be compensated with money damages for any defects?

- Did the promisor act in good faith?

The following case deals with several of these issues.

CASE SUMMARY

FOLK v. CENTRAL NATIONAL BANK & TRUST CO.

210 Ill. App. 3d 43, 1991 Ill. App. LEXIS 308
Illinois Court of Appeals, 1991

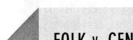

FACTS: Byron Dragway, a drag strip located in Byron, Illinois, needed work, including concrete retaining walls and resurfacing of the racing strip. Leek hired Randy Folk to do all of the work. When Folk finished, Leek refused to pay, claiming that the work was shabby and would need to be entirely redone. Folk sued. The trial court gave judgment for Folk in the amount of $140,000, finding that, although there were problems, he had substantially performed. Byron Dragway appealed.

The president of the nation's largest drag racing association testified that the new starting pads were too smooth and that the new concrete contained dangerous dips. One of the dips caused dragster tires to spin sideways. He observed hazardous puddles in both lanes. As he watched a meet, one car crashed and others struggled to negotiate the track. His organization refused to authorize events at Byron until the drag strip was resurfaced.

Other experts agreed that the problems were too severe for simple repairs, and that the surface would have to be ground off and replaced. Clearly, Folk did not substantially perform. The judgment is reversed in favor of Byron Dragway.

PERSONAL SATISFACTION CONTRACTS

Sujata, president of a public relations firm, hires Ben to design a huge multimedia project for her company, involving computer software, music, and live actors, all designed to sell frozen bologna sandwiches to supermarkets. His contract guarantees him two years' employment, provided all of his work "is acceptable in the sole judgment of Sujata." Ben's immediate supervisor is delighted with his work and his colleagues are impressed—all but Sujata. Three months later she fires him, claiming that his work is "uninspired." Does she have the right to do that?

This is a **personal satisfaction contract, in which the promisee makes a personal, subjective evaluation of the promisor's performance.** Employment contracts may require personal satisfaction of the employer, and agreements for the sale of goods may demand that the buyer be personally satisfied with the product. Judges must decide: When is it fair for the promisee to claim that she is not satisfied? May she make that decision for any reason at all, even on a whim?

A court applies a **subjective standard** only if assessing the work involves personal feelings, taste, or judgment and the contract explicitly demanded personal satisfaction. A "subjective standard" means that the promisee's personal views will greatly influence her judgment, even if her decision is foolish and unfair. Artistic or creative work, or highly specialized tasks designed for a particular employer, may involve subtle issues of quality and personal preference. Ben's work combines several media and revolves around his judgment. Accordingly, the law applies a subjective standard to Sujata's decision. Since she concludes that his work is uninspired, she may legally fire him, even if her decision is irrational.

Note that the promisee, Sujata, has to show two things: that assessing Ben's work involves her personal judgment and that their contract explicitly demands personal satisfaction. If the contract were vague on this point, Sujata would lose. Had the agreement merely said, "Ben will at all times make his best efforts," Sujata could not fire him.

GOOD FAITH

The parties to a contract must carry out their obligations in good faith. The Restatement (Second) of Contracts §205 states: **"Every contract imposes upon each party a duty of good faith and fair dealing in its performance and its enforcement."** The difficulty, of course, is applying this general rule to the infinite problems that may arise when two people, or companies, do business. How far must one side go to meet its good-faith burden? The Restatement emphasizes that the parties must remain faithful to the "agreed common purpose and justified expectations of the other party." Good-faith cases frequently arise between insurance companies and their customers.

Suppose that Doug causes a car accident, seriously injuring Virginia. She sues Doug, who is defended by his insurance company. Insurer's maximum liability is $100,000 and the company knows Doug is liable. Virginia is willing to accept $100,000 in full settlement, but Insurer refuses, even though it considers the figure reasonable. The company has a policy of refusing all early offers, in the hope that the long litigation process will wear down the other side and force a cheaper settlement. There is no risk to the company, since it can never be forced to pay more than $100,000, even if a jury returns a much larger verdict. The case goes to trial, and Virginia is awarded $500,000, meaning that Doug now personally owes $400,000. This is bad faith on the part of Insurer. If Doug sues the company, he will win. The company was obligated to fairly analyze the initial settlement offer, and deal fairly with its customer, Doug.

UPDATE | The last decade has seen an increase in bad-faith lawsuits against insurers. Find a new case making this claim. What is the dispute? What is your view? ◼

TIME OF THE ESSENCE CLAUSES

"Go, sir, gallop, and don't forget that the world was made in six days. You can ask me for anything you like, except time."

—*Napoleon, to an aide, 1803*

Generals are not the only ones who place a premium on time. Ask Gene LaSalle. The Seabreeze Restaurant agreed to sell him all of its assets. The parties signed a contract stating the price and closing date. Seabreeze insisted on a clause saying, "Seabreeze considers that time is of the essence in consummating the proposed transaction." Such clauses are common in real estate transactions and in any other agreement where a delay would cause serious damage to one party. LaSalle was unable to close on the date specified and asked for an extension. Seabreeze refused and sold its assets elsewhere. A Florida court affirmed that Seabreeze acted legally.

A time of the essence clause will generally make contract dates strictly enforceable. Seabreeze regarded a timely sale as important, and LaSalle agreed to the provision. There was nothing unreasonable about the clause, and LaSalle suffered the consequences of his delay. Notice, though, that merely including a date for performance does *not* make time of the essence.

Breach

When one party breaches a contract, the other party is discharged. The discharged party has no obligation to perform and may sue for damages. Edwin promises that on July 1 he will deliver 20 tuxedos, tailored to fit male chimpanzees, to Bubba's circus for $300 per suit. After weeks of delay, Edwin concedes he hasn't a cummerbund to his name. Bubba is discharged and obviously owes nothing. In addition, he may sue Edwin for damages. If Bubba is forced to pay $350 elsewhere to obtain similar tuxedos, he will recover the difference in cost. Twenty tuxedos, at $50 extra per suit, means that Bubba will get $1,000 from Edwin.

MATERIAL BREACH

Courts only discharge a contract if a party committed a material breach. A material breach is one that substantially harms the innocent party and for which it would be hard to compensate without discharging the contract. Suppose Edwin fails to show up with the tuxedos on June 1, but calls to say they will arrive under the big top the next day. He has breached the agreement. Is his breach material? No. This is a trivial breach, and Bubba is not discharged. When the tuxedos arrive, he must pay.

ANTICIPATORY BREACH

Sally will receive her bachelor's degree in May and already has a job lined up for September, a two-year contract as window display designer for Surebet Department Store. The morning of graduation, she reads in the paper that Surebet is going out of business that very day. Surebet has told Sally nothing about her status. Sally need not wait until September to learn her fate. Surebet has committed an anticipatory breach by making it unmistakably clear that it will not honor the contract. Sometimes a promisor will actually inform the promisee that it will not perform its duties. At other times, as here, the promisor takes some step that makes the breach evident. Sally is discharged and may immediately seek other work. She is also entitled to file suit for breach of contract. The court will treat Surebet's anticipatory breach just as though the store had actually refused to perform on September 1.

STATUTE OF LIMITATIONS

A party injured by a breach of contract should act promptly. **A statute of limitations begins to run at the time of injury and will limit the time within which the injured party may file suit.** Statutes of limitation vary from state to state and even from issue to issue within a state. In some states, for example, an injured party must sue on oral contracts within three years, on a sale-of-goods contract within four years, and on some written contracts within five years. Failure to file suit within the time limits discharges the party who breached the contract.

Impossibility

If performing a contract is truly impossible, a court will discharge the agreement. But if honoring the deal merely imposes a financial burden, the law will generally enforce the contract.

True impossibility means that something has happened making it utterly impossible to do what the promisor said he would do. Françoise owns a vineyard that produces Beaujolais nouveau wine. She agrees to ship 1,000 cases of her wine to Tyrone, a New York importer, as soon as this year's vintage is ready. Tyrone will pay $50 per case. But a fungus wipes out her entire vineyard. Françoise is discharged. It is theoretically impossible for Françoise to deliver wine from her vineyard, and she owes Tyrone nothing.

Meanwhile, though, Tyrone has a contract with Jackson, a retailer, to sell 1,000 cases of any Beaujolais nouveau wine at $70 per case. Tyrone has no wine from Françoise, and the only other Beaujolais nouveau available will cost him $85 per case. Instead of earning $20 per case, Tyrone will lose $15. Does this discharge Tyrone's contract with Jackson? No. It is possible for him to perform, just undesirable. He must fulfill his agreement.

True impossibility is generally limited to these three causes:

* Destruction of the Subject Matter, as happened with Françoise's vineyard.

* Death of the Promisor in a personal services contract. When the promisor, say a portrait painter, agrees personally to render a service that cannot be transferred to someone else, her death discharges the contract.

* Illegality. If the purpose of a contract becomes illegal, that change discharges the contract. Kitty hires Kato to work in her new Keno Klub (a club with electronic gambling games), but a month later the state legislature KO's keno, declaring that "Keno korrupts." Kitty's contract is discharged.

COMMERCIAL IMPRACTICABILITY AND FRUSTRATION OF PURPOSE

It is rare for contract performance to be truly impossible, but common for it to become a financial burden to one party. Suppose Bradshaw Steel in Pittsburgh agrees to deliver 1,000 tons of steel beams to Rice Construction in Saudi Arabia at a given price, but a week later the cost of raw ore increases 30%. A contract once lucrative to the manufacturer is suddenly a major liability. Does that change discharge Bradshaw? Absolutely not. Rice signed the deal precisely to protect itself against price increases.

Yet there may be times when a change in circumstances is so extreme that it would be unfair to enforce a deal. What if a strike made it impossible for Bradshaw to ship the steel to Saudi Arabia, and the only way to deliver would be by air, at five times the sea cost? Must Bradshaw fulfill its deal? What if war in the Middle East meant that any ships or planes delivering the goods might be fired upon? Other changes could make the contract undesirable for Rice. Suppose the builder wanted steel for a major public building in Riyadh, but the Saudi government decided not to go forward with the construction. The steel would then be worthless to Rice. Must the company still accept it? Courts use the related doctrines of commercial impracticability and frustration of purpose to decide when a change in circumstances should permit one side to escape its duties.

Commercial impracticability means some event has occurred that neither party anticipated, and fulfilling the contract would now be extraordinarily difficult and unfair to one party. If a shipping strike forces Bradshaw to ship by air, the company will argue that neither side expected the strike and that Bradshaw should not suffer a fivefold increase in shipping cost. Bradshaw will probably win the argument.

Frustration of purpose means some event has occurred that neither party anticipated and the contract now has no value for one party. If Rice's building project is canceled, Rice will argue that the steel now is useless to the company. Frustration cases are hard to predict. Some states would agree with Rice, but others would hold that it was Rice's obligation to protect itself with a government guarantee that the project would be completed. Courts consider the following factors in deciding impracticability and frustration claims:

- Mere financial difficulties will never suffice to discharge a contract.

- The event must have been truly unexpected.

- If the promisor must use a different means (such as transportation) to accomplish her task, at a greatly increased cost, she probably does have a valid claim of impracticability.

- A *force majeure* clause may help. A typical *force majeure* clause might permit the seller of goods to delay or cancel delivery in the event of "acts of God, fire, labor disputes, accidents or transportation difficulties." A court will consider such a clause, but may not enforce it if one party is trying to escape from routine financial problems.

CASE SUMMARY

CAPE-FRANCE ENTERPRISES v. PEED

29 P.3d 1011
Montana Supreme Court, 2001

FACTS: Cape-France Enterprises owned a large tract of land in Montana. Lola Peed and her granddaughter Marthe Moore offered to buy 5 acres of the property to build a hotel, and the parties signed a written agreement. However, the Department of Environmental Quality (DEQ) warned the parties that there was an underground pollution plume of perchloroethylene (PCE) near the property. The DEQ would not permit the subdivision and sale unless the parties dug a well and tested the water. DEQ letters acknowledged that no one knew the contamination's extent, but cautioned that drilling a well could cause it to spread further, creating liability for whoever owned the land.

Cape-France sued to rescind the contract. The buyers counterclaimed, seeking specific performance of the agreement. The trial court ordered the contract rescinded, based on impracticability. The buyers appealed.

ISSUE: Did impracticability prevent enforcement of the contract?

DECISION: Yes, impracticability prevented enforcement. Affirmed.

REASONING: Peed and Moore argue that the contract should not be rescinded because it remains possible to drill the well. Because there is no proof that drilling would cause the contamination to spread, they conclude that this is not a case of commercial impracticability.

PCE is a dangerous substance that has been linked to cancer, nerve damage, and other major illnesses. The chemical is also toxic to aquatic life. Although a new well *might* not cause the PCE to spread, there is a substantial risk it would do so. Both seller and buyer could be exposed to major, unquantifiable liability. All parties refused to assume responsibility if the contamination broadened.

The Montana Constitution guarantees everyone within the state a clean, healthful environment. Enforcing this contract would expose our citizens to potentially major environmental damage, violating the state's Constitution and leaving the parties liable for untold sums. Public policy requires that the contract be rescinded.

Chapter Conclusion

Negotiate carefully. A casually written letter may imply a condition that the author never intended. Never assume that mere inconvenience or financial loss will discharge contractual duties.

Chapter Review

1. A condition is an event that must occur before a party becomes obligated.

2. Strict performance, which requires one party to fulfill its duties perfectly, is unusual. In construction and service contracts, substantial performance is generally sufficient to entitle the promisor to the contract price, minus the cost of defects in the work.

3. Good-faith performance is required in all contracts.

4. Time of the essence clauses result in strict enforcement of contract deadlines.

5. A material breach is the only kind that will discharge a contract; a trivial breach will not.

6. True impossibility means that some event has made it impossible to perform an agreement.

7. Commercial impracticability means that some unexpected event has made it extraordinarily difficult and unfair for one party to perform its obligations.

8. Frustration of purpose may occur when an unexpected event renders a contract completely useless to one party.

PRACTICE TEST

Matching Questions

Match the following terms with their definitions:

___ **A.** Strict performance

___ **B.** Material

___ **C.** Discharged

___ **D.** Substantial performance

___ **E.** Condition

1. An event that must occur before a party becomes obligated under a contract.

2. Entitles a party to most or all of the contract price.

3. May be required in a personal services contract.

4. A type of breach that substantially harms the innocent party.

5. When a party has no more obligations under a contract.

True/False Questions

Circle true or false:

1. T   F   Frustration of purpose means that a contract has become a financial liability for one party.

2. T   F   A statute of limitations begins to run at the time of injury.

3. T   F   Contract dates and deadlines are strictly enforceable unless the parties agree otherwise.

4. T   F   Parties must use good faith in performing their contractual duties.

5. T   F   When one party breaches a contract the other party is still obligated to perform.

Multiple-Choice Questions

6. Jody is obligated under a contract to deliver 100,000 plastic bottles to a spring water company. Jody's supplier has just gone bankrupt; any other suppliers will charge her more than she expected to pay. This is

    (a) Frustration of purpose.   (d) Substantial performance
    (b) Impossibility.   (e) Legally irrelevant.
    (c) Commercial impracticability.

7. Strict performance

    (a) Is the norm in contract cases.   (d) Used to be the norm in contract cases but is now illegal.
    (b) Is required in services contracts, but not sale of goods.
    (c) May be required concerning payment, in a sale-of-goods case.   (e) Only applies when there has been a material breach.

8. Monica agrees to buy Kelly's house for $600,000 "on July 10, provided that by July 5 buyer has obtained financing of at least $500,000 at no more than 6% interest." Both parties sign the agreement. Monica is unable to obtain financing. Kelly sues to enforce the deal.

    (a) Monica wins, because the contract is impossible.   (d) Kelly wins, because the clause is against public policy.
    (b) Monica wins, because the condition failed.
    (c) Monica wins, because of frustration of purpose.   (e) Kelly wins, because there was no "time of the essence" clause.

9. Contracting parties are most commonly discharged by

    (a) Impracticability.   (d) Public policy.
    (b) Full performance.   (e) Strict performance.
    (c) Part performance.

10. An example of true impossibility is

    (a) Strict performance.   (d) Material breach.
    (b) Failure of condition.   (e) Novation.
    (c) Illegality.

Short-Answer Questions

11. Stephen Krogness was a real estate broker. He signed an agreement to act as an agent for Best Buy Co., which was interested in selling several of its stores. The contract provided that Best Buy would pay Krogness a commission of 2% for a sale to "any prospect submitted directly to Best Buy by Krogness." Krogness introduced Corporate Realty Capital (CRC) to Best Buy, and the parties negotiated a possible sale but could not reach agreement. CRC then introduced Best Buy to BB Properties (BB). Best Buy sold several properties to BB for a total of $46 million. CRC acted as the broker on the deal. After the sale, Krogness sought a commission of $528,000. Is he entitled to it?

12. Evans built a house for Sandra Dyer, but the house had some problems. The garage ceiling was too low. Load-bearing beams in the great room cracked and appeared to be steadily weakening. The patio did not drain properly. Pipes froze. Evans wanted the money promised for the job, but Dyer refused to pay. Comment.

13. ETHICS: Ken Ward was an Illinois farmer who worked land owned by his father-in-law, Frank Ruda. To finance his operation, he frequently borrowed money from Watseka First National Bank, paying back the loans with farming profits. But Ward fell deeper and deeper into debt, and Watseka became concerned. When Ward sought additional loans, Watseka insisted that Ruda become a guarantor on all of the outstanding debt, and the father-in-law agreed. The new loans had an acceleration clause, permitting the bank to demand payment of the entire debt if it believed itself "insecure," that is, at risk of a default. Unfortunately, just as Ward's debts reached more than $120,000, Illinois suffered a severe drought, and Ward's crops failed. Watseka asked Ruda to sell some of the land he owned to pay back part of the indebtedness. Ruda reluctantly agreed but never did so. Meanwhile, Ward decreased his payments to the bank because of the terrible crop. Watseka then "accelerated" the loan, demanding that Ruda pay off the entire debt. Ruda defended by claiming that Watseka's acceleration at such a difficult time was bad faith. Who wins the legal case? Analyze the ethical issues.

14. In August 1985, Colony Park Associates signed a contract to buy 44 acres of residential land from John Gall. The contract stated that "closing will take place August 20, 1986." The year's delay was to enable Colony Park to obtain building permits to develop condominiums. Colony Park worked diligently to obtain all permits and kept Gall abreast of its efforts. But delays in sewer permits forced Colony Park to notify Gall it could not close on the agreed date. Colony Park suggested a date exactly one month later. Gall refused the new date and declined to convey the property to Colony Park. Colony Park sued.

Gall argued that since the parties specified a date, time was of the essence and Colony Park's failure to buy on time discharged Gall. Please rule.

15. Omega Concrete had a gravel pit and factory. Access was difficult, so Omega contracted with Union Pacific Railroad (UP) for the right to use a private road that crossed UP property and tracks. The contract stated that use of the road was solely for Omega employees and that Omega would be responsible for closing a gate that UP planned to build where the private road joined a public highway. In fact, UP never constructed the gate; Omega had no authority to construct the gate. Mathew Rogers, an Omega employee, was killed by a train while using the private road to reach Omega. Rogers's family sued Omega, claiming, among other things, that Omega failed to keep the gate closed as the contract required. Is Omega liable based on that failure?

16. Krug International, an Ohio corporation, had a contract with Iraqi Airways to build aeromedical equipment for training pilots. Krug then contracted for Power Engineering, an Iowa corporation, to build the specialized gearbox to be used in the training equipment, for $150,000. Power did not know that Krug planned to resell the gearbox to Iraqi Airways. When Power had almost completed the gearbox, the Gulf War broke out and the United Nations declared an embargo on all shipments to Iraq. Krug notified Power that it no longer wanted the gearbox. Power sued. Please rule.

17. ROLE REVERSAL: Write a multiple-choice question focusing on a contractor's claim to substantial performance. The answers should contain dollar amounts that the contractor could possibly recover, from zero to the full value of the contract.

Internet Research Problem

Using the Internet, find a contract that contains a "commercial impracticability" clause and/or a "frustration of purpose" clause. They often go together. A good place to look is at **http://www.findlaw.com**, although many other sites will contain such clauses. What is the subject of the contract generally? What did the drafters of the contract hope to achieve with the clause you have located? In your opinion, will a court enforce the clause? (Refer to the bulleted list of criteria on page 224) Why or why not? If the clause is valid, will it accomplish the purpose you have described?

You can find further practice problems in the Online Quiz at **http://beatty.westbuslaw.com** or in the Study Guide that accompanies this text.

16

Remedies

Anybody can wrestle an alligator. But Freddie could wrestle an alligator and a python simultaneously. Kira watched Freddie clamp the snake on the gator's back and pin them both to the hard red soil; and when the small roadside crowd screamed approval, she knew she was looking at profit. She immediately signed Freddie to a two-year contract, promising him $500 per week plus room and board. They agreed that Rasslin' Reptiles would start its tour in a month, as soon as Kira had everything ready. Kira then spent $20,000 on a used mobile home and paid $8,000 for two more alligators and another python. Next, she hustled out on the road, drumming up business. Country bars and suburban malls were intrigued by her promotional pitch, though slow with guarantees.

Some suggested they would pay her $500 to put on a show, if and when she arrived. Others promised to rent space to her, allowing her to charge admission. Everything was looking great, and Kira went back to collect her star performer. But Freddie had met the girl of his dreams.

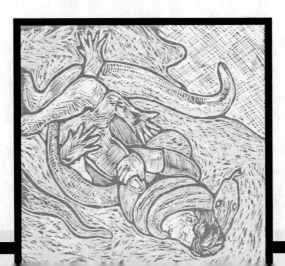

Breaching the Contract

The young woman had read Freddie one of her original sonnets, and the wrestler had fallen in love with poetry. He planned to enroll in State University's creative writing program. Kira hissed and thrashed to no avail, and finally sued. Freddie had certainly breached his contract. **Someone breaches a contract when he fails to perform a duty, without a valid excuse.** When the case gets to trial, a court will declare that Freddie is in breach of the agreement. But what will Kira's remedy be? **A remedy is the method a court uses to compensate an injured party.** How will a court help Kira? Should the court force Freddie to return to rasslin'? An order forcing someone to do something, or refrain from doing something, is an **injunction.** Courts seldom grant injunctions to compel a party to perform a job, since that would force two antagonistic people to work together. The court could prohibit Freddie from working elsewhere, and perhaps from going to school. Is that sensible?

The most common remedy, used in the great majority of lawsuits, is money damages. If the court decides to award Kira damages, how much money should she get? Kira may claim that she could have performed 8 to 10 shows a week, at $500 per show, for a total of $4,000 to $5,000 per week. Lost profits are considered *expectation* damages. Freddie will respond that all of the "shows" were hypothetical, since not one penny of income had been guaranteed. If Kira is not entitled to lost profits, should she receive the money spent on tour preparations? Such a remedy is called *reliance* damages.

How to help an injured party, without unfairly harming the other person, is the focus of remedies. Courts have struggled with remedies for centuries, but we will master them in one chapter. Kira will not obtain an injunction forcing Freddie to wrestle. An order barring him from college is also unlikely. And she will be hard pressed to prove lost profits, since she had no guarantee of earnings. She should win something for her reliance on Freddie's deal, since she spent $28,000 on major purchases. But she may not get that full amount because in losing Freddie's services she also shed the expense of an unproven road tour. The questions and issues created by Kira's broken road tour are typical remedy problems.

Though a court may have several alternative remedies available, it is important to note that almost all of them have one thing in common: The focus is on compensating the injured party, rather than punishing the party in breach. A court must decide whether to give Kira her lost profits or her expenses, but it will not consider sending Freddie to jail or assessing damages to punish him.

IDENTIFYING THE "INTEREST" TO BE PROTECTED

The first step that a court takes in choosing a remedy is to decide what interest it is trying to protect. An **interest** is a legal right in something. Someone can have an interest in property, for example, by owning it, or renting it to a tenant, or lending money to buy it. He can have an interest in a contract if the agreement gives him some benefit. There are four principal contract interests that a court may seek to protect:

- *Expectation interest.* This refers to what the injured party reasonably thought she would get from the contract. The goal is to put her in the position she would have been in if both parties had fully performed their obligations.

- *Reliance interest.* The injured party may be unable to demonstrate expectation damages, perhaps because it is unclear he would have profited. But he may still prove that he expended money in reliance on the agreement and that in fairness he should receive compensation.

- *Restitution interest.* The injured party may be unable to show an expectation interest or reliance. But perhaps she has conferred a benefit on the other party. Here, the objective is to restore to the injured party the benefit she has provided.

- *Equitable interest.* In some cases, money damages will not suffice to help the injured party. Something more is needed, such as an order to transfer property to the injured party (specific performance) or an order forcing one party to stop doing something (an injunction).

In this chapter, we look at all four interests.

Expectation Interest

This is the most common remedy that the law provides for a party injured by a breach of contract. **The expectation interest is designed to put the injured party in the position she would have been in had both sides fully performed their obligations.** A court tries to give the injured party the money she would have made from the contract. If accurately computed, this should take into account all the gains she reasonably expected and all the expenses and losses she would have incurred. The injured party should not end up better off than she would have been under the agreement, nor should she suffer serious loss.

William Colby was a former director of the CIA. He wanted to write a book about his 15 years of experiences in Vietnam. He paid James McCarger $5,000 for help in writing an early draft and promised McCarger another $5,000 if the book was published. Then he hired Alexander Burnham to coauthor the book. Colby's agent secured a contract with Contemporary Books, which included a $100,000 advance. But Burnham was hopelessly late with the manuscript, and Colby missed his publication date. Colby fired Burnham and finished the book without him. Contemporary published *Lost Victory* several years late, and the book flopped, earning no significant revenue. Because the book was so late, Contemporary paid Colby a total of only $17,000. Colby sued Burnham for his lost expectation interest. The court awarded him $23,000, calculated as follows:

$100,000	Advance, the only money Colby was promised.
−10,000	Agent's fee.
= 90,000	Fee for the two authors combined.
Divided by 2 = 45,000	Colby's fee.
5,000	Owed to McGarger under the earlier agreement.
= 40,000	Colby's expectation interest.
−17,000	Fee Colby received from Contemporary.
= 23,000	Colby's expectation damages, that is, the amount he would have received had Burnham finished on time.

The Colby case presented an easy calculation of damages. Other contracts are complex. Courts typically divide the expectation damages into three parts: (1) compensatory (or "direct") damages, which represent harm that flowed directly from the contract's breach; (2) consequential (or "special") damages, which represent harm caused by the injured party's unique situation; and (3) incidental damages, which are minor costs such as storing or returning defective goods, advertising for alternative goods, and so forth. The first two, compensatory and consequential, are the important ones. We look at them one at a time.

COMPENSATORY DAMAGES

Compensatory damages are the most common monetary awards for the expectation interest. Courts also refer to these as "direct damages." **Compensatory damages are those that flow directly from the contract.** In other words, these are the damages that inevitably result from the breach. Suppose Ace Productions hires Reina to star in its new movie, *Inside Straight.* Ace promises Reina $3 million, providing she shows up June 1 and works until the film is finished. But in late May, Joker Entertainment offers Reina $6 million to star in its new feature, and on June 1 Reina informs Ace that she will not appear. Reina has breached her contract, and Ace should recover compensatory damages.

What are the damages that flow directly from the contract? Ace obviously has to replace Reina. If Ace hires Kween as its star and pays her a fee of $4 million, Ace is entitled to the difference between what it expected to pay ($3 million) and what the breach forced it to pay ($4 million), or $1 million in compensatory damages. Suppose the rest of the cast and crew are idle for two weeks because of the delay in hiring a substitute, and the lost time costs the producers an extra $2.5 million. Reina is also liable for those expenses. Both the new actress and the delay are inevitable.

Reasonable Certainty

The injured party must prove the breach of contract caused damages that can be quantified with reasonable certainty. What if *Inside Straight,* now starring Kween, bombs at the box office? Ace proves that each of Reina's last three movies grossed over $60 million, but *Inside Straight* grossed only $28 million. Is Reina liable for the lost profits? No. Ace cannot prove that it was Reina's absence that caused the film to fare poorly. The script may have been mediocre, or Kween's costars dull, or the publicity efforts inadequate. Mere "speculative damages" are worth nothing.

CONSEQUENTIAL DAMAGES

In addition to compensatory damages, the injured party may seek consequential damages or, as they are also known, "special damages." **Consequential damages are those resulting from the unique circumstances of *this injured party*.** The rule concerning this remedy comes from a famous 1854 case, which all American law students read. Now it is your turn.

CASE SUMMARY

HADLEY v. BAXENDALE

9 Ex. 341, 156 Eng. Rep. 145
Court of Exchequer, 1854

FACTS: The Hadleys operated a flour mill in Gloucester. The crankshaft broke, causing the mill to grind to a halt. The Hadleys employed Baxendale to cart the damaged part to a foundry in Greenwich, where a new one could be manufactured. Baxendale promised to make the delivery in one day, but he was late transporting the shaft, and as a result the Hadleys' mill was shut for five extra days. They sued, and the jury awarded damages based in part on their lost profits. Baxendale appealed.

ISSUE: Should the defendant be liable for profits lost because of his delay in delivering the shaft?

DECISION: The defendant is not liable for lost profits. Reversed.

REASONING: When one side breaches a contract, the other party's damages should be those that arise inevitably from the breach or those that *both* parties reasonably anticipated when they made the agreement. If the contract involves special circumstances, and the plaintiff tells the defendant about them when they make the deal, then the defendant is liable for all injuries. On the other hand, if the plaintiff never informed the defendant about the unique situation, then the defendant should only be liable for harm that might occur in the normal course of events.

The Hadleys only told Baxendale that the article to be carried was a broken shaft from their mill. How could Baxendale have realized that a delay in delivery would prevent the mill from operating? He might have assumed very reasonably that the Hadleys owned a second shaft, and were sending this one for repairs while the mill ground on. It would be unfair to presume Baxendale realized that delay would halt the mill. The case should be retried, and the jury may *not* consider the Hadleys' lost profits.

The rule from Hadley v. Baxendale has been unchanged ever since: **the injured party may recover consequential damages only if the breaching party should have foreseen them.**

Let us return briefly to *Inside Straight*. Suppose that, long before shooting began, Ace had sold the film's soundtrack rights to Spinem Sound for $2 million. Spinem believed it would make a profit only if Reina appeared in the film, so it demanded the right to discharge the agreement if Reina dropped out. When Reina quit, Spinem terminated the contract. Now, when Ace sues Reina, it will also seek $2 million in consequential damages for the lost music revenue. If Reina knew about Ace's contract with Spinem when she signed to do the film, she is liable for $2 million. If she never realized she was an essential part of the music contract, she owes nothing for the lost profits.

INCIDENTAL DAMAGES

Incidental damages are the relatively minor costs that the injured party suffers when responding to the breach. When Reina, the actress, breaches the film contract, the producers may have to leave the set and fly back to Los Angeles to hire a new actress. The cost of travel, food, and audition-room rental are incidental damages.

SALE OF GOODS

Under the Uniform Commercial Code (UCC), remedies for breach of contract in the sale of goods are similar to the general rules discussed throughout this chapter. UCC §§2-703 through 2-715 govern the remedies available to buyers and sellers.

Seller's Remedies

If a buyer breaches a sale-of-goods contract, the seller generally has at least two remedies. She may resell the goods elsewhere. If she acts in good faith, she will be awarded **the difference between the original contract price and the price she was able to obtain in the open market.** Assume that Maud, the manufacturer, had a contract to sell her shoes to Foot the Bill for $55 per pair, and Foot the Bill's breach forces her to sell them on the open market, where she gets only $48 per pair. Maud will win $7 per pair times 5,000 pairs, or $35,000, from Foot the Bill.

Alternatively, the buyer may choose not to resell and settle for the difference between the contract price and the market value of the goods. Maud, in other words, may choose to keep the shoes. If she can prove that their market value is $48 per pair, for example, by showing what other retailers would have paid her for them, she will still get her $7 each, representing the difference between what the contract promised her and what the market would support. In either case, the money represents compensatory damages. Maud is also entitled to incidental damages, such as the storage and advertising expenses described above. But there is one significant difference **under the UCC: Most courts hold that the seller of goods is not entitled to consequential damages.** Suppose Maud hired two extra workers to inspect, pack, and ship the shoes for Foot the Bill. Those are consequential damages, but Maud will not recover them because she is the seller and the contract is for the sale of goods.

Buyer's Remedies

The buyer's remedies under the Code are similar to those we have already considered. She typically has two options. First, the buyer can "cover" by purchasing substitute goods. To **cover** means to make a good faith purchase of goods similar to those in the contract. The buyer may then obtain **the difference between the original contract price and her cover price.** Alternatively, if the buyer chooses not to cover, she is entitled to the difference between the original contract price and the market value of the goods.

Suppose Mary has contracted to buy 1,000 6-foot Christmas trees at $25 per tree from Elmo. The market suddenly rises, and in the spirit of the season Elmo breaches his deal and sells the trees elsewhere. If Mary makes a good-faith effort to cover but is forced to pay $40 per tree, she may recover the difference from Elmo, meaning $15 per tree times 1,000 trees, or $15,000. Similarly, if she chooses not to cover but can prove that $40 is now the market value of the trees, she is entitled to her $15 per tree.

Under the UCC, the buyer *is* entitled to consequential damages provided that the seller could reasonably have foreseen them. If Mary tells Elmo, when they sign their deal, that she has a dozen contracts to resell the trees, for an average price of $50 per tree, she may recover $25 per tree, representing the difference between her contract price with Elmo and the value of the tree to her, based on her other contracts. If she failed to inform Elmo of the other contracts, she would not receive any money based on them. The buyer is also entitled to whatever incidental damages may have accrued.

We turn now to cases where the injured party cannot prove expectation damages.

Reliance Interest

George plans to manufacture and sell silk scarves during the holiday season. In the summer, he contracts with Cecily, the owner of a shopping mall, to rent a high-visibility stall for $100 per day. George then buys hundreds of yards of costly silk and gets to work cutting and sewing. But in September, Cecily refuses to honor the contract. George sues and easily proves Cecily breached a valid contract. But what is his remedy?

George cannot establish an expectation interest in his scarf business. He hoped to sell each scarf for a $40 gross profit, and wanted to make $2,000 per day. But how much would he actually have earned? Enough to retire on? Enough to buy a salami sandwich for lunch? A court cannot give him an expectation interest, so George will ask for reliance damages. **The reliance interest is designed to put the injured party in the position he would have been in had the parties never entered into a contract.** This remedy focuses on the time and money the injured party spent performing his part of the agreement.

Assuming he is unable to sell the scarves to a retail store (which is probable since retailers will have made purchases long ago), George should be able to recover the cost of the silk fabric he bought and perhaps something for the hours of labor he spent cutting and sewing. However, reliance damages can be difficult to win because they are harder to *quantify.* Judges dislike vague calculations. How much was George's time worth in making the scarves? How good was his work? How likely were the scarves to sell? If George has a track record in the industry, he will be able to show a market price for his services. Without such a record, his reliance claim becomes a tough battle.

RELIANCE DAMAGES AND PROMISSORY ESTOPPEL

In one type of case, courts use reliance damages exclusively. Recall the doctrine of promissory estoppel, which sometimes permits a plaintiff to recover damages even without a valid contract. The plaintiff must show that the defendant made a promise knowing that the plaintiff would likely rely on it, that the plaintiff did rely, and that the only way to avoid injustice is to enforce the promise. **In promissory estoppel cases, a court will generally award *only* reliance damages.** It would be unfair to give expectation damages for the full benefit of the bargain when, legally, there has been no bargain. Lou says to Costas, who lives in Philadelphia, "You're a great chef. Come out to Los Angeles. My new restaurant needs you, and I can double your salary if not more." Costas quits his job and travels out west, but Lou has no job for him. There is no binding contract, because the terms were too vague; however, the chef will *probably* obtain some reliance damages based on lost income and moving costs.

AT RISK ❙ Costas's reliance damages are uncertain. How should he have protected himself? ◾

Restitution Interest

Jim and Bonnie Hyler bought an expensive recreational vehicle (RV) from Autorama. The salesman promised the Hylers that a manufacturer's warranty covered the entire vehicle for a year. The Hylers had a succession of major problems with their RV, including windows that wouldn't shut, a door that fell off, a loose windshield, and defective walls. Then they learned that the manufacturer had gone bankrupt. In fact, the Autorama salesman knew of the bankruptcy when he made the sales pitch. The Hylers returned the RV to Autorama and demanded their money back. They wanted restitution.

The restitution interest is designed to return to the injured party a benefit that he has conferred on the other party, which it would be unjust to leave with that person. Restitution is a common remedy in contracts involving fraud, misrepresentation, mistake, and duress. In these cases, restitution often goes hand-in-hand with **rescission,** which means to "undo" a contract and put the parties where they were before they made the agreement. The court declared that Autorama had misrepresented the manufacturer's warranty by omitting the small fact that the manufacturer itself no longer existed. Autorama was forced to return to the Hylers the full purchase price plus the value of the automobile they had traded. The dealer, of course, was allowed to keep the defective RV and stare out the ill-fitting windows.

Courts also award restitution in cases of quasi-contract, which we examined in Chapter 9. In quasi-contract cases, the parties never made a contract, but one side did benefit the other. A court may choose to award restitution where one party has conferred a benefit on another and it would be unjust for the other party to retain the benefit. Suppose Owner asks Supplier to install a new furnace in her home. Supplier forgets to ask Owner to sign a contract. If the furnace works properly, it would be unfair to let Owner keep it for free, and a court might order full payment as restitution, even though there was no valid contract.

Other Equitable Interests

In addition to restitution, the other three equitable powers that concern us are specific performance, injunction, and reformation.

Specific Performance

Leona Claussen owned Iowa farmland. She sold some of it to her sister-in-law, Evelyn Claussen, and, along with the land, granted Evelyn an option to buy additional property at $800 per acre. Evelyn could exercise her option anytime during Leona's lifetime or within six months of Leona's death. When Leona died, Evelyn informed the estate's executor that she was exercising her option. But other relatives wanted the property, and the executor refused to sell. Evelyn sued and asked for specific performance. She did not want an award of damages; she wanted the land itself. The remedy of specific performance forces the two parties to perform their contract.

A court will award specific performance, ordering the parties to perform the contract, only in cases involving the sale of land or some other asset that is unique. Courts use this equitable remedy when money damages would be inadequate to compensate the injured party. If the subject is unique and irreplaceable, money damages will not put the injured party in the same position she would have been in had the agreement been kept. So a court will order the seller to convey the rare object and the buyer to pay for it.

Historically, every parcel of land has been regarded as unique, and therefore specific performance is always available in real estate contracts. Evelyn Claussen won specific performance. The Iowa Supreme Court ordered Leona's estate to convey the land to Evelyn, for $800 per acre. Generally speaking, either the seller or the buyer may be granted specific performance.

Other unique items, for which a court will order specific performance, include such things as rare works of art, secret formulas, and patents. By contrast, a contract for a new Cadillac Escalade is not enforceable by specific performance. An injured buyer can use money damages to purchase a virtually identical auto.

INJUNCTION

You move into your new suburban house on two acres of land, and the fresh air is exhilarating. But the wind shifts to the west, and you find yourself thinking of farm animals, especially pigs. It turns out that your next-door neighbor just started an organic bacon ranch, and the first 15 porkers have checked in. You check out the town's zoning code, discover that it is illegal to raise livestock in the neighborhood, and sue. But money damages will not suffice, because you want the bouquet to disappear. You seek the equitable remedy of injunction. **An injunction is a court order that requires someone to do something or refrain from doing something.**

The court will order your neighbor immediately to cease and desist raising any pigs or other farm animals on his land. "Cease" means to stop, and "desist" means to refrain from doing it in the future. The injunction will not get you any money, but it will move the pigs out of town, and that was your goal. (The Web site **http://www.kinseylaw.com/ATTY%20SERV/civil/complaints/injunction.html** provides a sample complaint requesting an injunction.)

In the increasingly litigious world of professional sports, injunctions are commonplace. Brian Shaw was playing professional basketball in Italy when the Boston Celtics flipped him a contract offer. In January, Shaw inked a five-year deal with the Celtics, to begin playing the following October. The player grabbed a $450,000 bonus and a guaranteed salary of over $1 million per year. In June, Shaw reversed direction, informing the Celtics that he would remain with his Italian team. Boston ran a fast break into federal court, seeking an injunction. Shaw argued that when he signed the Celtics' contract he had been homesick for America, and depressed by criticism in the Italian press. He added that no agent had been available to assist. The court rejected his claims, noting that Shaw was a college graduate and the contract was a simple, standard-form agreement. The judge granted the injunction, blocking Shaw from playing anywhere except Boston.

REFORMATION

The final remedy, and perhaps the least common, is **reformation,** a process in which a court will partially "rewrite" a contract. Courts seldom do this, because the whole point of a contract is to enable the parties to control their own futures. But a court may reform a contract if it believes a written agreement includes a simple mistake. Suppose that Roger orally agrees to sell 35 acres to Hannah for $600,000. The parties then draw up a written agreement, accidentally describing the land as including 50 additional acres that neither party considered part of the deal. Roger refuses to sell. Hannah sues for specific performance, but asks the court to reform the written contract to reflect the true agreement. Most but not all courts would reform the agreement and enforce it.

A court may also reform a contract to save it. If Natasha sells her advertising business to Joseph and agrees not to open a competing agency in the same city anytime in the next 10 years, a court may decide that it is unfair to force her to wait a decade. It could reform the agreement and permit Natasha to compete, say, three years after the sale. But some courts are reluctant to reform contracts and would throw out the entire noncompetition agreement rather than reform it. Parties should never settle for a contract that is sloppy or overbroad, assuming that a court will later reform errors. They may find themselves stuck with a bargain they dislike or with no contract at all.

Special Issues of Damages

MITIGATION OF DAMAGES

There is one major limitation on *all* contract remedies: **A party injured by a breach of contract may not recover for damages that he could have avoided with reasonable efforts.** In other words, when one party perceives that the other has breached or will breach the contract, the injured party must try to prevent unnecessary loss. A party is expected to **mitigate** his damages, that is, to keep damages as low as he reasonably can. If you breach your lease by moving out of the apartment six months early, your landlord must make reasonable attempts to find a new tenant.

LIQUIDATED DAMAGES

It can be difficult or even impossible to prove how much damage the injured party has suffered. So lawyers and executives negotiating a deal may include in the contract a **liquidated damages clause, a provision stating in advance how much a party must pay if it breaches.** Is that fair? The answer depends on two factors: A court will generally enforce a liquidated damages clause if

- At the time of creating the contract it was very difficult to estimate actual damages; *and*

- The liquidated amount is reasonable. In any other case, the liquidated damage will be considered a penalty and will prove unenforceable.

In the following case, a private school provided special tutoring in liquidated damages—but not for free.

CASE SUMMARY

LAKE RIDGE ACADEMY v. CARNEY

66 Ohio St. 3d 376, 613 N.E.2d 183, 1993 Ohio LEXIS 1210
Supreme Court of Ohio, 1993

FACTS: In March, Mr. Carney reserved a spot in the 4th grade class at Lake Ridge Academy for his son, Michael. He paid a $630 deposit and agreed in writing to pay the balance of the tuition, $5,610, later that year. The contract permitted Carney to cancel the agreement and withdraw his son with no further obligation provided he did so before August 1. If he failed to notify the school before that date, he became liable for the full tuition.

Carney wrote a letter notifying Lake Ridge that Michael would not attend. He dated the letter August 1, mailed it August 7, and the school received it August 14. Lake Ridge demanded its full tuition, Carney refused, and the school sued. One of the disputed issues was whether the liquidated damages clause was a penalty. The trial court found for Carney, but the court of appeals reversed, finding that the clause was valid. Carney appealed to the state's highest court.

ISSUE: Is the liquidated damages clause enforceable?

DECISION: Yes, the liquidated damages clause is enforceable.

REASONING: The question in cases like this is whether the contract clause creates legitimate liquidated damages or unacceptable punitive damages. The answer depends on how easily the parties might have calculated the damages of a breach, and also on the size of the stipulated sum, compared to the value of the contract and the consequences of the breach.

When Carney and Lake Ridge entered into their contract, the damages that Lake Ridge might suffer from a breach were uncertain in amount and difficult to prove. Creating the school's budget is an uncertain science. The process begins in January and ends in the fall. The tuition money from all students is pooled and goes toward staff salaries, department budgets, maintenance, improvements, and utilities. Lake Ridge would be unable to calculate the precise damages caused by the loss of one student's tuition.

The school designated August 1 as the cutoff date so that it could meet its financial commitments. Carney had almost five months in which to cancel. By August 1, Lake Ridge reasonably relied on full tuition payment. This is a valid, enforceable liquidated damages clause.

Chapter Conclusion

The powers of a court are broad and flexible and may suffice to give an injured party what it deserves. But problems of proof and the uncertainty of remedies demonstrate that the best solution is a carefully drafted contract and socially responsible behavior.

Chapter Review

1. Someone breaches a contract when he fails to perform a duty, without a valid excuse.

2. A remedy is the method a court uses to compensate an injured party.

3. An interest is a legal right in something, such as a contract. The first step that a court takes in choosing a remedy is to decide what interest it is protecting.

4. The expectation interest puts the injured party in the position she would have been in had both sides fully performed. It has three components:

   (a) Compensatory damages, which flow directly from the contract.

   (b) Consequential damages, which result from the unique circumstances of the particular injured party.

   (c) Incidental damages, which are the minor costs an injured party incurs responding to a breach.

5. The reliance interest puts the injured party in the position he would have been in had the parties never

entered into a contract. It focuses on the time and money that the injured party spent performing his part of the agreement. If there was no valid contract, a court might still award reliance damages under a theory of promissory estoppel.

6. The restitution interest returns to the injured party a benefit that she has conferred on the other party, which it would be unjust to leave with that person. Restitution can be awarded in the case of a contract created, for example, by fraud, or in a case of quasi-contract, where the parties never created a binding agreement.

7. Specific performance, ordered only in cases of land or a unique asset, requires both parties to perform the contract.

8. An injunction is a court order that requires someone to do something or refrain from doing something.

9. Reformation is the process by which a court will—occasionally—rewrite a contract to ensure that it accurately reflects the parties' agreement and/or to maintain the contract's viability.

10. The duty to mitigate means that a party injured by a breach of contract may not recover for damages that he could have avoided with reasonable efforts.

11. A liquidated damages clause will be enforced if and only if, at the time of creating the contract, it was very difficult to estimate actual damages and the liquidated amount is reasonable.

PRACTICE TEST

Matching Questions

Match the following terms with their definitions:

___ **A.** Liquidated
___ **B.** Specific performance
___ **C.** Restitution
___ **D.** Injunction
___ **E.** Consequential

1. A remedy that typically accompanies rescission.
2. Damages that can be recovered only if the breaching party should have foreseen them.
3. A court order to do (or refrain from doing) something.
4. Damages agreed upon in advance, in the contract.
5. A remedy that requires the parties to perform the contract.

True/False Questions

Circle true or false:

1. T F Courts award the expectation interest more often than any other remedy.
2. T F Consequential damages are those that arise whenever one party breaches a contract.
3. T F In a case of promissory estoppel, a court is most likely to award liquidated damages.
4. T F In a case of quasi-contract, a court is most likely to award restitution.
5. T F Where one party has clearly breached, the injured party must mitigate damages.

Multiple-Choice Questions

6. Rodney and Katerina enter into an agreement. Both parties know exactly what the damages will be if either party breaches. This contract

(a) Is appropriate for liquidated damages.
(b) Is not appropriate for liquidated damages.
(c) Is appropriate for restitution.
(d) Is not appropriate for rescission.
(e) Cannot include consequential damages.

7. Museum schedules a major fundraising dinner, devoted to a famous Botticelli picture, for September 15. Museum then hires Sue Ellen to restore the picture, her work to be done no later than September 14. Sue Ellen is late with the restoration, forcing the Museum to cancel the dinner and lose at least $500,000 in donations. Sue Ellen delivers the picture, in excellent condition, two weeks late. Museum sues.

(a) Museum will win.

(b) Museum will win if, when the parties made the deal, Sue Ellen knew the importance of the date.

(c) Museum will win provided that it was Sue Ellen's fault she was late.

(d) Museum will win provided that it was *not* Sue Ellen's fault she was late.

(e) Museum will lose.

8. Which contract interest is designed to put the injured party in the position she would have been in had both sides fully performed?

(a) Reliance.

(b) Restitution.

(c) Expectation.

(d) Injunction.

(e) Quasi-contract.

9. Max has developed "Sky Juice," a new sports power drink. He signs a contract with the Crushers, a professional hockey team, which allows Max to sell Sky Juice at all Crusher home games, from three booths located inside the stadium. The Crushers, however, run into financial trouble, and cancel their season. Max sues. His best remedy is going to be

(a) Expectation interest.

(b) Reliance interest.

(c) Restitution.

(d) Rescission.

(e) Injunction.

10. Tara is building an artificial beach at her lakefront resort. She agrees in writing to buy 1,000 tons of sand from Frank for $20 per ton, with delivery on June 1, at her resort. Frank fails to deliver any sand, and Tara is forced to go elsewhere. She buys 1,000 tons from Maureen at $25 per ton, and then is forced to pay Walter $5,000 to haul the sand to her resort. Tara sues Frank. Tara will recover

(a) Nothing.

(b) $5,000.

(c) $10,000.

(d) $15,000.

(e) $30,000.

Short-Answer Questions

11. Mr. and Ms. Beard contracted for S/E Joint Venture to build a house on property it owned, and then sell the completed house to the Beards for $785,000. S/E was late with construction and ultimately never finished the house or conveyed anything to the Beards, who sued. Evidence at trial demonstrated that S/E had clearly breached the contract and that the Beards had spent about $32,000 in rent because of the delay. There was testimony that the market value of the house as promised would have been about $100,000 more than the contract price, but this point was not clearly established because the trial judge considered it irrelevant. The judge awarded only the rental payments. Both sides appealed. Is the market value of the house, as it should have been built, relevant? How much money are the Beards entitled to?

12. Lewis signed a contract for the rights to all timber located on Nine Mile Mine. He agreed to pay $70 per thousand board feet ($70/mbf). As he began work, Nine Mile became convinced that Lewis lacked sufficient equipment to do the job well and forbade him to enter the land. Lewis sued. Nine Mile moved for summary judgment. The mine offered proof that the market value of the timber was exactly $70/mbf, and Lewis had no evidence to contradict Nine Mile. The evidence about market value proved decisive. Why? Please rule on the summary judgment motion.

13. Racicky was in the process of buying 320 acres of ranch land. While that sale was being negotiated, Racicky signed a contract to sell the land to Simon. Simon paid $144,000, the full price of the land. But

Racicky then went bankrupt, before he could complete the purchase of the land, let alone its sale. Which of these remedies should Simon seek: expectation, restitution, specific performance, or reformation?

14. Ambrose hires Bierce for $25,000 to supervise the production of Ambrose's crop, but then breaks the contract by firing Bierce at the beginning of the season. A nearby grower offers Bierce $23,000 for the same growing season, but Bierce refuses to take such a pay cut. He stays home and sues Ambrose. How much money, if any, will Bierce recover from Ambrose, and why?

15. ETHICS: The National Football League owns the copyright to the broadcasts of its games. It licenses local television stations to telecast certain games and maintains a "blackout rule," which prohibits stations from broadcasting home games that are not sold out 72 hours before the game starts. Certain home games of the Cleveland Browns team were not sold out, and the NFL blocked local broadcast. But several bars in the Cleveland area were able to pick up the game's signal by using special antennas. The NFL wanted the bars to stop showing the games. What did it do? Was it unethical of the bars to broadcast the games that they were able to pick up? Apart from the NFL's legal rights, do you think it had the moral right to stop the bars from broadcasting the games?

16. ROLE REVERSAL: Write a multiple-choice question involving a contract for the sale of goods. The seller breaches, and the buyer definitely has compensatory damages. The test taker must decide whether there are also consequential damages, and the total amount of damages to which the buyer is entitled.

Internet Research Problem

You represent a group of neighborhood residents in a large city who are protesting construction of a skyscraper that will violate building height limitations. Draft a complaint, requesting an appropriate injunction. You may use the sample injunction complaint found at **http://www.kinseylaw.com/ATTY%20SERV/civil/complaints/injunction.html**.

You can find further practice problems in the Online Quiz at **http://beatty.westbuslaw.com** or in the Study Guide that accompanies this text.

Glossary

A

Accepted check A check that the drawee bank has signed. This signature is a promise that the bank will pay the check out of its own funds. (Chapter 24)

Accession The use of labor and/or materials to add value to the personal property of another. (Chapter 44)

Accommodation party Someone who does not benefit from an instrument but agrees to guarantee its payment. (Chapter 24)

Accord and satisfaction An agreement to settle a debt for less than the sum claimed. (Chapter 11)

Accounts Any right to receive payment for goods sold or leased, other than rights covered by chattel paper or instruments. (Chapter 26)

Accredited investor Under the Securities Act of 1933, an accredited investor is an institution (such as a bank or insurance company) or any individual with a net worth of more than $1 million or an annual income of more than $200,000. (Chapter 37)

Acquit To find the defendant not guilty of the crime for which he was tried. (Chapter 7)

Act of State doctrine A rule requiring American courts to abstain from cases if a court order would interfere with the ability of the President or Congress to conduct foreign policy. (Chapter 8)

Actus reus The guilty act. The prosecution must show that a criminal defendant committed some proscribed act. In a murder prosecution, taking another person's life is the *actus reus*. (Chapter 7)

Adhesion contract A standard form contract prepared by one party and presented to the other on a "take it or leave it" basis. (Chapter 12)

Adjudicate To hold a formal hearing in a disputed matter and issue an official decision. (Chapter 4)

Administrative law Concerns all agencies, boards, commissions, and other entities created by a federal or state legislature and charged with investigating, regulating, and adjudicating a particular industry or issue. (Chapter 1)

Administrator A person appointed by the court to oversee the probate process for someone who has died intestate (that is, without a will). (Chapter 45)

Administratrix A female administrator. (Chapter 45)

Adverse possession A means of gaining ownership of land belonging to another by entering upon the property, openly and notoriously, and claiming exclusive use of it for a period of years. (Chapter 42)

Affidavit A written statement signed under oath. (Chapter 7)

Affirm A decision by an appellate court to uphold the judgment of a lower court. (Chapter 1)

Affirmative action A plan introduced in a workplace for the purpose of either remedying the effects of past discrimination or achieving equitable representation of minorities and women. (Chapter 30)

After-acquired property Items that a debtor obtains after making a security agreement with the secured party. (Chapter 26)

Agent A person who acts for a principal. (Chapter 7)

Alternative dispute resolution Any method of resolving a legal conflict other than litigation, such as: negotiation, arbitration, mediation, mini-trials, and summary jury trials. (Chapter 3)

Amendment Any addition to a legal document. The constitutional amendments, the first ten of which are known collectively as the Bill of Rights, secure numerous liberties and protections directly for the people. (Chapter 1)

Annual report Each year, public companies must send their shareholders an annual report that contains detailed financial data. (Chapter 36)

Answer The pleading, filed by the defendant in court and served on the plaintiff, which responds to each allegation in the plaintiff's complaint. (Chapter 3)

Apparent authority A situation in which conduct of a principal causes a third party to believe that the principal consents to have an act done on his behalf by a person purporting to act for him when, in fact, that person is not acting for the principal. (Chapter 29)

Appellant   The party who appeals a lower court decision to a higher court. (Chapter 3)

Appellate court   Any court in a state or federal system that reviews cases that have already been tried. (Chapter 3)

Appellee   The party opposing an appeal from a lower court to a higher court. (Chapter 3)

Arbitration   A form of alternative dispute resolution in which the parties hire a neutral third party to hear their respective arguments, receive evidence, and then make a binding decision. (Chapter 3)

Arson   Malicious use of fire or explosives to damage or destroy real estate or personal property. (Chapter 7)

Assault   An intentional act that causes the plaintiff to fear an imminent battery. (Chapter 5)

Assignee   The party who receives an assignment of contract rights from a party to the contract. (Chapter 15)

Assignment   The act by which a party transfers contract rights to a third person. (Chapter 15)

Assignor   The party who assigns contract rights to a third person. (Chapter 15)

Attachment   A court order seizing property of a party to a civil action, so that there will be sufficient assets available to pay the judgment. (Chapter 4)

Authorized and unissued stock   Stock that has been approved by the corporation's charter, but has not yet been sold. (Chapter 34)

Authorized and issued stock   Stock that has been approved by the corporation's charter and subsequently sold. (Chapter 34)

B

Bailee   A person who rightfully possesses goods belonging to another. (Chapter 12)

Bailment   Giving possession and control of personal property to another person. (Chapter 12)

Bailor   One who creates a bailment by delivering goods to another. (Chapter 12)

Battery   The intentional touching of another person in a way that is unwanted or offensive. (Chapter 5)

Bearer paper   An instrument payable "to bearer." Any holder in due course can demand payment. (Chapter 22)

Bilateral contract   A binding agreement in which each party has made a promise to the other. (Chapter 9)

Bill of lading   A receipt for goods, given by a carrier such as a ship, that minutely describes the merchandise being shipped. A **negotiable** bill of lading may be transferred to other parties, and entitles any holder to collect the goods. (Chapter 8)

Bill of Rights   The first ten amendments to the Constitution. (Chapter 4)

Bill   A proposed statute that has been submitted for consideration to Congress or a state legislature. (Chapter 4)

Blue sky laws   State securities laws. (Chapter 37)

Bona fide occupational qualification   A job requirement that would otherwise be discriminatory is permitted in situations in which it is *essential* to the position in question. (Chapter 30)

Bona fide purchaser   Someone who buys goods in good faith, for value, typically from a seller who has merely voidable title. (Chapter 19)

Bonds   Long-term debt secured by some of the issuing company's assets. (Chapter 34)

Brief   The written legal argument that an attorney files with an appeal court. (Chapter 3)

Bulk sale   A transfer of most or all of a merchant's assets. (Chapter 19)

Burden of proof   The allocation of which party must prove its case. In a civil case, the plaintiff has the burden of proof to persuade the factfinder of every element of her case. In a criminal case, the government has the burden of proof. (Chapter 3)

Business judgment rule   A common law rule that protects managers from liability if they are acting without a conflict of interest, and make informed decisions that have a rational business purpose. (Chapter 35)

Buyer in ordinary course of business   Someone who buys goods in good faith from a seller who routinely deals in such goods. (Chapter 26)

Bylaws   A document that specifies the organizational rules of a corporation or other organization, such as the date of the annual meeting and the required number of directors. (Chapter 34)

C

Capacity   The legal ability to enter into a contract. (Chapter 9)

Certificate of deposit   An instrument issued by a bank which promises to repay a deposit, with interest, on a specified date. (Chapter 22)

Certified check A check that the drawee bank has signed. This signature is a promise that the bank will pay the check out of its own funds. (Chapter 24)

Certiorari, writ of Formal notice from the United States Supreme Court that it will accept a case for review. (Chapter 3)

Challenge for cause An attorney's request, during *voir dire*, to excuse a prospective juror because of apparent bias. (Chapter 3)

Chancery, court of In medieval England, the court originally operated by the Chancellor. (Chapter 1)

Charging order A court order granting the creditor of a partner the right to receive that partner's share of partnership profits. (Chapter 33)

Chattel paper Any writing that indicates two things: (1) a debtor owes money and (2) a secured party has a security interest in specific goods. The most common chattel paper is a document indicating a consumer sale on credit. (Chapter 26)

Check An instrument in which the drawer orders the drawee bank to pay money to the payee. (Chapter 22)

Chicago School A theory of antitrust law first developed at the University of Chicago. Adherents to this theory believe that antitrust enforcement should focus on promoting efficiency and should not generally be concerned about the size or number of competitors in any market. (Chapter 37)

CISG See Convention on Contracts for the International Sale of Goods. (Chapter 10)

Civil law The large body of law concerning the rights and duties between parties. It is distinguished from criminal law, which concerns behavior outlawed by a government. (Chapter 1)

Class action A method of litigating a civil lawsuit in which one or more plaintiffs (or occasionally defendants) seek to represent an entire group of people with similar claims against a common opponent. (Chapter 3)

Classification The process by which the Customs Service decides what label to attach to imported merchandise, and therefore what level of tariff to impose. (Chapter 8)

Close corporation A corporation with a small number of shareholders. Its stock is not publicly traded. (Chapter 33)

Codicil An amendment to a will. (Chapter 45)

Collateral The property subject to a security interest. (Chapter 26)

Collateral promises A promise to pay the debt of another person, as a favor to the debtor. (Chapter 14)

Collective bargaining Contract negotiations between an employer and a union. (Chapter 32)

Collective bargaining unit The precisely defined group of employees who are represented by a particular union. (Chapter 32)

Comity A doctrine that requires a court to abstain from hearing a case out of respect for another court that also has jurisdiction. **International comity** demands that an American court refuse to hear a case in which a foreign court shares jurisdiction if there is a conflict between the laws and if it is more logical for the foreign court to take the case. (Chapter 8)

Commerce clause One of the powers granted by Article I, §8 of the Constitution, it gives Congress exclusive power to regulate international commerce and concurrent power with the states to regulate domestic commerce. (Chapter 4)

Commercial impracticability After the creation of a contract, an entirely unforeseen event occurs which makes enforcement of the contract extraordinarily unfair. (Chapter 16)

Commercial paper Instruments such as checks and promissory notes that contain a promise to pay money. Commercial paper includes both negotiable and non-negotiable instruments. (Chapter 22)

Commercial speech Communication, such as television advertisements, that has the dominant theme of proposing a commercial transaction. (Chapter 4)

Common carrier A transportation company that makes its services available on a regular basis to the general public. (Chapter 44)

Common law Judge-made law, that is, the body of all decisions made by appellate courts over the years. (Chapter 1)

Common stock Certificates that reflect ownership in a corporation. Owners of this equity security are last in line for corporate pay-outs such as dividends and liquidation proceeds. (Chapter 34)

Comparative negligence A rule of tort law that permits a plaintiff to recover even when the defendant can show that the plaintiff's own conduct contributed in some way to her harm. (Chapter 6)

Compensatory damages Those that flow directly from the contract. (Chapter 17)

Complaint A pleading, filed by the plaintiff, providing a short statement of the claim. (Chapter 3)

Concerted action Tactics, such as a strike, used by a union to gain a bargaining advantage. (Chapter 32)

Condition A condition is an event that must occur in order for a party to be obligated under a contract. (Chapter 16)

Condition precedent A condition that must occur before a particular contract duty arises. (Chapter 16)

Condition subsequent A condition that must occur after a particular contract duty arises, or the duty will be discharged. (Chapter 16)

Confiscation Expropriation without adequate compensation of property owned by foreigners. (Chapter 8)

Conforming goods Items that satisfy the contract terms. If a contract calls for blue sailboats, then green sailboats are non-conforming. (Chapter 21)

Consent order An agreement entered into by a wrongdoer and an administrative agency (such as the Securities and Exchange Commission or the Federal Trade Commission) in which the wrongdoer agrees not to violate the law in the future. (Chapter 39)

Consequential damages Those resulting from the unique circumstances of *this injured party*. (Chapter 17)

Consideration In contract law, something of legal value that has been bargained for and given in exchange by the parties. (Chapter 11)

Constitution The supreme law of a political entity. The United States Constitution is the highest law in the country. (Chapter 1)

Contract A legally enforceable promise or set of promises. (Chapter 9)

Contract carrier A transportation company that does not make its services available to the general public but engages in continuing agreements with particular customers. (Chapter 44)

Contributory negligence A rule of tort law that permits a negligent defendant to escape liability if she can demonstrate that the plaintiff's own conduct contributed in any way to the plaintiff's harm. (Chapter 6)

Control security Stock owned by any officer or director of the issuer, or by any shareholder who holds more than 10 percent of a class of stock of the issuer. (Chapter 37)

Convention on Contracts for the International Sale of Goods A United Nations sponsored agreement that creates a neutral body of law for sale of goods contracts between companies from different countries. (Chapter 10)

Conversion A tort committed by taking or using someone else's personal property without his permission. (Chapter 5)

Cookie A small computer file that identifies the user of a computer. Internet sites typically place cookies on a computer's hard drive to track visitors to their site. (Chapter 40)

Copyright Under federal law, the holder of a copyright owns a particular expression of an idea, but not the idea itself. This ownership right applies to creative activities such as literature, music, drama, and software. (Chapter 41)

Corporation by estoppel Even if a corporation has not actually been formed, courts will sometimes enforce contracts entered into in the belief that the corporation did indeed exist. (Chapter 34)

Counter-claim A claim made by the defendant against the plaintiff. (Chapter 3)

Cover The buyer's right to obtain substitute goods when a seller has breached a contract. (Chapter 3)

Creditor beneficiary When one party to a contract intends to benefit a third party to whom he owes a debt, that third party is referred to as a creditor beneficiary. (Chapter 15)

Criminal law Rules that permit a government to punish certain behavior by fine or imprisonment. (Chapter 1)

Cross-examination During a hearing, for a lawyer to question an opposing witness. (Chapter 3)

Cure The seller's right to respond to a buyer's rejection of non-conforming goods; the seller accomplishes this by delivering conforming goods before the contract deadline. (Chapter 21)

D

Damages (1) The harm that a plaintiff complains of at trial, such as an injury to her person, or money lost because of a contract breach. (2) Money awarded by a trial court for injury suffered. (Chapter 5)

De facto corporation Occurs when a promoter makes a good faith effort to incorporate (although fails to complete the process entirely) and uses the corporation to conduct business. The state can challenge the validity of the corporation, but a third party cannot. (Chapter 34)

De jure corporation The promoter of the corporation has substantially complied with the requirements for incorporation, but has made some minor error. No one has the right to challenge the validity of the corporation. (Chapter 34)

De novo The power of an appellate court or appellate agency to make a new decision in a matter under appeal, entirely ignoring the findings and conclusions of the lower court or agency official. (Chapter 4)

Debentures Long-term, unsecured debt, typically issued by a corporation. (Chapter 34)

Debtor A person who owes money or some other obligation to another party. (Chapter 26)

Decedent A person who has died. (Chapter 45)

Defamation The act of injuring someone's reputation by stating something false about her to a third person. Libel is defamation done either in writing or by broadcast. *Slander* is defamation done orally. (Chapter 5)

Default The failure to perform an obligation, such as the failure to pay money when due. (Chapter 26)

Default judgment Court order awarding one party everything it requested because the opposing party failed to respond in time. (Chapter 3)

Default rules Under the Uniform Partnership Act, these rules govern the relationship among the partners unless the partners explicitly make a different agreement. (Chapter 33)

Definiteness A doctrine holding that a contract will only be enforced if its terms are sufficiently precise that a court can determine what the parties meant. (Chapter 10)

Delegation The act by which a party to a contract transfers duties to a third person who is not a party to the contract. (Chapter 15)

Deponent The person being questioned in a deposition. (Chapter 3)

Deposition A form of discovery in which a party's attorney has the right to ask oral questions of the other party or of a witness. Answers are given under oath. (Chapter 3)

Derivative action A lawsuit brought by shareholders in the name of the corporation to enforce a right of the corporation. (Chapter 36)

Deterrence Using punishment, such as imprisonment, to discourage criminal behavior. (Chapter 7)

Devisee Someone who inherits under a will. (Chapter 45)

Direct examination During a hearing, for a lawyer to question his own witness. (Chapter 3)

Directed verdict The decision by a court to instruct a jury that it must find in favor of a particular party because, in the judge's opinion, no reasonable person could disagree on the outcome. (Chapter 3)

Disaffirmance The act of notifying the other party to a contract that the party giving the notice refuses to be bound by the agreement. (Chapter 13)

Discharge (1) A party to a contract has no more duties. (2) A party to an instrument is released from liability. (Chapter 16)

Disclaimer A statement that a particular warranty does not apply. (Chapter 20)

Discovery A stage in litigation, after all pleadings have been served, in which each party seeks as much relevant information as possible about the opposing party's case. (Chapter 3)

Dishonor An obligor refuses to pay an instrument that is due. (Chapter 24)

Dismiss To terminate a lawsuit, often on procedural grounds, without reaching the merits of the case. (Chapter 3)

Dissociation A dissociation occurs when a partner leaves a partnership. (Chapter 33)

Diversity jurisdiction One of the two main types of civil cases that a United States district court has the power to hear. It involves a lawsuit between citizens of different states, in which at least one party makes a claim for more than $75,000. (Chapter 3)

Domestic corporation A corporation is a domestic corporation in the state in which it was formed. (Chapter 34)

Donee A person who receives a gift. (Chapter 44)

Donee beneficiary When one party to a contract intends to make a gift to a third party, that third party is referred to as a donee beneficiary. (Chapter 15)

Donor A person who makes a gift to another. (Chapter 44)

Draft The drawer of this instrument orders someone else to pay money. Checks are the most common form of draft. The drawer of a check orders a bank to pay money. (Chapter 22)

Drawee The person who pays a draft. In the case of a check, the bank is the drawee. (Chapter 22)

Drawer The person who issues a draft. (Chapter 22)

Due Process Clause Part of the Fifth Amendment. *Procedural due process* ensures that before depriving anyone of liberty or property, the government must go through procedures which ensure that the deprivation is fair. *Substantive due process* holds that certain rights, such as privacy, are so fundamental that the government may not eliminate them. (Chapter 4)

Dumping Selling merchandise at one price in the domestic market and at a cheaper, unfair price in an international market. (Chapter 8)

Durable power of attorney An instrument that permits an attorney-in-fact to act for a principal. A durable power is effective until the principal revokes it or dies. It continues in effect even if the principal becomes incapacitated. (Chapter 45)

Duress (1) A criminal defense in which the defendant shows that she committed the wrongful act because a third person threatened her with imminent physical harm. (2) An improper threat made to force another party to enter into a contract. (Chapter 7)

Duty A tax imposed on imported items. (Chapter 8)

E

Easement The right to enter land belonging to another and make a limited use of it, without taking anything away. (Chapter 42)

Economic loss doctrine A common law rule holding that when an injury is purely economic, and arises from a contract made between two businesses, the injured party may only sue under the UCC. (Chapter 20)

Element A fact that a party to a lawsuit must prove in order to prevail. (Chapter 5)

Embezzlement Fraudulent conversion of property already in the defendant's possession. (Chapter 7)

Eminent domain The power of the government to take private property for public use. (Chapter 4)

Employee at will A worker whose job does not have a specified duration. (Chapter 30)

Enabling legislation A statute authorizing the creation of a new administrative agency and specifying its powers and duties. (Chapter 4)

Entrapment A criminal defense in which the defendant demonstrates that the government induced him to break the law. (Chapter 7)

Equal Protection Clause Part of the Fourteenth Amendment, it generally requires the government to treat equally situated people the same. (Chapter 4)

Equity The broad powers of a court to fashion a remedy where justice demands it and no common

law remedy exists. An injunction is an example of an equitable remedy. (Chapter 1)

Error of law A mistake made by a trial judge that concerns a legal issue as opposed to a factual matter. Permitting too many leading questions is a legal error; choosing to believe one witness rather than another is a factual matter. (Chapter 3)

Estate The legal entity that holds title to assets after the owner dies and before the property is distributed. (Chapter 45)

Estoppel Out of fairness, a person is denied the right to assert a claim. (Chapter 29)

Evidence, rules of Law governing the proof offered during a trial or formal hearing. These rules limit the questions that may be asked of witnesses and the introduction of physical objects. (Chapter 3)

Exclusionary rule In a criminal trial, a ban on the use of evidence obtained in violation of the Constitution. (Chapter 7)

Exclusive dealing agreement A potential violation of §1 of the Sherman Act, in which a distributor or retailer agrees with a supplier not to carry the products of any other supplier. (Chapter 37)

Exculpatory clause A contract provision that attempts to release one party from liability in the event the other party is injured. (Chapter 12)

Executed contract A binding agreement in which all parties have fulfilled all obligations. (Chapter 9)

Executive agency An administrative agency within the executive branch of government. (Chapter 4)

Executive order An order by a president or governor, having the full force of law. (Chapter 1)

Executor A person chosen by the decedent to oversee the probate process. (Chapter 14)

Executory contract A binding agreement in which one or more of the parties has not fulfilled its obligations. (Chapter 9)

Executrix A female executor. (Chapter 45)

Exhaustion of remedies A principle of administrative law that no party may appeal an agency action to a court until she has utilized all available appeals within the agency itself. (Chapter 4)

Expectation interest A remedy in a contract case that puts the injured party in the position he would have been in had both sides fully performed. (Chapter 17)

Expert witness A witness in a court case who has special training or qualifications to discuss a specific issue, and who is generally permitted to state an opinion. (Chapter 3)

Export   To transport goods or services out of a country. (Chapter 8)

Express authority   Conduct of a principal that, reasonably interpreted, causes the agent to believe that the principal desires him to do a specific act. (Chapter 29)

Express contract   A binding agreement in which the parties explicitly state all important terms. (Chapter 9)

Express warranty   A guarantee, created by the words or actions of the seller, that goods will meet certain standards. (Chapter 20)

Expropriation   A government's seizure of property or companies owned by foreigners. (Chapter 8)

F

Factfinder   The one responsible, during a trial, for deciding what occurred, that is, who did what to whom, when, how, and why. It is either the jury or, in a jury-waived case, the judge. (Chapter 4)

Fair representation, duty of   The union's obligation to act on behalf of all members impartially and in good faith. (Chapter 32)

False imprisonment   The intentional restraint of another person without reasonable cause and without her consent. (Chapter 5)

Federal question jurisdiction   One of the two main types of civil cases that a United States district court has the power to hear. It involves a federal statute or a constitutional provision. (Chapter 3)

Federalism   A form of national government in which power is shared between one central authority and numerous local authorities. (Chapter 1)

Fee simple absolute   The greatest possible ownership right in real property, including the right to possess, use, and dispose of the property in any lawful manner. (Chapter 42)

Fee simple defeasible   Ownership interest in real property that may terminate upon the occurrence of some limiting event. (Chapter 42)

Felony   The most serious crimes, typically those for which the defendant could be imprisoned for more than a year. (Chapter 7)

Fiduciary duty   An obligation to behave in a trustworthy and confidential fashion toward the object of that duty. (Chapter 28)

Financing statement   A document that a secured party files to give the general public notice that the secured party has a secured interest in the collateral. (Chapter 26)

Firm offer   A contract offer that cannot be withdrawn during a stated period. (Chapter 10)

Fixtures   Goods that are attached to real estate. (Chapter 26)

Foreign corporation   A corporation formed in another state. (Chapter 34)

Foreign Sovereign Immunity Act   A federal statute that protects other nations from suit in courts of the United States, except under specified circumstances. (Chapter 8)

Formal rulemaking   The process whereby an administrative agency notifies the public of a proposed new rule and then permits a formal hearing, with opportunity for evidence and cross-examination, before promulgating the final rule. (Chapter 4)

Founding Fathers   The authors of the United States Constitution, who participated in the Constitutional Convention in Philadelphia in 1787. (Chapter 1)

Framers   *See* Founding Fathers. (Chapter 4)

Franchise   An arrangement in which the franchisee buys from a franchiser the right to establish a business using the franchiser's trade name and selling the franchiser's products. Typically the franchiser also trains the franchisee in the proper operation of the business. (Chapter 33)

Fraud   Deception of another person to obtain money or property from her. (Chapter 5)

Freedom of Information Act (FOIA)   A federal statute giving private citizens and corporations access to many of the documents possessed by an administrative agency. (Chapter 4)

Freehold estate   The present right to possess property and to use it in any lawful manner. (Chapter 42)

Frustration of purpose   After the creation of a contract, an entirely unforeseen event occurs that eliminates the value of the contract for one of the parties. (Chapter 16)

Fully disclosed principal   If the third party in an agency relationship knows the identity of the principal, that principal is fully disclosed. (Chapter 29)

Fundamental rights   In constitutional law, those rights that are so basic that any governmental interference with them is suspect and likely to be unconstitutional. (Chapter 4)

G

GAAP Generally accepted accounting principles. Rules set by the Financial Accounting Standards Board to be used in preparing financial statements. (Chapter 38)

GAAS Generally accepted auditing standards. Rules set by the American Institute of Certified Public Accountants (AICPA) to be used in conducting audits. (Chapter 38)

GATT *See* General Agreement on Tariffs and Trade. (Chapter 8)

General Agreement on Tariffs and Trade (GATT) A massive international treaty, negotiated in stages between the 1940s and 1994 and signed by over 130 nations. (Chapter 8)

General deterrence *See* Deterrence. (Chapter 7)

General intangibles Potential sources of income such as copyrights, patents, trademarks, goodwill and certain other rights to payment. (Chapter 26)

Gift A voluntary transfer of property from one person to another without consideration. (Chapter 44)

Gift *causa mortis* A gift made in contemplation of approaching death. (Chapter 44)

Goods Anything movable, except for money, securities, and certain legal rights. (Chapter 26)

Grantee The person who receives property, or some interest in it, from the owner. (Chapter 42)

Grantor (1) An owner who conveys property, or some interest in it. (2) Someone who creates a trust. (Chapter 42)

Greenmail If a company is threatened with a hostile takeover, its board of directors may offer to buy the stock of the attacker at an above-market price with the hope that the attacker will take her profits and leave the company alone. (Chapter 35)

H

Hacking Gaining unauthorized access to a computer system. (Chapter 40)

Harmless error A ruling made by a trial court which an appeals court determines was legally wrong but not fatal to the decision. (Chapter 3)

Heir Someone who inherits from a decedent who died intestate (that is, without a will). (Chapter 45)

Holder in due course Someone who has given value for an instrument, in good faith, without notice of outstanding claims or other defenses. (Chapter 22)

Holographic will A handwritten will that has not been witnessed. (Chapter 45)

Horizontal agreement or merger An agreement or merger between two potential competitors. (Chapter 37)

Hybrid rulemaking A method of administrative agency procedure incorporating some elements of formal and some elements of informal rulemaking, typically involving a limited public hearing with restricted rights of testimony and cross-examination. (Chapter 4)

I

Identify In sales law, to designate the specific goods that are the subject of a contract. (Chapter 21)

Illegal contract An agreement that is void because it violates a statute or public policy. (Chapter 12)

Illusory promise An apparent promise that is unenforceable because the promisor makes no firm commitment. (Chapter 11)

Implied authority When a principal directs an agent to undertake a transaction, the agent has the right to do acts that are incidental to it, usually accompany it, or are reasonably necessary to accomplish it. (Chapter 29)

Implied contract A binding agreement created not by explicit language but by the informal words and conduct of the parties. (Chapter 9)

Implied warranty Guarantees created by the Uniform Commercial Code and imposed on the seller of goods. (Chapter 20)

Implied warranty of habitability A landlord must meet all standards set by the local building code, or otherwise ensure that the premises are fit for human habitation. (Chapter 42)

Import To transport goods or services into a country. (Chapter 8)

In camera "In the judge's chambers," meaning that the judge does something out of view of the jury and the public. (Chapter 3)

Incidental damages The relatively minor costs, such as storage and advertising, that the injured party suffered when responding to a contract breach. (Chapter 17)

Incorporator The person who signs a corporate charter. (Chapter 34)

Indemnification A promise to pay someone else's obligations. (Chapter 28)

Independent agency An administrative agency outside the executive branch of government, such as the Interstate Commerce Commission. (Chapter 4)

Independent contractor Someone who undertakes tasks for others and whose work is not closely controlled. (Chapter 29)

Indictment The government's formal charge that a defendant has committed a crime. (Chapter 7)

Indorser Anyone, other than the issuer or acceptor, who signs an instrument. (Chapter 24)

Infliction of emotional distress A tort. It can be the *intentional infliction of emotional distress,* meaning that the defendant behaved outrageously and deliberately caused the plaintiff severe psychological injury, or it can be the *negligent infliction of emotional distress,* meaning that the defendant's conduct violated the rules of negligence. (Chapter 5)

Informal rulemaking The process whereby an administrative agency notifies the public of a proposed new rule and permits comment but is then free to promulgate the final rule without a public hearing. (Chapter 4)

Initial public offering (IPO) A company's first public sale of securities. (Chapter 37)

Injunction A court order that a person either do or stop doing something. (Chapter 1)

Instructions or charge The explanation given by a judge to a jury, outlining the jury's task in deciding a lawsuit and the underlying rules of law the jury should use in reaching its decision. (Chapter 3)

Instruments Drafts, checks, certificates of deposit and notes. (Chapter 26)

Insurable interest A person has an insurable interest if she would be harmed by the danger that she has insured against. (Chapter 12)

Insured A person whose loss is the subject of an insurance policy. (Chapter 46)

Insurer The person who issues an insurance policy. (Chapter 46)

Integrated contract A writing that the parties intend as the complete and final expression of their agreement. (Chapter 14)

Intentional tort An act deliberately performed that violates a legally imposed duty and injures someone. (Chapter 5)

Inter vivos gift A gift made "during life," that is, when the donor is not under any fear of impending death. (Chapter 44)

Inter vivos trust A trust established while the grantor is still living. (Chapter 44)

Interest A legal right in something, such as ownership or a mortgage or a tenancy. (Chapter 46)

Interference with a contract *See* Tortious interference with a contract. (Chapter 5)

Interference with a prospective advantage See Tortious interference with a prospective advantage. (Chapter 5)

Internet An international computer network that connects smaller groups of linked computer networks. (Chapter 40)

Interpretive rules A formal statement by an administrative agency expressing its view of what existing statutes or regulations mean. (Chapter 4)

Interrogatory A form of discovery in which one party sends to an opposing party written questions that must be answered under oath. (Chapter 3)

Intestate Without a will. (Chapter 45)

Inventory Goods that the seller is holding for sale or lease in the ordinary course of its business. (Chapter 26)

Invitee Someone who has the right to be on property, such as a customer in a shop. (Chapter 6)

Issue All direct descendants such as children, grandchildren, and so on. (Chapter 1)

Issuer The maker of a promissory note or the drawer of a draft. (Chapter 22)

J

Joint and several liability All members of a group are liable. They can be sued as a group, or any one of them can be sued individually for the full amount owing. (Chapter 33)

Joint liability All members of a group are liable and must be sued together. (Chapter 33)

Joint venture A partnership for a limited purpose. (Chapter 33)

Judgment *non obstante verdicto* (n.o.v.) "Judgment notwithstanding the verdict." A trial judge overturns the verdict of the jury and enters a judgment in favor of the opposing party. (Chapter 3)

Judicial activism The willingness shown by certain courts (and not by others) to decide issues of public policy, such as constitutional questions (free speech, equal protection, etc.) and matters of contract fairness (promissory estoppel, unconscionability, etc.). (Chapter 4)

Judicial restraint A court's preference to abstain from adjudicating major social issues and to leave such matters to legislatures. (Chapter 4)

Judicial review The power of the judicial system to examine, interpret, and even nullify actions taken by another branch of government. (Chapter 4)

Jurisdiction The power of a court to hear a particular dispute, civil or criminal, and to make a binding decision. (Chapter 3)

Jurisprudence The study of the purposes and philosophies of the law, as opposed to particular provisions of the law. (Chapter 1)

Justification A criminal defense in which the defendant establishes that he broke the law to avoid a greater harm. (Chapter 7)

L

Larceny Taking personal property with the intention of preventing the owner from ever using it. (Chapter 7)

Law merchant The body of rules and customs developed by traders and businesspersons throughout Europe from roughly the fifteenth to the eighteenth century. (Chapter 18)

Lease A contract creating a landlord-tenant relationship. (Chapter 43)

Legal positivism The legal philosophy holding that law is what the sovereign says it is, regardless of its moral content. (Chapter 1)

Legal realism The legal philosophy holding that what really influences law is who makes and enforces it, not what is put in writing. (Chapter 1)

Legal remedy Generally, money damages. It is distinguished from equitable remedy, which includes injunctions and other non-monetary relief. (Chapter 17)

Legislative history Used by courts to interpret the meaning of a statute, this is the record of hearings, speeches, and explanations that accompanied a statute as it made its way from newly proposed bill to final law. (Chapter 4)

Legislative rules Regulations issued by an administrative agency. (Chapter 4)

Letter of credit A commercial device used to guarantee payment in international trade, usually between parties that have not previously worked together. (Chapter 8)

Libel *See* Defamation. (Chapter 5)

License To grant permission to another person (1) to make or sell something or (2) to enter on property. (Chapter 42)

Licensee A person who is on the property of another for her own purposes, but with the owner's permission. A social guest is a typical licensee. (Chapter 6)

Lien A security interest created by rule of law, often based on labor that the secured party has expended on the collateral. (Chapter 26)

Life estate An ownership interest in real property entitling the holder to use the property during his lifetime, but which terminates upon his death. (Chapter 42)

Limited liability company An organization that has the limited liability of a corporation but is not a taxable entity. (Chapter 33)

Limited liability limited partnership In a limited liability limited partnership, the general partner is not personally liable for the debts of the partnership. (Chapter 33)

Limited partnership A partnership with two types of partners: (1) limited partners who have no personal liability for the debts of the enterprise nor any right to manage the business, and (2) general partners who are responsible for management and personally liable for all debts. (Chapter 33)

Liquidated damages A contract clause specifying how much a party must pay upon breach. (Chapter 17)

Liquidated debt The amount of the indebtedness is not in dispute. (Chapter 11)

Litigation The process of resolving disputes through formal court proceedings. (Chapter 3)

Living trust A trust established while the grantor is alive. *See inter vivos* trust. (Chapter 45)

Living will An instrument that permits adults to refuse medical treatment. It can also appoint a health care proxy to make medical decisions for a person who has become incompetent. (Chapter 45)

Lockout A management tactic, designed to gain a bargaining advantage, in which the company refuses to allow union members to work (and hence deprives them of their pay). (Chapter 32)

M

Mailbox rule A contract doctrine holding that acceptance is effective upon dispatch, that is, when it is mailed or otherwise taken out of the control of the offeree. (Chapter 10)

Maker   The issuer of a promissory note. (Chapter 22)

Material   Important or significant. Information that would affect a person's decision if he knew it. (Chapter 13)

Mediation   The process of using a neutral person to aid in the settlement of a legal dispute. A mediator's decision is non-binding. (Chapter 3)

Mens rea   Guilty state of mind. (Chapter 7)

Merger   An acquisition of one company by another. (Chapter 36)

Mini-trial   A form of alternative dispute resolution in which the parties present short versions of their cases to a panel of three "judges." (Chapter 3)

Minor   A person under the age of 18. (Chapter 13)

Minority shareholders   Shareholders who do not own enough stock to control their corporation. (Chapter 36)

Minute book   Records of shareholder meetings and directors' meetings are kept in the corporation's minute book. (Chapter 34)

Mirror image rule   A contract doctrine that requires acceptance to be on exactly the same terms as the offer. (Chapter 10)

Misdemeanor   A less serious crime, typically one for which the maximum penalty is incarceration for less than a year, often in a jail, as opposed to a prison. (Chapter 7)

Misrepresentation   A factually incorrect statement made during contract negotiations. (Chapter 13)

Mitigation   One party acts to minimize its losses when the other party breaches a contract. (Chapter 17)

Modify   An appellate court order changing a lower court ruling. (Chapter 3)

Money laundering   Taking the profits of criminal acts and either (1) using the money to promote more crime or (2) attempting to conceal the money's source. (Chapter 7)

Monopolization   A company acquires or maintains a monopoly through the commission of unacceptably aggressive acts. A violation of §2 of the Sherman Act. (Chapter 37)

Mortgage   A security interest in real property. (Chapter 42)

Mortgagee   A creditor who obtains a security interest in real property, typically in exchange for money

given to the mortgagor to buy the property. (Chapter 42)

Mortgagor   A debtor who gives a mortgage (security interest) in real property to a creditor, typically in exchange for money used to buy the property. (Chapter 42)

Motion   A formal request that a court take some specified step during litigation. A motion to compel discovery is a request that a trial judge order the other party to respond to discovery. (Chapter 3)

Motion to suppress   A request that the court exclude evidence because it was obtained in violation of the Constitution. (Chapter 7)

Multinational enterprise   A corporation that is doing business in more than one country simultaneously. (Chapter 8)

N

NAFTA   *See* North American Free Trade Agreement. (Chapter 8)

National Labor Relations Board   (NLRB) The administrative agency charged with overseeing labor law. (Chapter 4)

Nationalization   A government's seizure of property or companies. (Chapter 8)

Natural law   The theory that an unjust law is no law at all, and that a rule is only legitimate if based on an immutable morality. (Chapter 1)

Negative or dormant aspect of the Commerce Clause   The doctrine that prohibits a state from any action that interferes with or discriminates against interstate commerce. (Chapter 4)

Negligence per se   Violation of a standard of care set by statute. Driving while intoxicated is illegal; thus, if a drunk driver injures a pedestrian, he has committed negligence per se. (Chapter 6)

Negotiable instrument   A type of commercial paper that is freely transferable. (Chapter 22)

Negotiation   The transfer of an instrument. To be negotiated, order paper must be indorsed and then delivered to the transferee. For bearer paper, no indorsement is required—it must simply be delivered to the transferee. (Chapter 22)

Nominal damages   A token sum, such as one dollar, given to an injured plaintiff who cannot prove damages. (Chapter 17)

Noncompetition agreement A contract in which one party agrees not to compete with another in a stated type of business. (Chapter 9)

North American Free Trade Agreement A commercial association among Canada, the United States, and Mexico designed to eliminate almost all trade barriers. (Chapter 8)

Note An unconditional, written promise that the maker of the instrument will pay a specific amount of money on demand or at a definite time. When issued by a corporation, a note refers to short-term debt, typically payable within five years. (Chapter 22)

Novation If there is an existing contract between *A* and *B*, a novation occurs when *A* agrees to release *B* from all liability on the contract in return for *C*'s willingness to accept *B*'s liability. (Chapter 15)

Nuncupative will An oral will. (Chapter 45)

O

Obligee The party to a contract who is entitled to receive performance from the other party. (Chapter 15)

Obligor The party to a contract who is required to do something for the benefit of the other party. (Chapter 15)

Obscenity Constitutional law doctrine holding that some works will receive no First Amendment protection because a court determines they depict sexual matters in an offensive way. (Chapter 4)

Offer In contract law, an act or statement that proposes definite terms and permits the other party to create a contract by accepting those terms. (Chapter 10)

Offeree The party in contract negotiations who receives the first offer. (Chapter 10)

Offeror The party in contract negotiations who makes the first offer. (Chapter 10)

Order paper An instrument that includes the words "pay to the order of" or their equivalent. (Chapter 22)

Output contract An agreement that obligates the seller of goods to sell everything he produces during a stated period to a particular buyer. (Chapter 10)

Override The power of Congress or a state legislature to pass legislation despite a veto by a president or governor. A congressional override requires a two-thirds vote in each house. (Chapter 4)

P

Parol evidence Written or oral evidence, outside the language of a contract, offered by one party to clarify interpretation of the agreement. (Chapter 14)

Parol evidence rule In the case of an integrated contract, neither party may use evidence outside the writing to contradict, vary, or add to its terms. (Chapter 14)

Part performance An exception to the statute of frauds permitting a buyer of real estate to enforce an oral contract if she paid part of the price, entered the property, and made improvements, with the owner's knowledge. (Chapter 14)

Partially disclosed principal If the third party in an agency relationship knows that the agent is acting for a principal, but does not know the identity of the principal, that principal is partially disclosed. (Chapter 29)

Partnership An association of two or more persons to carry on as co-owners of a business for profit. (Chapter 33)

Partnership at will A partnership that has no fixed duration. A partner has the right to resign from the partnership at any time. (Chapter 33)

Partnership by estoppel If a person who is not a partner implies that he is a partner or does not object when other people imply it, he is liable as if he really were a partner. (Chapter 33)

Patent The right to the exclusive use of an invention for 20 years. (Chapter 41)

Payable on demand The holder of an instrument is entitled to be paid whenever she asks. (Chapter 22)

Payee Someone who is owed money under the terms of an instrument. (Chapter 22)

Per se violation of an antitrust law An automatic breach. Courts will generally not consider mitigating factors. (Chapter 37)

Peremptory challenge During *voir dire,* a request by one attorney that a prospective juror be excused for an unstated reason. (Chapter 3)

Perfect tender rule A rule permitting the buyer to reject goods if they fail in any respect to conform to the contract. (Chapter 21)

Perfection A series of steps a secured party must take to protect its rights in collateral against people other than the debtor. (Chapter 26)

Personal property All property other than real property. (Chapter 44)

Plain meaning rule In statutory interpretation, the premise that words with an ordinary, everyday significance will be so interpreted, unless there is some apparent reason not to. (Chapter 4)

Pleadings The documents that begin a lawsuit: the complaint, the answer, the counter-claim and reply. (Chapter 3)

Positive aspect of the Commerce Clause The power granted to Congress to regulate commerce between the states. (Chapter 4)

Precedent An earlier case that decided the same legal issue as that presently in dispute, and which therefore will control the outcome of the current case. (Chapter 1)

Predatory pricing A violation of §2 of the Sherman Act in which a company lowers its prices below cost to drive competitors out of business. (Chapter 37)

Preemption The doctrine, based on the Supremacy Clause, by which any federal statute takes priority whenever (1) a state statute conflicts or (2) there is no conflict but Congress indicated an intention to control the issue involved. (Chapter 4)

Preferred stock Owners of preferred stock have a right to receive dividends and liquidation proceeds of the company before common shareholders. (Chapter 34)

Preponderance of the evidence The level of proof that a plaintiff must meet to prevail in a civil lawsuit. It means that the plaintiff must offer evidence that, in sum, is slightly more persuasive than the defendant's evidence. (Chapter 3)

Presentment A holder of an instrument makes a demand for payment. (Chapter 24)

Pretermitted child A child omitted from a parent's will. (Chapter 45)

Prima facie "At first sight." A fact or conclusion that is presumed to be true unless someone presents evidence to disprove it. (Chapter 30)

Principal In an agency relationship, the principal is the person for whom the agent is acting. (Chapter 28)

Privacy Act A federal statute prohibiting federal agencies from divulging to other agencies or organizations information about private citizens. (Chapter 4)

Privity The relationship that exists between two parties who make a contract, as opposed to a third party who, though affected by the contract, is not a party to it. (Chapter 20)

Probable cause In a search and seizure case, it means that the information available indicates that it is more likely than not that a search will uncover particular criminal evidence. (Chapter 7)

Probate The process of carrying out the terms of a will. (Chapter 45)

Procedural due process *See* Due Process Clause. (Chapter 4)

Procedural law The rules establishing how the legal system itself is to operate in a particular kind of case. (Chapter 1)

Proceeds Anything that a debtor obtains from the sale or disposition of collateral. Normally, proceeds refers to cash obtained from the sale of the secured property. (Chapter 26)

Production of documents and things A form of discovery in which one party demands that the other furnish original documents or physical things, relating to the suit, for inspection and copying. (Chapter 3)

Product liability The potential responsibility that a manufacturer or seller has for injuries caused by defective goods. (Chapter 20)

Professional corporation A form of organization that permits professionals (such as doctors, lawyers, and accountants) to incorporate. Shareholders are not personally liable for the torts of other shareholders, or for the contract debts of the organization. (Chapter 33)

Profit The right to enter land belonging to another and take something away, such as minerals or timber. (Chapter 42)

Promissory estoppel A doctrine in which a court may enforce a promise made by the defendant even when there is no contract, if the defendant knew that the plaintiff was likely to rely on the promise, the plaintiff did in fact rely, and enforcement of it is the only way to avoid injustice. (Chapter 9)

Promissory note The maker of the instrument promises to pay a specific amount of money. (Chapter 22)

Promoter The person who creates a corporation by raising capital and undertaking the legal steps necessary for formation. (Chapter 34)

Promulgate To issue a new rule. (Chapter 4)

Prosecution The government's attempt to convict a defendant of a crime by charging him, trying the case, and forcing him to defend himself. (Chapter 7)

Prospectus Under the Securities Act of 1933, an issuer must provide this document to anyone who purchases a security in a public transaction. The prospectus contains detailed information about the issuer and its business, a description of the stock, and audited financial statements. (Chapter 37)

Protective order A court order limiting one party's discovery. (Chapter 3)

Proxy (1) A person whom the shareholder designates to vote in his place. (2) The written form (typically a card) that the shareholder uses to appoint a designated voter. (Chapter 36)

Proxy statement When a public company seeks proxy votes from its shareholders, it must include a proxy statement. This statement contains information about the company, such as a detailed description of management compensation. (Chapter 36)

Publicly traded corporation A company that (1) has completed a public offering under the Securities Act of 1933, or (2) has securities traded on a national exchange, or (3) has 500 shareholders and $10 million in assets. (Chapter 35)

Punitive damages Money awarded at trial not to compensate the plaintiff for harm but to punish the defendant for conduct that the factfinder considers extreme and outrageous. (Chapter 5)

Purchase money security interest A security interest taken by the person who sells the collateral to the debtor, or by a person who advances money so that the debtor may buy the collateral. (Chapter 26)

Q

Quantum meruit "As much as she deserves." The damages awarded in a quasi-contract case. (Chapter 9)

Quasi-contract A legal fiction in which, to avoid injustice, the court awards damages as if a contract had existed, although one did not. (Chapter 9)

Quid pro quo A Latin phrase meaning "this for that." It refers to a form of sexual harassment in which some aspect of a job is made contingent upon sexual activity. (Chapter 30)

Quiet enjoyment A tenant's right to use property without the interference of the landlord. (Chapter 43)

Quorum The number of voters that must be present for a meeting to count. (Chapter 36)

R

Ratification When someone accepts the benefit of an unauthorized transaction or fails to repudiate it once he has learned of it, he is then bound by it. (Chapter 29)

Real property Land, together with certain things associated with it, such as buildings, subsurface rights, air rights, plant life and fixtures. (Chapter 42)

Reasonable doubt The level of proof that the government must meet to convict the defendant in a criminal case. The factfinder must be persuaded to a very high degree of certainty that the defendant did what the government alleges. (Chapter 3)

Reciprocal dealing agreement An agreement under which Company *A* will purchase from

Company *B* only if Company *B* also buys from Company *A*. These agreements are rule of reason violations of the Sherman Act. (Chapter 37)

Record date To vote at a shareholders meeting, a shareholder must own stock on the record date. (Chapter 36)

Red herring A preliminary prospectus. (Chapter 37)

Reformation The process by which a court rewrites a contract to ensure its accuracy or viability. (Chapter 17)

Refusal to deal An agreement among competitors that they will not trade with a particular supplier or buyer. Such an agreement is a rule of reason violation of the Sherman Act. (Chapter 37)

Registration statement A document filed with the Securities and Exchange Commission under the Securities Act of 1933 by an issuer seeking to sell securities in a public transaction. (Chapter 37)

Reliance interest A remedy in a contract case that puts the injured party in the position he would have been in had the parties never entered into a contract. (Chapter 17)

Remand The power of an appellate court to return a case to a lower court for additional action. (Chapter 1)

Reply A pleading, filed by the plaintiff in response to a defendant's counter-claim. (Chapter 3)

Repossess A secured party takes collateral because the debtor has defaulted on payments. (Chapter 26)

Repudiation An indication made by one contracting party to the other that it will not perform. (Chapter 21)

Request for admission A form of discovery in which one party demands that the opposing party either admit or deny particular factual or legal allegations. (Chapter 3)

Requirements contract An agreement that obligates a buyer of specified goods to purchase all of the goods she needs during a stated period from a particular seller. (Chapter 10)

Res ipsa loquitur A doctrine of tort law holding that the facts may imply negligence when the defendant had exclusive control of the thing that caused the harm, the accident would not normally have occurred without negligence, and the plaintiff played no role in causing the injury. (Chapter 6)

Resale price maintenance A *per se* violation of the Sherman Act in which a manufacturer enters into an agreement with retailers about the prices they will charge. (Chapter 37)

Rescind   To cancel a contract. (Chapter 11)

Respondeat superior   A rule of agency law holding that a principal is liable when a servant acting within the scope of employment commits a tort that causes physical harm to a person or property. (Chapter 29)

Restitution   Restoring an injured party to its original position. (Chapter 13)

Restitution interest   A remedy in a contract case that returns to the injured party a benefit that he has conferred on the other party, which it would be unjust to leave with that person. (Chapter 17)

Restricted security   Any stock purchased in a private offering (such as one under Regulation D). (Chapter 37)

Retribution   Giving a criminal defendant the punishment he deserves. (Chapter 7)

Reverse   The power of an appellate court to overrule a lower court and grant judgment for the party that had lost in the lower court. (Chapter 3)

Revocation   The act of disavowing a contract offer, so that the offeree no longer has the power to accept. (Chapter 10)

Rule of reason violation   An action that breaches the antitrust laws only if it has an anticompetitive impact. (Chapter 37)

Rulemaking   The power of an administrative agency to issue regulations. (Chapter 4)

S

S corporation   A corporation that is not a taxable entity. (Chapter 33)

Sale on approval   A transfer in which a buyer takes goods intending to use them herself, but has the right to return the goods to the seller. (Chapter 19)

Sale or return   A transfer in which the buyer takes the goods intending to resell them, but has the right to return the goods to the original owner. (Chapter 19)

Scienter   In a case of securities fraud, the plaintiff must prove that the defendant acted willfully, knowingly, or recklessly. (Chapter 37)

Secondary boycott   Picketing, directed by a union against a company, designed to force that company to stop doing business with the union's employer. (Chapter 32)

Security   Any purchase in which the buyer invests money in a common enterprise and expects to earn a profit predominantly from the efforts of others. (Chapter 37)

Security agreement   A contract in which the debtor gives a security interest to the secured party. (Chapter 26)

Security interest   An interest in personal property or fixtures that secures the performance of some obligation. (Chapter 26)

Separation of powers   The principle, established by the first three articles of the Constitution, that authority should be divided among the legislative, executive, and judicial branches. (Chapter 4)

Servant   An agent whose work is closely controlled by the principal. (Chapter 29)

Service mark   A type of trademark used to identify services, not products. (Chapter 41)

Settlor   Someone who creates a trust. (Chapter 45)

Sexual harassment   Unwanted sexual advances, comments or touching, sufficiently severe to violate Title VII of the 1964 Civil Rights Act. (Chapter 30)

Shilling   A seller at auction either bids on his own goods or agrees to cross-bid with a group of other sellers. (Chapter 40)

Short-swing trading   Under §16 of the Securities Exchange Act, insiders must turn over to the corporation any profits they make from the purchase and sale or sale and purchase of company securities in a six-month period. (Chapter 37)

Signatory   A person, company, or nation that has signed a legal document, such as a contract, agreement, or treaty. (Chapter 8)

Single recovery principle   A rule of tort litigation that requires a plaintiff to claim all damages, present and future, at the time of trial, not afterwards. (Chapter 5)

Slander   *See* Defamation. (Chapter 5)

Sole proprietorship   An unincorporated business owned by a single person. (Chapter 33)

Sovereign immunity   The right of a national government to be free of lawsuits brought in foreign courts. (Chapter 8)

Spam   Unsolicited commercial or bulk e-mail. ("To spam" is to send such e-mail.) (Chapter 40)

Specific deterrence   *See* Deterrence. (Chapter 7)

Specific performance   A contract remedy requiring the breaching party to perform the contract, by conveying land or some unique asset, rather than by paying money damages. (Chapter 17)

Stakeholders Anyone who is affected by the activities of a corporation, such as employees, customers, creditors, suppliers, shareholders, and neighbors. (Chapter 35)

Stale check A check presented more than six months after its due date. (Chapter 25)

Stare decisis "Let the decision stand." A basic principle of the common law, it means that precedent is usually binding. (Chapter 1)

Statute A law passed by a legislative body, such as Congress. (Chapter 1)

Statute of frauds This law provides that certain contracts are not enforceable unless in writing. (Chapter 14)

Statute of limitations A statute that determines the period within which a particular kind of lawsuit must be filed. (Chapter 16)

Statute of repose A law that places an absolute limit on when a lawsuit may be filed, regardless of when the defect was discovered. (Chapter 20)

Statutory interpretation A court's power to give meaning to new legislation by clarifying ambiguities, providing limits, and ultimately applying it to a specific fact pattern in litigation. (Chapter 4)

Strict liability A tort doctrine holding to a very high standard all those who engage in ultrahazardous activity (e.g., using explosives) or who manufacture certain products. (Chapter 6)

Strike The ultimate weapon of a labor union, it occurs when all or most employees of a particular plant or employer walk off the job and refuse to work. (Chapter 32)

Strike suit A lawsuit without merit that defendants sometimes settle simply to avoid the nuisance of litigation. (Chapter 36)

Subpoena An order to appear, issued by a court or government body. (Chapter 4)

Subpoena duces tecum An order to produce certain documents or things before a court or government body. (Chapter 4)

Substantial performance The promisor performs contract duties well enough to be entitled to his full contract price, minus the value of any defects. (Chapter 16)

Substantive due process *See* Due Process Clause. (Chapter 4)

Substantive law Rules that establish the rights of parties. For example, the prohibition against slander is substantive law, as opposed to procedural law. (Chapter 1)

Summary judgment The power of a trial court to terminate a lawsuit before a trial has begun, on the grounds that no essential facts are in dispute. (Chapter 3)

Summary jury trial A form of alternative dispute resolution in which a small panel of jurors hears shortened, summarized versions of the evidence. (Chapter 3)

Supermajority voting Typically, shareholders can approve charter amendments by a majority vote. However, sometimes corporations require more than a majority of shareholders (e.g., 80 percent) to approve certain charter amendments, such as a merger. These provisions are designed to discourage hostile takeovers. (Chapter 35)

Superseding cause An event that interrupts the chain of causation and relieves a defendant from liability based on her own act. (Chapter 6)

Supremacy Clause From Article VI of the Constitution, it declares that federal statutes and treaties take priority over any state law, if there is a conflict between the two or, even absent a conflict, if Congress manifests an intent to preempt the field. (Chapter 4)

T

Takings Clause Part of the Fifth Amendment, it ensures that when any governmental unit takes private property for public use, it must compensate the owner. (Chapter 4)

Tariff A duty imposed on imported goods by the government of the importing nation. (Chapter 8)

Tenancy by the entirety A form of joint ownership available only to married couples. If one member of the couple dies, the property goes automatically to the survivor. Creditors cannot attach the property, nor can one owner sell the property without the other's permission. (Chapter 42)

Tender To make conforming goods available to the buyer. (Chapter 21)

Tender offer A public offer to buy a block of stock directly from shareholders. (Chapter 35)

Term partnership When the partners agree in advance on the duration of a partnership. (Chapter 33)

Testamentary trust A trust created by the grantor's will. (Chapter 45)

Testator Someone who dies having executed a will. (Chapter 45)

Testatrix A female testator. (Chapter 45)

Third party beneficiary Someone who stands to benefit from a contract to which she is not a party. An *intended* beneficiary may enforce such a contract; an *incidental* beneficiary may not. (Chapter 15)

Three-Fifths Clause A clause in Article 1, section 2 of the United States Constitution, now void and regarded as racist, which required that for purposes of taxation and representation, a slave should be counted as three-fifths of a person. (Chapter 4)

Tort A civil wrong, committed in violation of a duty that the law imposes. (Chapter 5)

Tortious interference with a contract A tort in which the defendant deliberately impedes an existing contract between the plaintiff and another. (Chapter 5)

Tortious interference with a prospective advantage A tort in which the defendant deliberately obstructs a developing venture or advantage that the plaintiff has created. (Chapter 5)

Trade acceptance A draft drawn by a seller of goods on the buyer and payable to the seller or some third party. (Chapter 22)

Trade secret A formula, device, process, method, or compilation of information that, when used in business, gives the owner an advantage over competitors who do not know it. (Chapter 41)

Trademark Any combination of words and symbols that a business uses to identify its products or services and that federal law will protect. (Chapter 41)

Treasury stock Stock that has been bought back by its issuing corporation. (Chapter 34)

Trespass A tort committed by intentionally entering land that belongs to someone else, or remaining on the land after being asked to leave. (Chapter 5)

Trial court Any court in a state or federal system that holds formal hearings to determine the facts in a civil or criminal case. (Chapter 3)

Trust An entity that separates legal and beneficial ownership. (Chapter 45)

Tying arrangement A violation of the Sherman and Clayton Acts in which a seller requires that two distinct products be purchased together. The seller uses its significant power in the market for the tying product to shut out a substantial part of the market for the tied product. (Chapter 37)

U

Ultra vires An activity that is not permitted by a corporation's charter. (Chapter 34)

Ultrahazardous activity Conduct that is lawful yet unusual and much more likely to cause injury than normal commercial activity. (Chapter 6)

Unconscionable contract An agreement that a court refuses to enforce because it is fundamentally unfair as a result of unequal bargaining power by one party. (Chapter 12)

Undisclosed principal If a third party in an agency relationship does not know that the agent is acting for a principal, that principal is undisclosed. (Chapter 29)

Undue influence One party so dominates the thinking of another party to a contract that the dominant party cannot truly consent to the agreement. (Chapter 13)

Unfair labor practice An act, committed by either a union or an employer, that violates the National Labor Relations Act, such as failing to bargain in good faith. (Chapter 32)

Unilateral contract A binding agreement in which one party has made an offer that the other can accept only by action, not words. (Chapter 9)

Unliquidated debt A claimed debt that is disputed, either because the parties disagree over whether there is in fact a debt or because they disagree over the amount. (Chapter 11)

Usury Charging interest at a rate that exceeds legal limits. (Chapter 12)

V

Valuation A process by which the Customs Service determines the fair value of goods being imported, for purposes of imposing a duty. (Chapter 8)

Verdict The decision of the factfinder in a case. (Chapter 3)

Vertical agreement or merger An agreement or merger between two companies at different stages of the production process, such as when a company acquires one of its suppliers or distributors. (Chapter 37)

Veto The power of the president to reject legislation passed by Congress, terminating the bill unless Congress votes by a $\frac{2}{3}$ majority to override. (Chapter 4)

Void agreement   An agreement that neither party may legally enforce, usually because the purpose of the bargain was illegal or because one of the parties lacked capacity to make it.   (Chapter 9)

Voidable contract   An agreement that, because of some defect, may be terminated by one party, such as a minor, but not by both parties.   (Chapter 9)

Voir dire   The process of selecting a jury. Attorneys for the parties and the judge may inquire of prospective jurors whether they are biased or incapable of rendering a fair and impartial verdict.   (Chapter 3)

W

Warranty   A guarantee that goods will meet certain standards.   (Chapter 20)

Warranty of fitness for a particular purpose   An assurance under the Uniform Commercial Code that the goods are fit for the special purpose for which the buyer intends them and of which the seller is aware.   (Chapter 20)

Warranty of merchantability   An assurance under the Uniform Commercial Code that the goods are fit for their ordinary purpose.   (Chapter 20)

Whistleblower   Someone who discloses wrongful behavior.   (Chapter 30)

Winding up   The process whereby the assets of a partnership are sold and the proceeds distributed.   (Chapter 33)

World Wide Web   A decentralized collection of documents containing text, pictures and sound that is accessible from Internet sites. It is a sub-network of the Internet. (Chapter 40)

Writ   An order from a government compelling someone to do a particular thing.   (Chapter 1)

The Constitution
of the United States

Preamble   We the People of the United States, in Order to form a more perfect Union, establish Justice, insure domestic Tranquility, provide for the common defense, promote the general Welfare, and secure the Blessings of Liberty to ourselves and our Posterity, do ordain and establish this Constitution for the United States of America.

ARTICLE I

Section 1.

All legislative Powers herein granted shall be vested in a Congress of the United States, which shall consist of a Senate and House of Representatives.

Section 2.

The House of Representatives shall be composed of Members chosen every second Year by the People of the several States, and the Electors in each State shall have the Qualifications requisite for Electors of the most numerous Branch of the State Legislature.

No Person shall be a Representative who shall not have attained to the Age of twenty five Years, and been seven Years a Citizen of the United States, and who shall not, when elected, be an Inhabitant of that State in which he shall be chosen.

Representatives and direct Taxes shall be apportioned among the several States which may be included within this Union, according to their respective Numbers, which shall be determined by adding to the whole Number of free Persons, including those bound to Service for a Term of Years, and excluding Indians not taxed, three fifths of all other Persons. The actual Enumeration shall be made within three Years after the first Meeting of the Congress of the United States, and within every subsequent Term of ten Years, in such Manner as they shall by Law direct. The number of Representatives shall not exceed one for every thirty Thousand, but each State shall have at Least one Representative; and until such enumeration shall be made, the State of New Hampshire shall be entitled to chuse three, Massachusetts eight, Rhode Island and Providence Plantations one, Connecticut five, New-York six, New Jersey four, Pennsylvania eight, Delaware one, Maryland six, Virginia ten, North Carolina five, South Carolina five, and Georgia three.

When vacancies happen in the Representation from any State, the Executive Authority thereof shall issue Writs of Election to fill such vacancies.

The House of Representatives shall chuse their Speaker and other Officers; and shall have the sole Power of Impeachment.

Section 3.

The Senate of the United States shall be composed of two Senators from each State, chosen by the Legislature thereof, for six Years; and each Senator shall have one Vote.

Immediately after they shall be assembled in Consequence of the first Election, they shall be divided as equally as may be into three Classes. The Seats of the

Senators of the first Class shall be vacated at the Expiration of the second Year, of the second Class at the Expiration of the fourth Year, and of the third Class at the Expiration of the sixth Year, so that one third may be chosen every second Year; and if Vacancies happen by Resignation or otherwise, during the Recess of the Legislature of any State, the Executive thereof may make temporary Appointments until the next Meeting of the Legislature, which shall then fill such Vacancies.

No Person shall be a Senator who shall not have attained to the Age of thirty Years, and been nine Years a Citizen of the United States, and who shall not, when elected, be an Inhabitant of that State for which he shall be chosen.

The Vice President of the United States shall be President of the Senate, but shall have no Vote, unless they be equally divided.

The Senate shall chuse their other Officers, and also a President pro tempore, in the Absence of the Vice President, or when he shall exercise the Office of President of the United States.

The Senate shall have the sole power to try all Impeachments. When sitting for that Purpose, they shall be an Oath or Affirmation. When the President of the United States is tried, the Chief Justice shall preside: And no Person shall be convicted without the Concurrence of two thirds of the Members present.

Judgment in Cases of Impeachment shall not extend further than to removal from Office, and disqualification to hold and enjoy any Office of honor, Trust or Profit under the United States: but the Party convicted shall nevertheless be liable and subject to Indictment, Trial, Judgment and Punishment, according to Law.

Section 4.

The Times, Places and Manner of holding Elections for Senators and Representatives, shall be prescribed in each State by the Legislature thereof: but the Congress may at any time by Law make or alter such Regulations, except as to the Places of chusing Senators.

The Congress shall assemble at least once in every Year, and such Meeting shall be on the first Monday in December, unless they shall by Law appoint a different Day.

Section 5.

Each House shall be the Judge of the Elections, Returns and Qualifications of its own Members, and a Majority of each shall constitute a Quorum to do Business; but a smaller Number may adjourn from day to day, and may be authorized to compel the Attendance of absent Members, in such Manner, and under such Penalties as each House may provide.

Each House may determine the Rules of its Proceedings, punish its Members for disorderly Behaviour, and, with the Concurrence of two thirds, expel a Member.

Each House shall keep a Journal of its Proceedings, and from time to time publish the same, excepting such Parts as may in their Judgment require Secrecy; and the Yeas and Nays of the Members of either House on any question shall, at the Desire of one fifth of those Present, be entered on the Journal.

Neither House, during the Session of Congress, shall, without the Consent of the other, adjourn for more than three days, nor to any other Place than that in which the two Houses shall be sitting.

Section 6.

The Senators and Representatives shall receive a Compensation for their Services, to be ascertained by Law, and paid out of the Treasury of the United States. They shall in all Cases, except Treason, Felony and Breach of the Peace, be privileged from Arrest during their Attendance at the Session of their respective Houses, and in going to and returning from the same; and for any Speech or Debate in either House, they shall not be questioned in any other Place.

No Senator or Representative shall, during the Time for which he was elected, be appointed to any civil Office under the Authority of the United States, which shall have been created, or the Emoluments whereof shall have been encreased during such time; and no Person holding any Office under the United States, shall be a Member of either House during his Continuance in Office.

Section 7.

All Bills for raising Revenue shall originate in the House of Representatives; but the Senate may propose or concur with Amendments as on other Bills.

Every Bill which shall have passed the House of Representatives and the Senate, shall, before it become a Law, be presented to the President of the United States; If he approve he shall sign it, but if not he shall return it, with his Objections to that House in which it shall have originated, who shall enter the Objections at large on their Journal, and proceed to reconsider it. If after such Reconsideration two thirds of that House shall agree to pass the Bill, it shall be sent, together with the Objections, to the other House, by which it shall likewise be reconsidered, and if approved by two thirds of that House, it shall become a Law. But in all such Cases the Votes of both Houses shall be determined by Yeas and Nays, and the Names of the Persons voting for and against the Bill shall be entered on the Journal of each House respectively. If any Bill shall not be returned by the President within ten Days (Sundays excepted) after it shall have been presented to him, the Same shall be a Law, in like Manner as if he had signed it, unless the Congress by their Adjournment prevent its Return, in which Case it shall not be a Law.

Every Order, Resolution, or Vote to which the Concurrence of the Senate and House of Representatives may be necessary (except on a question of Adjournment) shall be presented to the President of the United States; and before the Same shall take Effect, shall be approved by him, or being disapproved by him, shall be repassed by two thirds of the Senate and House of Representatives, according to the Rules and Limitations prescribed in the Case of a Bill.

Section 8.

The Congress shall have Power to lay and collect Taxes, Duties, Imposts and Excises, to pay the Debts and provide for the common Defence and general Welfare of the United States; but all Duties, Imposts and Excises shall be uniform throughout the United States;

To borrow Money on the credit of the United States;

To regulate Commerce with foreign Nations, and among the several States, and with the Indian Tribes;

To establish an uniform Rule of Naturalization, and uniform Laws on the subject of Bankruptcies throughout the United States;

To coin Money, regulate the Value thereof, and of foreign Coin, and fix the Standard of Weights and Measures;

To provide for the Punishment of counterfeiting the Securities and current Coin of the United States;

To establish Post Offices and post Roads;

To promote the Progress of Science and useful Arts, by securing for limited Times to Authors and Inventors the exclusive Right to their respective Writings and Discoveries;

To constitute Tribunals inferior to the supreme Court;

To define and punish Piracies and Felonies committed on the high Seas, and Offenses against the Law of Nations;

To declare War, grant Letters of Marque and Reprisal, and make Rules concerning Captures on Land and Water;

To raise and support Armies, but no Appropriation of Money to that Use shall be for a longer Term than two Years;

To provide and maintain a Navy;

To make Rules for the Government and Regulation of the land and naval Forces;

To provide for calling forth the Militia to execute the Laws of the Union, suppress Insurrections and repel Invasions;

To provide for organizing, arming, and disciplining, the Militia, and for governing such Part of them as may be employed in the Service of the United States, reserving to the States respectively, the Appointment of the Officers, and the Authority of training the Militia according to the discipline described by Congress;

To exercise exclusive Legislation in all Cases whatsoever, over such District (not exceeding ten Miles square) as may, by Cession of particular States, and the Acceptance of Congress, become the Seat of the Government of the United States, and to exercise like Authority over all Places purchased by the Consent of the Legislature of the State in which the Same shall be, for the Erection of Forts, Magazines, Arsenals, dock-Yards, and other needful Buildings;—And

To make all Laws which shall be necessary and proper for carrying into Execution the foregoing Powers, and all other Powers vested by this Constitution in the Government of the United States, or in any Department or Officer thereof.

Section 9.

The Migration or Importation of such Persons as any of the States now existing shall think proper to admit, shall not be prohibited by the Congress prior to the Year one thousand eight hundred and eight, but a Tax or Duty may be imposed on such Importation, not exceeding ten dollars for each Person.

The Privilege of the Writ of Habeas Corpus shall not be suspended, unless when in Cases of Rebellion or Invasion the public Safety may require it.

No Bill of Attainder or ex post facto Law shall be passed.

No Capitation, or other direct, Tax shall be laid, unless in Proportion to the Census or Enumeration herein before directed to be taken.

No Tax or Duty shall be laid on Articles exported from any State.

No Preference shall be given by any Regulation of Commerce or Revenue to the Ports of one State over those of another; nor shall Vessels bound to, or from, one State, be obliged to enter, clear, or pay Duties in another.

No Money shall be drawn from the Treasury, but in Consequence of Appropriations made by Laws; and a regular Statement and Account of the Receipts and Expenditures of all public Money shall be published from time to time.

No Title of Nobility shall be granted by the United States: And no Person holding any Office of Profit or Trust under them, shall, without the Consent of the Congress, accept of any present, Emolument, Office, or Title, of any kind whatever, from any King, Prince, or foreign State.

Section 10.

No State shall enter into any Treaty, Alliance, or Confederation; grant Letters of Marque and Reprisal; coin Money; emit Bills of Credit; make any Thing but gold and silver Coin a Tender in Payment of Debts; pass any Bill of Attainder, ex post facto Law, or Law impairing the Obligation of Contracts, or grant any Title of Nobility.

No State shall, without the Consent of the Congress, lay any Imposts or Duties on Imports or Exports, except what may be absolutely necessary for executing its inspection Laws: and the net Produce of all Duties and Imposts, laid by any State on Imports or Exports, shall be for the Use of the Treasury of the United States; and all such Laws shall be subject to the Revision and Controul of the Congress.

No State shall, without the Consent of Congress, lay any Duty of Tonnage, keep Troops, or Ships of War in time of Peace, enter into any Agreement or Compact with another State, or with a foreign Power, or engage in War, unless actually invaded, or in such imminent Danger as will not admit of delay.

ARTICLE II

Section 1.

The executive Power shall be vested in a President of the United States of America. He shall hold his Office during the Term of four Years, and, together with the Vice President, chosen for the same Term, be elected, as follows:

Each State shall appoint, in such Manner as the Legislature thereof may direct, a Number of Electors, equal to the whole Number of Senators and Representatives to which the State may be entitled in the Congress: but no Senator or Representative, or Person holding an Office of Trust or Profit under the United States, shall be appointed an Elector.

The Electors shall meet in their respective States, and vote by Ballot for two Persons, of whom one at least shall not be an Inhabitant of the same State with themselves. And they shall make a list of all the Persons voted for, and of the Number of Votes for each; which List they shall sign and certify, and transmit sealed to the Seat of the Government of the United States, directed to the President of the Senate. The President of the Senate shall, in the presence of the Senate and House of Representatives, open all the Certificates, and the Votes shall be counted. The Person having the greatest Number of Votes shall be the President, if such Number be a Majority of the whole Number of Electors appointed; and if there be more than one who have such Majority, and have an equal Number of Votes, then the House of Representatives shall immediately chuse by Ballot one of them for President; and if no Person have a Majority, then from the five highest on the List the said House shall in like Manner chuse the President. But in chusing the President, the Votes shall be taken by States, the Representation from each State having one Vote; A quorum for this Purpose shall consist of a Member or Members from two thirds of the States, and a Majority of all the States shall be necessary to a Choice. In every Case, after the Choice of the President, the Person having the greatest Number of Votes of the Electors shall be the Vice President. But if there should remain two or more who have equal Votes, the Senate shall chuse from them by Ballot the Vice President.

The Congress may determine the Time of Chusing the Electors, and the Day on which they shall give their Votes; which Day shall be the same throughout the United States.

No Person except a natural born Citizen, or a Citizen of the United States, at the time of the Adoption of this Constitution, shall be eligible to the Office of President; neither shall any Person be eligible to that Office who shall not have attained to the Age of thirty five Years, and been fourteen Years a Resident within the United States.

In Case of the Removal of the President from Office, or of his Death, Resignation, or Inability to discharge the Powers and Duties of the said Office, the Same shall devolve on the Vice President, and the Congress may by Law provide for the Case of Removal, Death, Resignation or Inability, both of the President and Vice President, declaring what Officer shall then act as President, and such Officer shall act accordingly, until the Disability be removed, or a President shall be elected.

The President shall, at stated Times, receive for his Services, a Compensation, which shall neither be encreased nor diminished during the Period for which he shall have been elected, and he shall not receive within that Period any other Emolument from the United States, or any of them.

Before he enter on the Execution of his Office, he shall take the following Oath or Affirmation:—"I do solemnly swear (or affirm) that I will faithfully execute the

Office of President of the United States, and will to the best of my Ability, preserve, protect and defend the Constitution of the United States."

Section 2.

The President shall be Commander in Chief of the Army and Navy of the United States, and of the Militia of the several States, when called into the actual Service of the United States; he may require the Opinion, in writing, of the principal Officer in each of the executive Departments, upon any Subject relating to the Duties of their respective Offices, and he shall have Power to grant Reprieves and Pardons for Offenses against the United States, except in Cases of Impeachment.

He shall have Power, by and with the Advice and Consent of the Senate, to make Treaties, providing two thirds of the Senators present concur; and he shall nominate, and by and with the Advice and Consent of the Senate, shall appoint Ambassadors, other public Ministers and Consuls, Judges of the supreme Court, and all other Officers of the United States, whose Appointments are not herein otherwise provided for, and which shall be established by Law: but the Congress may by Law vest the Appointment of such inferior Officers, as they think proper, in the President alone, in the Courts of Law, or in the Heads of Departments.

The President shall have Power to fill up all Vacancies that may happen during the Recess of the Senate, by granting Commissions which shall expire at the End of their next Session.

Section 3.

He shall from time to time give to the Congress Information of the State of the Union, and recommend to their Consideration such Measures as he shall judge necessary and expedient; he may, on extraordinary Occasions, convene both Houses, or either of them, and in Case of Disagreement between them, with Respect to the Time of Adjournment, he may adjourn them to such Time as he shall think proper, he shall receive Ambassadors and other public Ministers; he shall take Care that the Laws be faithfully executed, and shall Commission all the Offices of the United States.

Section 4.

The President, Vice President and all civil Officers of the United States, shall be removed from Office on Impeachment for, and Conviction of, Treason, Bribery, or other high Crimes and Misdemeanors.

ARTICLE III

Section 1.

The judicial Power of the United States, shall be vested in one supreme Court, and in such inferior Courts as the Congress may from time to time ordain and establish. The Judges, both of the supreme and inferior Courts, shall hold their Offices during good Behaviour, and shall, at Times, receive for their Services, a Compensation, which shall not be diminished during their Continuance in Office.

Section 2.

The judicial Power shall extend to all Cases, in Law and Equity, arising under this Constitution, the Laws of the United States, and Treaties made, or which shall be made, under their Authority;—to all Cases affecting Ambassadors, other public Ministers and Consuls;—to all Cases of admiralty and maritime Jurisdiction;—to Controversies to which the United States shall be a Party;—to controversies between two or more States;—between a State and Citizens of another State;—between Citizens of different States;—between Citizens of the same State claiming Lands under Grants of different States; and between a State, or the Citizens thereof, and foreign States, Citizens or Subjects.

In all Cases affecting Ambassadors, other public Ministers and Consuls, and those in which a State shall be Party, the supreme Court shall have original Jurisdiction. In all the other Cases before mentioned, the supreme Court shall have appellate Jurisdiction, both as to Law and Fact, with such Exceptions, and under such Regulations as the Congress shall make.

The Trial of all Crimes, except in Cases of Impeachment, shall be by Jury; and such Trial shall be held in the State where the said Crimes shall have been committed; but when not committed within any State, the Trial shall be at such Place or Places as the Congress may by Law have directed.

Section 3.

Treason against the United States, shall consist only in levying War against them, or in adhering to their Enemies, giving them Aid and Comfort. No Person shall be convicted of Treason unless on the Testimony of two Witnesses to the same overt Act, or on Confession in open Court.

The Congress shall have Power to declare the Punishment of Treason, but no Attainder of Treason shall work Corruption of Blood, or Forfeiture except during the Life of the Person attainted.

ARTICLE IV

Section 1.

Full Faith and Credit shall be given in each State to the public Acts, Records, and judicial Proceedings of every other State. And the Congress may by general Laws prescribe the Manner in which such Acts, Records and Proceedings shall be proved, and the Effect thereof.

Section 2.

The Citizens of each State shall be entitled to all Privileges and Immunities of Citizens in the several States.

A Person charged in any State with Treason, Felony, or other Crime, who shall flee from Justice, and be found in another State, shall on Demand of the executive Authority of the State from which he fled, be delivered up, to be removed to the State having Jurisdiction of the Crime.

No Person held to Service or Labour in one State, under the Laws thereof, escaping into another, shall, in Consequence of any Law or Regulation therein, be discharged from such Service or Labour, but shall be delivered up on Claim of the Party to whom such Service or Labour may be due.

Section 3.

New States may be admitted by the Congress into this Union; but no new State shall be formed or erected within the Jurisdiction of any other State; nor any State be formed by the Junction of two or more States, or Parts of States, without the Consent of the Legislatures of the States concerned as well as the Congress.

The Congress shall have Power to dispose of and make all needful Rules and Regulations respecting the Territory or other Property belonging to the United States; and nothing in this Constitution shall be so construed as to Prejudice any Claims of the United States, or of any particular State.

Section 4.

The United States shall guarantee to every State in this Union a Republican Form of Government, and shall protect each of them against Invasion; and on Application of the Legislature, or of the Executive (when the Legislature cannot be convened) against domestic Violence.

ARTICLE V

The Congress, whenever two thirds of both Houses shall deem it necessary, shall propose Amendments to this Constitution, or, on the Application of the Legislatures of two thirds of the several States, shall call a Convention for proposing Amendments, which, in either Case, shall be valid to all Intents and Purposes, as Part of this Constitution, when ratified by the Legislatures of three fourths of the several States, or by Conventions in three fourths thereof, as the one or the other Mode of Ratification may be proposed by the Congress; Provided that no Amendment which may be made prior to the Year One thousand eight hundred and eight shall in any Manner affect the first and fourth Clauses in the Ninth Section of the first Article; and that no State, without its Consent, shall be deprived of its equal Suffrage in the Senate.

ARTICLE VI

All Debts contracted and Engagements entered into, before the Adoption of this Constitution, shall be as valid against the United States under this Constitution, as under the Confederation.

This Constitution, and the Laws of the United States which shall be made in Pursuance thereof; and all Treaties made, or which shall be made, under the Authority of the United States, shall be the supreme Law of the Land; and the Judges in every State shall be bound thereby, any Thing in the Constitution or Laws of any State to the Contrary notwithstanding.

The Senators and Representatives before mentioned, and the Members of the several State Legislatures, and all executive and judicial Officers, both of the United States and of the Several States, shall be bound by Oath or Affirmation, to support this Constitution; but no religious Test shall ever be required as a Qualification to any Office or public Trust under the United States.

ARTICLE VII

The Ratification of the Conventions of nine States, shall be sufficient for the Establishment of this Constitution between the States so ratifying the Same.

Amendment I [1791]. Congress shall make no law respecting an establishment of religion, or prohibiting the free exercise thereof; or abridging the freedom of speech, or the press; or the right of the people peaceably to assemble, and to petition the Government for a redress of grievances.

Amendment II [1791]. A well regulated Militia, being necessary to the security for a free State, the right of the people to keep and bear Arms, shall not be infringed.

Amendment III [1791]. No Soldier shall, in time of peace be quartered in any house, without the consent of the Owner, nor in time of war, but in a manner to be prescribed by law.

Amendment IV [1791]. The right of the people to be secure in their persons, houses, papers, and effects, against unreasonable searches and seizures, shall not be violated, and no Warrants shall issue, but upon probable cause, supported by Oath or Affirmation, and particularly describing the place to be searched, and the persons or things to be seized.

Amendment V [1791]. No person shall be held to answer for a capital, or otherwise infamous crime, unless on a presentment or indictment of a Grand Jury, except in cases arising in the land or naval forces, or in the Militia, when in actual service in time of War or public danger; nor shall any person be subject for the same offense to be twice put in jeopardy of life or limb; nor shall be compelled in any criminal case to be a witness against himself, nor be deprived of life, liberty, or property, without due process of law; nor shall private property be taken for public use, without just compensation.

Amendment VI [1791].

In all criminal prosecutions, the accused shall enjoy the right to a speedy and public trial, by an impartial jury of the State and district wherein the crime shall have been committed, which district shall have been previously ascertained by law, and to be informed of the nature and cause of the accusation; to be confronted with the Witnesses against him; to have compulsory process for obtaining witnesses in his favor, and to have the Assistance of counsel for his defence.

Amendment VII [1791].

In suits at common law, where the value in controversy shall exceed twenty dollars, the right of trial by jury shall be preserved, and no fact tried by a jury, shall be otherwise re-examined in any Court of the United States, than according to the rules of the common law.

Amendment VIII [1791].

Excessive bail shall not be required, no excessive fines imposed, nor cruel and unusual punishments inflicted.

Amendment IX [1791].

The enumeration in the Constitution, of certain rights, shall not be construed to deny or disparage others retained by the people.

Amendment X [1791].

The powers not delegated to the United States by the Constitution, nor prohibited by it to the States, are reserved to the States respectively, or to the people.

Amendment XI [1798].

The judicial power of the United States shall not be construed to extend to any suit in law or equity, commenced or prosecuted against one of the United States by Citizens of another State, or by Citizens or Subjects of any Foreign State.

Amendment XII [1804].

The Electors shall meet in their respective states and vote by ballot for President and Vice-President, one of whom, at least, shall not be an inhabitant of the same state with themselves; they shall name in their ballots the person voted for as President, and in distinct ballots the person voted for as Vice-President, and they shall make distinct lists of all persons voted for as President, and of all persons voted for as Vice-President, and of the number of votes for each, which lists they shall sign and certify, and transmit sealed to the seat of the government of the United States, directed to the President of the Senate;—The President of the Senate shall, in the presence of the Senate and House of Representatives, open all the certificates and the votes shall then be counted;—The person having the greatest number of votes for President, shall be the President, if such number be a majority of the whole number of Electors appointed; and if no person have such majority, then from the persons having the highest numbers not exceeding three on the list of those voted for as President, the House of Representatives shall choose immediately, by ballot, the President. But in choosing the President, the votes shall be taken by states, the representation from each state having one vote; a quorum for this purpose shall consist of a member or members from two-thirds of the states, and a majority of all the states shall be necessary to a choice. And if the House of Representatives shall not choose a President whenever the right of choice shall devolve upon them, before the fourth day of March next following, then the Vice-President shall act as President, as in the case of the death or other constitutional disability of the President. The person having the greatest number of votes as Vice-President, shall be the Vice-President, if such number be a majority of the whole number of Electors appointed, and if no person have a majority, then from the two highest numbers on the list, the Senate shall choose the Vice-President; a quorum for the purpose shall consist of two-thirds of the whole number of Senators, and a majority of the whole number shall be necessary to a choice. But no person constitutionally ineligible to the office of President shall be eligible to that of the Vice-President of the United States.

Amendment XIII [1865].

Section 1. Neither slavery nor involuntary servitude, except as a punishment for crime whereof the party shall have been duly convicted, shall exist within the United States, or any place subject to their jurisdiction.

Section 2. Congress shall have power to enforce this article by appropriate legislation.

Amendment XIV [1868].

Section 1. All persons born or naturalized in the United States, and subject to the jurisdiction thereof, are citizens of the United States and of the State wherein they reside. No State shall make or enforce any law which shall abridge the privileges or immunities of citizens of the United States; nor shall any State deprive any person of life, liberty, or property, without due process of law; nor deny to any person within its jurisdiction the equal protection of the laws.

Section 2. Representatives shall be appointed among the several States according to their respective numbers, counting the whole number of persons in each State, excluding Indians not taxed. But when the right to vote at any election for the choice of electors for President and Vice President of the United States, Representatives in Congress, the Executive and Judicial officers of a State, or the members of the Legislature thereof, is denied to any of the male inhabitants of such State, being twenty-one years of age, and citizens of the United States, or in any way abridged, except for participation in rebellion, or other crime, the basis of representation therein shall be reduced in the proportion which the number of such male citizens shall bear the whole number of male citizens twenty-one years of age in such State.

Section 3. No person shall be a Senator or Representative in Congress, or elector of President and Vice President, or hold any office, civil or military, under the United States, or under any State, who, having previously taken an oath, as a member of Congress, or as an officer of the United States, or as a member of any State legislature, or as an executive or judicial officer of any State, to support the Constitution of the United States, shall have engaged in insurrection or rebellion against the same, or given aid or comfort to the enemies thereof. But Congress may by a vote of two-thirds of each House, remove such disability.

Section 4. The validity of the public debt of the United States, authorized by law, including debts incurred for payment of pensions and bounties for services in suppressing insurrection or rebellion, shall not be questioned. But neither the United States nor any State shall assume or pay any debt or obligation incurred in aid of insurrection of rebellion against the United States, or any claim for the loss or emancipation of any slave; but all such debts, obligations and claims shall be held illegal and void.

Section 5. The Congress shall have power to enforce, by appropriate legislation, the provisions of this article.

Amendment XV [1870].

Section 1. The right of citizens of the United States to vote shall not be denied or abridged by the United States or by any State on account of race, color, or previous condition of servitude.

Section 2. The Congress shall have power to enforce this article by appropriate legislation.

Amendment XVI [1913].

The Congress shall have power to lay and collect taxes on incomes, from whatever source derived, without apportionment among the several States, and without regard to any census or enumeration.

Amendment XVII [1913].

The Senate of the United States shall be composed of two Senators from each State, elected by the people thereof, for six years; and each Senator shall have one vote. The electors in each State shall have the qualifications requisite for electors of the most numerous branch of the State legislatures.

When vacancies happen in the representation of any State in the Senate, the executive authority of each State shall issue writs of election to fill such vacancies; *Provided,* That the legislature of any State may empower the executive thereof to make temporary appointments until the people fill the vacancies by election as the legislature may direct.

This amendment shall not be construed as to affect the election or term of any Senator chosen before it becomes valid as part of the Constitution.

Amendment XVIII [1919].

Section 1. After one year from the ratification of this article the manufacture, sale, or transportation of intoxicating liquors within, the importation thereof into, or the exportation thereof from the United States and all territory subject to the jurisdiction thereof for beverage purposes is hereby prohibited.

Section 2. The Congress and the several States shall have concurrent power to enforce this article by appropriate legislation.

Section 3. This article shall be inoperative unless it shall have been ratified as an amendment to the Constitution by the legislatures of the several States, as provided in the Constitution, within seven years from the date of the submission hereof to the States by the Congress.

Amendment XIX [1920].

The right of citizens of the United States to vote shall not be denied or abridged by the United States or by any State on account of sex.

Congress shall have power to enforce this article by appropriate legislation.

Amendment XX [1933].

Section 1. The terms of the President and Vice President shall end at noon on the 20th day of January, and the terms of Senators and Representatives at noon on the 3d day of January, of the years in which such terms would have ended if this article had not been ratified; and the terms of their successors shall then begin.

Section 2. The Congress shall assemble at least once in every year, and such meeting shall begin at noon on the 3d day of January, unless they shall by law appoint a different day.

Section 3. If, at the time fixed for the beginning of the term of the President, the President elect shall have died, the Vice President elect shall become President. If a President shall not have been chosen before the time fixed for the beginning of his term, or if the President elect shall have failed to qualify, then the Vice President elect shall act as President until a President shall have qualified; and the Congress may by law provide for the case wherein neither a President elect nor a Vice President elect shall have qualified, declaring who shall then act as President, or the manner in which one who is to act shall be selected, and such person shall act accordingly until a President or Vice President shall have qualified.

Section 4. The Congress may by law provide for the case of the death of any of the persons from whom the House of Representatives may choose a President whenever the right of choice shall have devolved upon them, and for the case of the death of any of the persons from whom the Senate may choose a Vice President whenever the right of choice shall have devolved upon them.

Section 5. Sections 1 and 2 shall take effect on the 15th day of October following the ratification of this article.

Section 6. This article shall be inoperative unless it shall have been ratified as an amendment to the Constitution by the legislatures of three-fourths of the several States within seven years from the date of its submission.

Amendment XXI [1933].

Section 1. The eighteenth article of amendment to the Constitution of the United States is hereby repealed.

Section 2. The transportation or importation into any State, Territory, or possession of the United States for delivery or use therein of intoxicating liquors, in violation of the laws thereof, is hereby prohibited.

Section 3. This article shall be inoperative unless it shall have been ratified as an amendment to the Constitution by conventions in the several States, as provided in the Constitution, within seven years from the date of the submission hereof to the States by the Congress.

Amendment XXII [1951].

Section 1. No person shall be elected to the office of the President more than twice, and no person who has held the office of President, or acted as President, for more than two years of a term to which some other person was elected President shall be elected to the office of the President more than once. But this Article shall not apply to any person holding the office of President when this Article was proposed by the Congress, and shall not prevent any person who may be holding the office of President, or acting as President, during the term within which this Article becomes operative from holding the office of President, or acting as President during the remainder of such term.

Section 2. This article shall be inoperative unless it shall have been ratified as an amendment to the Constitution by the legislatures of three-fourths of the several States within seven years from the date of its submission to the States by the Congress.

Amendment XXIII [1961].

Section 1. The District constituting the seat of Government of the United States shall appoint in such manner as the Congress may direct:

A number of electors of President and Vice President equal to the whole number of Senators and Representatives in Congress to which the District would be entitled if it were a State, but in no event more than the least populous State; they shall be in addition to those appointed by the States, but they shall be considered, for the purposes of the election of President and Vice President, to be electors appointed by a State; and they shall meet in the District and perform such duties as provided by the twelfth article of amendment.

Section 2. The Congress shall have power to enforce this article by appropriate legislation.

Amendment XXIV [1964].

Section 1. The right of citizens of the United States to vote in any primary or other election for President or Vice President, for electors for President or Vice President, or for Senator or Representative in Congress, shall not be denied or abridged by the United States or any State by reason of failure to pay any poll tax or other tax.

Section 2. The Congress shall have power to enforce this article by appropriate legislation.

Amendment XXV [1967].

Section 1. In case of the removal of the President from office or of his death or resignation, the Vice President shall become President.

Section 2. Whenever there is a vacancy in the office of the Vice President, the President shall nominate a Vice President who shall take office upon confirmation by a majority vote of both Houses of Congress.

Section 3. Whenever the President transmits to the President pro tempore of the Senate and the Speaker of the House of Representatives his written declaration that he is unable to discharge the powers and duties of his office, and until he transmits to them a written declaration to the contrary, such powers and duties shall be discharged by the Vice President as Acting President.

Section 4. Whenever the Vice President and a majority of either the principal officers of the executive departments or of such other body as Congress may by law provide, transmit to the President pro tempore of the Senate and the Speaker of the House of Representatives their written declaration that the President is unable to discharge the powers and duties of his office, the Vice President shall immediately assume the powers and duties of the office as Acting President.

Thereafter, when the President transmits to the President pro tempore of the Senate and the Speaker of the House of Representatives his written declaration that no inability exists, he shall resume the powers and duties of his office unless the Vice President and a majority of either the principal officers of the executive department or of such other body as Congress may by law provide, transmit within four days to the President pro tempore of the Senate and the Speaker of the House of Representatives their written declaration that the President is unable to discharge the powers and duties of his office. Thereupon Congress shall decide the issue, assembling within forty-eight hours for that purpose if not in session. If the Congress, within twenty-one days after receipt of the latter written declaration, or, if Congress is not in session, within twenty-one days after Congress is required to assemble, determines by two-thirds vote of both Houses that the President is unable to discharge the powers and duties of his office, the Vice President shall continue to discharge the same as Acting President; otherwise, the President shall resume the powers and duties of his office.

Amendment XXVI [1971].

Section 1. The right of citizens of the United States, who are eighteen years of age or older, to vote shall not be denied or abridged by the United States or by any State on account of age.

Section 2. The Congress shall have power to enforce this article by appropriate legislation.

Amendment XXVII [1992].

No law, varying the compensation for the services of the Senators and Representatives, shall take effect, until an election of Representatives shall have intervened.

index

index